CW00926970

Telephone: 01-340 3343

HIGHGATE LITERARY & SCIENTIFIC INSTITUTION
11 SOUTH GROVE N6 6BS

920 WHI

A2669

Time allowed 21 days

Date Issued	Date Issued	Date Issued
2 2 MAR 1980		
-8 MAY 1980		

THE IMPROBABLE PURITAN

HIC DEPOSITA SUNT
IACOBI WHITELOCK

THE IMPROBABLE PURITAN

A LIFE OF BULSTRODE WHITELOCKE

1605–1675

by

RUTH SPALDING

Quodcunque evenerit optimum

FABER & FABER   3 QUEEN SQUARE
LONDON

First published in 1975
by Faber and Faber Limited
3 Queen Square London WC1
Printed in Great Britain by
Western Printing Services Ltd
Bristol

ISBN 0 571 10626 9

Contents

Preface 9

Acknowledgements 15

List of Illustrations 19

Family Tree 20

One 'The Best School in Christendom' 23

Two Rebecca 38

Three Frances 58

Four 'A Spirit of Division and Contradiction' 78

Five Matters of Life and Death 98

Six 'The Business of the Widow Wilson' 120

Seven Ambassador Extraordinary 136

Eight Christina 158

Nine Abdication 184

Ten The Last Years in Office 200

Eleven 'Bonfires and Joys' 221

Twelve Pardon – and Oblivion 232

Postscript: *A Needle in an Irish Haystack* 254

Principal Manuscript Sources *with Notes* 262

Bibliography 266

Abbreviations 269

Reference Notes 270

Index 301

Preface

I first came across Bulstrode Whitelocke when I visited Stockholm as a student. Swedish histories devoted a page or more to the months he spent in Uppsala as Ambassador to Queen Christina, and gave extracts from the highly entertaining conversations they had together, including the much-quoted, good-humoured exchange about a mastiff and a great English cheese sent as a present by the army chaplain, Hugh Peter. In common with several English historians, the Swedish authors poked fun at Whitelocke as a stiff and pompous Puritan, and it took me some years to rid myself of that image. All the same he had aroused my curiosity, and when I returned to Oxford I successfully advertised for a second-hand copy of his record, last published in 1853, *A Journal of the Swedish Embassy*. This account runs from August 1653 to July 1654.

The English Ambassador was in his late forties, the Queen of Sweden in her late twenties. It was intriguing to find that he recorded his long interviews with her in detail, as he did many of his talks with Oliver Cromwell, with the Swedish Chancellor, Axel Oxenstierna, with a Dutch skipper and an English boatswain, and with his wife, Mary, setting them down like the dialogue for a play. I wondered and have continued to wonder how far these conversations, which occur in several of his manuscripts, give a trust-worthy account of what was said. Not at all, if we are to believe Thomas Carlyle who sneered at 'dull Bulstrode', nicknamed him 'Dry-as-dust' and dismissed his 'dramaturgic turn' and 'occasional poetic friskiness' which he found 'most unexpected, as if the hippopotamus should show a tendency to dance; which painfully deducts from one's confidence in Bulstrode's entire accuracy on such occasions!'[1] Yet the man about whom Carlyle was con-sistently scathing was a scholar, one of the foremost lawyers of his day, a Judge in Chancery, a friend of Hampden, Thurloe and Selden and, remark-ably, a Parliamentarian whose advice was sought by Charles I and Charles II, Oliver Cromwell and Queen Christina. It seems reasonable to suppose that, as a distinguished lawyer, he had developed an attentive ear and that his habit of writing down the day's events, and sometimes the day's con-versations, sharpened this skill while a knowledge of shorthand enabled him to take quick notes with an interview fresh in mind. He may have been one of those fortunate people who can memorize a conversation verbatim. The remarks he attributed to his astute, emotional third wife or to one of his tenant farmers have an authentic ring; he recorded Oliver Cromwell using clumsy reiteration reinforced by the word *indeed*: 'I think no man can serve his country more than you may herein, *indeed I think so*,' or 'They consider you are most fit for this employment: *you are so indeed*.' These turns of phrase were characteristic; Cromwell was reported by another writer as saying of his eldest son's death, 'It went as a dagger to my heart, *indeed it did*,' while his death-bed words were said to be: 'Truly God is good, *indeed he is*.' Whitelocke's private conversations with Christina are in a different category, for when they were alone they spoke French together, but in spite of the effects of his translation the Queen comes through as a quick-minded, fascinating young woman of unusual charm. With Oxenstierna he talked in Latin and there the translation reflects an aggressive, genial, didactic old man. The dialogue stands the test of being spoken as I discovered when I devised a feature on the Swedish mission for the B.B.C. Third Programme, using Whitelocke's words. The programme was fortunate in having Terence Tiller as producer with Carleton Hobbs and Nicolette Bernard playing Whitelocke and Christina; yet even allowing for that advantage the language rang true, sounding strangely modern and idiomatic.

Much of the material in this book, particularly that concerning White-locke's private life, appears in print for the first time. His previous biographer, Professor R. H. Whitelocke, writing in the mid-nineteenth century, only had access to one important manuscript, the volume of the memoirs or 'Annals' covering the first twenty-nine years, from 1605–34. Although he speculated as to the survival of other autobiographical material, the Professor knew nothing about two volumes which had lain for decades unrecognized on the library shelves at Luton Hoo. They belonged to the Marquess of Bute and had been catalogued vaguely in 1820 as 'MS. on English Affairs 2 volumes 4to'. In 1848, five years after a disastrous fire, the second Marquess sold Luton Hoo. The two manuscripts were among the volumes which had been salvaged and they were sent to London where, in about 1870, they were identified as a work of Whitelocke's. Shortly afterwards the Third Report of the *Historical Manuscripts Commission* described them flatly as 'English Affairs 1605–1675', adding an incorrect speculation as to what they were.

I had been working for some months on the present book and reckoned I must make a trip to the Isle of Bute to look at these manuscripts when Lord Bute, to whom I had written, kindly had them sent to London. I opened one volume at random, expecting from the title to find a history of the seventeenth century. Instead, I found myself reading Whitelocke's

'Diary'. It starts autobiographically with his birth and early years, in the manner of John Evelyn's *Diary*; it turns into the transcript of a monthly and then of a daily record, and finally becomes his day-by-day jottings which end with a shaky entry made about a week before his death. Tucked inside the second volume I discovered a letter written in 1895 by the eminent historian Dr. S. R. Gardiner. He wrote that, having completed his major work on the Stuart period, he would be glad to carry out an earlier proposal that he should edit the 'Diary'. For some reason his offer was not taken up; consequently it is my good fortune, with Lord Bute's kind permission, to prepare an edition of the 'Diary' for a Ph.D. thesis, which I hope will later be published. In that study I intend to take a harder, longer look at Whitelocke's political and religious position than seems appropriate to the present book. The greatest difficulty I have experienced in this biography has been that of selection and of trying not to be submerged under an unexpected wealth of material.

Whitelocke's 'Diary' is written in the third person, except sometimes in moments of stress. 'The Annals of his Life dedicated to his Children', in five (or it can be argued seven) large volumes, with two more covering the Swedish embassy, are in the first person. These 'Annals' are made up of autobiographical sections interspersed with a history of his times and with reflections on religious, political, historical and legal subjects. Seven years after his death the 'Annals' were edited for publication under the title *Memorials of the English Affairs from the Beginning of the Reign of Charles the First to the Happy Restoration of Charles the Second*. Besides giving the book this fancy title the first editor, who was almost certainly Lord Anglesey the Lord Privy Seal, emasculated the text, paraphrased, inserted passages of his own, turned it into a third person narrative and cut out most of the personal details which enlivened the original. The Quaker, William Penn, who as a young man had known and admired Whitelocke, expressed dismay that the work had been 'castrated' and so, in more genteel terms, did Dr. Charles Morton, the first under-librarian and afterwards Librarian of the British Museum. Benjamin Disraeli's father, Isaac, later expressed a similar regret in his *Curiosities of Literature*. Already in the 1732 edition of the *Memorials* some of the passages had been restored, but the text in all editions remains inaccurate and a pitfall to those who quote from it. Yet it is by this mutilated, much-quoted publication that Whitelocke has usually been judged, supplemented by Sir Charles Firth's long and in some respects misleading article in the *Dictionary of National Biography*. Many well-read people have never even heard of Whitelocke, and those who have some knowledge of him may approach this biography with strong preconceptions, which perhaps they will find reason to modify.

It has been claimed that William Prynne, the lawyer and pamphleteer, was the most prolific writer of his century.[2] Whitelocke must have run him very close. Over thirty manuscript volumes of various sizes, nearly all in his own handwriting, have survived; most of them are now in the British Museum as well as a few of his letters. He also left a richly indiscriminate mass of personal papers. He treasured correspondence with Cromwell, Queen Christina, Milton, Moncke, Selden, Thurloe and other prominent figures; he stored up legal and political documents, important and trivial alike; he kept papers of sentimental value, ranging from his seating plans for the musicians at the royal masque in the Banqueting House to illuminated marriage verses, and a heavily blacked dirge on the occasion of his second wife's death. He hoarded family letters, notes about sowing crops or putting horses out to grass, coachmakers' and saddlers' accounts, bills for the family tomb, for Master James's coat and for dressing a beaver hat. The main collection of these miscellaneous papers belongs to the Marquess of Bath, and the admirable index and calendar at Longleat make the business of studying them easy and delightful. In addition to thirty folio volumes in the muniments room, the library houses the 'Book of Expenses' for the Swedish embassy and the original version of the 'Journal of the Swedish Embassy'; this came to light at Longleat in 1859 in a room adjoining the library. Unfortunately many of its pages are missing. The University Library at Cambridge has a Parliamentary Diary for 1626, attributed to Whitelocke, and a member of the family owns an autograph manuscript covering his activities and meditations in August 1653. He was a good linguist, and his endearing manuscript phrase-book has recently been bought by the University of Lund in Sweden; it contains paragraphs in Latin, French and English for use in negotiations with Queen Christina and Chancellor Oxenstierna, or when entertaining Swedish guests to dinner. It is astonishing that so much has survived, for on three occasions many of his papers were destroyed, first by royalist soldiers, then by an anxious wife and finally in the Fire of London. The manuscripts which escaped are now collated for the first time. They throw new light on Whitelocke's character and beliefs as well as reflecting the activities of a large family across three-quarters of a century.

At some points I have been unable to find evidence against which to check

Whitelocke's account of events, and secondary sources to which I turned often quoted his *Memorials* as their authority. Where I have been able to test his statements they have usually proved to be accurate in substance, although he made blunders over dates, figures and other details. Apart from the destruction of many of his personal papers he lived, after the age of thirty, in more than a dozen different houses and the mind boggles at the thought of packing, unpacking and co-ordinating the mountain of papers and notebooks he needed for reference. Historians have criticized the use he made of newspaper reports, hinting that he passed them off as eye-witness accounts, but in the 'Annals' he stated frankly the use he made of them to fill gaps in his experience. His statements as to whether he was present on some historic occasion or was only relying on hearsay were usually omitted by the editors of the *Memorials*.

References in the 'Diary' and *Journal* to receiving highly complimentary letters from prominent men and women of his day are confirmed by the letters themselves, and I have spent many hours at Longleat matching his exuberant claims against the supporting documents. He was conceited in matters of small importance but assessed himself objectively on larger issues. He never disguised his pleasure at being treated as a man of distinction, but he could be equally candid in reporting the snubs when he was out of office.

In retirement, he copied out his pocket diaries from the early and middle years of his life, retaining even their trivialities and adding, now and then, a bitter after-thought. I have traced only one sheet of the original 'Diary', a small page torn from a note-book, neatly ruled with margins on all four sides; the brief entry tallies exactly with that in the final version. The fair copy of the 'Diary', although transcribed after the Restoration, describes his political activities before 1660 without glossing over his allegiance. He may, after that date, have accentuated his puritan wife's distrust of Cromwell, and his own occasional hostility, as he did in the final version of 'A Journal of the Swedish Embassy', but an account he wrote before 1660 was also boldly critical, especially of Cromwell assuming power as Protector.[3] Despite this, Whitelocke was consistently generous in maintaining that the Protector had been free from personal ambition. The 'Diary' is of particular interest in that it provides the only account of Whitelocke's harassed years from the Restoration in 1660 to his death fifteen years later.

He always wrote with sepia ink, in an attractive italic hand, usually ruling the pages into two neat columns. He must have written at extraordinary speed, but in spite of the enormous output his handwriting is almost always clear and strong. He liked to use a wide quill and if he sometimes cut it sharp and fine, after a few pages he would revert to a wider one. When writing a sequence of volumes he identified them with a number or date on the fore-edge. Below the surface of a strong intellect and discipline he was an artistic and emotional man, and at times of strain this showed through his handwriting.

In most cases, I have quoted from the manuscripts in preference to the printed editions of his work and in doing so I have modernized the spelling and punctuation. When quoting from the printed text of Sir James Whitelocke's *Liber Famelicus* I have, after some hesitation, modernized the spelling to bring it into line with the extracts taken direct from the manuscripts. Where, on the other hand, a printed *title* adopts the original spelling I have not tampered with it. Bigoted consistency in style, as in anything else, seems to me absurd. On the awkward question of recording dates I have, where possible, followed the 'new style' with the year starting on 1st January. When quoting, however, from manuscripts in which the 'old style' is used with the new year starting on 25th March, I have added the 'new style' in square brackets, for example, 24 March 1653 [4]. Where I am not quoting directly but there could, for some reason, be ambiguity, I show the two dates like this: January 1653-4.

After Whitelocke's disappearance from the political scene in 1659, a satirist and at least one contemporary dramatist lampooned him as a calculating time-server, a charge which I shall scrutinize in my edition of the 'Diary'. There are historians, up to the present day, who show a strangely personal animosity when writing about him, depicting him as a 'plodder' and a 'trimmer', as one whose motto might have been 'never resign!' and as a man of tedious and overweening conceit. Perhaps he had too good an opinion of himself, an unpardonable offence in the eyes of educated Englishmen. He possessed that physical gusto and exuberance which make a man good company and allow him to praise himself without offence. The same boasting in cold print antagonizes some readers. I once asked a nun what she understood by humility and she told me it was knowing your place, your value. She recalled a priest who was asked by a parishioner what she should read on humility. 'Mine' he replied accurately 'is the best book you can buy on the subject.' In that sense Whitelocke possessed humility, untainted by mock modesty.

Acknowledgements

To name all the people who have contributed to the progress of this book would be impossible, for they are too many, but I am grateful to every one of them. In the early stages, when I most needed encouragement, I received it from Dame Veronica Wedgwood and Dr. Christopher Hill and I thank them for their kindness.

To those who have made my researches possible I record my deep indebtedness: to the Marquess of Bute for allowing me to borrow and quote from Whitelocke's unpublished manuscript 'Diary', and to his archivist Miss Catherine Armet for her help; to the Marquess of Bath for granting permission to study and quote from the thirty folio volumes and nine parcels of Whitelocke Papers in the muniments room at Longleat, and the 'Journal of the Swedish Embassy' and 'Book of Expenses', the embassy accounts housed in the Library; also to his former Comptroller, Mr. R. H. Ingleton. To Mr. T. C. Skeat, Keeper of Manuscripts at the British Museum, as well as to Miss C. H. Olorenshaw and all other staff in the Students' Room, I am grateful for advice and information and for their Job-like patience with my sometimes tiresome requests; when, for example, a shelf-full of Whitelocke manuscripts suddenly disappeared, they responded to my howl of despair by rescuing them from the dextrous hands of the binders (some volumes already stripped of their leather spines and tied with tape) and restored them to me for several months of checking. To the staff in the Museum's Reading Room and North Library I also record my gratitude.

I am grateful to Mr. Mackworth Young, Librarian at Windsor Castle and to Mr. A. E. B. Owen at the Cambridge University Library, to librarians at the Bodleian in Oxford, Guildhall London, at the South Audley Street branch of the Westminster Public Library, at the Holborn Central Library and Cheltenham Public Library, also to those in Dr. Williams's, the Fawcett and the Senate House Libraries. I thank them all for their courtesy and efficiency in helping me to trace obscure books, documents or information.

County archivists in Wiltshire, Bedfordshire and East Suffolk and the City archivist in Bristol have supplied me with relevant data, and I have been helped with erudite replies to my queries from incumbents at Bromham, Chilton Foliat, Fawley near Henley-on-Thames, Hedgerley and Wokingham, and from the Baptist minister at Cotton End near Bedford. Mrs. Rosalind Gibbs who found me pottering inquisitively in Hunsdon Church, Herts, lent a valuable book on the great house and the parish to me, a total stranger.

For advice on medical questions which arise in the manuscripts I am indebted to Dr. Esther Welbourn of New Hall, Cambridge and to Mr. E. Gaskell, Librarian of the Wellcome Institute of the History of Medicine.

Miss M. Mackenzie, Father Paul and Father Pecz, who have all had personal links with Fawley Court, and Colonel E. J. S. Ward, M.V.O., M.C., at Chilton Foliat, have helped me to piece together details relating to two of Whitelocke's homes, although both houses were rebuilt after his death.

I am particularly grateful to Mrs. Madeleine Whitelocke for lending me a manuscript in her possession, a family tree, and most of all for allowing me to look through her late husband's papers. One of these, supplemented by her memory for detail, set me on a trail which took me across the Republic of Ireland, in pursuit of Bulstrode Whitelocke, an adventure which is described in a Postscript to this book. In Eire I was greatly helped by Miss Winifred Whitelocke Lloyd, by two firms of solicitors, by Mr. Osmond Dowling, Director of the Dublin Diocesan Press Office, by Dame Agnes Finnigan the Lady Abbess at Kylemore Abbey and by Dr. Raymond Cross. On a second visit to Dublin I received help from Father Carton and Mr. William Kirkpatrick as well as from Sister Benvenuta, with whom I talked seventeenth-century history for five hours one Saturday evening; on the Sunday morning she commandeered a friend with a car who kindly drove us to Priorswood House, to the north-east of Dublin, a Georgian mansion which had belonged to Whitelocke's grandson, John Carleton Whitelocke. We found it was to be demolished within a month. Many, many other people in Eire showed me great kindness.

Portraits of the leading characters in a biography, and pictures of the places they knew, add a seasoning of understanding and enjoyment. For help in that direction I thank Mr. John Piper, C.H. for most generously drawing details of the Whitelocke tomb in Fawley Church, as one of the illustrations to this book. I am also indebted to Mr. David Piper, C.B.E. for his advice on the portraits, while for Swedish illustrations I thank the administrators of the Council of Europe's Christina Exhibition and Miss Eva Benedicks of the Swedish Institute in Stockholm. She and Dr. Rudberg of the University of Uppsala also went to considerable trouble answering my enquiries, and the information they supplied helped me to retrace Whitelocke's coach journey from Gothenburg to Uppsala and then down to Stockholm.

I have met or corresponded with a surprising number of descendants of the Whitelocke and Bulstrode families (as well as people who hope they are descendants); several of them have allowed me to borrow genealogies and other material, notably Dr. John Bulstrode, Mr. A. J. Bulstrode Whitelocke, Mrs. M. A. Hawksley and members of her family, also Group Captain F. W. Wiseman-Clarke and his daughter Mrs. Richard Carr who allowed me to study interesting family portraits as well as lending me a family tree. Trafford Whitelock of the B.B.C. gave me the opportunity to collaborate over a programme on Bulstrode Whitelocke in John Carroll's series 'People Past and Present' in the National Portrait Gallery, and in a subsequent radio programme; Daniel Massey played Whitelocke in both programmes, with subtlety and panache, with Sheila Allen gracefully playing Queen Christina and all the other ladies; Robert Spencer, the lutanist, effectively revived 'Whitelocke's Coranto', composed in 1634.

To my friends in general, and particularly to those in the Association of Head Mistresses who have listened to me talking endlessly about Whitelocke, and some of whom have commented on parts of the book, or helped translate obscure Latin tags, I am very grateful. I also wish to thank Lieut.-Commander Peter Kemp, O.B.E., formerly head of the Naval Historical Branch and Naval Librarian, Ministry of Defence, for scrutinizing and correcting the nautical terms used in several chapters. The most continuously stimulating and heartening help has come from members of the seventeenth-century seminars led at first by Mr. Robert Latham, and subsequently by Mr. Roger Lockyer, Dr. Henry Roseveare and Dr. Ian Roy at the Institute of Historical Research of the University of London. It would need a long list to name all the research students who have given me references and notes as a result of questions and discussion in seminars or casual encounters in the British Museum. To Dr. Roy I extend my warmest thanks for reading the penultimate draft of the script and making valuable suggestions which I have tried to incorporate. Any errors and shortcomings in the book are my own, unaided work.

I thank Eric Wyatt for his good humour in the face of the domestic turmoil occasioned by this book and for his painstaking work on Whitelocke's family tree. Finally, I thank his wife, Marjorie Wyatt, who has pursued Whitelocke with me, notebook in hand, around Longleat and the British Museum, through Ireland and across Sweden, and who typed the script of this book with scholarly care.

List of Illustrations

Frontispiece The tomb of Judge Sir James Whitelocke and his wife Elizabeth, Fawley Church. Drawn for the book by John Piper.

Between pages 48 and 49

1 Bulstrode Whitelocke by kind permission of the Trustees of the *National Portrait Gallery*.
2 Judge Sir James Whitelocke by kind permission of the Trustees of the *National Portrait Gallery*.
3 Bulstrode Whitelocke by kind permission of the President and Fellows of *St. John Baptist College, Oxford*.
4 Bulstrode Whitelocke, Ambassador Extraordinary to the Swedish Court, by kind permission of the Trustees of the *National Portrait Gallery*.

Between pages 64 and 65

5 Queen Christina by Sebastian Bourdon by kind permission of *Baron Carl Gripenstedt*.
6 Ambassador Coenraad van Beuningen by Caspar Netscher by kind permission of *Statens Museum for Kunst, Copenhagen*.
7 Chancellor Axel Oxenstierna by David Beck, in a private Swedish collection, reproduced by kind permission of the owner.

Between pages 192 and 193

8 Queen Christina, 1645 drawing by P. Holsteyn, by kind permission of *Kungliga Biblioteket, Stockholm*.
9 Don Antonio Pimentel de Prado by Frederik Bouttats, by kind permission of *Nationalmuseum, Stockholm*.
10 Uppsala from the South, showing the Edenberg House, woodcut by O. Rudbeck, in *Atlantica*, by kind permission of *Kungliga Biblioteket, Stockholm*.

Between pages 208 and 209

11 Uppsala Castle, woodcut by O. Rudbeck, in *Atlantica*, by kind permission of *Kungliga Biblioteket, Stockholm*.
12 Edward Hyde, 1st Earl of Clarendon, after G. Soest, by kind permission of the Trustees of the *National Portrait Gallery*.
13 George Cokain (believed) by kind permission of the Lay Pastor and Elders of *Harecourt United Reformed Church*.
14 George Moncke, 1st Duke of Albemarle, by kind permission of the Trustees of the *National Portrait Gallery*.
15 Archbishop Sheldon by kind permission of the Trustees of the *National Portrait Gallery*.

JOHN WHITELOCK *m. circa 1454* AGNES *dr.and heir of Robert de la Beche of Beches nr Wokingham, Berks.*
of Beches, nr Wokingham WILLIAM WHITELOCK = COWDREY

RICHARD WHITELOCK = GROVE *from Fingest, Bucks*

m.7 Feb.1563-4

RICHARD = JOAN BROCKHURST *née* COLTE *widow*
d.Bordeaux 7 Nov.1570 *d.21 Feb.1606-7*
buried Aldermary Church chancel

WILLIAM
Eton and King's Coll. Cantab.
Vice-Provost of King's
Canon of Wells and Lichfield

JOHN
=
ANN
dr.of John Planer of Wokingham

HIEROM

twins

RICHARD
b.28 Dec.1565

WILLIAM
b.28 Nov.1570
d.circa 1597

JUDGE JAMES WHITELOCK Kt
b.28 Nov.1570 in Thames Street
in parish of St Dunstan's-in-the-East
d.22 June 1632
buried Fawley

m.9 Sept.1602 at Beaconsfield ELIZABETH BULSTRODE
dr.of Edward Bulstrode of
Hedgerley Bulstrode, Bucks.
b.31 July 1575
d.28 May 1631
buried Fawley

EDMUND
b.10 Feb.1564
Parish of Fenchurch
died Newhall Essex

MARY
b.6 Oct.1606 at
Hedgerley
d.3 June 1611
buried St Dunstan's-
in-the-West

CECILIA
b.10 Mar.1607-8
in Fleet St, Christ-
ened St Dunstan's-
in-the-West
m.1632
=
EDWARD DIXON
of Hilden, Tonbridge, Kent

JOAN
b.6 Aug.1609
at Hedgerley
d.8 May 1610
buried Beaconsfield

DOROTHY
b.15 Sept.1610
in Fleet St
Christened St
Dunstan's-in-
the-West
d.30 Sept.1610
buried St Dunstan's
in-the-West

JAMES
b.17 May 1612
at Fleet St
Christened St Duns-
tan's-in-the-West
d.in infancy

ELIZABETH
b.6 Oct.1603
Beaconsfield
d.1668-9
m.24 May 1623
at Stanton Lacy
=
THOMAS MOSTYN
of Flint
|
ROGER

m.June 1630

BULSTRODE WHITELOCKE Kt === REBECCA BENNET
b.6 Aug.1605 in Fleet St · dr.of Thos.Bennet, Alderman of London. d.May 1634 at Bow
Christened St Dunstan's-in-the-West
19 Aug.1605. d.28 July 1675

JAMES Kt === MARY PILCHARD widow. dr.of George Pyke of Trumpington
m.1657
b. 13 July 1631 at
Mrs Bennet's house, Cheapside. d.Oct.1701

runaway marriage at Fawley Court 9 Nov.1634
2 === FRANCES WILLOUGHBY dr.of Lord Willoughby of Parham. d.16 May 1649

FRANCES 1
b.26 Dec.1635
d.Dec.1654

WILLIAM Kt
b.27 Dec.1636
Treasurer of
Middle Temple
‖ m.1671
MARY
dr.of Sir Thos.Overbury

ELIZABETH
b.1638
‖ m.1653
RICHARD
PRYCE Kt

MARY
bapt.
Apr.1639
‖ m.1657
GEORGE
NEVILL
of Sheffield Park,
Sussex. d.1665

ANNE
b.Apr.1640
d.1661
‖ m.1657
GEORGE
HILL

CECILIA
b.21 June
1641
d.27 May 1662
‖ m.1658
SAMUEL HARVEY
d.Jan.1662

HESTER
b.8 Aug.
1642
PRYCE Jr in Wales

WILLOUGHBY BULSTRODE
b.7 Oct.1645
d.1670–71

BULSTRODE
b.17 Nov.1647

m.Bronham Church, Beds.5 Aug.1650   m.Hackney Church, London 5 Sept.1650
3 === MARY WILSON
widow of Rowland Wilson. Buried Chilton Foliat, Wilts. July 1684

SAMUEL
b.30 May 1651
‖ m.27 Dec.1671
ELIZABETH GOUGH

CARLETON
b.13 July 1652
at Whitehall
d.6 Aug.1706

BIGLEY
b.6 Nov.
1653

FRANCES 2
b.17 May 1655
‖ m.11 Apr.1672
FRANCIS PILE

JOHN
b.26 Sept.1656
at Bishopsgate St

REBECCA
b.7 Mar.1657–8
at Bishopsgate St

STEPHEN
b.7 Oct.1659 at
Scotland Yard,
Whitehall

KATHERINE HENLEY
2 === MARY ALWYN

Chapter One

'The Best School in Christendom'

Bulstrode Whitelocke, who was born in Fleet Street in 1605, was a rich mixture of a man. A scholar and an obsessive writer, a distinguished lawyer and Parliamentarian, he also had something about him of an Elizabethan swashbuckler. He was sensitive but tough, a gifted musician and keen falconer, a man who enjoyed pranks as well as poetry, and relished philosophical meditation as he did food and wine. He had reached his late forties when Cromwell and the Council appointed him Ambassador to the young Queen Christina of Sweden, and a very good choice it was for he had the manners of a courtier with the wary astuteness of a diplomat. He liked ceremony, especially when he was at the centre of it, but he was also drawn to solitude and was happy riding through the woods, overseeing the building of a wall or following the plough. Tolerant, ironical, uncoercive by nature, he could put on the grand manner when it was called for, and enjoy it. He valued women for their judgement as well as for their charms and within a span of twenty years he had three wives, was married four times in unusual circumstances, and became the indulgent father of seventeen children. He was in short, according to the popular image, a most improbable puritan.

It must be admitted that there were a good many improbable puritans: men who delighted in music, in dancing or in falconry, in good living, ceremonial, or in making love; but few of them enjoyed Whitelocke's rich assortment of talents and pleasures, and no other left behind such a mass of detail, reflecting an intense interest in history, politics, and in himself. Men who were labelled puritan in the seventeenth century held widely divergent views. They included tailors, cobblers and labourers, merchants, clergymen and lawyers, scholars and noblemen yet, like other radical groups which threaten the established order, they were bundled together under the one contemptuous nickname and caricatured as seditious workmen or Philistine prigs, devoid of social grace.[1]

Bulstrode Whitelocke claimed descent from the family of de la Beche, whose recumbent seven-foot effigies, from the fourteenth century, fill the small church of Aldworth, near Pangbourne. Nicholas de la Beche had served at the Courts of Edward II and Edward III, he had been Constable of the Tower of London, Seneschal of Gascony, and had supervised the education of the young Black Prince.[2] A branch of the family had owned the Manor of Beeches at Bearwood near Wokingham from the year 1231; Robert de la Beche, the last male heir, died in about 1453 and his daughter

Agnes inherited the Manor; soon afterwards she married John Whitelocke and the property passed into the hands of a sturdy but at that time undistinguished family. Down the years the Whitelockes produced the occasional clergyman and scholar but they were, in the main, modest Berkshire gentry. Writing early in the seventeenth century James Whitelocke commented on 'the moderation of this family, that hath continued their patrimony for almost 400 years without increase or diminution; it hath been more impaired by the now owner than by all his ancestors . . . neither do I find that in all this time they have purchased any land, neither that they have sold any'.[3] The same could not be said of James Whitelocke himself nor of his son Bulstrode, both of whom thrust their way upward professionally, socially and as acquisitive landowners.

Bulstrode's grandfather, Richard Whitelocke, was born in 1533, the year in which Henry VIII married Anne Boleyn and was excommunicated by the Pope. Being the youngest son Richard was obliged to work for his living, which he did as a merchant, importing goods from Italy, Spain, Russia and France.

He used to go in person into foreign countries and, having a purpose to leave that dangerous course of life, was taken away by death in that voyage he made account should have been his last. He went from London towards Bordeaux in France, the emporium for Gascoyne wines, 22 September 1570, and there fell into a pleurisy, 21 October next following, of which he died 7 November following, and was buried with great difficulty.[4]

He was excommunicated on his death-bed for refusing the sacrament of extreme unction 'and such popish ceremonies', and so was denied Christian burial. But a hundred or more English merchants, living in Bordeaux, armed themselves with guns and carried his body to a vineyard outside the town where he was buried with honour, not among the corpses in sanctified ground, but among the living vines. He was only thirty-seven. His widow Joan, the executrix to his will, inherited his large house in Thames Street, 'over against the Bear Key', and enough money to support a young family. Edmund was six years old, Richard not yet five, while twin brothers, William and James, were born in the Thames Street house three weeks after their father's death.

With her heavy responsibilities Joan Whitelocke decided to marry a third time, but as she was (by her own reckoning) nearing her mid-forties and had four sons under the age of seven she was hardly in a position to pick or choose. Again she married a merchant, but she soon discovered that Thomas Price was 'a very unkind and insolent husband'.[5] If Price married her for the legacy, he too came in for a disappointment. Joan had a head for business and 'by means underhand' protected the boys' inheritance, buying up leases of properties and displaying, according to her son James, an 'admirable wisdom, almost not to be looked for in one of her sex, so afflicted with the daily miseries wrought to her from her husband'. Her object was to provide a good schooling for all her sons; this must include the attainments of an English gentleman, singing, dancing and playing the lute as well as a knowledge of Latin, Greek, Hebrew and French. Apart from that she wished to have them trained 'every one of them to that he was likeliest to do good in'.[6] Their talents varied. Edmund excelled as a dilettante and a polished parasite. After going down from Christ's College, Cambridge he studied at the Universities of Rostock, Rome, Prague, Paris and Wittenberg, where he picked up several languages and could pass for a Frenchman, but he learned little in the way of wisdom or judgement. To his familiars the merchant's son became 'Captain' Whitelocke, having held a commission in the French infantry. He was a well-known figure in London society, witty, sophisticated and on drinking terms with a number of noblemen at whose expense he lived without working. His patrons included Henry Percy, Earl of Northumberland, and Roger Manners, Earl of Rutland.[7] He numbered among his acquaintances the young Inigo Jones who visited King James's Court in 1605, and the middle-aged Walter Ralegh. At various times in his life he became an inmate of Newgate, the Marshalsea, the Fleet and the Tower. On 7 February 1601 he met the young Earl of Rutland in the street, went along with him to a meeting and so became an innocent suspect in Essex's plot to depose Queen Elizabeth. Four years later he happened to dine with the catholic Earl of Northumberland and that nobleman's relative, Sir Thomas Percy. The date was 4 November 1605. When Guy Fawkes's Gunpowder Plot was exposed on the following day Percy was found to be deeply implicated. Edmund Whitelocke was arrested as an associate, but was released after a long spell in jail since nothing was found against him. His bizarre life and death were summed up by Dudley Carleton in a caustic letter dated 20 September 1608: 'Captain Whitelocke . . . is so lamented by all boon companions as if the world had not been worthy of him. His death was sudden, as were all the actions of his life, and as he lived amongst lords, so was he buried in a vault amongst my Lord of Sussex' ancestors, at whose house he died.'[8]

In contrast Joan's second son, Richard, became a respectable merchant like his father. He spent most of his life abroad, in or near Danzig, married a woman of property from Elbing in Prussia, and founded the continental branch of the Whitelocke family. James's twin brother William was a tall, flaxen-haired lad who threw up a London apprenticeship for the life of a buccaneer. After fighting in Portugal he served in the West Indies under Sir Francis Drake. He told the family that in January 1595-6 (when Drake was dying of dysentery) he buckled the Admiral into his armour 'that he might die like a soldier'. William also claimed that Sir Francis on his death-bed gave him 'divers rich legacies of plate and jewels', but that Drake's brother Thomas stripped him of the gift. The matter was not pursued; the bequest did not appear in the Admiral's Will, executed the day before his death, and William himself died a year or two later in an encounter with the Spaniards.[9]

Bulstrode's father, James, grew up to be the most distinguished of the four brothers. From Merchant Taylors' School, under its famous headmaster Richard Mulcaster, he went to St. John's College, Oxford, where he was industrious and chronically hard up. The University usually kept aloof from events in the world outside, but even they felt a tremor in 1588 from 'the terrible show of the sea armada from Spain, which was a little distemper to the quiet course of studies'. The number of students at Oxford from aristocratic and wealthy homes had risen steeply in the previous century.[10] There were young men in the colleges with horses, servants and money. James had none of these, but made the acquaintance of some of his well-born or well-to-do contemporaries. He made friends too with a student from a modest background like his own, a clothier's son from Reading, William Laud. As the two men matured their religious and political convictions diverged sharply, but the friendship survived. In later years however James prophesied trouble, since Laud was 'too full of fire, though a just and good man, and . . . his want of experience in state matters and his too much zeal for the Church and heat (if he proceeded in the ways he was then in) would set this nation on fire.'[11] In 1593 James Whitelocke was admitted to the Middle Temple and, at the late age of thirty, was called to the Bar in 1600. His eldest brother Edmund's imprisonment the next year in connection with the Essex plot reflected for some time on James's career.[12]

In spite of his difficulties, James set out in the world with two assets, a devoted mother and a good education. In 1602 he added to his resources by marrying Elizabeth Bulstrode of Hedgerley Bulstrode near Beaconsfield. Her widowed mother, Cecilia, set her up with clothes and jewelry and provided five hundred pounds in cash, as well as board and lodging at a house in Fleet Street during the first eighteen months of their married life. Although it was not a large dowry there were hidden benefits. The Bulstrode family were no longer wealthy but they were influential. Their forbears had given service at Court; one had been a servant to Henry VI's wife Queen Margaret, another a maid of honour in the household of Katherine of Aragon. They had shown themselves adaptable to the times. Three of them had been gentlewomen of the bedchamber in the service of Anne Boleyn, while a maternal great-grandfather of Elizabeth Bulstrode's had been one of the first clerks in holy orders to marry after the break with Rome. More important, from James's point of view, were the immediate family connections. The Bulstrodes were related by marriage to successful lawyers, the Untons of Chequers and the Crokes. Elizabeth's uncle John Croke, Recorder of London, was currently Speaker of the House of Commons in what was to be Queen Elizabeth's last Parliament. The next summer, in May 1603, King James I, arriving from Scotland to a great welcome from his new subjects, knighted John Croke with half a dozen other gentlemen. One of them was Queen Elizabeth's famous Attorney General, Edward Coke, a friend of the Crokes.[13] John Croke was shortly afterwards appointed a King's Bench Judge, his brother George became a Judge of Common Pleas, while their friend Edward Coke was made Lord Chief Justice, first of Common Pleas and later of the King's Bench. Altogether it was a most desirable marriage for James Whitelocke, a barrister with little money and no standing. It also proved to be a deeply happy one. A year later they had a daughter whom they named Elizabeth.

On 6 August 1605 a son was born to them at George Croke's house in Fleet Street.[14] The infant was baptized in the church of St. Dunstan in the West, where his mother's parents had been married in 1571;[15] his notorious uncle Edmund Whitelocke, 'a man of excellent parts and wit but of a wild fancy', being one of the godfathers, announced at the christening that the child was to be called Bulstrode. This halted the vicar in his tracks; he asked if the godparents would suggest something else. Something scriptural would no doubt have been acceptable. Uncle Edmund insisted however that the infant must bear one of its mother's names, ' "Bulstrode or Elizabeth let them choose which they pleased" and thereupon he was named Bulstrode.'[16]

In 1606, with the next child on the way, Elizabeth placed her year-old son in the care of a village woman at Wooburn, Buckinghamshire, an easy ride from Hedgerley; but when she visited the cottage she was not satisfied that her son was being properly fed. The nurse of course blamed the 'testy child' who refused to eat his shaffling broth though she made it 'yellow as the golden noble'.[17] Elizabeth was not impressed by eel and rusty-bacon soup as a baby's diet, so she picked up her testy child and took him home. The Whitelocke parents were not afraid to show affection towards their children and Bulstrode came in for a great deal of attention and thrived on it. His mother was widely read with a good knowledge of history and French, and was giving him lessons by the time he was four; his father sometimes fortified her teaching with 'solid instruction to heighten the mind', while at other times 'he delighted to sport with his child.'[18]

Of seven children, only Elizabeth, Bulstrode and Cecilia survived infancy. Their father held a series of rewarding posts – as Land Steward of his old college in Oxford, as Steward of Eton and later as a Steward of Westminster College or, as it is commonly called, Westminster School. He and his son always referred to it as 'Westminster College'. He sharpened his wits fighting legal battles for himself and for the colleges who employed him, and earned the disapproval of Lord Chancellor Ellesmere, a man of rigid views; he met people of influence, named his children after them and roped them in as godparents; he cultivated the friendship of lawyers of independent outlook notably John Selden, and Lord Chief Justice Sir Edward Coke to whom in later years he sent gifts of turkey, swan and expensive salmon; Coke liked him and returned the compliment with an occasional piece of venison or an invitation to dinner at Stoke Poges.[19]

James Whitelocke began to make his mark in London as spokesman for those men who were demanding, with growing insistence, that the King should acknowledge certain limits on his prerogative. In 1606, King James had unobtrusively increased the import duty on currants from two shillings and sixpence to seven shillings and sixpence a hundredweight. A Levant merchant named Bate challenged the legality of this measure, imposed without reference to Parliament, but the Court of Exchequer upheld the King's action, for which there was ample precedent, and when the Commons assembled in 1608 they raised no objection.

In 1610, in his fortieth year, James Whitelocke entered Parliament as Member for Woodstock, and during a debate in July made a speech which set the scene for much that was to follow. Impositions, he conceded, were of such importance to the nation that it was right that they should be determined by the sovereign power of the State. But where, he asked, did sovereign power lie? In an elaborate argument he propounded that the King by

THE BEST SCHOOL IN CHRISTENDOM'

himself enjoyed limited power, while the King in Parliament wielded supreme power.[20] He was at first alone in challenging the Court's decision against Bate; gradually, however, it occurred to Members of Parliament that by acquiescing in the King's action they forfeited any prospect of controlling his revenue.

James Whitelocke's stand made enemies for him at Court, and the age-old machinery for dealing with trouble-makers was slowly trained in his direction. In 1613 he faced a trumped up charge – 'to give him an item for old deserts.' He was scarcely allowed to defend himself and was sneered at and vilified by the Master of the Rolls before being imprisoned in the Fleet.[21] For an ambitious man it is more profitable to be abused than to be ignored, and he accepted the sentence philosophically, thankful that his family had left London for the Easter vacation. But he had no intention of languishing in jail, however good the cause, so after a month he made a plausible apology for his great error and misdemeanour, which obtained his release. After that he resumed the struggle.

As time went on, Lord Chief Justice Coke, although nearly twenty years his senior, began to treat him like a colleague. One Sunday, in September 1615, as the morning service at Windsor ended, Coke beckoned to James to help him to his coach. As he hobbled down the aisle on the younger man's arm he growled that he could not dine with the King because His Majesty would persist in asking questions, and took it badly when the answers were not what he wanted. The King, encouraged by Lord Chancellor Ellesmere, had been asserting that he was above the law while Coke insisted defiantly 'the King is under God and the law.' Coke's belief in the supremacy of the common law, and the conclusions that followed from this, had profoundly influenced some lawyers of his day. James Whitelocke was one of them.[22]

Bulstrode was growing up in a home where the liberating views of Edward Coke and John Selden were taken for granted, views which often ran counter to those of King James and the churchmen; it was a home in which his mother's unfanatical puritanism and his father's learning and passion for music permeated his life. James Whitelocke was kindly, hot-tempered, ambitious, the merchant's son making good; he demanded much from his heir, driving him to work harder than other boys and, as it happened, his son responded.

At the age of six Bulstrode had been sent away to a school where he remained, for three years, in the care of a schoolmaster who beat boys twice if they failed to yell the first time. In the holidays he returned to his father's house at Clewer, near Eton, and spent much of his time in the stables, until one day he was kicked in the face by a horse. His mother could deal with most emergencies, and stitched the wound so neatly that in later years his lip showed only a faint scar. Soon afterwards he was sent to Eton, but that year's schooling seems to have been uneventful.

From the year 1615 his education followed the same pattern as his father's. As a pupil at Merchant Taylors' School he was grounded in Greek, Latin and Hebrew, music, dancing and fencing; he studied shorthand which he used in later years for jotting down sermons or private notes and he performed in the school masque. At twelve years old Bulstrode was clever, self-assured, aggressive; the boys accepted his leadership in street fighting against their enemies from Paul's School and 'many a black eye and bloody nose was had among them'. Eventually the masters decided the feud must stop, and picked on young Whitelocke to lead a deputation to the rival school, where he delivered an oration in Latin offering terms for peace. After appropriate consultations the others replied, also in Latin, accepting the proposals. It was his first taste of diplomacy and he liked it.

In spite of the short spell in prison his father continued to consolidate his position, and by the year 1616 was able to raise £9,000 for the purchase of Fawley Court near Henley-on-Thames.[23] In 1632 he bought Fillets or Phyllis Court, the adjoining estate on the Henley side, for £1,200. Fawley was to be Bulstrode's home during most of his life; he loved the place with its beech woods and deer park, the steep ride up the knoll and lands stretching down to the wide, complacent Thames.[24]

At the age of fifteen he went to his father's college in Oxford to study logic and philosophy. William Laud, the President of St. John's, kept an eye on his friend's son, and occasionally invited him round to his lodging for a talk; he was responsible for appointing the boy's tutor, Philip Parsons, a man of twenty-six who 'not only read to him, but much conversed with him as his companion'.[25] Bulstrode spent his leisure time with music groups, reading English history, or hunting; he was taught the finer points in the hunting field by William Juxon, the mild and orthodox vicar of Summertown on the outskirts of Oxford. When Juxon succeeded Laud as President he gave up hunting with the students; he was later appointed Bishop of London, and it was he who ministered to King Charles on the scaffold.

Laud's zeal to suppress puritanism had already made its mark on Oxford and Bulstrode found himself surrounded by the champions of religious orthodoxy; at home, however, puritan as well as anti-Court views were the daily currency, and in spite of conformist pressures at college, he gained a reputation for making puritanical jibes at the Church.[26]

The family income was by this time substantial but his father, who had known what it was to be poor, kept him short of money. Bulstrode later advised his own children against imposing this form of discipline on their sons, for in his own case it had an unfortunate sequence. He could not afford to keep a horse at Oxford, as many boys did, so when his friends rode off for a day's hunting he trudged along on foot.[27] One day he had walked nearly six miles to join them at Islip, when he injured his leg and had to lie down on the damp ground, where he fell asleep. He woke in great pain to find that he could not get to his feet, and in some consternation he sounded his huntsman's horn. He was rescued and driven back to St. John's in a farm cart; doctors prescribed medicines and poultices but could not relieve the pain in the hollow of his thigh. Eventually his parents sent the coach, piled up with blankets and pillows, to bring him back to Fawley. It was feared he would never walk again but his mother called in an unlicensed German practitioner, Dr. Matthews, who told the servants to heat a brick in the fire, drench it in a solution of herbs, ox-marrow and muskadine, then wrap it in cloths and apply it to the injured limb; as one brick cooled down it was replaced by a hot one, and the treatment was continued for about ten days.[28] Whitelocke was soon able to get about on crutches but it was nearly a year before he could walk without a stick, and for the rest of his life he had trouble with his leg. Yet he never allowed this to spoil his enjoyment of dancing, riding or hawking. The accident deprived him of a university degree but, more important, it steered him away from the forces of reaction in Oxford and into the political hurly-burly of conflicting views at the Inns of Court.

He was seventeen when he was admitted a law student to the Middle Temple; there he made friends with several young men who later became famous. One of them, Edward Hyde, had a great admiration for him; this came out in colourful, untidy letters which, incidentally, conveyed scant reverence for some of the men in authority. The correspondence, and the admiration, lasted until some twenty years later when their political paths diverged. Both students came under the influence of the eminent scholar and lawyer John Selden. In later years Hyde made excuses for the old man's allegiance to Parliament. He never forgot Selden's 'stupendous learning' or his 'faculty of making hard things easy'.[29] Whitelocke, who became a life-long friend of Selden's, recalled years later some of the advice the older man used to give him: always, even when he came home late, to read something before he fell asleep; also, to master the main points of the law and then specialize, rather than waste time on 'common known' subjects. Selden stimulated his interest in English history, taught him to make notes and jot down sources, showed him how to study old records and manuscripts, and awakened in him an interest in oriental languages. Whitelocke could say with satisfaction he 'so well liked my company that he gave me the freedom of his rare library'. Above all Selden encouraged him to make a study of men, saying that there was even more to be learned from the conversation of intelligent men than there was from books.[30]

As often happens to a rebel if he lives long enough, James Whitelocke's earlier exploits came to be remembered with indulgence or respect, and in 1624 he was knighted and appointed a King's Bench Judge. He had started life with the disadvantages of a youngest son and a stepson. He had built a career on office-holding, on voicing a grievance in Parliament before others had recognized it, and on aligning himself with those distinguished lawyers who were chipping at the foundations of royal prerogative. He believed in justice, free from corruption or pressure. By the age of fifty-four he had reached the heights of his profession and was recognized as a man of substance and influence. None of his ancestors had risen in this spectacular way by their own efforts, nor had they been able to invest extensively in land as he had done. He was also a devoted father, ambitious for his son, inclined to be crusty. He had never been outside his own country and when Bulstrode asked for permission to travel abroad Sir James insisted that there were places in England worth a visit before crossing the Channel. By way of inducement he asked some of his brother judges to allow the boy to attend their Assizes. The response was cordial and Bulstrode, accompanied by a groom, set off from Fawley in high spirits riding 'a good nag, the first whereof he was master' given him by their neighbour at Greenlands, Sir Cope D'Oyly.[31] At Gloucester he left the Assizes to explore the Forest of Dean, then rode farther west to see 'other memorable places that way'. This meant crossing the Wye in a small, flat-bottomed horse-ferry, propelled by a woman with a 'scoop' or paddle. It was foolhardy to take two horses over at once but Bulstrode was inexperienced and headstrong. In midstream the baggage horse 'began to flounce' and finished back to front, its hind quarters in the river. The groom was helpless with fear so Bulstrode started to push the animal overboard to swim, but the horse was not having that; it dragged its quarters into the boat and staggered to its feet, twisting round with such violence that Bulstrode was nearly thrown into the water. By the time they reached the bank the boat was waterlogged, and they floundered ashore sopping wet and badly shaken.

It is not clear whether Whitelocke was still travelling or whether he was at the Middle Temple in March 1625, at the time of King James's death and the accession of Charles I. He later recounted the events as if they were items of history which scarcely touched his life, and in the same spirit he described the First Parliament of the new reign and the outcry against the disastrous expedition to Cadiz. This had been mismanaged by the Duke of Buckingham, in his role as Lord High Admiral, assisted by the corrupt James Bagg whom he commissioned to victual the ships before they left Plymouth. 'Where the fault lay hath not yet been determined, nor any punished for it,' Whitelocke wrote. He could not have made that comment after the Second Parliament had met, since it laid the blame firmly on the Duke, but it is significant that years later when he wrote his memoirs, 'The Annals of his own Life Dedicated to his Children', he apparently copied the note he had made as a boy of twenty.

The bubonic plague, carried by black rats, was decimating the population of London. Even in Henley and the nearby village of Remenham whole families were obliterated. Sir James isolated his household. The gates of Fawley Court were shut and no one was allowed in or out without good cause. To avoid contagion a tub of water was set at the gate; the labourers' wages were dropped in it and they had to fish for their pay. In London the number of victims had gone down from 5,000 a week to half that number when it fell to Judge Whitelocke, in the Michaelmas term 1625, to adjourn the King's Bench to Reading. Bulstrode insisted on accompanying his father on this dangerous visit and they set off together in the coach, accompanied by servants on horseback. After stopping for a night with relatives at Horton, near Colnbrook, they arrived next day at Hyde Park Corner. To avoid infection, they had brought their own food and drink and the Judge made his company sit on the ground for an open air meal. Then he and his son were driven at speed through deserted streets in which the grass was beginning to grow. At Westminster Hall he went to the King's Bench, adjourned the Court and set off again for Hyde Park Corner and home, thanking God that there were no signs of the plague among his people.

In February 1626 Bulstrode found himself, through his father's influence, returned as Burgess for Stafford in King Charles's Second Parliament and was able to write with pride 'I was an eye and ear-witness of all these great transactions.'[32] In spite of his effortless entry, not unusual at that date, Bulstrode was punctilious in attending debates and committees of the House of Commons and in recording the activities of this short-lived but 'great, warm and ruffling Parliament'. The word ruffling conveyed a sense of turbulence and aggression. He saw the Parliament of England as 'the best school in Christendom' but it was a tough school, in which the theories he had heard discussed were beginning to take flesh. His father advised him to avoid committing himself to any party or faction, and to vote according to his conscience; Bulstrode claimed that he did this, using the light and reason which God had given him regardless of popular pressure or court flattery. Light and reason, in the event, prompted him to vote against the Court party.[33]

Some forty years later he imagined that he had encountered Edward Coke and Thomas Wentworth in this Parliament. In fact, their activities in the previous Parliament had brought them into collision with the Court party, and in consequence they had been appointed sheriffs to make them ineligible to stand for Parliament. This attempt by the King's friends to create a docile House which would vote supplies failed, for the Commons found new and formidable fighters in men like their three Johns – Pym, Hampden and their leader Sir John Eliot.

The Lord Keeper informed the new Parliament that they were summoned in order to make good laws and to execute justice; the Speaker, too, 'made a harangue suitable to the times'. But the Commons had their own notion of their functions, reaching far beyond the maintenance of law and order or the voting of supplies. In defiance of what was expected of them 'the Commons began to fall upon the public grievances: the miscarriage of the late voyage to Cadiz; the misemployment of the King's revenue; evil counsel; favouring of Papists; the loans; taxes' and other controversial issues.[34] In spite of messages from the King and Lords urging them to vote supplies they pressed their demand for redress of grievances. On 10 March 1626 Sir Edward Coke's youngest son Clement ('fighting Clem' he was called because of his taste for duelling) expressed the mood of the Commons: 'it were better to die by an enemy than to suffer at home.'[35] Next day, Dr. Samuel Turner asked some pertinent questions about the Duke of Buckingham's fitness to hold such a large number of important posts, basing his criticism on 'common fame'.[36] The King responded with a sharp letter to the Speaker, pressing for supplies. He promised redress of grievances on condition they were 'presented in a dutiful, mannerly way' but to the

Commons' criticism of the Duke, his father's favourite and his own close friend and adviser, he replied loftily 'I will not allow any of my servants to be questioned among you, much less such as are of eminent place and near unto me.' He required the House to discipline Coke and Turner for 'foolish impudence' and the message ended with menace: 'I would you would hasten for my supply, or else it will be worse for yourselves.'

The wrangle continued. The Commons compelled every Member in turn to say whether he had heard Clement Coke speak the words attributed to him and every one of them denied it. This curious defence of a Member who had only said what they were thinking made a deep impression on Whitelocke, who was extremely nervous when his turn came to speak. The King made one concession. He said there had been a misunderstanding and he ordered Buckingham to explain his actions to both Houses. The Commons were not placated; Sir Dudley Digges and Sir John Eliot instituted proceedings for the Duke's impeachment, at which the King committed them both to the Tower. After that the Commons sat stubbornly behind closed doors 'and would not proceed in any other business till they were righted in their liberties'. Before long the two Members were released but on 15 June 1626, as neither side was prepared to give way over Buckingham, the King dissolved Parliament. The Commons had already prepared their Remonstrance against Buckingham and, in spite of the King's proclamation against it, copies were circulated to the public.

Whitelocke does not explain why he was left out of the next Parliament but it was probably because his father was displeased with him for sitting in the gallery of the House, the resort of political extremists.

The short spell as a Member of Parliament had done nothing to subdue his high spirits or his taste for escapades. He enjoyed plotting the elopement of a young heiress, Eleanor Hanham, with John Pyne, and he acted as decoy to put her uncle-guardian off the scent. Pyne was a friend from their student days and remained one until, in the Long Parliament, he joined the 'more rigid party' of the Presbyterians, and became so hostile that Whitelocke regretted having helped him to a rich wife. Another friend, Harbottle Grimston, married Whitelocke's kinswoman, a daughter of Judge Croke's. After their marriage in London the couple drove down to Essex to visit the bridegroom's father, and 'in a youthful frolic' Whitelocke insisted on playing the bride's coachman. On the journey they called at the house of friends, who came to the door to toast the couple and offer refreshments. 'I sat mannerly with my hat in my hand on the coach box, all powdered over with dust.' The lady, perhaps seeing through the livery and under the dust, advanced with a cup of wine in her hand, and staring intently said:

'Sir, I do not use to drink to coachmen, but you seem to be an extraordinary one and therefore I present my service to you.'

I then came off the coachbox and spake to the lady.

'Madam, I believe you do not use to give leave to coachmen to salute you, but let one whom you judge extraordinary have that extraordinary favour from you'
and so I saluted the lady, and went up to my coachbox again.

He returned to his travels, this time riding the western circuit; but the Assizes did not offer enough excitement and he set off on a one-thousand-mile ride, stopping on his journey at the places that a dedicated sight-seer has to visit: Chichester Cathedral and Winchester College, Salisbury, Old Sarum and Stonehenge, Dorchester and Maiden Castle, Weymouth and Chesil Beach; after Bridport he and his horse contended with the 'troublesome hilly ways to Lyme'. He took with him Speed's maps and William Camden's indispensable guide book, *Britannia*, which had been translated from Latin into English in 1610. He was never without a notebook and, as in later life, he jotted down everything that caught his interest. Sea walls and fortifications held a special fascination for him; he studied them all along the south coast, and stopped at Lyme Regis for a good look at the Cobb, the finest harbour in the whole sweep of Lyme Bay – a fact which was to benefit Parliament in the Civil War.[37] As in other towns he was received by the Mayor, to whom his father sent a letter of introduction; this led to a ridiculous incident which he recorded in his notebook. The Mayor invited him and some other young lawyers to dinner. During the meal one of them said to the Mayoress, ingratiatingly, that they were putting her to some trouble and he must offer her his apology. The first lady bridled at what she took to be a gross affront and replied that she was astonished he dared to insult her in front of her husband; they were not so backward in Lyme as he evidently supposed. When they got away the young men wrote a piece of student nonsense at the lady's expense, and the recollection amused Whitelocke enough, as an old man, for him to copy it out for his children.

When we had seen
    the famous Cobb of Lyme,
With Mr. Mayor
    we spent our dinner time,

But Mrs. Mayoress,
   sitting at board's end,
Took great exceptions
   at my noble friend
Because he spake
   the word *apology*
Which Mrs. Mayoress
   said was 'speech too high'
And unbefitting
   both the time and place
Spoken to her
   and to her husband's face . . .
   I dare not for her make *apology* –
   Since she my friend's took so offensively.[38]

He travelled on through Devon to Cornwall, where he was shown St. Michael's Mount by the hospitable Mr. St. Aubyn. After Penzance he recorded 'I rode till I could ride no further, to the land's end, 240 miles from London.'[39] He then set off for Flintshire to visit his sister Elizabeth and her husband Thomas Mostyn, stopping on the way to see Wookey Hole by candlelight – a frightening experience – and to look at cathedrals, abbeys and holy wells on the way north. After a short stay with his sister and her irascible husband, Whitelocke paid a visit to her wealthy father-in-law, Sir Roger Mostyn, who made his money in the coal mines of North Wales. He wrote dryly 'I had a kind outward welcome, but I had rather sit at coarser fare myself than . . . my horse to want provender.'

Wherever he went he had introductions to the leading citizens and his reception was flattering enough to turn any young man's head. He, a young law student, was *persona grata* with a number of judges and not only listened to them in Court but talked and ate and drank with them. It gave him great self-assurance and ease of manner. He was Judge Whitelocke's son; heir to one of the richest estates in Buckinghamshire. He only realized later that the favours he was receiving were not directed to him, but to his father.

Chapter Two

Rebecca

By the time Bulstrode was twenty-two years old he had been given a gentleman's education, a horse of his own and a seat in Parliament. It only remained to provide him with a wife. His father tried to negotiate a match, first with the daughter of a wealthy Mr. Willcox and then with the daughter of a Hertfordshire knight; but although he delineated his son's character and expectations in a most businesslike manner, the deal in each case fell through.[1]

Bulstrode took the disappointment philosophically. He had been called to the Bar when he was twenty-one and two years later, in the autumn of 1628, he was appointed Master of the Revels at the Middle Temple; it was an office which nourished his social ambitions and his taste for being in the centre of the picture. The revellers rehearsed their dances in the evenings at St. Dunstan's tavern; on the opening night, as at successive performances, the Middle Temple hall was packed with spectators. Whitelocke was responsible both for the production and for the front of house arrangements; several indignant gentlemen who were unable to obtain seats sent him challenges, but he was not to be provoked into fighting a duel, 'it being' he considered 'a great folly and sin . . . to hazard your own and another's life and salvation.'[2] The glittering audiences included visitors from abroad, some of whom Whitelocke entertained lavishly at his own expense. As producer he received flattering invitations to dance with the Queen's ladies at Court, where he was treated as a person of consequence. He was climbing the social ladder fast; already he had one foot firmly planted in the Middle Temple, the other in the Palace of Whitehall.

It was not until the new year that he had to face his creditors. He dared not tell his father that he had been borrowing money and he saw no prospect, on his modest allowance, of extricating himself from a jungle of debt. Up to that time he had looked on his legal training as no more than a gentlemanly accomplishment, like the study of Latin and Greek; brooding over the predicament it occurred to him that if he practised as a barrister he could gradually pay off his debts. Sir James approved, but insisted that he would show no more favour towards his son than to any other young lawyer. There were, however, hidden benefits in being a judge's son, and even in the first year Bulstrode earned over £150.

He had not been practising for long when the nation received news that the Duke of Buckingham, the hated power at Court, had been assassinated. According to hearsay, which Whitelocke recorded, the Duke died with the

conventional cry on his lips 'The villain hath slain me.' When the wrong
man was nearly arrested Felton stepped forward saying 'I am he that did it.
Let no innocent man suffer.' Under interrogation he denied that the murder
was a puritan plot or that anybody else was implicated. He claimed to have
committed it because of the wrongs exposed in Parliament's Remonstrance,
for which the Duke was blamed. Grateful Englishmen visited Felton in
prison and admirers all over the country drank his health. The Judges had
the courage to rule that he could not lawfully be tortured, as the King
wished, nor would they consent to his own suggestion that his offending
hand should be cut off. In the end he was sentenced to death and hanged in
chains. Whitelocke was present at the trial, a fact which was omitted when
his 'Annals' were published posthumously as *Memorials of the English Affairs*.[3]
   Sir James eventually succeeded in arranging a match for his son with
Rebecca Bennet, the niece of his old friend Sir Humphrey May who had
been a student with him at St. John's and at the Middle Temple.[4] 'This made
the proposal the better liked', Whitelocke wrote 'and her portion helped it
on, which was three thousand pounds.' The girl's widowed mother arranged
for the wedding to be celebrated in June 1630, in the private chapel of her
house at Mortlake; Whitelocke put on his finery and sailed up the Thames
accompanied by a gallant crowd of young men from the Temple. His
exuberance was short-lived. Rebecca was in a highly nervous state induced
by fear of the marriage bed, and relatives told him he should postpone the
ceremony, or at least its consummation; during the day, however, the bride
recovered her composure and Sir James advised his son to proceed with the
wedding. Bulstrode needed no encouragement. The service was followed by
dancing and revels, and when at last these were over the guests left for home
and Judge Whitelocke returned contentedly to London. It was late at night
when the bride was put to bed by her servants. She lay there in dread of her
husband, who came to her 'expecting marriage joys'. As soon as he climbed
into bed and started claiming those joys she gave way to such a hysterical
outburst that he had to call for help, and for the rest of the night she remained stricken and unapproachable, leaving him to reflect grimly on a
night 'so different from that which new married men look for and enjoy'.[5]
   Rebecca was very contrite the next morning and her husband, hiding his
disappointment, tried to reassure her. Apart from the two accidents when
he was a boy, the sun had always shone for him. Now, he knew suddenly
in his own flesh the terrible frailty of happiness. It was the beginning of
maturity. He turned for solace to his books, and found the pagan authors

sometimes offered more than Christians to a man in adversity. He struggled
to find a meaning in what seemed like senseless misery and was strengthened
by a phrase from Epictetus: *Quodcunque evenerit optimum.* He adapted the
words as his motto: 'Whatever happens is best – if I make it so.' It was not a
tight-lipped resignation nor a grudging 'Thy will be done.' It was a creative
welcome to the inevitable. He could have said with Boethius 'Every lot is
good be it harsh or be it pleasing.' This philosophy was to colour his outlook
and even his political judgement in the years to come.

'Finding music no small refreshment in any trouble', he wrote some
mournful verses and set them to a lute accompaniment.

> The comforts of this life are fading joys,
> Pleasures are toys,
> Honours are vapours, riches fly away
> And friends decay.
> God orders all things to those for the best
> That in him rest.
> Then let our fortunes rise or fall
> Happen what will 'tis best of all.
>
> Seest thou a man in full prosperity
> Mounted on high,
> The wheel of fortune turning round again
> He's in the wain,
> And down he tumbles to that low estate
> Where first he sate
> And more sure, for on earth who lies
> Can never fall, but yet may rise.
>
> If thou art raised to an high degree
> Labour to be
> As good as great; when thy condition's low
> Yet, surely know,
> God loves the poor and indigent as well
> As those that swell
> In wealth; let fortunes rise or fall
> Happen what will 'tis best of all.
>
> If thou are disappointed in the things
> Which thy hope brings

Ne'er to fruition, if the joys of love
Afflictions prove,
When all thy comforts and desires are crossed
And thou art lost
In seas of trouble, waves of gall,
Look up to him that orders all.

He, in a moment, can to us restore
And add much more
Than we have lost. He turns our joys to grief
And gives relief
And can our sorrows unto comforts turn, even from the urn.
Then let our fortunes rise or fall
Happen what will, 'tis best of all;
Quodcunque evenerit optimum.[6]

Whitelocke was patient and tender with Rebecca and not long after their marriage she submitted to its consummation. Her health improved and he found her 'for the most part cheerful and pleasant and very good company'. As time went on he could write 'We took much satisfaction and contentment in one another, and all the testimonies of conjugal affection did mutually appear between us.' When he was riding the circuit nine months after their marriage he wrote lightheartedly, but as if to a timid child:

Dear Wife
I have thrived well at Oxford, especially in my health . . . I have a care of my diet and hours, and I never take better physic than when my clients are with me. . . .
If this weather hold on, our travail will be a great deal the more pleasant. We wish it for our sakes and the country's. I am buying a horse of my cousin Unton Croke that I think will serve my turn. . . .
Prithee remember my kind love to my sister and to Mrs. Hungerford. Thus wishing you all health and courage and freedom from all fear, which you may well enjoy considering your security and the stillness of rogues at this time, I take leave and rest
    Your truly loving husband
        Bulstrode Whitelocke[7]
from Oxon
Mar.13 1630 [31]

Sir James Whitelocke who was 'a very wise and discerning man' admitted later that he and his wife were anxious about Rebecca's dark moods, but they kept their thoughts to themselves.

Just before Whitsun 1631 Bulstrode and his mother travelled together from London to Fawley Court; she had been in poor health since Easter, and talked on the journey about the need to accept death without fear. When they reached the elm walk, leading to the house, she insisted on getting out of the coach and asked her son to help her walk up the path, as she wished to do so once more before she died. 'Though she was very weak yet she took much content in it, and came to her husband with much joy to meet him and her children there. She supped with them in the hall for coolness and was very cheerful, and said nothing to her husband of her expectation of death, but drank to all her children as in a way of taking leave of them, and went early to bed.'[8] She was heard praying and at about eleven o'clock she called to her maid to prepare some medicine. The servant went to warm it and heard nothing more, but when she returned to the room her mistress was dead. It was so gentle an end that Whitelocke was reminded of a commentary on God calling Moses to go up and die: 'if he had invited him to a meal, it could not have been in a more sociable compellation.'

When the Judge opened his eyes next morning, and saw his son and daughter and the servants standing at his bedside, he asked simply 'Is my wife dead?' and when they assented, though he was a man of great courage, he broke down and cried without restraint. They had been married for twenty-nine years. Elizabeth, like her parents, had been 'of the number of those whom worldlings in scorn used to style Puritans'.[9] But in practical matters she was no less alert than the worldlings, and for years Sir James had entrusted her with the management of his estate. Shortly before her death he had remarked casually that he wished he could put up a new barn. Elizabeth said nothing, but when next he set off for the Assizes she had timber cut and supervised the construction of a barn as a surprise for his return.[10] Sir James recognized that with her death the springs of his own life began to dry up, and when the servants brought out a winding sheet for her burial he told them to put aside another, as it would soon be needed.

Bulstrode's life was clouded by his mother's death but his thoughts, unlike his father's, were striding into the future. Rebecca was expecting a child. He gave up the summer circuit to be with her in London until their son was born on 13 July 1631. They called him James, after his grandfather, and he was christened in the church of Pancras, Soper Lane. A month later Bulstrode wrote confidently to his father:

May it please you Sir,

I find my wife so well recovered after her lying in that she saith she is ready for her journey sooner than I thought she would have been able to endure travel. . . .

If you shall please to think fit to send your coach hither on Thursday next, my wife and I and our company will come to Fawley Court on Friday next. She is willing to go through a day, but if she should be weary on the way we can rest ourselves at Horton one night and come on Saturday. If this time be too soon for your horses to travel after the circuit if you be pleased to appoint any other, more convenient, and send word of it we will provide ourselves ready against that time. . . .

My wife desires to have her duty remembered unto you, and my mother-in-law remembereth her to you and saith that ere long she will come and be merry with you at Fawley Court.

Thus, with my prayer for your health, I humbly crave your blessing and rest

Your dutiful son

Bulstrode Whitelocke[11]

Cheapside, London

August 13 1631

While the young parents stayed at Fawley their baby was entrusted to a wet nurse in Wooburn, some ten miles away, where Bulstrode himself had been nurtured on eel and bacon broth.

The family had always enjoyed making music together. When Bulstrode and his sisters were younger they and their parents held a weekly music meeting at home, and it was said that to obtain a post even as clerk to Judge James Whitelocke a man had to be a good musician.[12] So it seemed to them perfectly natural to take a pile of song books and music in the coach when they went to Wooburn to see the child. The Judge was delighted by the way his grandson listened to the impromptu concert. He put a golden twenty-shilling piece into the tiny fist but the infant flung it on the floor, at which the Judge gave the money to the nurse and his blessing to the baby, saying that the boy would grow up to throw his money away – a joke which turned out to be true.

As the year drew to an end Sir James busied himself with the completion of a private chapel at Fawley Court. Bulstrode attended its consecration by a family friend, John Williams, Bishop of Lincoln, in the presence of the Bishop of Bristol and a number of distinguished neighbours. There was a good deal of criticism. Some guests found the style of the chapel too puritanical. The altar was not railed off; the pulpit was in line with it, implying that the word was of equal importance to the holy sacrament and there were neither images nor crucifixes on the walls. William Laud would have frowned on such austerity. Some puritanical guests objected for the opposite reason. They took exception to the splendid new organ, the lutanists, viol-players, and the singers supported by the Judge's own 'very sweet tenor'.[13] They were somewhat mollified, however, when it was pointed out that the anthems were taken from holy scriptures and that the congregation had the words in front of them. The Bishop of Lincoln, an enemy of Laud's in the years ahead, saw nothing wrong either with the chapel or the music, for his views coincided with those of the family.[14] He was able to assure Sir James that the music was the best to be heard in any private chapel in Christendom and second only to that of the King's chapel. They parted cordially, with the Bishop joking about his host's coachman who, he insisted, drove like a younger son of Nimshi.[15]

Sir James was outwardly calm but he spoke sometimes of how deeply he missed his wife and said that he would hasten to meet her. While he was in London, during the summer of 1632, he caught a severe cold which he could not throw off, although a number of ladies sent syrups and medicines to cure it. He refused to consult a doctor because it was 'only a cold, and he was no lover of physic'. Instead, he decided to go to Fawley 'hoping that the fresh air which he loved would do him good'. His manner was cheerful when he shook hands with his fellow Judges and officials in Court, but his son over-heard him saying 'God be with you. I shall never see you again.' Bulstrode was anxious to accompany him to Fawley but after they had travelled a few miles together his father sent him back to London, confiding to the servants that he did not wish the boy to see him die for fear it made too deep an impression. At Fawley the Judge's cold developed into a hard, painful cough; the servants called in a local physician, and later sent for Bulstrode.[16] On 22 June their master got up and dressed as usual. He had difficulty in breathing and refused to eat anything but he gave instructions with his usual composure. He informed members of the household, in his matter-of-fact way, that he was going to die and in the afternoon lay on his bed talking to them. After speaking of his confidence in God's love he gave two or three little groans, and with that he died. Bulstrode arrived within the hour; he ran upstairs and kissed his father's cheek. It was still warm.[17]

Summing up the Judge's qualities he wrote 'for a husband, a father, a master and neighbour he was one of the best in the world'; his relationship towards everyone, from his wife to the servants, was 'to all with love'; but Bulstrode did not gloss over his father's shortcomings, in particular his hot temper. He remembered the time the Judge had been furiously angry with Anthony Bull, a gentleman of the household, and told him to get out; Bull stayed where he was and, being asked the reason, answered, ' "If you do not know when you have a good servant I know when I have a good master, and therefore I will never leave you", which soft and drolling answer pacified the master's wrath and reconciled him to his old servant, who left him not till he left this world.'[18] The locked cabinet, in which the Judge had kept his private papers, was found to contain three important documents: a Deed of Gift of his personal estate made in his son's favour (a legal device to avoid it being inventoried by the Ecclesiastical Court); a Will written on a half sheet of paper, making individual bequests; and finally, the manuscript of his autobiography 'Liber Famelicus'.[19] According to Bulstrode the estate was worth £7,000; this did not include the horses, household goods and family plate, nor the unspecified bonds and securities for loans which the Judge had made out in his son's name, again to avoid disclosing the amount of the legacy. Because of this reticence it is impossible to calculate its total value. In addition to profitable woodlands and a deer park the estate included copyhold farms and probably the Bell Inn, Henley, which Bulstrode certainly owned some years later. He did not indicate what rents and other income the estate yielded but £7,000 was an under-estimate of its capital value, even after deducting marriage portions of £2,500 each for his sisters, Elizabeth and Cecilia. It was not a large fortune but it was a comfortable one, and he could at last indulge in a spending spree. Within a week of his father's death he incurred tailors' bills amounting to £160.[20] Soon afterwards he had his portrait painted for the first time.

He needed both mourning and wedding clothes, for the funeral was hardly over before his sister Cecilia asked his consent to her marriage. Sir James had unfortunately written her marriage portion of £2,500 into his Will, but had subsequently paid £1,200 of it in advance to her future father-in-law, Henry Dixon. Bulstrode's uncle, Judge George Croke, and Bartholomew Hall, a friend and adviser, agreed that there was no need to pay more than Sir James had intended. With doubtful propriety Bulstrode suppressed the Will and only produced the Deed of Gift. Old Henry Dixon was suspicious and when, just before they went into the chapel, he was asked to sign a receipt for the balance of £1,300 in settlement, he and his friends 'did boggle'. Whitelocke made it clear that he too could boggle, by withholding the balance and refusing to allow the wedding to take place in his chapel, or anywhere else if he could help it; he might even demand repayment of the advance on his sister's dowry. Eventually Henry Dixon gave in, undermined by his son Edward's eagerness to possess Cecilia rather than the money.[21] When the terms of the Will were later revealed Henry Dixon felt he had been cheated, but young Dixon was satisfied.

Not long after Sir James Whitelocke's death his old friend William Laud had occasion to travel to Oxford, where he was Chancellor of the University. Breaking his journey at the Bell in Henley he sent for his former pupil to enquire about his plans. He commended the young man's intention to continue in legal practice, for he considered that too many gentlemen led unhappy and ungodly lives, wasting their time on hunting or hawking, if not in worse pursuits; but he 'wished him not to sweat too much at it' now that he was a man of substance.[22] Whitelocke stayed at the Bell for supper and noticed how respectfully he was treated because of his host's attitude.[23] During his father's lifetime he had been appointed Recorder of Abingdon which enabled him, as the new master of Fawley Court, to live at home while attending the Quarter Sessions but since Judge Whitelocke's death less work came his way and his fees, which had risen to over £300 in the previous year, dropped disconcertingly to under £50. Rebecca seemed happier, although she was in poor health and was still subject to fits of depression; William Kitson, the Rector of Fawley, had granted her a licence to eat meat on fish days, since it was stated that she could not eat fish without danger to her health.[24]

In July 1633 Whitelocke noted briefly the routine appointment of a young man named Thomas Napper, who was bound apprentice to him. Twenty-seven years later the incident was to assume dramatic importance.

If his professional and home life were disappointing he had two activities which, for a time, absorbed his energies. His father had left money for the construction of a family vault and monument in Fawley church, near to the pew in which he used to sit as Lord of the Manor. Bulstrode obtained a licence for the work from the Bishop of Lincoln and apparently arranged for a south transept to be built onto the little church to house the monument. Underneath was the well-ventilated vault. He planned the tomb himself and engaged William Wright, a 'graver in stone' of St. Martin-in-the-Fields, to build it in London. It was mainly of black and white marble, with falcons poised round the painted effigy of Sir James in his Judge's robes and his wife Elizabeth in her everyday clothes. Perched above an arch of black marble, justice, peace and plenty (done in alabaster) watched over the recumbent figures. A tablet, engraved in letters of gold, bore an epitaph which the

Judge himself had composed. William Wright charged one hundred pounds for the sculpture, and Thomas Babb was paid fourteen pounds for painting it. The finished work was 'plain yet rich, beautiful yet substantial'. It cost three times the sum Sir James had allocated, but Bulstrode was content to meet the extra cost and it was gratifying that people came from far and wide to admire the tomb.[25] When the Whitelockes' neighbour Sir Cope D'Oyly of Greenlands died in August 1633, his heirs kept in step by erecting their own marble and alabaster monument in Hambleden church.

Rebecca became discontented with life in the country and partly for that reason her husband took a house in London, on the corner of Salisbury Court and Fleet Street, for which he paid a rent of nine pounds a quarter. Soon after they moved he became involved in a new and demanding activity. The four Inns of Court decided to collaborate in presenting a masque before the King and Queen. It was their repudiation of William Prynne's book *Histriomastix*. Whitelocke seems to have dissociated himself from this objective while taking a full share in the production. Prynne was a bencher of Lincoln's Inn, a man of great courage but a sour Puritan; Whitelocke describes how six weeks after *Histriomastix* appeared, with its condemnation of stage plays and interludes, Queen Henrietta Maria had performed in a pastoral at Somerset House. The next day Laud maliciously showed the book to the King and Queen, pointing to an entry in the table of contents: 'Women actors notorious whores'. Ignoring the date of publication Laud made out that it had been written as an attack on Her Majesty. In spite of their annoyance the King and Queen did not take any action; Laud, however, had a grudge to settle so he gave a copy of the book to Prynne's enemy Dr. Heylyn, inviting him to pick out any objectionable passages; this done, he took Heylyn's notes to Attorney General Noy and instructed him to prosecute. As a result, Prynne was imprisoned in the Tower and in February 1634 the Star Chamber sentenced him to be expelled from Lincoln's Inn, fined £5,000, to have his ears cut off in the pillory and to be imprisoned for life.

Ironically, the royal masque was an allegory by James Shirley in praise of peace, law and justice, entitled *The Triumph of Peace*. It was an ambitious production. Two representatives from each of the Inns of Court served on the organizing committee; Edward Hyde and Whitelocke were appointed by the Middle Temple while other Inns chose senior members like Selden and Noy; Inigo Jones designed the scenery and costumes and Whitelocke was responsible for the music. For this he engaged well-known composers including William Lawes and Simon Ives; he himself wrote several airs one of which, 'Whitelocke's Coranto', proved to be a hit and was played in London and throughout the country for nearly thirty years.[26] The Queen, with her taste for French music, said flatteringly that she could not believe it was by an Englishman, 'because, she said, it was fuller of life and spirit than the English airs use to be.'

Music rehearsals were held at Whitelocke's house in Salisbury Court, where there were sometimes as many as forty lutanists with other instrumentalists and singers including English, French, Italian and German musicians. The noise in the narrow courtyard must have been deafening. Nor was it the only home where music was practised; in a modest house across the court John Pepys the tailor liked to play the bass viol in the evenings, accompanied by members of his family. At that time his son Samuel was just one year old.[27]

In due course, it fell to Whitelocke and Hyde to consult the Earl of Pembroke, in his capacity as Lord Chamberlain, and Sir Henry Vane the elder, as Comptroller of the Household. The two young lawyers had been deputed to discuss both backstage and front of house arrangements and to book rehearsals in the Banqueting House. Pembroke had an unfortunate reputation; according to one report he could be 'intolerable choleric and offensive', and Hyde later dismissed him as pretending 'to no other qualifications than to understand dogs and horses'. On this occasion, however, he seems to have gone out of his way to be helpful to the producers; whereas Sir Henry had 'a scornful, slighting way of expressing himself' which they found insufferable. He too was known to be quarrelsome; he had fallen out years earlier with the Duke of Buckingham and in 1631, when Charles had sent him to Germany, to try to persuade King Gustavus Adolphus to fight for restitution of the Palatinates, Vane had made a hopeless mission the worse by picking a personal quarrel with the Swedish King. Now he seemed to think that because he was Comptroller of the King's House he should also be 'Comptroller of all other men's judgements' in matters of music and stage management. Whitelocke stood his ground, supported by Hyde; eventually Pembroke intervened in the dispute, granting all that the young men asked.

The masque was performed on Monday 3 February. The procession paraded from Ely House in Holborn, down Chancery Lane, through the Temple Bar, along to Charing Cross, then down to Whitehall Palace. It was night time but the hundreds of torches made it look like noonday, only more glittering. All along the route houses and streets were packed with

1 Bulstrode Whitelocke 1634, after his marriage to Rebecca. Artist unknown

2 Judge James Whitelocke, said to have been taken from his death mask. Artist unknown

3   Bulstrode Whitelocke after he had met
Frances Willoughby.
Artist unknown

spectators. Twenty men marched at the head of the procession to clear the
roadway. They wore scarlet liveries with silver lace and swords at their
sides; each man carried a baton in one hand and a torch in the other. Behind
them rode the Marshal on one of the King's finest horses with two lackeys
beside him, bearing torches, and a page carrying his cloak. Then came
trumpeters followed by a hundred gentlemen from the four Inns of Court,
gorgeously attired and mounted on the best horses the King's and noblemen's stables could provide. They too were escorted by lackeys and pages.
The next spectacle was an antimasque, by tradition a grotesque contrast,
often introducing comedy. This one provided a reminder of ugly realities,
with beggars and cripples riding on lean horses borrowed from the dirt-
carts; they were heralded by the clanging of tongs and keys snapped
together in unison. Whistles and pipes brought on another antimasque of
small boys dressed as birds clustering round a large owl in an ivy bush,
symbolizing perhaps the envy of the weak for the strong. Bagpipes and
north-country music preceded the third antimasque. Here was a man wearing
a bridle on his head with an outsize bit; his horse too had a large bit in its
mouth. It was a mute criticism of projectors who obtained patents from the
King for every day necessities and held the community to ransom. Such
monopolies were a source of grievance, both in Scotland and in England.
In the masque itself, on stage, the audience saw the same theme simply as
an endorsement of enterprise and invention. There the words explained that
the large bit and bridle were hollow and contained a vapour which prevented the horse from growing tired. A projector of patents followed, in
the procession, with a capon in his hand and a bunch of carrots on his head,
implying facetiously that he held the monopoly for fattening capons on
carrots. Surprisingly Attorney General Noy, who had gone over to the side
of the Court, had a hand in planning the satirical antimasques, using them
to highlight the people's grievances.

There were musicians, on horseback, dressed as heathen priests and a
group, got up as pagan gods and goddesses, riding in an open chariot; then
more musicians playing very loudly before the entry of the grand masquers
themselves who were driven in specially built Roman-style chariots, drawn
by four horses abreast, with oval seats at the back to avoid disputes over
precedence. The societies had thrown dice to determine their colours and
their place in the procession. Grays Inn led with costumes of silver and crimson. The Middle Temple took second place, their chariot drawn by Whitelocke's own horses caparisoned in coverings of silver and blue reaching down

to their hocks, with huge plumes springing from their heads and haunches. They were driven by his coachman in a livery of silver and blue, colours which Whitelocke later adopted as his own.

Whitelocke and Hyde went ahead and found a great crush in the Banqueting House; even the King and Queen had to push their way to the window but they were enchanted by the spectacle and sent word for the masquers to go round by the Tilt Yard, to give a second view of the procession before the players entered the hall to present the masque itself. When it was over the Queen and her ladies danced with the masquers until morning, after which they all sat down to a banquet. The Queen wished to see a further performance, so the Lord Mayor of London arranged for it to be repeated some ten days later in Merchant Taylors' Hall. It is impossible for a producer to please everyone and Whitelocke had his share of rehearsal problems. Nicholas Lanier, Master of the King's Music, felt that he and his companions were slighted when they learned that they were to be replaced by professional musicians from the City, for the second performance. Whitelocke wrote soothingly, 'I perceive by your letter some apprehension of distress by the King's servants . . . because you were not engaged to the employment of playing in the chariots . . . because I thought the service too mean for those you write for; but since your letter, guided by your advice, I esteem it not so and very earnestly request your undertaking of it.'[28]

The production cost over £21,000, of which the music alone came to nearly £1,000 and Whitelocke claimed, perhaps accurately, that it was the finest that had ever been heard in England.[29] Ives and Lawes were paid a fee of one hundred pounds each and Whitelocke invited the four musicians of the Queen's chapel, who had taken part, to dine with him in a large room known as the Oracle of Apollo at St. Dunstan's Tavern. When his guests took the covers off their plates each one found his dish filled with forty gold coins. Whitelocke, with an eye to the future, thought that this gesture would please the Queen.[30] The part he had played in the revels and then in the masque no doubt appeared to be a stepping stone in his profession. He had done well for himself at Court and had no personal grounds for objecting to the King's decision, five years earlier, to govern without Parliament. He was still viewing life as a barrister not as a politician.

Suddenly there were no more rehearsals; no more flatterers; no more royal compliments. He could no longer blind himself to unhappiness at home. Rebecca's emotional scenes were becoming worse. He was too much distressed to record her illness in detail, and wrote simply 'tears blot the page'. He was advised to place her in the care of Dr. Bartlett, a physician with a reputation for curing emotional disorders; the doctor was prepared to accept her as his patient on condition she lived under his roof for five or six months and that during that time no one visited her. His fees were exceedingly high: two hundred pounds for treatment and fifty shillings a week for board and lodging. Whitelocke agreed to pay this and arranged, unknown to Rebecca, for a trustworthy woman to look after her and 'to see that she should have no ill usage'. It was an enlightened attitude in an age when mental illness often evoked brutal punishment.

At the doctor's suggestion Whitelocke decided to go to France, and so avoid the temptation of visiting his wife, but he took precautions not to let his mother-in-law know where he was going. The Lord Chamberlain provided him with letters of introduction and a licence to leave the country with another young lawyer, Robert Cole, and their two servants. They sailed from Rye to Dieppe where they paid a courtesy call on the Governor and then booked rooms at an inn. The landlord's wife asked why the dark-haired Englishman looked so sad and stayed upstairs when the others came down for supper. She even went to his bedroom, begged him to forget his sorrows, talked 'as if she had been my near kinswoman' and 'told me there was nothing in her house that might be serviceable to me, but I should command it'. He was not so blunted by grief as to be insensitive to feminine charm and he summed her up as 'a handsome, well-fashioned and well-spoken woman and clothed more like a lady than an hostess'.[31]

During the coach ride to Rouen and on to Paris, he and his friend admired the neat orchards, thriftily laid out with vines twining up the fruit trees and bands of corn between the rows of trees. He enjoyed long conversations in Latin with their travelling companion, a learned French prior of the Celestine order, who asked him whether he was a Catholic. 'I told him that I was, as I still am and hope ever to be, in the true sense of that word catholic.'[32] When they settled into their Paris lodgings Whitelocke was again much taken with the inn-keeper's wife. 'The mien of those women far exceeds others of their condition in other countries', he wrote, and a few days later he sent a request to his father's discreet old friend and servant, John Cely. After describing the French King's edict for dress reform, an economy measure which forbade the wearing of silver and gold embroidery, he came to the point, 'This new plain fashion makes me desire your trouble to send me a present for a lady here to whom I am much engaged. I desire six dozen yards of plain ribbon such as gentlewomen usually wear in knots – one dozen yards black, one other dozen yards scarlet colour, the other four dozen yards of several like colours, but all plain, without any gold or silver.' Seventy-two yards is a lot of ribbon. He never divulged what act of kindness had earned such a festoon.

He himself went about Paris in a cinnamon-coloured suit of fine English cloth with a richly-lined cloak. People stopped him in the street to feel the texture, to ask the price of the cloth and even to enquire if he would order them a length; he noted that the French liked to imitate English fashions just as the English copied the French. He was visited by King Charles's representative in Paris and by members of the French Court to whom his friends had sent introductions. He was invited to call on Cardinal Richelieu who, he was told, had thoughts of appointing him Secretary for British Affairs. Whitelocke pondered what such a post might involve. It would advance his career but since he was afraid it would also mean betraying his King, his country and his religion he 'sought civilly to waive that business', on the pretext that he had been offered the command of a troop of horse with the French army in Picardy.[33]

He was in constant correspondence with friends and servants in England and with Rebecca's doctor, to whom he wrote an anxious, self-absorbed letter:

To his worthy friend Mr. Doctor Bartlett at his house at Bow near London, these
Sir,
I take this first opportunity after my being settled at Paris to present my service to you . . . I came hither but three days agone, the wind having been very contrary in our passage, and since my being here I have not enjoyed one night's good rest, having been miserably tormented with rheums and catarrhs and in danger of a fever through the raging of the toothache; but now I thank God I receive some ease, and still my heart is strong, hoping that ere long in England I shall give you thanks for your many favours to me and your real endeavours for the recovery of my happiness in my wife. ..
        Your most respectful kinsman and servant
                Bulstrode Whitelocke   ˎ
From Paris
May 5–15 1634.

Other letters from France reflect his disturbed state of mind and mood of intense secrecy. Edward Hyde wrote reproaching him for leaving England without a word and later sent cheerful messages about 'little friend' James; he rallied Whitelocke with hopes that the change of air would restore him

and the French language expel his English distractions, although he admitted
that 'Paris has as few antidotes against a troubled soul as London.'

Whitelocke wrote again to John Cely at Clifford's Inn, asking him to keep
an eye on a young French boy who was going to London with his father, a
Paris goldsmith; if M. Piccart could satisfy himself about the household in
Salisbury Court, and its master, the boy was to stay as a servant and must be
well looked after. In another letter he addressed Cely:

at Mr. Whitelocke's house, being the first house on the right hand in Salisbury Court near
Fleet Conduit.
Mr. Cely
. . . In my study at Salisbury Court there is the key of my study in the Temple. I
pray do not stick to go into either of them for any papers, or upon any other occasion
you shall think fit. I would they did contain such treasure as I should willingly trust
with you. . . .

He concluded a long, unhappy letter about Rebecca and Mrs. Bennet, and a
'sea of troubles' with the words:

All my comfort is in my child's health . . . I can never read enough concerning my
domestic affairs, nor give you thanks enough for your perfect relations of them. . . .
    Your true friend
        Bulstrode Whitelocke
I would fain know what particular scandals my wife's mother lays upon me. . . .
Paris
May 20–30 1634.

He was still anxious not to let his mother-in-law know where he was, as he
showed in an endearing letter to his clerk:

Thomas Napper,
    Give the packet which this bearer brings unto Mrs. Hinckson. There is in it two
coats for my boy. Let her give it out (if any say they are like French coats) that the
French woman in London made them. If they be too long they may be tucked up at
the bottom. One is for every day, the other for holidays. . . .
    Commend me to Mrs. Hinckson and tell her I hope ere long to see my boy playing
in one of his new coats.
    Let nobody know from any of you where you guess I am,
        Your master
            Bulstrode Whitelocke
May 20
1634

His last letter from France gives a full account of events reported to him by his friends. It survives as the draft of a letter to Elizabeth Mostyn, scrawled in a cramped handwriting:

Dear Sister,

Let me entreat your patience to hear a sad relation of my unhappiness, which I write . . . that you may know the certainty . . . and not be troubled at flying reports. . .

Six weeks agone my wife grew into a distraction of mind in greatest extremity and raging. . . . By the advice of her mother and friends, we placed her with the doctor where her sister then was (and yet is) under cure at a place called Bow, some two miles out of London, where she was to remain in a course of physic for six months, during which time neither myself nor any of her friends might see her, for the doctor affirmed that if we did it might cause her relapse and death.

I being miserably perplexed in my own thoughts and unfit for any business . . . that I might not be importunate to see her, which I could hardly have forborne if I had been near her, . . . on a sudden resolution I went into France for some two or three months. . . .

My wife's mother, hearing of the hopeful way her daughter was in of recovery, . . . went to the doctor's house with a most earnest desire to see her daughter and, notwithstanding divers denials, at last was brought to speak with her. Immediately whereupon, whilst her mother was with her, my wife fell into a relapse and increased to the highest extremity and raging, without taking any sustenance for twelve days together, and the fourteenth day after, which was Friday the 9 of this month, she died. This news of the saddest affliction of my life, came to me in a strange country.

He did not finish the copy but endorsed it *Sur la mort de ma femme*.[34] His mother-in-law had taken Rebecca aside for a private talk which lasted for about an hour, but he could never discover what had passed between them; he knew enough, however, to suspect Mrs. Bennet of telling the distracted girl that he had deserted her. Ned Hyde wrote advising him to come home immediately, since Mrs. Bennet was saying that her son-in-law had died abroad; she intended to appropriate his estate and to apply for custody of her grandson. Hyde told Whitelocke not to reproach himself; his friends knew the truth and would not listen to Mrs. Bennet's story that he had abandoned his wife.

Whitelocke, Cole and their two menservants left Paris at seven o'clock on a Wednesday evening and rode night and day for the coast, covering two hundred miles in thirty-six hours. In Picardy the army was much in evidence and 'many bullets came whistling by their ears'; the French soldiers had a way of climbing into trees or skulking at a turn in the road to take a shot at passing travellers. If a man fell they killed him and picked his pockets; if he escaped their bullets they let him go. At Amiens the Englishmen were held for questioning but, after a courteous cross-examination, were allowed to go on their way. Whitelocke was in mourning while Robert Cole wore a splendid suit of scarlet yet, to their surprise, it was Whitelocke who was served first with wine and given the first horse at the posting-inns. He understood the power of his black suit when he heard himself addressed as *mon père*.

They reached Boulogne harbour early on the Friday morning. Cole's servant, a Frenchman, stayed behind to see to the heavy luggage which was following by carrier. The other three went aboard a small vessel which was sailing for England with a crew of ten French sailors. After two nights and a day on the road Robert Cole and the servant fell into a deep sleep on the hard boards of their cabin; Whitelocke walked about on deck tormented by his thoughts.

Suddenly a calm descended and in the stillness he heard the sailors discussing, in low tones, a plan to throw the passengers overboard and seize their possessions. He walked over casually and started talking to them and handing round tobacco. The Frenchmen spoke aggressively about England's invasion of the Isle of Ré off la Rochelle in 1627, an ill-conceived adventure of the Duke of Buckingham's. It had ended in humiliation for England and the Protestant cause but the incident still rankled and the sailors declared that it was a Frenchman's duty to cut an Englishman's throat whenever he had the chance. Whitelocke did not attempt to justify his country's action but tried to persuade the mariners that ordinary people of all nations were friendly towards each other, and that enmity was nourished by the men in power; as for the invasion, except in obedience to their rulers 'the common people were not concerned'. The Frenchmen's response was discouraging: 'Your tobacco is good', one of them said, 'but your action at the Isle of Ré was very bad and bloody and you are all guilty of it.' They asked pointedly whether their passengers had helped the Huguenot rebels at la Rochelle against the King of France, to which he thought fit to reply 'I and my companions here are Catholics'; but the sailors were not impressed and holding up clenched fists made further dark threats. Whitelocke changed the subject: 'Some of you want pipes, and some want tobacco. I make this proclamation – that all of you that will fetch their pipes I will fill every man's pipe out of my box; and I will take another pipe with you.' It was a naïve offer; there was little to stop the seamen disposing of the travellers, yet five or six of them

ran off to fetch their pipes which Whitelocke filled slowly, while the men
sat watching in silence; they were soon joined by Cole and the servant who
had been wakened by the commotion; then there was a sudden gust of wind
and the Frenchmen 'fell to the business of their sails', which kept them
occupied until they brought the boat into Dover and their passengers disembarked.

Was this a tall story, invented by Whitelocke to impress his children?
It is impossible to verify the account but it seems too artless to be false; in a
fiction the hero would have fought ten brawny sailors, unarmed and single-
handed. It was in character for Whitelocke to deal with a dangerous situation
in this informal, good-humoured way and years later he used similar tactics
to deal with a minor mutiny on the journey across Sweden.

He took post from Dover to London and went straight to Salisbury
Court to see little James. The servants told him that Piccart, the French boy,
had been left in their care and as he was well-mannered, good-looking and
an accomplished lutanist Whitelocke appointed him as a personal servant,
glad of an opportunity to keep up his French. Among the friends who welcomed him home none, he thought, was happier to see him than Edward
Hyde.

After a few days, he forced himself to call on his mother-in-law; he felt
strongly tempted to reproach her for his wife's death but was persuaded not
to pick a quarrel; instead they talked about Rebecca without bitterness or
recrimination.

He soon realized that his preoccupation with the masque followed by the
trip to France had set him back in his profession. Judges no longer helped
him as they had done during his father's lifetime; coming into a fortune and
making friends at Court had not advanced his career and the year's income
from his practice had dwindled to £37.10.0d. He decided that he must work
harder. As he was living beyond his means he gave up the house in London
and moved back to Fawley Court; but he still entertained his musical friends
with hectic extravagance and squandered £500 constructing ornamental
ponds and building what he was pleased to call his 'Banqueting House', a
little room twelve-foot square set above an arch, close to the river, with
floors and steps of blue and white Bletchington marble. Owing to faulty
construction the arch collapsed and he incurred further expense rebuilding
it on higher ground; this time he sited it on part of his estate which was in
Oxfordshire so that, as a Justice of the Peace for that county, he could transact
their business from home. Fawley Court itself was in Buckinghamshire.

He was coming to the end of a deeply unhappy phase in his life. Spending and entertaining were a form of escape but they brought no relief. His philosophy 'Whatever happens is best – if I make it so' had strengthened him during four troubled years; but in spite of a brave creed and a sturdy spirit, his body had been cheated and his mind bruised.

Chapter Three

Frances

'I was now as it were turned loose into the world again, and had but few friends upon whose advice I could depend.' One of those few was William Cooke, a tenant farmer at Fawley who had served the family for many years. Whitelocke strolled round the estate one day consulting him about its management as well as about more personal matters, and afterwards wrote concerning their conversation 'I have thought fit here to insert it dialoguewise.'[1]

Tell me your opinion William Cooke, for I account you an honest man and one that loves me, what do you think of the present ordering of my affairs?

Cooke replied warily:

If you will give me leave to speak plainly to you, and not be angry, I will tell you what my opinion is, and what I say to you will be in love to you and yours.

I pray speak your opinion with all plainness and freedom, and I assure you I shall be so far from being angry that I shall give you thanks for it.

Why then, landlord, I say this to you. I loved my lady your mother and the Judge your father, and they were good people and are gone to heaven, and we must all go after them out of this world one time or another; and whilst we are here we must do what we can to provide for those we shall leave behind us, I mean our children.

The hint of criticism in the last sentence was lost on his master.

I know you loved my father and mother well, and so I hope you do love me and my child. . . .

Indeed Sir I do; and my little young landlord.

Then William tell me plainly, what do you think of my business?

This was all the encouragement Cooke needed.

I'll tell you what I do think of it.[2] I think that odds will beat any gentleman.

What do you mean by odds?

In reply Cooke expounded the timeless, Micawberan theory of money.

I mean this. If a gentleman have £500 a year and he spend £600 a year I call that odds. . . . It will at last beat him out of his estate.

But I hope you do not think me at this odds?

I know not well what to make out. 'Tis true that your father – God's peace be with him – hath left you good means, such as you may live on very well; but if you spend more than your means comes to it will not be well at last.

Whitelocke attempted to justify himself.

I do not yet find my expenses to be beyond my revenue, and after I am a little settled I shall look carefully into my accounts, and see that I keep all even.

I know your revenue annest as well as yourself, and I likewise see the great resort of company to your house – them and their horses, which are worse than the men; and there must be good store of provisions to maintain them, and that will cost money, and still more guests will come because they find good entertainment, and there must be more going to the market – which cannot be without money – and all this spends apace.

It is true that much company now comes to me, at my first coming home, but that will not continue. I hope e're long to be rid of most of this company.

When they have once got a haunt of a place they are not easily put off again.

But I shall forbear to invite them. . . .

They that come most expect least invitation. Besides, Sir, you want skill in ordering the affairs of a house to the best advantage. There wants a woman to govern those things.

I confess I am not skilful in these matters.

Cooke pressed his advantage.

There is the more reason for you to get a good wife, that may order them better than you can.

Disturbed, perhaps, to find himself interested in the proposition, Whitelocke replied shortly.

I have lately lost a dear wife, and to think of another is not agreeable to my thoughts.

Cooke knew enough about Rebecca to answer guardedly:

I say nothing to that. It has pleased God that she is gone, and you want another in her stead that may govern your family and see that your goods be not embezzled, as I am afraid many of them now are for want of a mistress to look after them.

A servant may look after such things; and it is no pleasing discourse to me of my marrying again, the thought whereof is rather hateful to me.

You have no reason to take ill what I say. It is in love to you. I see your linen and goods every day wasted and some of them carried away, and all is for want of a wife to take account of them; and a servant will hardly be so careful as a wife.

That's true. But my thoughts are averse to marriage.

I am sorry for it, because I think you wrong yourself by that fancy. I had thought to have named one to you that lives hard by, if you would have given me leave. . . .

It was irresistible. His master answered loftily:

I take well your care of me and you may name whom you will to me. I am neither the further off from marriage thereby nor the nearer to it.

She that I mean is the Countess's niece that lives with her aunt at Hambleden, Mistress Willoughby by name, and she seems to me to be a comely, housewifely maiden and that she would make a very good wife for you.

Whitelocke, who had only been a widower for two or three months, accepted the information coldly, remarking:

It may be so, but let that pass.[3]

The young lady recommended by William Cooke was Frances, elder daughter of the former William, Baron Willoughby of Parham. She was staying in the next village at New House, Hambleden, with her mother's sister, the dowager Countess of Sunderland, formerly Elizabeth Manners, whose brother was George Manners, 7th Earl of Rutland. Frances' father, who died in 1617, had appointed the Earl as one of his executors, the other surviving executor being a relative on the Willoughby side of the family, Robert, Lord Willoughby de Eresby, created Earl of Lyndsey in 1626.

Soon after the conversation with Cooke, Whitelocke visited the Isle of Wight where he prosaically studied the island's fortifications. When he returned home he thought it advisable to drain the moat at Fawley Court, since in summer the flood-waters from the Thames became stagnant and unhealthy. One of the servants, perhaps William Cooke, had the idea of borrowing a new type of dredging machine from Lady Sunderland.[4] Whitelocke thought himself 'obliged in civility' to call at New House and thank the Countess in person for the loan of the engine. He assured himself that he was 'so far from any thought of wooing' that he went with his hair and beard all overgrown on his face, wearing a black leather doublet with breeches of 'coarse, hair stuff' and looking about fifty. 'Only my horse was very handsome, and my French boy which waited on me was in plush and satin.'[5]

While he was talking to Lady Sunderland in the parlour a 'heavenly creature' appeared in the doorway.[6] It was Frances Willoughby. 'Her habit was plain but neat and her person most beautiful and lovely, so that upon the first sight of her I was strangely surprised, and struck with an high affection for her.' On her side, too, the attraction was immediate. She confessed later that, although she never normally intruded when her aunt had guests, on that occasion she said as a joke to her ladies, 'Let us go see the widower; perhaps we may have good of him.' Whitelocke 'concealed his wounds' but his mind was fixed on Frances while he was talking to the Countess and he was elated when he was invited to call again. He naturally said nothing about the encounter to William Cooke, and Piccart, knowing no English, was as silent as the horse.

Whitelocke could not immediately follow up his advantage as he was obliged to attend the Quarter Sessions in Abingdon. Complaints were addressed to him, as Recorder, against nonconformists in the town who refused to bow towards the altar and at the name of Jesus, to stand during the creed or to kneel when receiving the sacrament. The Mayor was sympathetic towards dissenters and Whitelocke, with a puritan upbringing and a growing faith in toleration, declined to proceed against them. Since Rebecca's death and the loosening of his ties with the Court, his belief in freedom of conscience for men of other persuasions than his own had taken root. In this he was ahead of many contemporaries who, a decade later, as Independents became champions of toleration in debate with rigid Presbyterians. Already in 1634 he was rashly flouting the policy of the Court and of the formidable Archbishop; before William Laud was translated to Canterbury he had divided the sheep from the goats, presenting King Charles with a list of clergy in which the letter O or P was written against each name: O for Orthodox, P for Puritan. In that alphabet it was O not P that stood for promotion.

As soon as Whitelocke returned to Fawley the romance began to blossom, and before long everybody in the neighbourhood knew about it from the servants at New House. He wisely kept the Countess in the centre of the picture, talking to her, taking her and Frances fishing on the Thames, then up to Fawley Court for a meal and a musical evening. She repaid him by occasionally allowing him to be alone with Frances and early in the courtship he wrote 'I took an opportunity of privacy with the young lady and frankly made known my affection and suit to her, and received a modest and general answer, and no denial.'[7] An impoverished gentlewoman in the household, Mrs. Thynne, who was a cousin of the Duchess of Buckingham and a relative of Frances', agreed to pass letters between them. A draft of one of them, stilted but tender, has survived:

Dear Lady

Having been hitherto so unhappy as to miss a longed for opportunity to speak my true affection to you, pardon me if I endeavour to express it in these lines. I craved to assure you that it is as unfeigned as can lodge in the heart of any man . . . none can, with more sincerity, love and honour you than I do.

This, with your goodness, can protect me from the censure of presumption in presenting myself an humble suitor to you for the acceptance of my service; to which, if you shall be pleased to give entertainment, that only can make me happy and I shall be ever constant most really to express myself.

    Your truly affectionate servant

      B.W.

Sep 23.1634

Scribbled on the draft is a copy of his tactful covering note to Mrs. Thynne:

Good Lady

Be pleased to present and obtain from my mistress the acceptance of this enclosed. Doubt not but you shall see cause to judge your courtesy very well placed, to produce an united happiness and an ever thankful acknowledgment of your great (though yet undeserved) favours bestowed upon

    Your most obliged servant

      B.W.[8]

James, who was three years old, took to Frances from the start. He called her his lady and behaved 'as if he had known his father's desires and affections towards her'. Whitelocke thought contentedly that 'oft-times such little accidents and circumstances testify a providence in the guiding of a man's business'.[9] He asked the Countess to plead his suit with her sister, the dowager Lady Willoughby, which she did with success; she also agreed to put the case to her brother the Earl of Rutland, and to her nephew the young Lord Willoughby of Parham.

Whitelocke's leniency towards nonconformists had been reported and he was summoned to London to reply before the Council to a charge of being 'disaffected to the Church'. He was undismayed, in spite of the pressure which Archbishop Laud was exerting against dissenters. He had the assurance that Frances and her aunt admired the stand he had taken and the volatile, charming Earl of Holland, who was High Steward of Abingdon, spoke in his defence. He had other weighty matters on his mind. While in town he had a good hair cut and ordered some coloured suits. His barber and his tailor between them transformed him from a heavily-bearded, studious-looking lawyer wearing sombre, old-fashioned clothes into a fashionable young man of the 1630s, with a neatly-trimmed beard and a lip-tuft.[10]

When his business was completed he went home and presented himself at Hambleden in his finery, to learn abruptly that he was no longer *persona grata*. Much had happened while he was away: the Earl of Rutland, in his capacity as Frances' uncle and trustee, and her brother Lord Francis Willoughby had descended on Fawley and, with gross impertinence, had questioned William Cooke about his master's financial position. After a family conclave the Earl had written to the dowager Lady Willoughby telling her that the courtship must cease. Lady Sunderland was charged with the embarrassing duty of informing Whitelocke, who concluded cynically that since Rutland controlled the marriage portion he had an interest in Frances remaining single. Frances managed to convey that she admired the new clothes and that her feelings had not changed. They could no longer meet but this did not put an end to the courtship, for 'love is a subtle and working passion'.[11] When William Cooke's wife took apples and other provisions to the kitchen at New House she carried love notes in the bottom of the basket. Whitelocke however was not prepared to pursue a hole-and-corner courtship so in view of their 'honest and just desires' he returned to London to plan the next move, and was joined by the conspiratorial Mrs. Thynne who, being a lady of 'decayed fortune', responded to gifts and flattery.

On the night of 8 November 1634 he returned to Fawley, accompanied by Mrs. Thynne and six stalwart young men. Next morning he and his body-guard set off again by coach, in the direction of Hambleden.[12] The strategy had been carefully planned; a short way down the lane they stopped and he went into a field on the Greenlands estate, where he and Frances had been accustomed to meet. She was walking towards him, escorted by a maid-servant and two elderly gentlemen of the household. He greeted her, remarked on the cold weather and invited her to join him in the coach. The old gentlemen 'began to bustle' but Whitelocke assured them that his purpose was honourable and put a hand on his sword, at which their resistance collapsed without the stalwarts even showing their faces. He helped his 'rich treasure' into the coach, jumped in beside her and they drove to Fawley Court. Servants barred the gates behind them. Mrs. Thynne welcomed the bride and Mr. Kitson, the local parson, married them in Whitelocke's private chapel.[13] After a hasty wedding breakfast the coachman drove them at full tilt for London.

They spent their honeymoon at the Ship in Fleet Street, close to the Middle Temple.[14] There they experienced 'the height of those joys and comforts which true love affords' and Whitelocke thought gratefully that God had made it up to him for the earlier sad fiasco. Lord Willoughby the outraged brother, a young man of twenty, arrived the same evening. He ignored Whitelocke and only spoke to Frances. Was the business 'past recovery'? His sister told him it was, *and* that they were married.

News of the runaway couple had reached London ahead of them and friends came round to offer congratulations. Ned Hyde in particular expressed unstinted approval of the way in which the elopement had been carried out. Everyone was discussing it. The ladies in general approved; the Lord Chamberlain, the fourth Earl of Pembroke, said publicly 'that he was glad of it and that he thought his cousin had done better for herself than any of her friends would have done for her',[15] while the King commented that he 'knew not but it might be well for both parties'. William Laud was furious. He sent for his former pupil and ranted at him for daring, as a commoner, to marry a nobleman's daughter without first obtaining his permission, as Archbishop, or that of the King. Whitelocke explained that there had not been time, adding boldly that he considered the eldest son of a Judge a very good match for the youngest daughter of a Peer; the Archbishop 'being in his usual passion' treated him 'more like a porter than a gentleman' and Whitelocke marched out in the middle of a tirade. Laud's concept of discipline and hierarchy had been affronted and no doubt the Abingdon affair rankled, but he quickly recovered from his fits of temper and, using his friend Dr. Bailie as an intermediary, invited Whitelocke to dinner when he excused the outburst as a sign of his affection. In later years Whitelocke admitted to himself that, as a young man, he rather enjoyed a rumpus.[16]

Members of the Willoughby family were not so quickly reconciled as Laud, and for a time refused to recognize the marriage. The young couple wrote to their relatives 'to clear mistakes and to justify (but not to excuse) ourselves' but Frances's mother and aunt would not receive the letters until Bishop John Williams intervened with an artful, persuasive appeal to the

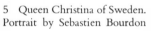

4 Bulstrode Whitelocke at the time of his ambassadorship to Sweden. Artist unknown

5 Queen Christina of Sweden. Portrait by Sebastien Bourdon

6 Coenraad Van Beuningen.
Portrait by Casper Netscher

7 Chancellor Axel Oxen-
stierna. Portrait by David Beck

dowager Lady Willoughby, in which he indicated that when God permits
a misalliance even the nobility must make the best of it:

... If your daughter who lived with her aunt, the Countess of Sunderland, had been
married to the greatest subject in England I should have esteemed him worthy of the
fortune. But considering these casualties often come to pass by God's providence and
permission ... it is wisdom ... not to make these accidents, which happen not so well
as we desire, much worse by our unprofitable and unreasonable impatience. Per-
adventure Mr. Whitelocke who hath married your daughter is not so well known
... unto your good ladyship as he is unto me ... I know him thoroughly, his friends
and his fortunes. He is a gentleman of fair descent both from the father and mother's
side. ... Your daughter shall lead as happy a life, for his person and usage, as she
could have done in any other place wheresoever. In a word, the gentleman is most
worthy ... of your pardon and fair reception because this is a business which may be
marred but cannot be mended but in this way. ...

He is a counsellor at law, indeed, and therein the more to be approved of, but a
gentleman besides richly and plentifully provided for, as I said before, and such a one
for his behaviour, in all respects, as your ladyship may have comfort of and a bishop be
bold to mediate for to any personage in England.[17]

The letter, larded with flattery, had the desired effect; Ned Hyde had a talk
with Lord Francis Willoughby, which brought the rest of the family into
line, and poor bewildered Lady Sunderland was able to be friends with the
young couple again.

It was disconcerting that the man who had thrust himself into this aristocratic circle was an experienced lawyer. It did not take Whitelocke long to
discover that, for eighteen years, his wife and her sister Elizabeth had been
cheated by the executors of substantial legacies from the estate of their
father, Lord William Willoughby. He thought the Earl of Rutland was
principally unbusinesslike, while the Earl of Lyndsey (Lord Willoughby de
Eresby) was 'pleased to waste others' fortunes as well as his own'. In an
attempt to settle the dispute Bulstrode and Frances accepted Lord Rutland's
invitation to visit him at Belvoir Castle. They took Bartholomew Hall as a
legal adviser and set off in mid-July with servants, five saddle horses and
four coach horses, which Whitelocke naïvely hoped would create a good
impression.

They called first on the dowager Lady Willoughby at her home in
Lincoln, who 'met them with much joy and the more seeing her daughter's
great belly'. As Frances was scarcely three months pregnant her mother's
enthusiasm seems exaggerated, but it was no doubt intended to show them

that they were forgiven. After spending a few days in Lincoln they visited Lord Willoughby at Knaith House, on the river Trent, about ten miles north-west of the city, and then drove back to Belvoir, the castle set on a hill in the great flat countryside near Grantham. The servants escorted them first to the Countess of Rutland, whom Whitelocke summed up as a lady 'more humble than high and more religious than stately'; he joined his host in the bowling alley, since the Earl had not come out to welcome them; they played bowls together until dusk when the bell rang and they all trooped into the great hall for prayers. At supper the Earl was in good spirits and after the meal he insisted on escorting his relatives to their rooms; Whitelocke was impressed by the gilt plate displayed on the cupboards and by the hospitable provision for the night of a loaf of bread and bottles of ale and wine.

The next day was Sunday, so the substantial breakfast of soup and beef was not served until nine o'clock. When it was over the bell rang again and they went into the simple chapel which was unadorned by crucifixes or images; one chaplain read the prayers and another preached the sermon. Dinner was at noon and afterwards the gentlemen withdrew to smoke their pipes; this was the only form of self-indulgence the Earl allowed on the Lord's Day. There was another service during the afternoon and a stroll in the gardens before supper, after which the men escaped for another smoke and everyone went early to bed as there was nothing to stay up for.

George Manners, seventh Earl of Rutland, was a man of about sixty with stooping shoulders and a face disfigured by the loss of an eye. Strict puritan observance took its toll of his Sundays; for the rest of the week hunting, hawking, racing, eating and drinking, playing bowls or cards and dancing absorbed most of his time. Whitelocke noticed, with the censoriousness of youth, that the Earl not only 'delighted to see young people dance and be frolic' but 'would sometimes go too far in example'.[18]

When the novelty of stately meals and wine in the bedroom began to wear off the young guests 'Grew weary of those great feastings and ceremonies and often wished themselves at home, with their meaner fare and family.' Whitelocke was claiming a legacy of £2,500 on behalf of his wife and £3,000 for her elder sister Elizabeth who wrote to him affectionately, in a childish handwriting, starting mysteriously 'Dear Husband'. This, he explained, was because he looked after her fortune.[19] He admitted to himself that the Earl 'understood business well and managed it providently when he would be troubled with it', but for the most part it was left to servants.

After ten days at the castle all that had been achieved, in a series of short and disagreeable talks, was a decision to appoint arbitrators to interpret the Will. It took two years of unremitting pressure before the Earls of Rutland and Lyndsey handed over most of the money they had held in trust.

Frances' first baby was expected in December 1635 so in the autumn, when her husband returned to London, she remained at Fawley where she proved herself as efficient as her mother-in-law had been in managing the estate. Whitelocke still enjoyed hunting and fishing but he found 'his greatest pleasure was in the most affectionate and sweet conversation of his dear wife and companion'; whenever he could get away from London he hurried home and she would come to meet him 'leaping for joy'. Their first child, a daughter, was born on St. Stephen's day and christened Frances, with old Lady Willoughby, Lady Sunderland and the Earl of Rutland as god-parents. It was a declaration that the rift in the family had been repaired.

The following year Whitelocke was drawn into a controversy of lasting significance and the legal advice he then gave helped to determine the course of his political career. John Hampden, whom he claimed as a kinsman, consulted him and other lawyers about the legality of the King's Ship-money levy. Charles had successfully exploited other sources of revenue which he could tap without resort to Parliament; besides rents from crown lands, payments were exacted from Knights to exempt them from military service, while fines were imposed on men with land worth £40 a year and over, for failure to take knighthood. There were fines, too, for breach of long-forgotten forest laws and fees were charged for patents of monopoly, which increased the price of some essential commodities. These fees and fines caused widespread discontent; but it was the assault on their purses in the form of Ship-money levies which finally goaded men of substance to defy the King's authority. In Hampden's case the levy was assessed against his property at Stoke Mandeville at one pound. The sum was derisory to a man reputed to be one of the wealthiest commoners in England, but the implications were far reaching and Whitelocke advised him not to pay. The point at issue was whether the levy could lawfully be imposed inland and without the authority of Parliament which had not met since 1629. The King had reason and precedent for imposing the levy, but it was argued in the country that if such a levy could once be established Parliament need never be recalled; it might serve, Edward Hyde wrote later, 'for a spring and magazine that should have no bottom, and for an everlasting supply of all occasions'.[20] The suspicion that Ship-money was being appropriated for other than naval purposes was unfounded. What mattered was that people thought this was happening.[21] Hampden's refusal to pay was to become the subject of the famous test case. Whitelocke attended the hearing in the Exchequer Court and noted, with disgust, what he considered the sub-missive attitude of most of the Judges.

It was irritating that Whitelocke's apprentice clerk, Thomas Napper, should choose that particular time to apply for a post with the new Attorney General, Sir John Bankes, the very man who was later to prosecute Hampden. There was an exchange of letters between the two masters and Whitelocke brought the correspondence to a close by writing, coldly, that he would not stand in the way of an ambitious servant whose

... hopes to obtain your favour made me seek out for another in his place, and I doubt his mind being upon other hopes his service to me would be but unwilling, which seldom proves continuing. Therefore I very willingly part with him, and shall be very glad for his preferment if you would be pleased to receive him.
Fawley Court
Nov 6.1636[22]

This promotion was to bring Napper into court circles, where he later climbed high above the rank of a diligent clerk.

At Christmas Whitelocke devoted himself to the pursuits of a country gentleman. Following his father's custom he entertained tenants, farm-workers and neighbours with feasting and music. He even allowed them to play cards, but only for low stakes. The day after their daughter's first birthday a son was born to the Whitelockes, whom they named William after the former Lord Willoughby of Parham.[23]

When James was six years old he developed smallpox and Lady Sunder-land invited his parents, with their two younger children, to stay at Hamble-den. The routine at New House was quiet and orderly, with none of the ostentation which Whitelocke had disliked at Belvoir Castle. The Countess was not wealthy. Emanuel Scrope, first Earl of Sunderland, had been a rich man and a notorious gambler. As far as he could he had willed his great estates away from his widow, for the benefit of his four illegitimate children by a servant.[24] The Countess may have found a vicarious pleasure in her niece's happy marriage. She certainly treated her young relatives with great consideration. Whitelocke was happy to be given his own study where no one was allowed to disturb him, and he worked there in the mornings while Frances helped her aunt to dress. He usually joined them in the drawing room between eleven and twelve o'clock and the Countess would consult him about her business affairs, until the servants brought in the simple two-course dinner. Lady Sunderland was quite informal, not troubling to carve the meat but inviting them to help themselves. At meal-times she would joke with the servants or with her guests, but there was no attempt at serious conversation. Dinner over, Whitelocke would join the gentlemen of the household for a smoke, then he and one of them spent an hour or two singing and playing for the Countess who was herself a good lutanist.[25] Between three and four o'clock in the afternoon Frances and Bulstrode accompanied her for a ride in the coach or took her fishing, and returned home by six o'clock. After a short rest they met again for supper; Whitelocke enjoyed another pipe in the parlour, followed by more music, and at nine or ten o'clock the household went to bed. This placid, secure existence impressed him, and he looked on the month he spent at New House as being one of the happiest of his life. Years later he still recalled the 'neatness, sweetness and civility' of the Countess's home. In future when he found peace in the country it was as a brief respite from work, or during periods of humiliation when he was out of office. He never again savoured such serenity.

To some extent Whitelocke's professional and domestic activities had blurred his perception of the mounting crisis north of the Border, which was the chief cause of King Charles's financial difficulties. Earlier, King James with his bumbling, canny instinct and readiness to compromise had been content to try to tone down Scottish Calvinism and restore Episcopalianism. His son was not so easily satisfied. Like others who suffer from the conviction that their principles must be right, he showed little discretion or human understanding when confronted by alien views. The Scots ought to be brought into line with the English style of worship approved by Archbishop Laud; a new Prayer Book had been imposed on them in 1636 but had been so violently rejected that it had to be withdrawn. In February 1638 and for many weeks afterwards vast numbers of Scots signed the Covenant, which meant rejection of Scottish Bishops and of any attempt to reintroduce the Service Book. The Covenanters invited support from dissident Englishmen. They assumed that Whitelocke was one of them since he spoke for freedom of conscience. In 1636 he had championed the freeholders against Lord Danby in a much-talked-of case concerning Wychwood Forest and, most important, he had supported John Hampden against the King. But the Covenanters were wrong in their deduction. Whitelocke

had no intention at that time of aligning himself with any faction; opposition
to Court policies did not in his case imply disloyalty to the King, any more
than sympathy for nonconformists meant support for Scottish Calvinists.
He appealed to his friends 'not . . . to be any means of encouraging a foreign
nation, proud and subtle, against their natural Prince, whereof great and
evil consequences might ensue.'

Many Englishmen however were in sympathy with the Covenanters
who, by June 1639, had created a formidable army for the encounter with
the English forces known as the first Bishops' War. Charles's soldiers had
little heart for the fight, and his poverty caused him to negotiate and pre-
varicate, postponing his plans to subdue the Scots.

Edward Hyde was still a faithful correspondent of Whitelocke's.[26] Down
the years he wrote in his scrawling hand, facetiously, admiringly or flip-
pantly, regretting that the plague had not taken any of the judges; missing
his friend's 'loved conversation', appealing to him to send some 'longed-for
cider'; sending messages to James, 'my young master', apologizing pro-
fusely about the doe, promised in an earlier letter, which somehow had
never been sent; he explained his delay in visiting Fawley because he was in
the doctor's hands and finished one of his letters 'I am very proud that you
are a friend to your most affectionate servant Edw. Hyde'.[27] He kept Whitelocke informed about events in London and in the latter part of 1639 told
him the great news that, after eleven years of personal rule, the King had
decided to summon Parliament. Charles had in fact no choice, being desperate for money to finance his war with Scotland. Hyde wrote that there
would be work for good men to do in the Commons, and urged his friend
to stand as Member for Abingdon. Whitelocke was reluctant to neglect a
successful legal practice for a precarious career in politics; but members of
the anti-Court party urged the 'argument of doing public good'.[28] Encouraged by letters from supporters in Abingdon, expressing confidence
that they could 'carry the election for him', he was persuaded to stand, only
to learn that the seat was contested by Sir George Stonehouse, J.P.; this
candidate 'employed his butcher, brewer, vintner, shoemaker, tailor, and
other like instruments to labour for him', reinforcing his appeal to the
electorate with gifts of beef, bacon and bag pudding topped by an invitation
to his constituents, on the eve of the election, to get drunk in the alehouses
at his expense. 'By these laudable means', Sir George's opponent wrote, 'he
convinced their judgements that therefore he was the ablest person to serve
for the town in this Parliament.'[29]

Friends urged Whitelocke to appeal, for although the 'eat 'n swill' style of electioneering was not uncommon it afforded grounds for complaint to the Committee of Privileges. But in May 1640, before a complaint could even be lodged, Parliament was summarily dissolved. Its members had sat for less than a month, infuriating the King by debating grievances instead of voting supplies.

In August Whitelocke received the news he had dreaded, of the second Bishops' War with Scotland. He purchased a number of swords, to hang in the hall at Fawley Court, as well as twenty carbines with ammunition and a barrel of gunpowder; it is not clear whether this armoury was to protect his family against Scottish or English invaders. 'Men differed much in opinion touching the war' he wrote, but 'most wished it had not been begun.' The Scots Covenanters were invading a divided country and met with half-hearted resistance as they marched south to occupy Northumberland and Durham. They proceeded to negotiate from strength, demanding that the English should pay for the maintenance of the occupying forces and pay again heavily to have them withdrawn. Once more the King had no choice but to recall Parliament.

This time Whitelocke agreed to stand for Oxfordshire, at the election to be held in November 1640, until he learned that he would be contesting the seat against Mr. James Fiennes whose father, Lord Say and Sele, was a powerful supporter of anti-Court policies and an opponent of the Ship-money levy; far from this creating any good will, Lord Say expressed astonishment that his son should be opposed by an 'upstart lawyer'. White-locke had already decided to withdraw but he believed that a man who allowed one insult invited another.[30] Accordingly he sent a sharp rejoinder, pointing out that his was an honourable profession and taking exception to the term 'upstart lawyer'; he added, with gratuitous effrontery, that his ancestors had been gentlemen in Oxfordshire before the name of Say and Sele was heard of in the county.

His prospect of entering politics seemed remote and he returned to his professional work. He was at his Middle Temple chambers in Essex Court, two or three days before Parliament was due to assemble, when he had a visit from a plainly dressed man named Toucher Carter. The stranger announced that he and his fellow townsmen in Great Marlow believed Whitelocke had been wronged in the Oxfordshire elections so, without even asking his consent, they had nominated him as their Burgess along with a Mr. Peregrine Hoby. Although the names of Hoby and Whitelocke had been shouted the loudest, at the election, the Sheriff had corruptly returned Hoby and another candidate, John Borlase (or Burlace), the son of an influential local family and son-in-law to Attorney General Bankes. Toucher Carter, with a back-handed compliment to Whitelocke, dismissed Borlase as 'too high for us'. To complicate the election further, Borlase's stepfather, Gabriel Hippesley, had also stood, sponsored by his relative Lord Paget who, having the lordship of the town, imagined he could impose his own candidate. 'But that' Toucher commented sturdily 'will not do in these times, blessed be God.' The townsmen were determined to have their own candidates and asked Whitelocke to support them. He was at first sceptical, objecting that he was hardly known to the electorate, but Toucher insisted that he was no stranger and was 'well heard of' among them. Reports must have reached them from servants and tenants at Fawley, only five miles from Marlow, and it is tempting to believe that the finger of William Cooke was active in the electoral pie. In the end Whitelocke agreed that if the information proved to be correct he would petition for a new election. This pleased Toucher Carter so much that he flung his hat on the floor and stamped on it.

The election at Marlow was not the only one to be disputed. The Committee of Privileges were confronted by thirty or forty petitions similar to Whitelocke's. John Maynard, an experienced barrister, was Chairman of the Committee and day by day petitions were heard in the order in which he picked them up. This meant a considerable delay before the last ones could be considered, but with good-natured chicanery Maynard made a little mark on his friend's paper and picked it up second or third. The Committee of Privileges was at that time manipulated by Pym and his friends who, like their opponents before them, were not above showing partiality towards men of their own persuasion. Yet Whitelocke's admission to the Long Parliament was not gained easily. He first submitted that his name had been shouted louder than that of his rival; later he pointed out that conflicting indentures had been made, one naming Hoby and Borlase, the other naming Borlase and Hippesley as the elected candidates; he accused Borlase of intimidating voters, and finally alleged that information as to the time of the election had been withheld. It was on this ground that the election was declared void and a new one ordered for 23 November.

On the appointed day Borlase, Hippesley and their followers forgathered in one alehouse, Hoby, Whitelocke and their allies in another. When the treating was over the candidates were hoisted onto the shoulders of their supporters and paraded through the streets to cries of 'A Hoby, a Whitelocke', or 'A Borlase, a Hippesley'; Whitelocke recorded soberly that at the election he came second to Hoby with some fifty votes more than Borlase. Later, Borlase disputed Hoby's election but accepted Whitelocke's; so on 5 January 1641 the Commons voted that Whitelocke should take his seat and he entered the Long Parliament through the patronage not of neighbouring landowners but of Marlow's tradesmen, shop-keepers, bargemen and labourers.[31]

The first debate in which he took part concerned five of the Members of Parliament (one of them being John Selden) who, in 1627, had refused to pay a forced loan required of them by the King.[32] They had been summarily imprisoned and later released on writs of *habeas corpus* to come before the King's Bench; there they had protested against their imprisonment without charge or trial by the King's special command. They now alleged that three of the Judges had refused them bail, ruling that their imprisonment was lawful. One of those three was said to have been Sir James Whitelocke.[33] George Croke was the only one whom they exonerated, and they demanded that reparations should be paid to them out of the estates of the other Judges. In a forthright maiden speech Whitelocke defended his father's memory and, indirectly, his own patrimony. Judge James Whitelocke, he said, had been 'a faithful, able and stout assertor of the rights and liberties of the free-born subjects of this kingdom' who had himself once suffered imprisonment, only for doing his duty, and in 1627 he had given the same judgement as George Croke. Whitelocke sat down to cries of 'well moved' as John Hampden rose to speak in his support, referring to Sir James with deep respect. At the close of the debate it was resolved that the late Judge White-locke should rank in this matter with Judge George Croke.[34]

In the Courts Whitelocke had already shown his quality in a number of legal actions concerning the liberty of the subject. His vindication of his father established him in the Commons as an effective speaker; he could present a case well, his style was economical, his voice clear. In Parliament, as in other assemblies, such a man is quickly picked out from the mumblers. Even so it is difficult to understand how he came to be appointed Chairman of the select committee which was to handle the evidence for the Earl of Strafford's impeachment. The committee included such powerful men as John Pym and John Selden, both of them lawyers and both nearly sixty years of age; Oliver St. John, in his forties, who had come into prominence through his defence of Hampden; John Hampden himself, aged forty-six, a man of great influence in the Commons; John Maynard, Chairman of the Committee of Privileges, and two other experienced barristers, John Glyn and Geoffrey Palmer; Lord Bristol's quick-witted son George Digby was the only young man among them; finally, the committee acquired a liability in the person of a wealthy middle-aged landowner, that active committee man and Puritan, Sir Walter Earle. At thirty-six, Whitelocke was virtually a newcomer to Parliament. He pleaded this as a reason for not accepting the chairmanship but 'after many excuses on my part and compliments on their part' he agreed to do so.[35] The older men had made up their minds.

Pym had been working on the impeachment since Parliament met in November 1640, if not earlier. He knew there must be no repetition of the blundering impeachment of Buckingham some fifteen years before. For the nation's sake Strafford had to die. He was widely regarded as the King's evil counsellor and the cause of the country's misfortunes. His death was envisaged even before he returned from Yorkshire to London on 11 November, with the King's promise that Parliament should not touch one hair of his head. Pym may have viewed Whitelocke, with his legal experience, powerful friends and property, as a promising newcomer, possibly as a future leader of the House, but in picking him for Chairman he must have been prompted by more immediate calculations. He was aware that a charge of high treason against Strafford might not prove good in law. A chairman who was known for his moderation and scarcely regarded as a House of Commons man could lend an air of impartiality to the proceedings. For Whitelocke it was a flattering if not a wholly welcome appointment.

During Strafford's trial, which opened in Westminster Hall on 22 March 1641, the Chairman earned the respect both of his colleagues and of his opponents; Strafford admitted to a friend that while Glyn and Maynard behaved like advocates towards him, Palmer and Whitelocke treated him like a gentleman, without however weakening their case. Queen Henrietta Maria, a regular spectator at the trial, said of Whitelocke that she 'never heard any man speak so audibly and clearly and with so little gaping'. This was the man she had praised, seven years before, for composing such a lively piece of music that she could not believe it was by an Englishman.

At the proceedings on 7 April (or two days earlier) Sir Henry Vane claimed to recall a highly significant proposal made by Strafford at a Council meeting. It was to the effect that he would bring over the Irish army to 'this country', the implication being that he had intended, with its help, to subdue not the Scots but the English. The allegation was, however, contradicted by other witnesses.[36] At the end of the day Whitelocke spoke to Sir Henry and others and satisfied himself that the prosecution's article 23, which hinged on this piece of evidence, could not be proved. Accordingly, he called an emergency meeting of his committee and told them he thought it wise to withdraw that article.[37] Before the barristers could comment Sir Walter Earle protested:

This article concerns matters of war and of the army which Mr. Whitelocke, being a gown man, hath no experience of nor can so well understand them as sword men do; and it were better that matters of this nature should be referred to those of the short robe, and matters of law to the gentlemen of that profession.

This was a gratuitous insult to nearly all the committee and the Chairman answered loftily:

. . . I suppose that gentlemen of the long robe are not . . . incapable to serve their country in other matters if there be occasion, besides . . . the law, and perhaps I may have seen almost as many armies as that noble Knight. But I shall not compare with him nor desire to hear my profession reflected upon. I am sure that a lawyer may be capable to understand and report whether witnesses do speak materially to a point or not, and I think the witnesses do not speak materially to the 24th article, and that it will be best to omit it in our proceedings.[38]

Lord Digby supported the Chair:

Mr. Whitelocke having spoken with the witnesses, and thereupon making this report to us, I think it will be best to omit this article.

John Hampden agreed:

If we should proceed upon it and not be able to make it out by our proofs it would reflect upon the House, and be ill taken by them.

Sir Walter Earle was undeterred:

I think the witnesses will fully prove the matter of that article, and I dare undertake the management of it myself and to prove it as fully as any other article amongst them is proved.

Since the gentleman of the short robe was determined to make a fool of himself Whitelocke replied:

I dare not make such an undertaking, but since this noble Knight hath done it, if the committee please I shall be willing to resign up that article to his management. But I shall acquit myself if any slur happen by it.

Earle answered with obtuse confidence:

I will undertake it and shall give a good account of it to the House, and to all the world.

He seemed so sure of himself that Pym approved the proposal, for the article, if it could be proved, was important to the prosecution. Maynard declined to oppose the plan, although he thought it rash, but another member feared that they would 'receive a foil' and Whitelocke gave one final warning:

. . . I must deal faithfully with you and tell you that the proof will fail you.

To this the Knight replied:

That is but one man's opinion. I believe the contrary and shall take it upon me.

The Chairman concluded grimly:

Much good may the honour of it do you.

In the event, Sir Walter's arguments proved so inept that the proceedings became hilarious; Strafford pretended to cower before him and was able to explain at one point that the Irish army would have been obliged to take ship for England, Sir Walter having apparently supposed that Ireland was joined to the mainland.[39] During the merriment the Queen, in her curtained box, asked for the Knight's name. Perhaps she misheard the whispered 'Walter Earle' and thought it was 'Water Cur' for she replied gaily 'That Water Dog did bark but not bite, but the rest did bite close.'

When the prosecution failed in their charge of high treason the older men still held to the conviction that Strafford must die. There was only one course open to them, to destroy him by Act of Parliament using the ancient device of a Bill of Attainder, for which guilt need not be proved in the manner required by the Courts. The procedure was foreign to the tradition of law and justice in which Whitelocke had grown up, but he was too deeply committed to vote against it when fifty-nine Members, including Digby, dissented. Coinciding with the Bill of Attainder was a Bill to ensure that Parliament could not be dissolved without its own consent. Whitelocke was instructed to draft this second Bill, which was to earn the Long Parliament its name. He prepared it overnight but deplored the speed with which the measure was pushed through.[40]

Under severe pressure the King put his name to both Bills. He hoped, almost to the end, that he could save his minister; but on 12 May 1641

Strafford was executed on Tower Hill before a huge crowd of spectators. Whitelocke saw both sides of the case with perplexing clarity. He noted that the Lieutenant of the Tower defeated an escape plot, refusing a bribe of £2,000 and remaining true to the interest of his countrymen; yet he also wrote that Strafford died with charity and courage, leaving few men to equal him in wisdom, faithfulness and gallantry.[41] He was appalled by violence and bloodshed and never accepted the doctrine that arbitrary methods could rightly be used against high-handed and ruthless men; after Strafford's execution he refused ever again to take part in proceedings on a capital charge.

The trial, however, brought him fame. 'Whensoever I stood up to speak to any question I was heard before others', he wrote.[42] He noticed, too, that men who had fiercely opposed his election had begun to fawn on him. 'Though I understood them I would not give them the advantage to understand me, but kept it to myself and desired God to keep me from any exercise of revenge, which was then not a little in my power and temptation.'[43]

He spent the summer in the country with Frances. Almost every year brought an addition to their family and by June 1641 his wife had six children of her own, Frances, William, Elizabeth, Mary, Anne and Cecilia, as well as her ten-year-old stepson, James. She was a young woman of strong views. Although of royal descent, from the Plantagenets, she was a staunch Parliamentarian and if anyone questioned the justice of Parliament's cause she was immediately up in arms. She was interested in events at Westminster and her husband had no hesitation in consulting her about his work. Years later he wrote 'In the most perplexed and difficult matters which befell me in my public employments, I received sound and wise counsel from her beyond imagination to come from a woman's brain, unexperienced in such affairs.'[44] It is possible that, from the angle of worldly achievement, the good sense and happiness she brought to their marriage acted as a curb on his ambition. The height of his career was attained after her death, when he could bring himself to leave home for a full eight months. Had his first wife, Rebecca, lived he might have developed that feverish application, that savage devotion to work which drives a man to the pinnacle of his profession when he fails to find contentment at home. Frances helped him towards a different fulfilment. Two portraits, one painted before and the other after she came into his life, provide visual evidence of the change that came over him. The first shows a dedicated, cramped young man; the second a bold, humorous, almost rakish character. But under the surface of his new exuberance can be seen an essentially serious man, mature, alert and perceptive.[45]

Chapter Four

'A Spirit of Division and Contradiction'

There was nothing new about Parliament and the King being at logger-heads, but by the late summer of 1641 the antagonism had spread so that, in Whitelocke's words, 'the whole kingdom seemed to be moulded into a spirit of division and contradiction.'[1] Strafford's execution in May had done nothing to reconcile the two sides; John Pym had gone on systematically kicking away the props on which the King's prerogative rested. Some men disliked his manner of doing this, even if they agreed with his objective. The King had been disarmingly amenable when faced with legislation which curbed his powers. The Star Chamber and other Prerogative Courts were gone. Archbishop Laud was in the Tower. The Commons were determined to prevent bishops (who were appointed by the King) from voting in the House of Lords, and had also introduced the 'Root and Branch' Bill for their abolition. Impositions and tonnage and poundage could not in future be levied without Parliament's consent, while Ship-money levies had been pronounced illegal. Several judges who had shown themselves subservient to the Crown were in danger of impeachment.

At the end of October King Charles was in Scotland, playing golf, when news reached him of the rebellion in Ireland which was to last for a decade.[2] Thoughtful enquiry as to its cause, its possible cure and long-term results was not in Englishmen's minds. Parliament's remedy was simple: to raise money, recruit an army and crush the rebels, thereby protecting the English and Scottish settlers. The question of how to establish that Parliament, rather than the King, should control this armed force was not so simple. An emergency committee for Ireland was set up and Whitelocke was appointed to serve on it, but early in November he fell ill and could not attend. No doubt his illness was caused, as he said, by overwork in the Commons but it may have been aggravated by the conflicting political pressures to which he was being subjected.

Before he was taken ill he had made the acquaintance of the famous astrologer, William Lilly, who prescribed physic for him during his illness; thanks to that, or more probably to Frances' care and nursing, he was soon restored to health.[3] When he returned to the Commons, later in November, he found that the alignment of loyalties in support of King Charles or of 'King Pym' had become more sharply defined. The Grand Remonstrance, with its string of grievances against the King, had been introduced on 8 November 1641 and was finally voted on two weeks later. John Pym's objective was not to obtain satisfaction for these grievances. He and his supporters were determined to have a voice in the appointment of the King's Councillors and to gain control over the militia. The Remonstrance was to promote these aims by advertising the King's shortcomings to the nation and eroding the royal authority. Whitelocke believed that Pym and his circle courted him all the more eagerly because, although he usually agreed with them, he refused to give their cause his unqualified support. As the gap widened between Parliament and the Court, Hyde and other friends from Whitelocke's student days expected him to join them on the side of the King, but his father's advice to vote on the merits of every issue and to keep free from entanglement with any party or faction had gone deep. In theory, everybody deplored party and faction; Pym saw the Royalists as a disloyal, splinter group, while they saw him and his junta in the same light.

The final debate on the Remonstrance started on 22 November and went on, according to Whitelocke, from three o'clock that afternoon until ten o'clock next morning. (Simonds D'Ewes recorded that it started after mid-day, that it went on until the House divided at one o'clock next morning and that the House rose as the clock struck two. But he could have been wrong. He had left the debate at four o'clock in the afternoon, because he had a bad cold.) Whitelocke noted that during the night many Members 'through weakness or weariness' left the House, and someone remarked that the outcome was like 'the verdict of a starved jury'. The Remonstrance was only carried by 159 votes to 148; these figures contained about 40 uncommitted Members, whose votes were canvassed by both sides.[4] Whitelocke sat through the night next to his 'dear friend' Geoffrey Palmer. They were both opposed to the Remonstrance which Whitelocke objected to as 'somewhat roughly penned, both for the matter and expressions in it', while Palmer objected as a staunch Royalist. When it was passed by its narrow majority Palmer felt outraged. He wished to have a protest against it recorded and urged his friend to join him. Such a proposal was quite out of order in the Commons; it would advertise faction in the House; but Palmer was in a temper and demanded, with other Royalists, that their protest should go on record. 'I wished him not to do it', Whitelocke wrote, 'and pulled him down when he stood up.' Exhausted though they were, the indignant Members of the House of Commons had the offender arrested for his effrontery. 'The next day', Whitelocke recorded, 'I visited Mr. Palmer in

the Tower and we drolled about his imprisonment. He said that if he had
followed my advice he had not been a prisoner; but he was very cheerful
and glad to see his friends, and after a few days and some expenses . . . he was
released, and took his place again in the House.'[5]

Animosity between the Commons and the King continued to smoulder
and when it was rumoured that the House was planning to impeach the
Queen herself, on a charge of encouraging the Irish rebels, the King retaliated
by charging Pym, Hampden, Haselrig, Holles and Strode with high treason.
Not content with that, on the afternoon of 4 January 1642 he made his
notorious attempt to seize the five Members in the House of Commons. By
the time he arrived they were on their way to take refuge with friends in
Coleman Street, near Moor Gate (the street which later gave its name to the
famous riot and became known for its nonconformist sympathies, facts of
some importance in Whitelocke's life). The attempted breach of the Commons' privilege was a gift to Pym, and a stride in the direction of civil war.
Deeply shocked by it Whitelocke wrote, 'This action of the King filled the
discourses of all people, and it was much wondered at by many sober men,
and judged extremely to his prejudice and to the advantage of those that were
disaffected to him.'[6]

On the disputed question of whether the King or Parliament should raise
and control armed forces, recruited in the counties to meet an emergency,
Whitelocke stoutly opposed extremists on both sides. To those who maintained that power lay only with the King he observed, in a speech to the
Commons, 'the power of money is solely in this House, and without the
power of money to pay the soldiers, the power of the militia will be of little
force.' He suggested that there was merit in leaving the matter ambiguous
and that 'the power of the militia is neither in the King alone nor in the
Parliament but, if anywhere in the eye of our law, it is in the King and
Parliament both consenting together.' He dissociated himself from those
who wished Parliament to assume sole control, he urged them to approach
His Majesty again for an acceptable settlement of the matter and ended with
the hope that whoever took the responsibility, singly or jointly, would be
more ready to keep the sword sheathed than to draw it.[7]

In February 1642, Parliament passed an Act for the Speedy Reducing of
the Rebels in Ireland, to which the King gave reluctant assent. An invitation
was extended to those well affected to the House of Commons to subscribe
towards a fund for raising a private army to subjugate the rebels. This
speculative venture depended for its success on rendering many Irishmen

and their families destitute. Repayment was to be made by handing over good Irish lands to the investors, or Adventurers. Most of the prominent House of Commons men put up money. John Pym subscribed £600, Oliver Cromwell £300 and Bulstrode Whitelocke £400. John Hampden subscribed £1,000 and there were sums of £2,000 and more, as well as contributions from small tradesmen, grocers, bakers, tailors and clothiers, girdlers, carpenters, salters and skinners, for as little as £50, or even £10. Earlier, there had been those who asked, tentatively, whether the Irish were not simply defending themselves against a conqueror, as the English had done against the Norman invader. These suggestions were countered with tales of Irish atrocities (some probably true and some fictitious), which enabled Englishmen to think of Irishmen as little better than wild beasts. Propaganda made it plain that it was a righteous deed to contribute to the fund, and Whitelocke was among those who advertised the trade in rebel lands as offering 'very good bargains'. Altogether, 1,188 subscribers promised a total of £249,305.19.8d. To avoid paying it into the exchequer, where the King might lay hands on it, the money was entrusted to a committee composed of House of Commons men and other Adventurers.[8]

The King had left London and was moving from place to place. Parliament pressed him to grant them command of the Tower, which was London's armoury, and of the militia; but as often as they asked it he refused. After a final attempt, at the beginning of March, they decided to take matters into their own hands by passing a Militia Ordinance. The measure empowered Parliament to appoint County Lieutenants and their Deputies, with authority to recruit and also to make officers. The Ordinance was condemned as illegal by King Charles. Hyde and Palmer were among those who repudiated it and they left the Commons when it was passed, vainly urging Whitelocke to join them. Other lawyers, however, notably Sir Edward Littleton, the Lord Keeper, declared that there was precedent in certain circumstances for Parliament to raise an army. In the case under review, the King's absence from London was the pretext. Whitelocke only voted in favour of the measure after hearing 'the solemn protestations of the most powerful and active members' that their purpose was defensive and that there was no intention of declaring war on the King.[9] On personal grounds he had reason to dread war. It threatened a most happy marriage, a large family, a promising legal practice and an estate which in one year, according to his figures, yielded from the sale of timber and firewood alone a profit of over £3,800.[10] More objectively, he abhorred bloodshed. He favoured reform: the shift of power from the King to Parliament, with explicit limitation on the King's powers; increasingly he demanded liberty of conscience. But he was looking for these reforms within the existing constitutional framework.

Many people in the country wished, as he did, for a peaceful compromise. Parliament, on the other hand, under Pym's leadership, was in the mood to fight and after Charles's invasion of the House of Commons there was no turning back. In spite of Whitelocke's craving for peace he continued to be closely associated with Pym. Early in June 1642 he was appointed to Parliament's Committee of Safety and he supported Pym's attempt to force the King to accept the Nineteen Propositions. These would, in effect, have transferred most of what remained of the King's sovereign power to Parliament, notably control of the armed forces and control over the appointment of his counsellors. The implications of the Propositions would later be taken for granted by limited constitutional monarchs but to a King imbued with a belief in Divine Right they were an impertinent blasphemy. It is an indication of Whitelocke's prestige in the Commons that he was chosen as Chairman of the committee which was to consider the so-called Preamble of His Majesty's Answer to the Nineteen Propositions. This Answer reached the Lords and Commons on 21 June, with a demand from the King that it should be read to both Houses. It contained a concept of the balance of power which, though based on a classical theory, was significant because it came from him. Perhaps he propounded it as a romantic ideal of harmony, in the spirit of his court masques and metaphysical speculations; whatever the motive, his reply was quoted for decades to come and in the 1650s and 1660s was used by Whitelocke in debate and in his writing. Charles resorted, in his Answer, to the theory that the ideal form of government consisted in King, Lords and Commons balancing one another. He can hardly have recognized the implication that two-thirds of this trinity of power could out-weigh his decisions, undermining the authority which he claimed by Divine Right.[11]

In preparing for war Pym's supporters were confident that it would be over by Christmas. Whitelocke was not so sanguine. Close though he was to Pym and his policy-making, in July 1642 before the country was finally immersed in war he warned Parliament in a forceful, courageous speech against the course they were following:

. . . It seems to me to set us at the pit's brink, ready to plunge ourselves into an ocean of troubles and miseries. . . . It is strange to note how we have insensibly slid into this beginning of a civil war by one unexpected accident after another, as waves of the sea which have brought us thus far and we scarce know how, but from paper combats, by declarations, remonstrances, protestations, votes, messages, answers and replies we are now come to the question of raising forces and naming a general and officers of an army. . . . What the issue of it will be no man alive can tell. Probably few of us now here may live to see the end of it.

He conjured up the anguish that civil war would bring to the people of England, but he did not minimize the unrelenting assault that still had to be made on court policies in the interest of Parliament and the people, and he ended sturdily, 'I am not for a tame resignation of our religion, lives and liberties into the hands of our adversaries who seek to devour us. Nor do I think it inconsistent with your great wisdom to prepare for a just and necessary defence of them.'[12] He believed that a settlement could still be reached by hard bargaining. Pym knew better, recognizing that the King could not be altered by negotiation and that his word could not be trusted. It was a view that Whitelocke, acquainted with Charles in the friendly context of revels and masques, could never quite accept.

Whitelocke's description of the country sliding into undeclared civil war was apt. During the summer of 1642, with the 'paper combats' still in progress, the King had been recruiting an army through his Commissions of Array, issued to the Lords Lieutenant of the counties. In the meantime his enemies at Westminster, after issuing their Militia Ordinance, had themselves recruited through those Lords Lieutenant (and their Deputies) who supported Parliament's cause. As the tension grew and householders supplied themselves with arms and ammunition, there were inevitable skirmishes and some injuries were inflicted. On 15 July fighting broke out in the streets of Manchester and a supporter of Parliament was killed. It was seized on as the first death of the Civil War.

After some hesitation Whitelocke had accepted office as a Deputy Lieutenant both in Berkshire and in Oxfordshire, appointed to the one by Lord Paget, who later went over to the King, and to the other by the far from friendly Lord Say and Sele.[13] Like other Parliamentarians he clung to the quaint self-deception that they were recruiting an army 'for the safety of His Majesty's person, the Parliament and kingdom, in this time of imminent danger'.[14] If once the King would rid himself of 'evil counsellors' all would be well between him and Parliament. Although Whitelocke continued to speak for peace he dissociated himself from those wealthy Parliamentarians who, in the months ahead, kept out of the war and were derided as 'training commanders', their valour reserved for directing military exercises in the safety of Finsbury Fields, the former archery grounds near Moor Gate.[15] He scornfully rejected an appointment as a mere Captain of a troop of distinguished volunteers, noting that Hampden and Goodwin had been made Colonels. He never fought in a campaign but as a Deputy Lieutenant, later as a member (in name at least) of John Hampden's regiment and finally as Governor of a garrison, he came to know something of war and of army mentality. It confirmed his hatred of bloodshed but also made him understand how the men who risked their lives felt towards politicians who greedily picked up the prizes of peace.

In August 1642 the King's Commission of Array, for recruiting to his army, was to be read by the Earl of Berkshire at Watlington, a few miles from Fawley. Whitelocke, as a Deputy Lieutenant, was ordered by the Commons to disperse the gathering and he rode up Shirburn Hill, to the north-east of the town, with a troop of horsemen. He was joined there by parties of Colonel Goodwin's cavalry and by John Hampden with his infantry.[16] Hearing that their opponents were in the field the King's Commissioners hastily withdrew to a neighbouring mansion, pursued by Parliament's forces. After putting up a show of resistance the Earl of Berkshire surrendered. Whitelocke paid his captive the compliment of riding with him as far as Henley, but found him 'proud and peevish and sullen and empty in his discourse'. The Earl was subsequently imprisoned and 'lay for a long time after not enquired into nor missed'.[17] Whitelocke was glad to get home to Frances, who was nursing the latest baby, Hester. In the skirmish, some of his teeth had been knocked out with a blow from a pistol and he was in great pain; he wrote laconically that the injury caused 'much hindrance in my feeding, and some inconvenience in my speech'.[18]

On 28 August Sir John Byron captured Oxford for the King. Immediately, Lord Say and Sele as Lord Lieutenant of the County called on Lord St. John, the Lord Lieutenant of Bedfordshire, Lord Wenman, from Thame Park, Whitelocke and others, with such troops as they could raise, to support him in attacking the city. But Byron, like the Earl of Berkshire, had no wish to cause bloodshed, so hearing that a considerable force was mustered against him he withdrew and moved north. When Parliament's army entered the city on 12 September the inhabitants put up no resistance, thankful no doubt to be spared the horrors of a siege. Whitelocke noticed, however, that while the townspeople were friendly, heads of colleges seemed reserved although they prudently expressed their obedience to

Parliament. With a foresight which might have influenced the course of the war, he pointed out the strategic importance of Oxford, a rich city in a productive countryside, not far from London. It had been used in time of emergency as the seat of government, and it was obvious that the spirit of orthodoxy enveloping the University would ensure support for the King if the opportunity arose. With this in mind, Whitelocke advised Lord Say to fortify the city as a garrison under a Governor, and his own name was put forward on the grounds that his local connections would make him acceptable to the University, the town and the county. His friends even offered to raise the necessary forces. With fitting modesty, he protested that he lacked experience for such a post. He need not have troubled. The 'upstart lawyer' incident still rankled and Lord Say refused to act. A few weeks later Oxford fell to the King and became his headquarters for the duration of the war.[19] Whatever Whitelocke's motives may have been, his assessment was vindicated.

Robert Devereux, third Earl of Essex and the son of Queen Elizabeth's favourite, commanded Parliament's army. He was a veteran from the wars in Holland and the Palatinate and a skilful soldier, but unsure of his own judgement. He had been ten years old when his father died on the scaffold in 1601. At fourteen he had married Frances Howard. At twenty-two he had been exposed to ignominy when Frances, who had taken a fancy to Robert Carr, petitioned for divorce on grounds of her husband's impotence.[20] Essex insisted that he was only impotent towards her but the humiliating publicity of the divorce, after the earlier tragedy in his life, was enough to unnerve him not only for his second marriage years later, which again proved a failure, but also for his profession. Whitelocke knew him well and liked him personally but, with many others, criticized his indecisive conduct of the war.

After capturing Worcester in September 1642 Essex lingered in the city with his forces, enabling the King's army to leave Shrewsbury and reverse their earlier roles by barring the road to London. The private army which had been raised by the Adventurers, with the express purpose of crushing the Irish rebels, consisted by this time of something over 5,000 men. They were ready to embark for the invasion of Ireland when Parliament ordered Lord Wharton, who was in command, to march his men to the midlands, to confront the King. It was hardly what the Adventurers as a whole had intended. In the south it was like the eve of an invasion. Whitelocke decided to scatter his family. He had rented a house in London where Frances remained with their two elder daughters. The six other children stayed on at Fawley Court, under the eye of William Cooke and his wife. Whitelocke moved to Ditton Park, near Slough, to be with his friend Richard Winwood the Member for Windsor who, like himself, was a Deputy Lieutenant for Buckinghamshire. Conflicting rumours began to reach them, snatched from horsemen as they headed down the road for London. A battle in Warwickshire. Parliament's army broken. The King's army routed. The verdict depended on the rider's allegiance. Winwood sent an express messenger to Westminster who returned with news of the battle of Edgehill where, according to Parliament, their soldiers had won 'a little victory'. Royalists meanwhile claimed it as their victory, and with slightly more justification, but little use was made of it. Instead of following his nephew Prince Rupert's advice to march south and attack the capital, Charles was content to move by stages to Oxford, where the University gave him an ardent welcome.

Rupert, at twenty-three, had already created a formidable reputation for himself, and not only as a cavalry commander on the battlefield. From Oxford he made sorties into the countryside, foraging and spreading terror as part of his military policy. William Cooke knew what to expect when, early in November, he heard that the Prince was descending on Henley. He gathered up the Whitelocke children, took them to his farm on Fawley hill and told his wife to pass them off as grandchildren. Other devoted tenants grabbed what they could of their master's treasured books and papers, hiding them in their homes, at the rectory and even in the woods. Metal goods, which could be melted down by the enemy, were flung into the moat. The servants were starting to remove the furniture when the army arrived.

Prince Rupert took up quarters in Henley. It was his policy to requisition the homes of wealthy Parliament men so he despatched the two brothers, Sir John and Sir Thomas Byron, with a regiment of horse to commandeer Fawley Court. Unlike foreign invaders, however, officers on both sides knew each other and, with the respect which one English gentleman feels for another English gentleman's property, Sir John gave orders that Whitelocke's house was not to be damaged. In spite of this the soldiers, not being English gentlemen, tore the place apart. No doubt Prince Rupert, who had grown up abroad and did not share this feeling for English gentlemen, thought as the cavalry did. They stripped the house of curtains and hangings, chair covers and household linen; they broke open cupboards and chests and cut open mattresses, letting out a flurry of feathers, a favourite pastime of looting soldiers. They tore up such books as were left in the library and lit their pipes on precious manuscripts. Outside, they broke down fencing and killed most of the deer in the park, only sparing a tame stag which they presented to Prince Rupert. They went off with Whitelocke's coach and its four good horses, as well as all his saddle horses. In the stables they spoiled, in one night, a hundred loads of hay and corn, feeding and littering their horses on sheaves of wheat. William Cooke stood by impotent with rage and scandalized by the antics of horsemen and their women in his master's out-buildings. When he caught them throwing plough timber onto bonfires in the close he could bear it no longer and told them to use the faggots which had been stored for burning. The soldiers contemptuously threatened to throw him onto the bonfire for daring to speak to them. He went home, frightened and angry, to find Sir Thomas Byron paying undue attention to the Whitelocke children. Eventually Cooke had to confess that they were his landlord's, but he begged that they should not suffer on their father's account. To his relief Sir Thomas petted and kissed them, saying it would be barbarous to hurt the pretty infants.[21]

Some effort had been made to arrange peace talks. On Friday 11 November Parliament's Commissioners returned from a meeting with the King at Colnbrook, near Slough. The account they gave of his attitude was encouraging. The next day Parliament ordered their forces to suspend hostilities; they sent a messenger to tell the King of this decision and to express the hope that he would show the same restraint. The messenger never got through, for already a battle was raging in the streets and gardens of Brentford. Edward Hyde later condemned the Royalist assault as a grave blunder by Prince Rupert. The King, he thought, should have drawn back from Colnbrook to Reading while negotiations were under review, to avoid seeming to threaten London. Instead, Rupert 'exalted with the terror he heard his name gave to the enemy' had attacked Brentford at dawn on 12 November 'without any direction from the King', and Londoners found themselves beleaguered. Rupert had credulously accepted reports by Royalists that the army had only to show itself on the threshold and London would go over to the King.

At some time on 12 November, either before Parliament ordered a cessation of hostilities or as soon as they knew of the fighting, Whitelocke went on a deputation to the Common Council of London appealing to them, in Parliament's name, to mobilize their Trained Bands for the defence of the capital.[22] The Council responded and their forces marched across

London under the command of Major General Skippon. Riding with this staunch Puritan, a veteran from the Dutch wars, Whitelocke noticed how he moved from one company to another, encouraging his men. 'Come my boys, my brave boys', he would say, 'let us pray heartily and fight heartily. I will run the same fortunes and hazards with you' and more to that effect. At once serious and comradely it was typical of the new ways. The following day the Trained Bands rode past Parliament's gun-sites in a lane near Hammersmith, and joined the Commander-in-Chief at Turnham Green. Hyde noted the 'unspeakable expedition' with which Parliament's army was drawn together under Essex. They were a motley crowd composed of raw volunteers, Trained Bands and veterans, but they greatly outnumbered the King's army. Like Skippon, Lord General Essex rode among his men with words of encouragement, which moved them to throw their caps into the air shouting, with affectionate familiarity, 'Hey for old Robin!'

Whitelocke had left home early on the Sunday without telling Frances where he was going. The thought of volunteering had hardly crossed his mind but once among the soldiers, with the enemy breathing on London, even he was infected with the fever of loyalty to Parliament. Sir Philip Stapleton, a Yorkshireman of conspicuous courage, invited him to join the Life Guards, but somewhat nostalgically 'remembering the English custom to fight among the foot' he 'preferred to trail a pike' and enlisted with men of his own county in John Hampden's famous regiment. Under orders from Essex they marched up a lane to a point between Brentford and Acton from which they might surprise the King's forces. This was sound strategy but Essex had second thoughts and sent an officer galloping after them to countermand the order. Whitelocke's tenacious, argumentative nature was not subdued by enlisting and Hampden had to warn him, with good humour, to hold his tongue in case he were shot for mutiny. In the end the regiment marched back, reluctantly, to Turnham Green.

The two English armies, in full battle array, confronted one another across the Green. Essex had the advantage of strong reinforcements, entrenched behind him in lanes and gardens and skulking behind fruit trees. During that wintry afternoon he listened to advice from enthusiasts who urged him to attack and from veterans who knew the horrors of war and told him to hold his ground. Eventually the King withdrew his ordnance, after which Parliament's soldiers settled down to enjoy the food and wine provided, in cartloads, by their wives and friends. Presently the King's army withdrew, hungry and dispirited, accepting a bloodless defeat and Parliament's forces recaptured Brentford.[23] Royalists later confided to Whitelocke that they had been so short of ammunition that if Essex had attacked they could not have held out for more than fifteen minutes.

During the next weeks cities were stormed by both sides and the people of England suffered the hardship and losses, heavy taxation and terrors which accompany civil war. Denzil Holles, expressing the wishes of the peace party in Parliament and of many people in the country at large, demanded that negotiations should be initiated. Unlike extremists in the war party, Pym was not averse to negotiating for peace while preparing for war. From the outset, Whitelocke had made it clear that his chief interest was to help restore peace on reasonable terms and he believed that was why, early in 1643, he was appointed one of a twelve-man deputation to take proposals for a settlement to the King in Oxford. Although they travelled under safe-conduct their reception in the city was mortifying. Royalist soldiers shouted abuse at them in the streets, calling them rogues, rebels and traitors; Whitelocke was further dismayed to learn that the Governor of Oxford had allotted him rooms in which several people had recently died from the plague.

The first audience granted by the King was in the garden at Christ Church where he was in residence; it was a relief to be received with civility. Displaying their customary loyalty to His Majesty's person, the Members of Parliament advanced in turn to kiss his hand and were greeted with a few gracious words. Last in the line came Edmund Waller, the Member of Parliament for St. Ives, in Cornwall, and a poet of some standing. The King lowered his voice to say 'though you are the last yet you are not the worst, nor the least in my favour'; Whitelocke repeated the words to his colleagues but it was not until later that they understood the incident. When the formalities were over they settled down to business with the Earl of Northumberland putting forward Parliament's proposals. Once the King interrupted him but the Earl asked sharply 'Your Majesty will give me leave to proceed?' and the King meekly assented. When their mission was over the deputation returned to London. Parliament nominated as Commissioners for further negotiations the Earl of Northumberland, Lord Say and Sele, Sir William Armine and his wife's nephew William Pierrepont, Sir John Holland and Bulstrode Whitelocke. When the names were submitted to the King he refused to treat with Say and Sele, whom he classed as a traitor, but accepted the other names.

Negotiations were again conducted in a gentlemanly manner, as if old friends were patching up a quarrel. The Commissioners could not know that they were playing a charade while the leaders on both sides were cynically preparing to extend the war.[24] Northumberland set the style of living which was imitated more modestly by his companions. He took with him his own plate, linen and food; his stock of wine was replenished at intervals from London and when a particularly good consignment arrived he sent some to Christ Church, for the King to sample. Royalists said scornfully that the Parliamentarians gave them provisions believing they were on short rations, but they were not too proud to accept hospitality from their enemies, some of whom had been their friends in peace time. Apart from his longstanding friendship with Hyde, Whitelocke had met the King's physician, Dr. Samuel Turner, in happier times at dinner with John Selden and the Countess of Kent; although an enemy, the doctor dined at Merton as Whitelocke's guest.

The Commissioners had instructions only to negotiate with the King. During the talks Prince Rupert, the Earl of Southampton, Lord Chief Justice Bankes, Lord Keeper Littleton and other lords were usually present, but seldom joined in the discussions.[25] On the Parliamentary side the Earl of Northumberland again took the initiative but his fellow Commissioners felt free to speak whenever they thought fit. The atmosphere was informal. One day, in the course of conversation, the King looked across towards the Thames (or Isis as it was soon to be called) and spoke as if it were flowing north-west; Whitelocke corrected him. 'It is as I say', the King insisted, with the doggedness of a stammerer, 'and to convince you I will show you the map.' When the map proved him wrong he conceded, 'Indeed, I was mistaken. You are in the right Mr. Whitelocke and I see you know well your own country, which is commendable and fit for gentlemen.'[26]

Besides negotiating by day, Whitelocke sat up at night drafting for his colleagues, until the strain became too much and he was taken ill. Sir John Holland, from Norfolk, with whom he shared rooms in Merton, tried to look after him and sent for Whitelocke's old tutor, Dr. Parsons, who brought in another physician. They were at the bedside one day when Dr. Turner called. He was known to be a good doctor although 'much given to drollery or rather raillery'. Looking round the bedroom he asked bluntly who the other visitors were; on being told that they too were physicians he said loudly 'These fellows will kill you!' and to emphasize his unprofessional remark he swore volubly. His rivals understandably withdrew, leaving their patient at the mercy of the King's doctor.

For half an hour, Turner paced up and down the room smoking his pipe and questioning the sick man. Then he made his pronouncement:

I must tell thee Whitelocke that thou art very ill indeed, and worse than thou takest thyself to be. . . .

His patient replied with resignation:

I believe it, and feel it so doctor, and am willing to submit to the will of God in it.

The physician retorted:

Leave your soul's affairs and consider, now, how to save your body from death.

I cannot die in a better employment than labouring to make a peace between the King and Parliament.

That is a good work, but how came it to this pass?

Not wishing to embark on a political dispute the invalid replied wanly:

Let that alone at this time, good doctor, and advise what I shall do . . . for recovery of my health.

Hang thee rogue, thou are a rebel and a traitor and dost not deserve to live.

Whitelocke was in no condition to endure banter or abuse.

I am sick of a fever at this time, therefore I prithee prescribe something for me.

Dr. Turner ignored the appeal and roamed round the room appraising its ornaments:

Though thou art a traitor (and so are the rest of your companions) yet you are the gallantest of rebels that ever were. Witness these large silver candlesticks and dishes in your chamber, and the brave table you all keep here and the welcome you give to us Cavaliers.

Whitelocke was quick in his party's defence:

It is, I am sure, not displeasing to you and persons of honour here that we live hand-somely and for the honour of our masters.

Hang your masters, a company of rebels. But for thy part Whitelocke, I know thee to be an honest and brave fellow . . . and therefore I am resolved to save thy life at this time.

. . . I am confident you will use your best skill and endeavour for my recovery.

I am sure I have more skill than a hundred of these fellows that were here with you.

If I were not confident of your skill and good nature I should not trouble you now.

By God, I will do the best I can for thee . . . for thou art an honest fellow, drawn in too far by the rogues at Westminster.

That was Hyde's contention. At another time Whitelocke would have challenged it; now he protested faintly:

I prithee doctor, do not speak so of them to me.

Damme! they are rogues.

I pray think of my condition and let them alone.

The doctor finally relented and said reassuringly:

. . . I will give thee that shall cure thee. . . . Here, I have writ it down that you may see what it is, that there is no poison in it, although you deserve poison rather than physic.[27]

He told his patient to have the medicine made up by someone trustworthy and left, promising to call the next day. Whitelocke's friends begged him not to use a prescription written by an enemy, but he ignored their advice and a few days later was cheerfully thanking God who had been pleased to make 'this debauched man' the instrument for his recovery.

Encounters were not all so good-humoured. He was accosted in the street one day by a group of Royalists who saluted him derisively, calling him a rebel and expressing surprise that he went out alone 'without expecting to be cut in pieces'. He replied that, for his part, he was astonished they should threaten a man who held a safe-conduct and was received by the King. As a servant of Parliament he was not prepared to tolerate their insults. The Royalists retorted that the fellows at Westminster who pretended to be a parliament were rebels and traitors, 'damn me and sink me' they were, and so were their Commissioners. At that they put their hands on their swords. Fortunately for Whitelocke, Sir Humphrey Bennet happened to walk down the street. He was a well-known Royalist and seeing his brother-in-law at bay he went over and warned the Cavaliers that if any of them caused trouble 'he would thrust his sword into that party's guts.' The parties were sobered by this proposition and were further discomfited by a threat to report them to the King. In the silence which followed, Sir Humphrey took Whitelocke by the hand and led him into the safety of Merton College.

A further incident enlivened the stay in Oxford. When Sir John Holland and Whitelocke visited officers of Parliament's army who were imprisoned under appalling conditions in Oxford Castle, a rumour raced round the city that negotiations had broken down and the King had sent two of the Commissioners to prison, where they were seen in the custody of the Marshal.[28]

In Whitelocke's view the King showed ability as a negotiator but was too easily swayed by his advisers.[29] Late one evening Charles appeared, at last, to reach an understanding with the Commissioners. When they asked for written confirmation he said it was then too late but they should have it in the morning. Next day the statement was not forthcoming and when they reminded him that he had given his royal word Charles replied that he had changed his mind. They were told, unofficially, that gentlemen of the bed-chamber and others, fearing the negotiations might be too successful, had persuaded him to make fresh demands which were known to be unacceptable. So at the end of six weeks of barren diplomacy Parliament's Commissioners returned to London.

Waller's plot was uncovered at the end of May, accounting for the King's cryptic aside in Christ Church gardens. It amounted to a plan to seize London for the King; Waller had discussed the details with Royalists while he was in Oxford as a Commissioner for Parliament. Under cross-examination he betrayed his accomplices to save himself. When he was asked whether Selden, Pierrepont and Whitelocke were implicated he replied that he had indeed gone to Selden's lodgings one evening, intending to talk over his design with these three supporters of peace talks, but when he hinted at a conspiracy they condemned it so vehemently that he said no more, and even considered abandoning the plot. In view of Waller's readiness to incriminate others, this was powerful testimony of the three men's loyalty to Parliament.

A friend who defects in time of revolution is an embarrassment if not a danger. Geoffrey Palmer was such a friend. He and Whitelocke had been law students together and had met again as Members of the Long Parliament. They enjoyed each other's company and, in spite of the political rift between them which had become evident in the months after the Grand Remonstrance, they had shared the tenancy of a house in Ivy Lane, not far from Westminster, on a 'joint-stock' arrangement with another couple. By 1643, however, with the war building up against Parliament, it was no longer possible for politicians who were active on opposite sides to go on living under the same roof. The house they rented belonged to Thomas Fanshawe, a wealthy Royalist and Member of Parliament for Hertford until he absented himself in 1642; consequently it was Whitelocke, the Parliamentarian, who had to leave. This he did on the pretext of taking the children into the fresh air of Highgate, where the family shared a home for some time with Richard Winwood and his wife. Even then he kept in touch with his old friend until early the next year, when he wrote 'My correspondence ceased with Mr. Geoffrey Palmer and Mr. Edward Hyde, they being deeply engaged with the King as I was with the Parliament.' In general, he could see no reason for being on bad terms with a man because he held different views on politics or religion. He advised his children, if they became involved in public service, to speak their minds strongly but with good temper and at the same time to try to win the affection of 'all parties concerned'.[30]

The daily ride from Highgate to Westminster was long and tiring, and Whitelocke could not afford to replace the coach and horses which had been looted by the soldiers at Fawley. Sometimes he borrowed Winwood's; later, his wealthy friend and client, Sir William Drake, the Member of Parliament for Amersham, presented him with a coach and pair in payment for numerous legal services. Sir William was on the point of leaving the country not wishing, it seems, to be implicated in the civil war.[31]

Early in August 1643 Whitelocke asked the Speaker's permission to travel to Fawley. By that date the issuing of passes was severely restricted. Over a hundred Members had deserted to the King and anyone connected with the peace party was likely to be suspect. Parliament had suffered severe losses; John Hampden was among those who had died that year from wounds, and members of the peace party, expecting the King to be victorious, were prepared to negotiate a surrender. In spite of this, William Lenthall showed a special mark of trust by sending a pass 'with', as Whitelocke wrote, 'a blank to insert what place I pleased.' The terms of the warrant gave a measure of protection to the traveller, declaring:

These are to will and require all people, to whom this shall be shown, peaceably and quietly to permit and suffer Bulstrode Whitelocke Esq., a Member of the House of Commons, his wife, three men and two women, with their goods and horses, to pass from London to   without any let or hindrance whatsoever, and for so doing this shall be to every one of you a sufficient warrant.

The tide which had been pulling against Parliament's army suddenly seemed to turn. Young Colonel Massey, the Governor of Gloucester, with a steady nerve and great fortitude held the city against heavy siege from the

King's forces. Torrents of rain saved his garrison from destruction by mines even before Lord General Essex reached him on 5 September. On the way back to London Essex was confronted by Prince Rupert and his army who lay in wait for him at Newbury. The first battle in that town took place on 19 and 20 September, and again Parliament's army had the best of it. After suffering months of set-backs and criticism, Essex returned to London for a hero's welcome. The Trained Bands lined the streets while the Lord Mayor and Aldermen, in crimson gowns, acclaimed him protector of their wives and children and, they might have added, of the money they had reluctantly lent to Parliament. When the shouting was over Whitelocke told Essex laconically that had Parliament's army been defeated those same men would have shown nothing but contempt; the General agreed that they 'honoured no man for his own worth but for the good they received by him'.

In spite of Whitelocke's cynicism he recognized the courage and sacrifice of those who were prepared to

leave a soft bed, close curtains and a warm chamber to lodge *sub Dio* upon the hard and cold earth; to leave the choicest and most delicate fare of meats and wines for a little coarse bread and dirty water, with a foul pipe of tobacco; to leave the pleasing discourse and conversation of friends, wives and children for the dreadful whistling of bullets, and bodies dropping dead at one's feet.

Many gentlemen, he wrote, made this choice, himself among them.[32] At the same time he was dismayed by the waste of lives on both sides and wrote after Newbury, 'All were Englishmen, and pity it was that such courage should be spent in the blood of each other.'[33] His friend Lord Falkland, who had sympathy for both sides, also grieved at the war. When he dressed on 20 September he had a premonition of death and, following the quaint tradition which dictates that we must not be found dead in dirty underwear, he called for clean linen. He died at Newbury, fighting for the King, yet under the terms of his Will he left a ring to his Parliamentarian friend Bulstrode Whitelocke.

The earlier disastrous encounters in the field, coupled with the King's attempts to obtain military aid from Ireland, had driven Pym and his supporters to seek an ally north of the Border. The terms demanded by the Scots, for an alliance against the King, were set out in the Solemn League and Covenant, to which Members of the House of Commons pledged themselves on 25 September, less than a week after the first battle of Newbury. Presbyterianism was to be established as the official religion in England or, as a sly amendment to the Covenant put it, the Church of England was to be reformed 'according to the Word of God and the example of the best reformed churches'.[34] It sounded unexceptionable but in the event the ambiguous, all-embracing Word of God became the subject of bitter dispute.

The Assembly of Divines, joined at this point by the brethren from Scotland, had been set up to advise Parliament on reform of church liturgy, discipline and government. Whitelocke, as one of the small group of lay members in the Assembly, found himself talking on equal terms with the divines. Their earnest debates often deteriorated into wrangles about the Scriptures, in which Selden would confute the less learned brethren, with scholarly malice.[35] His outlook has been described as latitudinarian, although the word was not in current use until some twenty years later. Whitelocke was condemned by many Presbyterians as 'a disciple of Selden and an Erastian'.[36] He had been brought up an Anglican of the puritan tradition but even as a student, under the strict eye of William Laud, his nonconformity had been stronger than his churchmanship; 'You were always wont to have a puritanical jerk at the Church', Dr. Bailie of St. John's had reminded him in 1634.[37] Even at that date he had shown his belief in toleration at a time when, as he wrote, the 'spiritual men began to swell higher than ordinary'. Archbishop Laud and the men of the Star Chamber were evidently still in his mind when he claimed, in the Assembly of Divines, that civil government should have the last word in church affairs. This Erastian doctrine was common among English Puritans and lawyers welcomed it for financial reasons.[38] Whitelocke's allegiance was usually to the Independents, particularly after 1650, but it was their toleration rather than their congregational style of organization which appealed to him. He viewed church government not as a religious question, to which there was an answer ordained by God, but purely as an administrative one, the solution to which must include safeguards against oppression. On the congregational issue he actually opposed the Independents in the Assembly, claiming that the counterbalance of 'a power over a power', the State over the Church, was necessary to protect liberty of conscience.[39] In most debates, however, he supported the Independents in attacking the rigid Presbyterians with their measures against heretics, their belief in the weapon of excommunication and their claim that the presbyterian system of church government was by divine appointment.

The most impressive passages in Whitelocke's *Essays Ecclesiastical and*

Civil are those which deal with freedom of conscience. On this, his outlook remained firm to the end of his life. He believed that Christians should accept one another's differences and that they should even show charity towards infidels; this he illustrated with the story from the *Talmud* about Abraham, who offered a traveller a night's shelter in his tent, but when the stranger turned out to be a fire-worshipper Abraham, in righteous indignation, pitched him out. Then God spoke, saying He had put up with the fellow for one hundred years, could not Abraham do so for one night? This shamed the old man, who welcomed the fire-worshipper back into his tent. Several times Whitelocke argued that since God permitted heresy it was not for man to punish it. He could not believe that any absolute atheist existed, lacking all sense of divine power in his heart, nor that anybody in the whole world was beyond redemption.[40] It is not surprising that a man whose toleration went even beyond that of most Independents was anathema to rigid Presbyterians. Theirs was a harsh belief in dogma and discipline, and in the predestination of every soul, either for heaven or for hell.

Chapter Five

Matters of Life and Death

Like other war-time governments, Parliament's leaders were suspicious of their critics and apprehensive of harbouring traitors. It followed that White-locke took a risk when he bluntly refused to attend the committee, under the chairmanship of Miles Corbet, which was to draw up charges against William Laud. The Archbishop had been in the Tower awaiting trial since December 1640 and by 1643 he was old, frail and without influence; but to Puritans he was still the embodiment of oppression from Star Chamber days. His prosecution, which was later handled remorselessly by Prynne, was being staged partly with a view to impressing the brethren from Scotland. Corbet indignantly reported Whitelocke's negligence to the House of Commons and urged them to make an order compelling him to serve on the committee. Before anyone else could answer Whitelocke was on his feet:

Mr. Speaker. I am called up by that severe gentleman who spake last and hath charged me before you for not attending the charge against the Archbishop, wherein I hoped that I had given him satisfaction by the private information to him of the grounds. . . .

I see a great number of worthy and learned gentlemen in all parts of the House, who have had their education in our eminent universities, and have had their tutors and persons to read to them and to take care of their education and learning. I am willing to persuade myself that not one of these noble gentlemen would be forward, personally, to prosecute those to whom they have been thus obliged. . . . He that takes care of my breeding is next to him that gave me my breeding. Sir, the Archbishop, being then President of St. John's College in Oxford, did me the favour to take a special care of my breeding there. He appointed my tutor and examined me constantly of my proficiency in learning and of my morality of life. . . . I humbly pray to be discharged from this unpleasing employment, and if you will be pleased so far to indulge me I doubt not but to make it up again by my diligence in other services wherewith I am entrusted.

The House accepted the appeal and, according to the 'Diary', Corbet 'had some regret for his unkind and rugged accusation'.[1] This was not the only favour shown to Whitelocke. As a result of two sequestration ordinances in 1643, the goods of active Royalists were liable to be seized by officials and put up to public auction; Parliament could, however, intervene and place a house with its contents at the disposal of one of their supporters who had suffered losses on their account.[2] Accordingly in February 1644 Whitelocke, his wife and those of his children who were not still at Fawley with William Cooke, moved from Highgate to chambers in the Middle Temple, pro-

vided by order of the House of Commons to compensate for the extensive
damage Prince Rupert's army had done to Fawley Court. The chambers
and their contents had been appropriated from Richard Lane, whom the
King later appointed Lord Keeper of his Seal. Whitelocke, who disliked
sequestration, preserved his former friend's books and manuscripts, and later
wrote in his 'Diary' that he returned them to Sir Richard's son, after the
Restoration.[3]

Their new home was smaller than any house Frances had lived in before,
but she was happy to have a place of her own again and never complained
of their poverty. The family was almost without funds. The King's army
had fortified Greenlands as a garrison, and the soldiers commandeered whatever the Fawley estates yielded; consequently there was no revenue for
Whitelocke from rents, corn or timber. The profitable work of the Law
Courts had also dried up. His neglected legal practice had brought in a
meagre twenty-six pounds ten shillings, for the year ended 31 July 1643.[4] In
the coming months he was obliged to sell the coach and horses, given him by
Sir William Drake, and when the money from that source was spent he sold
the family plate for four hundred pounds; he buried some of the money in
the cellar under his Temple chambers but soon had to dig it up to buy food
for the family. At the beginning of March 1644 Frances received a rambling
letter from William Cooke, written in the capricious, phonetic spelling of a
man who seldom puts pen to paper. It was endorsed: *Deliver this to Mistriss
Whitelocke in the Middle Temple in Brick Court*, but it started:

Master and Mistress. . . . Upon Wenday nite there hapined a nill mischance at the
Bell at Henley about to of the cloke in the morning by fire. . . . It began at the Yal-
house, as we go to Filles Court . . . there is not much of the timber distroyed but the
tilles be distroid, the selling bet down, the walls bet down, the woman's household
stuff torn and lost to peces of hir great lose but she doth umbelie desier you that you
would be pleased to set your helping hand to mend it. . . .

I ham very willing to have it mended again, and had thought to set upon it without
trobilling of you, I have take a nottis of it, about 2 thousens of tilles will heale it
again, so that I thinge that the charge will amount to fiftie pounds to mend it if it be
suddenlie dun fiftie pounds will do more now than a hundrid will do twelve month
hence, and therefore if I do not hear from you to the contrary I will set upon it, to
mend it, that I will have it dun with in this month if God will give me leafe. . . .

I rest your loving servant
    William Cooke to command in anything that
        God shall give me leave.[5]

The damage had been done by Parliament's soldiers 'and I am a parliament man', Whitelocke complained, adding bitterly, 'common soldiers . . . know no distinction between friends and others.' Early that month Major General Skippon's men occupied Phyllis Court, making a garrison of it in retaliation against the garrison at Greenlands. Fawley Court, standing between them, was torn by cannon fire. In May Lord General Essex insisted, probably for friendship's sake as much as for strategic reasons, that Parliament should capture Greenlands and this was achieved in July by Major General Browne, a notoriously difficult man. Whitelocke's possessions, which had already been looted by the King's soldiers, were regarded as lawful spoils by Parliament's troops and Browne, as Governor, would do nothing to thwart his men. The following year there were difficulties with the garrison at Phyllis Court and Whitelocke was appointed its Governor.

With no country home to escape to, in the summer of 1644, he accepted an invitation from the Treasurer to the Navy, young Henry Vane, in return for various services, to borrow the Navy House at Deptford. While there he travelled by boat each day to the Temple or to Westminster. In the evenings Frances was often seen walking along the riverside to meet him, with her seven-year-old daughter 'Frank' in tow, and with easy familiarity the Thames watermen would call out 'There is the pinnace and her cockboat!'[6]

In the two years since the beginning of hostilities Whitelocke had served Parliament in a diversity of ways. He had been appointed to the committee set up to consider 'The Printing of Pamphlets of False News'; the royalist news-sheet, *Mercurius Aulicus*, did not appear until early in 1643 but printed propaganda was already rife in the summer of 1642; Whitelocke was to become an avid reader of the printed diurnals with which both sides battered each other. He was called upon to draft the pained protest sent from both Houses to the Low Countries, when it was learned that the Queen was sending officers and supplies to the King from Holland. He was Chairman of the committee which asked the Merchant Adventurers for a loan to Parliament of £60,000; they raised just half that sum. Up to the time of Pym's death, in December 1643, Whitelocke was frequently consulted on policy matters and particularly on foreign affairs. He was also trusted by Lord General Essex and his circle of presbyterian friends, Sir Philip Stapleton, Sir William Lewis and Denzil Holles. This group showed him 'much intimacy of friendship' and 'would seldom resolve of any great business' without first asking his advice. He was generally in sympathy with their concern for peace and was on cordial terms with them until the summer of 1645, while 'reserving' as usual 'his own freedom'.[7] In January 1644 Essex was approached by the King's 'anti-Parliament' in Oxford; Charles had already stated that he proposed to treat with Essex, as chief rebel, instead of with the revolutionary Parliament at Westminster. Whitelocke was one of those who advised the Commander-in-Chief to reply coldly that since the royalist letter did not acknowledge Parliament's existence he could not communicate it to them, and that his soldiers were resolved to spend their blood in defence of Parliament and its privileges, which were the foundation of their laws and liberties.

The mood in Parliament made it dangerous to speak of ending the war, yet Whitelocke continued to do so. In March 1644 a debate took place as to whether peace proposals should be considered by the Committee of Both Kingdoms or by an *ad hoc* committee. Whitelocke insisted that while they argued about it they were failing to work for peace. He was conscious of the war party's attitude when he told the Commons with passion and eloquence:

The land is weary of our discords being thereby polluted with our blood. The creatures are weary and groan to be delivered from them. Children are weary being robbed of their beds and food and of their parents. Women are weary of them being robbed of their children, of their chastity and of their husbands. Old men are weary being robbed of their rest, of their goods and of their liberty. Young men are weary of them being robbed of their strength, of their limbs and of their lives. . . . God hath given you great successes in many places against our enemies and sometimes he is pleased to give our enemies against us.

He could see no purpose in continuing the carnage and asked vehemently:

Whose goods, I pray Sir, are plundered? whose houses are burnt? whose limbs are cut or shot off? whose persons are thrown into loathsome dungeons? whose blood stains the walls of our towns and defiles our land? is it not all English? and is it not time for us, who are all Englishmen, to be weary of these discords and to use our utmost endeavours to put an end to them?

In Henley there had been an odious hanging, on orders from Prince Rupert, as well as blood flowing down the narrow streets.[8] Whitelocke was not speaking rhetorically. He was speaking from disgust. Towards the end of the speech he argued persuasively, 'There is as much gallantry in furthering a good peace as in making a good charge in the head of your forces. I have seen the one and should be glad to see the other.'[9] Events in the spring and summer offered little hope that this wish would be fulfilled. Whitelocke continued to record the encounters between Parliament's forces and those of the King, methodically if sometimes inaccurately, with a few lines added concerning the outcome. The newly-raised army from Scotland, joining the armies under Fairfax and Manchester, beleaguered the garrison at York without success. Then, early in July, their triumph over Prince Rupert at Marston Moor occasioned a spell of devout elation at Westminster; this was offset at the end of August when Essex and his army found themselves trapped in Cornwall. The Commander-in-Chief escaped by boat, leaving his infantry with Skippon to fend for themselves. Whitelocke did not condemn Essex, who he believed was 'brought into this noose by the wilfulness of others'. Later he wrote 'I think I knew as much of his mind as others did, and always observed him to wish for peace yet not upon any dishonourable or unjust terms. He was a lover of monarchy and nobility which, he suspected, some designed to destroy together with gentry, ministry and magistracy; which humour began then to boil up.'[10] Whitelocke himself had no wish to see the social hierarchy altered but his belief in toleration and freedom of conscience was soon to take him into unexplored territory, where his earlier concept of authority as well as his friendship with the Presbyterians would be undermined.

One morning, in November 1644, a Bill was presented to the Commons laying down the principle that the presbyterian form of church government was ordained by Divine Right. The promoters hoped by introducing the measure early in the day to have it passed before their opponents arrived. Indeed, when the debate began the only two Members present who spoke against the motion were Glyn and Whitelocke. Realizing the repression that would result from it they both spun out their arguments until the House gradually filled up, and when it was finally put to the vote the motion was defeated.

When new peace terms were proposed, later that month, Whitelocke was again chosen as one of Parliament's representatives for further negotiations in Oxford. The King received the English Commissioners with his usual courtesy but was extremely haughty towards the Scots who were included in the delegation, led by their Lord Chancellor, the Earl of Loudoun; Edward Hyde later described him as 'obnoxious for his loose, vicious life which was notorious' and as 'the principal manager of the rebellion'. It was agreed that the Commissioners should not visit their royalist friends without first informing one another; accordingly, Whitelocke says that he and Denzil Holles announced their intention of calling on Frances' relative Montagu, Earl of Lyndsey, at his lodgings. The young Earl had inherited the title when his father, Robert, died of wounds received at Edgehill. The two Commissioners were warmly welcomed by the Earl, who was ill in bed, and by other noblemen who were with him; in particular by Lord Savile. They had been with Lyndsey for about fifteen minutes when, to their embarrassment, the King arrived accompanied by Prince Rupert and other courtiers. Holles and Whitelocke were uncertain whether this visit coincided with theirs by chance or by design but they were immediately on guard. Charles drew them aside and after an exchange of courtesies concerning the peace talks he started asking their advice about Parliament's proposals. They explained stiffly that these were matters they could not discuss. He assured them he was not asking their advice as Commissioners but in their private capacity, and as his friends. They replied warily that, speaking in a private capacity, they thought he should meet Parliament in order to end the crisis. The King made the extraordinary request that they should go into another room and draft a letter for him to send to Parliament. They were disconcerted but obeyed. Aware of the dangerous construction which could be put on their action Whitelocke wrote in an assumed hand and left the unsigned paper for the King to pick up. He and Holles knew that what they had done was highly irregular but their motive, he claimed, was 'compassion to their distressed, bleeding country' and the desire for 'settlement of a just and happy peace'.[11]

The negotiations which followed proved disastrous. When the Earl of Denbigh read aloud Parliament's list of 'excepted persons', which included Prince Rupert and Prince Maurice, both of whom were present, it was greeted with gusts of laughter. This displeased the King; but when he learned that the Commissioners had not been given power to negotiate and could only receive his reply, he remarked that Parliament treated them as letter-carriers. To add to the insult he sealed his reply, as if for a common messenger, failed to hand them the customary copy and, as a slight to Parliament, omitted to address the letter.[12] The Commissioners were reluctant to accept the document on such terms, but they decided to do so rather than be responsible for breaking off negotiations. In the end the King relented and gave them a copy. On the Commissioners' return to Westminster the Commons made them go through the farce of standing up, one by one, to receive the thanks of the House. Yet only members of the peace party had had any hopes of a treaty. The rest were intent on victory.

Whitelocke's first reference to personal contact with Oliver Cromwell occurs at the end of the year 1644, but clearly they were already acquainted as Members of the House of Commons. The growing tension between the Earl of Manchester, an uninspired veteran, and Cromwell, his brilliant Lieutenant-General of Horse, was no longer a secret. Cromwell's prowess at the battle of Marston Moor in July had been acknowledged by his enemies, while the generals on his own side played it down.[13] That in itself did not trouble him unduly, but in the weeks which followed he had brooded over the lack of aggression shown by his superiors and in particular by Manchester, under whom he served. At the second battle of Newbury, in October 1644, Cromwell taxed him with holding back and Manchester's reply confirmed that he had no intention of defeating the King. In the Commons on 25 November Cromwell shocked his enemies and delighted his friends with an exposure of how the war was being conducted, laying bare Manchester's deliberate 'backwardness to all action'.

Whitelocke was in London at the beginning of December when he and John Maynard received a mysterious summons from the Earl of Essex. They arrived at his house in the Strand to find Denzil Holles, Philip Stapleton and John Meyrick there before them, with other Presbyterians including the Scottish Commissioners. Essex opened the proceedings by announcing that he wished to consult them on a matter of grave concern to the nation. He then invited the Earl of Loudoun to outline the problem. The Lord Chancellor of Scotland addressed himself to the two barristers in a speech which Whitelocke recorded with its distinctive 'You ken vary wele that General Lieutenant Cromwell is no friend of ours. . . . You ken vary weel the accord twixt the tway kingdoms' and 'whilke way wud be best to tak to . . . clepe his wings'. It was a denunciation of Cromwell as an 'incendiary', a religious and political trouble-maker between the English and the Scots. The question the Scots asked was whether action could be taken against him under English law.

A giant is sometimes cut down by a committee of stunted men. Whitelocke, however, supported by Maynard, insisted that Essex and his group 'must not accuse any but where they should be sure to make out what they alleged' and must not act without clear proof. In any case, Cromwell had done well for the nation and had influence in Parliament. The English Presbyterians were restive under this advice but the Scots recognized its wisdom and it was finally accepted. It says something for Whitelocke's standing as a lawyer that, although he had antagonized the Presbyterians the previous month by opposing their motion in Parliament, they consulted him on this important issue. They may have expected a more favourable opinion from a known moderate, but as an experienced lawyer he could only advise as he did. It is possible, too, that he was disillusioned by the negotiations in Oxford and was beginning to look towards Cromwell for the strong leadership which had died with Pym. Whatever his private thoughts, he was taken aback to learn that someone reported these secret talks to Cromwell, who suddenly showed a new respect for him and Maynard.[14]

At the end of January 1645 he was again appointed one of Parliament's Commissioners, this time to negotiate with the King at Uxbridge. The weather was cold and living conditions harder than they had been in Oxford. This time Whitelocke shared a room with his wealthy friend Lord Wenman of Thame Park, sleeping on a field-bed with only a quilt for a mattress. Since Uxbridge was in Parliament's hands their Members were responsible for the arrangements, in which protocol was studiously observed. Edward Hyde acknowledged that the King's Commissioners were given as good quarters as Parliament's, but he thought smugly that although the Royalists were in enemy territory they were more at ease than the rebels, for they enjoyed a quiet conscience. A large house was taken over for the meetings; the King's Commissioners were given the use of the front door while Parliament's Commissioners came in at the back. Each delegation had its own staircase. In the council chamber the King's Commissioners sat at one end and side of the large table and Parliament's at the other, with secretaries, advisers and divines ranked behind them. At both ends of the chamber there was a committee room into which either group could withdraw for private consultation. The Earl of Loudoun, attending again with Parliament's Commissioners, was sensitive about precedence. The Englishmen assured him that a Keeper of the Great Seal from Westminster no longer exercised his rights when visiting Scotland, but as the Earl of Northumberland was anxious to placate the Scots they set the Lord Chancellor at the top of the table and honour was satisfied. Loudoun was unaware that in England it was 'not taken for the chief but for the woman's place'.[15]

In the course of the negotiations Whitelocke had a sharp dispute with Edward Hyde about the militia insisting, as he had done before, that the King could not control it alone since he did not control the purse. Later Hyde wrote that Whitelocke 'used with . . . the King's Commissioners his old openness and professed his detestation of all the proceedings of the Parliamentarians, yet could not leave them'.[16] This sounds like malice for Whitelocke was a man of great discretion. His own records indicate that he championed Parliament's cause even when he had misgivings about it.[17] Repeated attempts to win him to the royalist side failed, which may account for Hyde's attempt to discredit him. Hyde stated, moreover, that none of Parliament's Commissioners would talk to the Royalists unless a fellow Commissioner were present, which makes nonsense of his allegation. At Uxbridge as at Oxford the talks came to nothing with each side blaming the other.

At the beginning of July Whitelocke was back at the Navy House in Deptford when the Commons heard an allegation which cast grave doubt on his loyalty. It was contained in a written statement by Lord Savile, purporting to explain that nobleman's transfer of allegiance from Parliament to the King and then back to Parliament. He wrote that he felt it his duty to report that Denzil Holles and Bulstrode Whitelocke were so well disposed towards the King that they had entered into private negotiations with him at Oxford, even giving him their advice in writing. The Commons were shocked and demanded an explanation. John L'Isle volunteered that Whitelocke was not in the House. Holles, who was, lost his head and gave a reply which prompted some Members to demand that both the accused men should be committed to the Tower on a charge of high treason. Sir William Lewis, a Presbyterian and a man of considerable influence, rebuked the House for distrusting two of its Members on the word of a turncoat, who had probably been sent by the Royalists 'to cast a bone among them'.

Whitelocke received a note from the officious John L'Isle informing him that the Commons required his presence the next day but giving no reason. He learned what had happened from Richard Winwood who hurried down to Deptford to see him. The seriousness of the charge was not lost on Whitelocke, who asked Winwood why he had risked his life to help a man suspected of high treason. The reply was simple. Whitelocke was his friend and he loved him. Without saying anything to alarm Frances the two men returned to Westminster the same evening. Some Members of Parliament were noticeably cool towards them while others went out of their way to be kind. Whitelocke stayed the night in London, thoughtfully sending a message to his wife.

When a Committee of Enquiry was appointed it became evident that some men were going to use the allegation as a means of settling old scores. The alignment of friends and enemies was complicated. Sir Arthur Haselrig and young Sir Henry Vane, who were no friends to the peace party, were among those who attacked both defendants. Enemies of the Earl of Essex were bent on destroying Denzil Holles, but offered inducements to Whitelocke to dissociate himself from his presbyterian acquaintance; this he refused to do. Whitelocke's supporters were for the most part associated with the peace party and the Presbyterians. They included Richard Winwood, Lord Wenman, the Earl of Denbigh and Sir Philip Stapleton, Sir William Lewis and John Maynard. Most of them were also friends of Holles's. Whitelocke's most dangerous opponent seemed at first to be Lord Say and Sele. On that occasion, however, 'Old Subtlety' over-reached himself by encouraging Lord Savile to write to Royalists in Oxford, in order to make good his case. When this came to light some members of the committee were so disgusted that they thought the whole business should be dropped, especially when they recalled that it had taken Savile five or six months to bring the charge. It seemed no mere coincidence that he should suddenly accuse two members of a committee appointed to examine his own allegiance. In spite of Lord Say being discredited the enquiry was not called off and there was talk of examining Holles and Whitelocke separately, until their friends pointed out that neither man was technically on trial and it would therefore be illegal to exclude them from the House. Once this principle was accepted Whitelocke withdrew voluntarily before Holles's case was heard.

Frances had to be warned that her husband's life was in danger. 'She was not terrified at it but told him that she knew his innocence and doubted not but that God would protect him.' As usual she was 'full of comfort' to him, and in spite of the gravity of the accusation Whitelocke too remained cheerful, except during the hours of suspense when he was waiting at a friend's house for the verdict. As soon as he heard that he and Holles had been cleared, on the reasonable grounds that they had not done any disservice to Parliament, he sent word to Frances. He wrote in the 'Annals' a detailed, if one-sided, account of this anxious time for the benefit of his children, admitting to them that he had not imparted the full facts at the enquiry; there were some aspects which 'all the examinations at committees and in the House of Commons could not get out of us'.[18] Holles's report of the event covered little more than a page of his *Memoirs*; in it he accused Whitelocke of telling what he, Denzil Holles, had said to the King in Oxford.[19]

Shortly after the investigation the plague broke out in Deptford and Whitelocke made that an excuse for returning to the Middle Temple, where Frances gave birth to her second son whom they named Willoughby.[20] Vane's wife wanted them out of the Navy House and they could hardly have remained there in view of Vane's hostility during the investigation.

They were glad to be back in their own home where Whitelocke contentedly 'set his books in order in his study and wrote, upon such as were of other men's, the names of their owners'.[21] There was not to be much leisure for scholarly pursuits. He was forty years old, with a large and increasing family to support. He had been seriously impoverished by the war but in the coming months there were opportunities to improve his fortunes. Although he was still active in the Commons, his legal practice was beginning to build up again, besides which he was appointed High Steward of Westminster School. He still had enemies in Parliament, but he also had a circle of powerful friends including Denzil Holles's father the Earl of Clare, the Earl of Pembroke, the Countess of Kent and her friend John Selden. His wealthy clients included the Earls of Northumberland, Winchilsea and Lincoln, Lord Grey and Sir William Waller. There was some rare quality of charm and independence about Whitelocke which enabled him to remain on familiar terms with the King as well as with Cromwell; to be lent a house in Deptford by Harry Vane and to be offered the Kensington home of the Earl of Holland. Women found him attractive, men enjoyed his company while ambitious politicians, sensitive to every shift of power, thought him a man to watch since he was consulted by the men in power.

The Savile affair made him more wary. He began to detach himself from Holles and the Presbyterians, but the danger he had been through did not make him noticeably more circumspect when stating his views in the Commons. In the late summer of 1645 the 'rigid' Presbyterians brought forward plans for excommunicating sinful members of a congregation. Whitelocke opposed them. 'Tyranny over men's consciences', he wrote, 'is far more grievous than any . . . over men's estates or persons.' He argued that, far from excommunication being a proper means of church discipline, it was unthinkable that pastors, charged with the instruction 'feed my sheep', should withhold spiritual food from those of their flock who were most in need of sustenance.[22] He could hardly, at that date, have been labelled an Independent in the religious sense; it is debatable whether he ever could. His church-going in August and September that year shows that he normally attended the nearest church to where he was staying. One Sunday he went to Deptford church where the Independent minister, Thomas Mallory, preached the sermon. Another week he went to the Temple church where the preacher was Thomas Tombes, a Baptist divine, who believed in presbyterian church government while remaining a communicant member of the Church of England. For good measure Tombes frequently preached antinomianism, the doctrine that the moral law is not binding on Christians. Although Whitelocke was under fire at the time from Presbyterians in the Commons he went to church another Sunday in the company of two prominent presbyterian acquaintances, Sir William Lewis and Sir Philip Stapleton, who had befriended him during the enquiry. In religion as in politics he was an individualist, whose beliefs defy being slotted into categories. Only in his concern for liberty of conscience was he consistently on the side of the Independents; when they debated the congregational form of church government they could no longer count on his support. In 1646 the presbyterian brethren attempted to make heresy and blasphemy a capital offence. This was partly so that they could condemn to death a man named Paul Best who had expressed doubts about the divinity of Christ, and who was also accused of writing a blasphemous pamphlet. Whitelocke, joining again with the Independents, opposed the measure.[23]

On 27 April 1646 the King escaped from Oxford and on 5 May he gave himself into the hands of the Scots army. A few days later Lord General Fairfax, who had replaced Essex as Commander-in-Chief, asked the Speaker to arrange with the Commons for Whitelocke to join him as an adviser during the siege of Oxford, and to help prepare terms for the city's surrender. Friends warned Whitelocke to keep the request to himself as it was likely to cause jealousy. The Speaker, William Lenthall, gave him a pass to visit Fawley and once there Whitelocke slipped over to Oxford, without calling attention to his mission. He was relieved to find that Fairfax shared his concern to protect Oxford's treasures from plunder by either side and this was written into the Articles of Agreement. Oxford capitulated on 24 June. Later, a grateful letter attributed to Whitelocke the preservation of the University.

Through his appointment as Governor of the Phyllis Court garrison, Whitelocke had found himself in an unfamiliar environment. On Councils of War he mixed as an equal with high-ranking officers, including Cromwell. Those officers who enjoyed power could not make out why he 'thirsted after the end of the war'. When Oxford had fallen and Wallingford belatedly surrendered, Whitelocke hurried to London to discuss plans for dismantling his own garrison. As usual he left Frances in charge, and on his return she told him that the officers obeyed her orders as if she herself had been Governor.[24] By August workmen were busy with pickaxes, shovels and mattocks breaking down the parapets and ramparts; Whitelocke paid his soldiers sixpence a day above their wages, to help speed the demolition. With the end of the First Civil War he and Frances made their home in

Fawley once again but this time at Phyllis Court. As they hated to be away from each other he bought a light, two-horse carriage in which he could drive the thirty-six miles to London in half a day, travelling up and down about twice a week.[25]

Faced by the hazards of victory, the Commons were occupied with two main problems: how to deal with the King now that he was in the hands of the Scots, under pressure to sign the Covenant and trying to play off the English and the Scots against one another (the problem remained intractable even when he was handed over to Parliament's Commissioners, early in 1647); more difficult still was the question of what to do with the army. Holles and his presbyterian supporters viewed members of the armed forces with suspicion, as potential revolutionaries. The soldiers had challenged authority within the Church, and that was only a step from challenging authority and privilege in general. For Holles and his friends almost any settlement with the King seemed preferable to power falling into the hands of the sectaries.[26]

Soldiers who have borne the brunt of a revolution are not inclined, when it is over, to hand back power to politicians who have kept their distance from the gunpowder and the blood. Yet the highly disciplined New Model Army might have done that, had the Commons honoured their obligations. Instead, Holles and the majority in the Commons, ignoring both the moral debt and the arrears of pay, spoke blithely of disbanding the army to reduce the burden on the tax-payer. Whitelocke had mixed enough with army officers to know how they were thinking. He feared that an exasperated army might defy their masters, explode into further civil war and take over the government. In May 1647 he recommended that some of the soldiers should be sent to Ireland (a proposal which did not commend itself to the army) and the rest be dispersed into small units until the impoverished exchequer could gradually pay them off. This was not to the liking of the Presbyterians, who thought up an appointment for Whitelocke as Lord Chief Justice of Ireland in order, their nominee supposed, that they could be 'honourably quit' of him. Cromwell being well disposed towards him defeated the scheme.

During the summer of 1647 hostility between Parliament and the army grew intense. Whitelocke was unable to sway the Commons and unwilling to be a party either to their policies or to those which the officers might try to impose. When the army threatened and later impeached Holles, Whitelocke was determined that their names should not again be linked so he kept away from Parliament and the Presbyterians as much as he dared, busying himself in his profession. There was much to repel him in the religious as well as the political scene, and in July he decided to escape to Fawley. He and Frances with his sister Elizabeth Mostyn, from Wales, rode through the night to avoid calling attention to their journey. He looked forward to a spell of peace in which to pursue his profession and his studies, but he had only been at Fawley for a few days when he received an embarrassing piece of news. On 2 June the King had been kidnapped, by troops, from Holmby House where he had been in Parliament's custody, and since then he had been under the control of the army. As usual he was turning to friends and enemies alike, trying with one scheme after another to bargain for a settlement. In July he had been moved from Newmarket to a house at Caversham, near Reading. He was allowed reasonable freedom; he planned to visit Henley on 14 July and spoke of dining at Phyllis Court, no doubt with a view of sounding his host. Whitelocke left home hurriedly. Since the recent charge against him he knew better than to entertain the King to dinner. The implication of his sudden return to London was not lost on the Commons, who already knew about the King's proposed visit. On 23 July Cromwell's son-in-law, Henry Ireton, put the army's Heads of the Proposals before the King. They offered a reasonable settlement but Charles gave them little serious consideration. He was indulging in fantasies of unconditional restoration with the help of the Earl of Lauderdale and a Scottish army.

With the ending of the war the Law Courts had again become active and financially Whitelocke was beginning to prosper; after the death of Lord Essex in September 1646 he had been appointed legal adviser to the executors, a post of prestige as well as profit. By March 1648 he claimed to have the largest practice in the land. He had become the senior lawyer riding the Oxford circuit and young barristers at the Assizes turned to 'the General', as they called him, for advice both on private and professional matters.

In Court one day, at the Gloucester Assizes, he looked so downcast that the attorney sitting next to him asked if he had received bad news. He replied that the news was as bad as any he had ever read and handed over a letter from Frances, with an enclosure announcing that he had been appointed a Keeper of the Great Seal. He was profoundly agitated. To use Parliament's Great Seal was technically an act of treason, yet after the fall of Oxford the King's Seal had been broken up by order of Parliament. In November 1647 the King had escaped from the army to Carisbrooke Castle on the Isle of Wight; he had hoped to find liberty but was again their prisoner. At

Westminster, Parliament remained in uneasy control and affairs of State had to be carried on. Owing to the danger of entrusting the Seal to a single Lord Chancellor, whose allegiance might change, Parliament had earlier appointed three Keepers whom they were now replacing. Whitelocke's scruples, or fears, were not shared by his fellow barristers or by the Assize Judges, who expected him to be elated by promotion to the highest appointment in their profession. He doubted whether this high office would add to his income, since his private practice must suffer, and he reflected ruefully that 'such an employment . . . seldom affords quiet, never safety'. His assessment of his fellow Keepers was objective: 'The Earl of Kent being a very honest, just man and of good rational parts and abilities. . . . Sir Thomas Widdrington being a gentleman of known integrity and of great abilities in his profession . . . I was less considerable than the other in all respects yet well known and understood in the House.'[27]

At the end of the Assizes he went home to a joyful welcome from Frances. William Cooke, always ready with shrewd advice, considered that Parliament had done well to pick on his master who was an honest man and well qualified for the work. After a few days' rest at Fawley Whitelocke took his wife to London, travelling by the public hackney coach. He called on the Speaker and announced that he did not wish to take office. He asked how best to extricate himself. William Lenthall proceeded to give him such a gloomy picture of long imprisonment in the Tower that the Keeper-designate quickly changed his mind. It appeared that the appointment had been settled by Cromwell and his junta before it was debated in the House. He would be ill-advised to refuse.

Whitelocke felt vulnerable in his new post and in the summer of 1648 decided to make his Will. To each of his children he left thirty pounds a year in trust until they were fifteen, forty pounds a year up to the age of twenty-one and after that one thousand pounds each, as a marriage portion for the girls and to pay for training or apprenticeships for the boys.[28] At the same time he arranged for James and William to go up to Oxford before they entered the Middle Temple. Peace was profitable and money plentiful. In three months he earned almost £600 and could expect over £2,000 on the year, apart from the income from his estate. He had become a man of substance.[29]

His friend the Earl of Holland, who for years had vacillated between the King and Parliament, called on him during the summer and in the course of a probing conversation criticized Parliament for their slowness in arranging a personal treaty with the King on which, he said, most people's hearts were set. Whitelocke agreed that many people would welcome a settlement but he rejected the suggestion that, given a lead, the country would rise in the King's support. He warned Holland that Parliament's army was strong, experienced and well equipped and that 'it would be a desperate and rash attempt for any to imagine to make a head against them with a new body; that there was no trust to be given to people's words or minds in such designs; they were giddy and would not stir except they saw the tide turning.' Holland argued 'how honourable, just and pious a thing it would be to rescue their country from the misery and slavery they were now under' especially, he said pointedly, if those men who had caused the misery took a hand in putting things right. Whitelocke replied that this would be treachery and breach of faith and he opposed the scheme 'with more than ordinary dislike and earnestness'.[30] In July he learned that, had he responded, he would have been consulted on Holland's conspiracy with the Earl of Peterborough and the Duke of Buckingham. Early that month they raised a troop of not more than 1,000 horsemen against Parliament and were promptly crushed, as were the Scots and the leaders of other sporadic risings which constituted the Second Civil War. Whitelocke felt a surprising affection for Holland, an attractive, pleasure-loving character, politically unstable and of slender judgement. When the Earl was beheaded the following year for his part in the rising, Whitelocke wrote about him at length and about the manner in which he overcame his terror and prepared himself for death.

On 31 July 1648 Whitelocke and Frances rode over from Fawley to Thame Park, to visit Lord and Lady Wenman. During the afternoon the rain came down in torrents and it turned so cold that the guests would have liked to stay the night, but as the Wenmans 'did very slenderly invite them' they declined and rode home through thirteen miles of drenching rain. Breaking for once into the first person, Whitelocke wrote in his 'Diary', 'we wondered at such unkindness.' Frances caught a cold that day from which she never fully recovered.

Although the political scene was very grave, for Whitelocke the summer finished uneventfully. He spent a good deal of time in the country; he played bowls or hunted with Sir Humphrey Forster at Aldermaston; he improved the gardens at Phyllis Court and had a new barn built. He was never too busy to record his children's achievements: how Frances at twelve years old 'rode in a day singly on horseback from Phyllis Court to London'; how James left school 'a well-grounded scholar' and was given a mare and a colt by William Cooke. Domestic incidents jostled in his record with urgent political news gleaned, while he was in the country, from newspapers or from his secretaries Daniel Earle and William Swift, writing from Westminster. The army officers in Parliament had left in order to crush the royalist uprisings; their departure, and the subsequent flight of many remaining Independents, left the Presbyterians in precarious control. At the beginning of September Earle reported that they had appointed Commissioners to negotiate with the King on the Isle of Wight; Whitelocke had been passed over, ostensibly because of his office as a Commissioner of the Great Seal. He could count himself fortunate that he was to have no part in negotiating the Treaty of Newport. Unlike the Presbyterians, the army had become convinced of the King's duplicity and the bloodshed of the Second Civil War, for which the Royalists were responsible, had inflamed their minds against any settlement with Charles. The man of blood had to be brought to trial.

The 'Diary' entries for the three months starting in November 1648 are terse and non-committal. Back at Westminster Whitelocke was deeply uneasy about the nation's future, dreading above all the establishment of a military dictatorship. He had little immediate cause for anxiety on his own account, for although there were rumours that the army might remove him from the House he had received a kindly letter from Fairfax.[31] The soldiers who marched into London on 2 December 1648 treated him with respect and his Chancery work provided an excuse for not attending Parliament, where the Presbyterians held angry debates about the army's revolutionary activities. On 6 December he and Thomas Widdrington, his fellow Keeper, were stopped by soldiers drawn up menacingly in Palace Yard but Colonel Pride, who was conducting his purge of the army's enemies in the House, allowed the two lawyers to proceed to the Chancery Court. When Cromwell arrived in London he took an early opportunity of consulting them both about the future of the Commons; during the discussion he insolently lay on one of the King's rich beds.

Two days before Christmas the debate took place in which 'the fierce party' in the Commons pressed that the King, whom they openly named as the greatest delinquent, should be brought to trial. More moderate opinion, in the newly-purged House, suggested that since the King had been defeated it remained only to protect Parliament against their enemies for the future. Whitelocke allied himself with this group which 'endeavoured to . . . put the business wholly upon the army, that if they would have the thing done they should do it themselves . . . but they were subtle enough to see and avoid that . . . and to make those whom they left sitting in the Parliament to be their stales, and to do their most dirty work for them.'[32] A committee of thirty-eight was appointed to draw up charges against the King. White-locke was inevitably named to serve but he informed the Commons that he was opposed to the trial and he never attended; Thomas Widdrington was of the same mind and their friend Henry Elsynge, the Clerk to Parlia-ment, resigned on a pretext of ill-health. When Whitelocke and Widdring-ton were called to attend the newly-appointed committee on 26 December, they ignored the summons and drove down to Phyllis Court where they stayed for a week. The country's two most eminent lawyers went hawking, while Cromwell and his supporters made out what case they could for the legality of a trial without precedent. Whitelocke's evasion was by no means heroic but there was no acceptable choice open to him. He could neither support the King nor be a party to his trial and execution. He could not stop what was going to happen. He was a man with a wife and ten children. Even to dissociate himself from the King's trial required courage.

Because of his opposition he was not named as a Commissioner for the trial itself and once the appointments were made he returned to the House of Commons, early in the new year. 'The times were full of danger, trouble and change.' He and Frances were appalled by the turn of events. On the fateful 30 January 1649 he 'went not to the House but stayed all day at home, troubled at the death of the King this day and praying to God to keep his judgements from us'.

Parliament was dazed and elated by what it had done but the nation, as well as the King, was without a head. In the weeks which followed, White-locke helped to make the necessary legal adjustments to enable government and the administration of justice to be carried on within the framework of a republic. It was the kind of work at which he excelled, with his knowledge of the law and meticulous attention to detail.

Parliament's Great Seal was broken and a new one cast. The Commons released Widdrington, on grounds of conscience, from serving again as Keeper but would not exempt Whitelocke, who was none too pleased to learn that John L'Isle and Sergeant Richard Keble were to serve with him; he regarded them as inexperienced and self-opinionated men. He was appointed to serve on the Council of State by a unanimous vote but Crom-well saw fit to refer, in the new Council, to certain members who had been opposed to 'the Great Business'. Whitelocke gave them his reasons, adding that he was now prepared to co-operate in planning for the future. There appears to have been no ill-will towards him. John Bradshaw, who had presided at the trial, invited him to dinner, and soon afterwards Cromwell and Ireton were Whitelocke's guests at supper and spent the evening, in high spirits, exchanging anecdotes of the war. They left him at about midnight and on the way home their coach was stopped by the guard; when they said who they were the Captain was sceptical and threatened to arrest them; Ireton lost his temper but Cromwell took it in good part and gave the guard twenty shillings, praising him for his vigilance. The Captain boasted afterwards that he knew very well who the officers were but had shown them he was doing his duty.

Some months earlier, when the Earl of Pembroke had been appointed Constable of Windsor Castle and Keeper of the Forest and Great Park he had chosen Whitelocke as his deputy and placed Manor Lodge at his disposal. This was a pleasant house in the Park, situated between two arms of the lake, on the north-west shore of Virginia Water.[33] When two of the children, Mary and Willoughby, contracted smallpox Whitelocke was anxious to take Frances away from the risk of infection, for she was expecting another child, so he took her to stay at the Lodge. There he could hunt in Windsor Park during the morning and return to London the same afternoon. One day he noticed two men taking land measurements and he asked on whose authority they were there. When they replied that they had permission from Oliver Cromwell he told them to be off. He resented liberties taken by Cromwell or anyone else in the new regime and when the Keeper of the Wardrobe, at the Castle, offered him some of the late King's hangings for Manor Lodge he haughtily refused them, as something on which he had no claim.

During the spring of 1649 he learned with dismay that the Council of State proposed sending him as Ambassador to Holland. He protested vigorously that he was unqualified for the appointment, that he was in poor health and that his wife was expecting a baby. Members of the Council were not easily put off by such excuses, but eventually he talked his way out of the ambassadorship and a former Cambridge lecturer, Dr. Isaac Dorislaus, was appointed. Dorislaus was a marked man, having helped draw up the charges against King Charles, and in May 1649 he was brutally murdered in the Hague by a gang of English Royalists. The Dutch government made very little effort to bring the assassins to justice.[34] The following year Whitelocke was to have a second narrow escape when he refused an ambassadorship to Spain; Anthony Ascham was appointed in his place and was murdered by royalist agents in Madrid. It was not a healthy time for a representative of the English government to travel abroad.

One evening, at the end of April 1649, Whitelocke had supper with John L'Isle and another acquaintance and went home late to his Temple chambers. His wife was not waiting up for him. That was not like Frances. 'My heart was suddenly struck at it', he wrote. Next day she complained of a severe headache but refused to see a doctor. Whitelocke attended to his Chancery work and hurried home to find her very feverish, having difficulty in swallowing and suffering attacks of vomiting. Her sister-in-law, Lady Anne Willoughby, advised them to consult a certain Dr. George Bate. Three others, Dr. Peter Chamberlain, Dr. Francis Prujean and Dr. John Hinton were later called in. They wrote deferentially in Latin to Sir Theodore de Mayerne, outlining the patient's symptoms.[35] Sir Theodore was the most distinguished physician of his day. He had signed John Pym's post-mortem certificate and had attended the birth of the Queen's last child. Not only were there five doctors in attendance on Frances but also an apothecary and a nurse. She was already six months pregnant. The doctors considered inducing a miscarriage but decided it was too dangerous. Instead they treated her with physic and sedatives, purges and poultices, blood-letting, enemas and vomits. In an attempt to draw off the poisons the apothecary bandaged fresh-killed pigeons, sliced in two, onto the soles of her feet. The doctors quarrelled among themselves. Dr. Hinton, who was a specialist on problems of childbirth, favoured less drastic treatment than the others, who protested that his methods would undo the good they had already done. In terrible perplexity Whitelocke dismissed Hinton, deciding to rely on the doctors recommended by the Willoughby family.[36]

Frances talked freely with her relatives begging them, if she died, to cherish her husband and to do what they could for the children. When Bulstrode sat holding her hand they were both silent for long spells, not trusting themselves to speak. She dreaded leaving him and the children and was for a time in a state of mental turmoil; later she gained command of herself and spoke with the greatest sweetness to her husband but when he tried to answer he broke down. Eventually for her sake he managed to check his tears. She had never had any pretensions to scholarship but he was stirred by the power of her words, and by the insight reflected in her prayers: 'Break the heavens O Lord, and come down into the heart of a poor sinner.' 'His mercies are greater than my sins.' 'I find it in my own spirit that Jesus is there, my comforter, and he will be my salvation.' 'There is combat in my soul but God is mighty and hath prevailed for me,' and near the end, in quiet thankfulness, 'He hath filled my heart with spiritual joy, which is more precious than life!'

Whitelocke could find little consolation. 'My heart panted within me to see her restlessness and hear her cries and groans' he wrote and, in total fear and desolation, 'My loss will be so great that I shall hardly be able to bear it.' If there was any comfort to be found it was in his wife's growing serenity. To her sister-in-law she could say calmly, 'I am stretching out myself for death' and by that time she seemed 'no more daunted at the pale and ugly face of death than at one of her maids coming to her bedside'. Yet she had lost none of her spirit and when, on the doctors' orders, the servants laid green herbs on her bed to cool her she said tartly 'That was a fine course!' and promptly had them removed, for rushes and herbs belonged to the laying-out.

At midnight on 16 May 1649 Bulstrode stood for a moment at Frances' bedside then bent down and kissed her. He noticed the faint, cold sweat on her face. 'It was the coldest and the last kiss that ever I had from her and never any sad one before.' He lay down in the next room and about an hour later William Willoughby came to tell him it was over. He could not believe it. He ran into her room 'and there looked upon her DEAD'. The word is written twice the normal size. Though blood was gushing from her nose and mouth he had to be restrained from kissing her again.

In minute detail, covering eight large pages, he wrote his recollections of this enchanting creature. It was the most healing exercise he could have undertaken and provided a picture of the woman who had been the centre of his life for nearly fifteen years or, as he measured it with a lover's precision, for fourteen years six months and six days. They had married, he wrote, for no other reason but love and during those years there had never been an angry word between them. Frances had been quick to reprove a fault in one of the children or servants, but it was soon over and 'then she would be meek and loving again'. He remembered little traits. How on their journeys 'she would be the first ready and the last weary; never, as the custom of ladies is, would she make the company wait for her but she commonly waited for the company.' She had been an excellent horse-woman. She loved the horses and used to oversee their feeding and grooming. Above all she had been unfailingly gay; even when they had faced poverty, hunger or danger she had been 'not one jot discouraged or less cheerful'.

William and Anne Willoughby took Whitelocke back to their house in
Charterhouse Yard and gave him a room leading onto the garden. He had
little appetite and slept fitfully but on the second night he found some
comfort when, for about fifteen minutes, he believed he saw Frances as she
was in life standing at his bedside. Anne Willoughby undertook all the
funeral arrangements. Frances was to lie in the family vault at Fawley,
where Whitelocke's parents and his first wife were buried. The procession
of coaches and riders followed the hearse from London and was joined,
outside Henley, by a large crowd of mourners.

The first months of 1649 had been the most terrible of Whitelocke's life.
There had been the shock of the King's execution, followed by that of the
Earl of Holland. Then had come the loss that he feared he could not endure.
After the funeral wherever he went in his house or in the grounds he was
reminded with anguish of Frances; when he stayed with friends he could
not bear to sleep in a room he had once shared with her.

Two weeks after her death he returned to London, pulled himself together and fulfilled an engagement to deliver a speech; but he found himself unable to carry out his legal duties, for as he sat in Chancery the tears
poured down his cheeks. His grief was so consuming that his friends feared
for his life.

Chapter Six

'The Business of the Widow Wilson'

The new republic was under threat from the north and from the west. In Scotland, within a week of the execution of Charles I in January 1649, the Scottish Estates had proclaimed his son, Prince Charles, King in his place. Shortly afterwards, in Ireland, the Earl of Ormonde had also proclaimed Charles II King, and Irish Catholics and Protestants, sinking their differences, had come out in support of the Crown.[1] Suddenly, Ireland seemed the likeliest spot from which the Royalists might invade England. Yet it took Parliament over three months to equip an expeditionary force to deal with the crisis.

On 10 July 1649 Cromwell left London for Ireland, holding the new rank of Lord Lieutenant of Ireland as well as Commander-in-Chief of the army in Ireland. He stopped at Windsor the following day, with an impressive retinue, and sent for Whitelocke who had returned to Manor Lodge after some weeks in London. Cromwell entertained him with great kindness, persuaded him to travel to Reading in his company and on the way consulted him about affairs of state. He knew from his own experience what bereavement could do to a man. Whitelocke refused an invitation to accompany him further, making out that he had work to do. In fact, he rode over to Phyllis Court to visit five of the children and returned the same evening to Windsor Park.

He felt too distracted to make a home for the family. There were James, Frances, William, Elizabeth, Mary, Anne, Cecilia, Hester, Willoughby, and Bulstrode who was not yet two years old. The children at Fawley were being looked after by William Cooke and his wife, three others were in the care of Lady Anne Willoughby while Elizabeth, who was eleven, was with her aunt in North Wales. James, a spirited boy of eighteen, came up from Bristol to ask his father's permission to volunteer for Cromwell's army in Ireland. His tutors, Farren of Oriel and Zankey of All Souls, wrote supporting him; Farren in fulsome terms implored Whitelocke to lend fortune the jewel that God and nature bestowed on him, and James made a high-minded if fanciful speech about wishing to escape from the debauchery of Oxford to come under the good influence of the army officers. To the objection that he was too young and that the Irish campaign would interrupt his studies, James replied with accuracy that his genius was better fitted to the army

than it was to academic work.[2] Whitelocke, who could never deny James
anything for long, gave his reluctant consent on condition the boy travelled
with his tutor Jerome Zankey.[3] He provided his son with a horse and credit
facilities but said he was not prepared to ask for any special favours. This
did not however prevent him mentioning his son's initiative in a letter to
Cromwell, who wrote back that James was 'the only gentleman of England
that went a volunteer with him and that he would have a care of him'.[4]

Whitelocke had, by that time, a large choice of houses in which to live.
He owned Fawley Court and Phyllis Court and had the use of Manor Lodge
and of his Temple chambers; in addition the Earl of Northumberland had
placed Syon House, Isleworth, at his disposal partly out of friendship (they
had served together on peace negotiations with the King) but more to save
it from being requisitioned. Next, John L'Isle made a proposal that they
should both ask Parliament to procure for them the Duke of Buckingham's
house in Chelsea, once the home of Sir Thomas More. With five other
places to look after, and distrusting sequestration, Whitelocke refused to
lend his name; L'Isle disregarded his wishes and persuaded Parliament that
the business of the Great Seal could be transacted more efficiently if two
of the Keepers shared a home; as a result they were granted a lease and on
reasonable terms, since the house was in need of repair. Whitelocke resented
his colleague's action and was even more irritated when L'Isle moved into
the best rooms, leaving him the dilapidated quarters. He eased his conscience
about the requisition by informing the brilliant, irresponsible Duke of
Buckingham. The Duke, being a kinsman of the Willoughby family,
genially promised that when he came into his own again he would repay
whatever had been spent on the place.

During the summer of 1649 Whitelocke occupied himself, with a small
group of barristers, in scrutinizing the procedures of the Chancery Court;
in the autumn they introduced a set of Orders for simplifying and speeding
up the hearing of suits and for removing abuses.[5] In November he helped
to defeat a move to prevent practising lawyers, who were very unpopular
in the country, from sitting in Parliament. He pointed out that many lawyers
had served with distinction in the war; their knowledge provided a defence
of the people's rights against oppression; if lawyers were to be excluded
unless they relinquished their posts, then merchants must give up trading,
physicians stop visiting their patients and country gentlemen desist from
selling their corn and wool while sitting as Members of Parliament.[6] A
further claim on Whitelocke's attention concerned the safeguarding of the

Royal Library. After the King's execution, practical Philistines like Hugh Peter, the army preacher, were in favour of selling the valuable books, manuscripts, medals and jewels at St. James's for what they would fetch at home or abroad. Selden and other scholars saw them as treasures to be saved for posterity. Whitelocke was appointed Chairman of the small committee set up to preserve the collection and was later made Librarian.[7]

In December Whitelocke was taken seriously ill. Since Frances's death he had largely lost interest in his career and said he had no wish to live, except on account of the children. At the turn of the year his doctors persuaded him to go into the country for a change of air and he accepted an invitation from the Earl of Suffolk, to stay at Audley End in Essex; he went hawking on the beautiful estate but even that could not free him from his listless melancholy. The only thing which held his attention was news from Ireland about his son. His preoccupation with that subject was obsessive. James had made friends with Captain Owen, 'the preacher's son'; that was a nice friendship for the boy. Contemporaries would have known at once that 'the preacher' was the famous independent minister, John Owen, who had preached the victory sermon after the fall of Colchester and preached to Parliament on the day after the King's execution; he was in Ireland as Cromwell's Chaplain and in March would be appointed preacher to the Council of State. There was also news that James had won the friendship of the Earl of Cork's son, Lord Broghill; that James earned the affection of his fellow soldiers; James lent his cloak to a sick comrade, and James was struck on the thigh with the butt of a musket, his horse was killed under him and a bullet went through his hat. Whitelocke was oblivious of the atrocities committed against the Irish at Drogheda, although he acknowledged the 'stoutness of the enemy who maintained the breach as gallantly as ever men did'.[8] His attention, wherever the fighting took place, was riveted on his son. James 'beat in the enemy' and James was made standard-bearer to the Life Guards, no mean recognition by Cromwell for a young boy. James also incurred enormous debts which he expected his father to pay.

Whitelocke's friends meantime were planning to provide an even more vivid interest than his son's career. At first the mention of marriage renewed his distress but gradually he allowed the thought to take hold of him and, on his return to London, he mustered enough strength to call several times on Lady Hungerford, a widow with a large fortune. Both parties understood the nature of the visits and when the time seemed auspicious he proposed to her. Lady Hungerford replied courteously that she was resolved not to marry again. That was the correct response. He persisted, noticing suddenly that the lady was not only intelligent but good-looking. They continued to meet and talked at some length, but whenever he touched on marriage she quoted the Epistle to Timothy in support of her widowed state. [9] He wanted a devout woman but this was too much. His friends made alternative suggestions. There was Lady Salter, a widow with several children, but he 'feared that would not be comfortable and convenient'. Bartholomew Hall thought he should remain a widower while William Cooke 'bluntly wrote to him to marry'. The Cookes had children and grand-children of their own besides being encumbered with five of their landlord's and, although Goodwife Cooke was kind to them, Whitelocke noticed with a pang that they looked in need of a mother.

In February 1650 a wealthy Member of Parliament, Colonel Rowland Wilson, died at his home in Bishopsgate Street. Some people thought he had committed suicide. [10] His attractive young widow Mary was overcome with grief, and only roused herself when she heard that her husband's parents planned to seize the estate, with the taunt that her marriage had been childless. Although she recoiled from the prospect of a wrangle over the inheritance, she was determined to fight back.

Within a few days of the Colonel's death Whitelocke's friends were assessing Mary as a possible bride. He thanked them but said he had no intention of marrying again, unless he met a woman who would be good to the children; in any case he thought it unseemly to consider a lady who had so recently lost her husband. He turned his mind to other matters. The University of Oxford was preparing to elect a Chancellor. Bradshaw and Fairfax were candidates, but Whitelocke's friends assured him that if he accepted nomination he himself would stand a good chance. He refused to do so 'for a feather in his cap' and argued that, as he had already been ap-pointed Steward and Recorder of Oxford, it would be inappropriate to stand. He tried to apply himself to Chancery work but his friends distracted him by returning to 'the business of the widow Wilson'. Mary, they insisted, would make a very good wife and would certainly be kind to the children.

He had known Rowland Wilson and planned to attend the funeral, which took place a month after the Colonel's death. In fact he set off in the august company of the Lord Mayor of London and Lord General Fairfax, walking directly behind them with Lord President Bradshaw. As the procession moved through streets lined with onlookers men in the crowd raised their sticks, shaking them and yelling 'Here is the rogue that judged the King!

Kill him. Kill him. Let us tear him in pieces!' Bradshaw had been threatened before and became alarmed. He appealed to Whitelocke to stay by him and the two men disappeared down a side street before the funeral cortege reached the church.[11] The ceremony was hardly over before Whitelocke's friends were again urging him to approach Mary Wilson. He still hesitated but was nettled to learn that other suitors lacked his delicacy. One of them was the Regicide, Colonel George Fleetwood, M.P. A friend offered to take Whitelocke to Pancras Church, Soper Lane, to have a look at the lady during the service but he objected that the setting was inappropriate. He did however agree to his suit being mentioned; Mary replied firmly that she had been approached by a number of well-known men but that she did not consider remarrying. Not long afterwards her father-in-law, old Rowland Wilson, told her she should not have a penny from her husband's estate beyond what she could win through the Courts. She decided to contest the case and, confident that her father-in-law would have no scruples, she decided to make discreet enquiries as to whether the Judges in Chancery took bribes. When she learned that Whitelocke was to hear her case she asked George Cokain, the minister of her church and her private chaplain, to find out what he could on her behalf. Cokain consulted George Fleetwood, in whose regiment he had served as a chaplain. The Colonel was perhaps unaware at that time that Whitelocke was his rival for Mary's hand. He replied categorically that this Lord Keeper would scorn to accept a bribe.

Whitelocke's prospect of winning Mary seemed slender. His intermediaries had failed to mention the matter of ten step-children but mischiefmakers had quickly made good the omission. Fortunately George Cokain favoured the match, believing that the care of step-children might help to 'divert her melancholy'. It was not until May 1650 that Whitelocke met the object of his great interest. Mary was staying in Hackney with (it seems) her sister and her sister's husband, Samuel Wilson, a prosperous vintner. They invited her distinguished suitor to visit her and to stay the night. By the following month he was calling regularly at her house in Bishopsgate Street. He was even beginning to feel possessive. It seemed that Colonel George Fleetwood and other men were still paying court to his lady, but Mr. Cokain assured him that Mary was not interested in them. Fleetwood took a different view and asked Mary's permission to challenge his rival to a duel; Whitelocke commented that there was little to fear from a gentleman who needed a lady's consent before he would fight.

In June 1650, Cromwell returned after crushing the main resistance in Ireland. He was welcomed and feted in London yet he found time to receive Whitelocke, with great cordiality, and regaled him with tales of James's courage in battle; but for once James had to take second place and when he sent home extravagant bills his father wrote sternly:

Son James,

I have not received from you so many letters as I wished concerning the public affairs but I have received many more than I expected for the payment of moneys taken up by you in Ireland, the sum whereof comes to above £400. I presume you will acknowledge me a loving and indulgent father and that your education hath not been narrow . . . neither can you forget your nine brothers and sisters who, by the smallness of my fortune and so large an expense out of it, will not be so well provided for as I hope yourself do wish . . . for them.

As I am unwilling to suspect any extravagancy or disorder in your ways, especially having received with much contentment from my Lord Lieutenant a very fair report of your civility and good carriage, so I cannot in love to you and your brothers and sisters, being all of you equal to me, any longer permit this expense of yours but admonish you to forbear it or I must forbear the payment of such bills. I am tender of putting any discountenance upon you, and surely you will be as careful not to displease me, or to prejudice my fortune and your own and those that are so near unto us. God hath laid sadness enough upon me. . . .

I shall pray for his blessing upon you,
        and remain your loving father
June 18
1650
                                                            B. Whitelocke[12]

James, whose debts in Ireland finally ran to £1,500, replied with the familiar excuse that his letters must have gone astray.

Having set his mind on marrying again Whitelocke was not to be trifled with; even in a letter to Mary he introduced a note of asperity, warning her not to listen to objections to his suit from interested parties.[13] He could not however devote himself exclusively to courting, for within days of Cromwell's return the nation was facing another grave crisis. With the defeat of his supporters in Ireland, the exiled and impoverished Charles Stuart had turned his mind towards Scotland as the base from which to conquer England. The cost was high. Although the Scots had proclaimed him King they were still determined he should sign the Covenant before he could expect their help. This he eventually did, under duress, only to find that they had worse in store. He was required to humiliate himself before

God for his father's opposition to presbyterian reform and for his mother's idolatry.[14] The Scots drove a hard bargain. At Westminster it was known that he planned to invade England and assume the Crown, supported by Scottish forces. Cromwell proposed that the English should attack first, to avoid being 'put to the after game'. Fairfax appeared to agree but under pressure from Presbyterians, and in particular from his wife, he later protested that he could not consent to an act of aggression against Parliament's former allies. A committee was appointed composed of Cromwell, Harrison, Lambert, Vane and Whitelocke to try to persuade him otherwise. Whitelocke took an active part in the long meeting, held behind locked doors, and recorded the debate in detail. In the end Fairfax resigned and Cromwell accepted supreme command, appointed by Parliament as Captain General and Commander-in-Chief.

It was a time of momentous decisions. But the defence of the realm was not the only thing on Whitelocke's mind. He had a letter in his pocket. It told him that Mary was going to stay with George Cokain's parents in Bedfordshire and he was invited to join her; George Cokain hinted that 'privacy might be an advantage to his suit'. Whitelocke only waited until Cromwell had left for Scotland before hurrying down to Fawley and across country to Cotton End, a hamlet between Shefford and Bedford. He took with him Bartholomew Hall and four servants, all well horsed to create a good impression. Old Mr. Cokain and his wife lived modestly in 'a pretty little gentleman's house'. Because of the national emergency Whitelocke could only spare five days but he 'made use of his time'. When he returned to London Mary was left pondering and praying about the daunting question of those ten step-children. In the end she found encouragement in the Psalmist's words that a man is blessed who has his quiver full of children. Clearly, Mr. Whitelocke was abundantly blessed and might make good the humiliation she had suffered in her childless marriage to Rowland Wilson.[15]

When he returned to Bedfordshire Whitelocke told Mary exactly how he was placed financially. There was no debt on his land and his income was substantial but he made it clear that Fawley Court was to go to James, his eldest son, and Phyllis Court to William, the eldest son of his second marriage, while the rest of the land must be divided between his eight other sons and daughters. If Mary were to bear him children she would have to provide for their inheritance out of her own fortune. She said she liked him for being so frank with her and agreed to marry him; if she were to die leaving children she hoped he would be equally good to them. Once she had made up her mind 'she cast herself wholly upon his affection and honesty . . . and put her estate into his hands.' Bartholomew Hall drew up a short marriage settlement which they signed and sealed.

Whitelocke could not tolerate further delay so on 5 August 1650, the day after the agreement was signed, he invited Mary to go riding with him accompanied by George Cokain, Bartholomew Hall and some of the servants. A few miles west of Bedford they rode up the short, steep hill and across a stretch of grass to the village church of Bromham. There they dismounted and went in search of the clerk to unlock the door and the minister to conduct an impromptu wedding.[16] The small party of riders witnessed the ceremony and afterwards Whitelocke appealed to them to keep it a secret for he intended, as soon as he could obtain consent from the Wilson family, to have a public wedding in London. The eve of his forty-fifth birthday was a very agreeable one; his bedroom 'being next to his mistress's there was the more convenience of lodging together, and none of the family took notice of it'. In the following weeks, when guests came to the house he made out that he was still courting and Mary, too, kept up the pretence.

At the end of the month they presented themselves at the Wilsons' house in Hackney; Mary announced that she had made up her mind to marry Bulstrode and asked Samuel to negotiate a settlement. The Wilsons revered money and position and were delighted; 'brother Wilson', as Whitelocke usually called him, agreed to a settlement similar to the one already signed, of which he remained in ignorance. Whitelocke prudently slept at the Middle Temple and he and Mary only met by day, visiting the church together to arrange for their second wedding. Two days before the ceremony troublemakers warned Mary that her suitor had debts amounting to £4,000. She was distressed but urged her husband to tell her the truth so that she could help pay off his creditors; he was able to assure her that the rumour was invented by 'pickthanks, knaves and liars' and that his total debts amounted to some twenty or thirty pounds for household expenses.

On 5 September, a month after their secret wedding, Bulstrode and Mary were married a second time. The ceremony in St. John's Church, Hackney, was followed by a reception at which many Members of Parliament were present, including the Speaker of the House of Commons and, in spite of the grave happenings in Scotland, 'they were very merry, as is usual upon such an occasion.'[17]

Two days later the newly-married couple were driving towards Chelsea when they met a messenger bringing news of Cromwell's triumph at

Dunbar. Whitelocke's thoughts were jerked back to politics and he set off for Parliament to hear a full account of the victory.

After some weeks, finding the daily journey tedious between Bishopsgate and Westminster, he persuaded Mary to move from her luxurious home to his Middle Temple chambers, where they could have the children with them. She was satisfied, provided she could take her kitchen utensils with her and her own bed. It was a modest home, 'Yet his new wife was well contented with it and was so careful and tender of his children that a stranger could not observe but that she was their own mother. Only in some things she was more indulgent to them than an own mother would have been.'

Mary was as generous towards the memory of his two previous wives as she was towards her step-children, and later named one of her daughters Rebecca and another Frances. Her fine character was not appreciated by Bartholomew and Frances Hall or by the Willoughby family, who did not disguise their disapproval of the marriage. Whitelocke was dismayed by people's pettiness. Apart from the unkindness towards his wife he was bewildered by the professional jealousy shown towards him by his fellow Keepers of the Great Seal. There were, however, happier duties to take his mind off the tensions in Chancery. His governorship of Charterhouse school and hospital was a source of considerable pleasure; the foundation's charitable and educational purposes appealed to him and it was flattering to be asked to serve, for, since Charterhouse reopened in 1611, Governors had been chosen from among the most prominent men of the day. He was also engaged in an exacting intellectual exercise. It was more than a century since the language of church worship had been translated into the vernacular and Parliament had, for some time, intended that the language used in the Law Courts should also be made intelligible. The French tongue roused resentment because it was the language of William the Conqueror, 'the Norman bastard'; to Puritans it had become a symbol of conquest and kingship.[18] Men who fretted against oppressive laws blamed the Normans for introducing them. Whitelocke was at pains to insist that English law was of Saxon origin, but he agreed that it ought to be administered in the mother tongue and he became an active member of the parliamentary committee appointed to prepare a translation.

At home, life resumed its accustomed pattern. Mary had been married to Rowland Wilson for fourteen childless years but after the secret wedding in Bedfordshire she conceived almost at once. This did not deter her from hunting with her husband, until one day she had a fall from her horse and was badly bruised; this was followed by attacks of vomiting and it was thought that as she was six months pregnant she would lose the child, but she was a sturdy young woman and soon recovered. She decided to go back to the familiar surroundings and comfort of her Bishopsgate home for the confinement, and her first child was born there on 30 May 1651. It was feared he was not going to live, until someone remembered an old practice of blowing tobacco smoke in a baby's face, causing it to gasp for breath and yell. It worked and the child thrived. He was Mary's answer to prayer and accordingly she named him Samuel, but it later appeared that he was not the answer she had expected.

Domestic events were suddenly overshadowed by news from the north. The Scottish campaign had continued through the winter, interspersed with Cromwell's attempts to win back England's former allies and persuade them to abandon Charles Stuart. Since February he had been ill and Parliament had sent two doctors to attend him, one of them being Dr. Bate who had treated Frances during her last weeks. By June Cromwell was in better health. He was determined not to expose his army to another winter in Scotland. On the other side, Leslie and the Scottish army had recovered from their defeat at Dunbar and a substantial part of their force had taken up an impregnable position at Stirling. They had to be drawn to fight. To achieve this Cromwell crossed the Firth of Forth, threatening the Scottish army's supply lines. The battle of Inverkeithing followed, with a notable victory for the English army. This was only the beginning of Cromwell's far-sighted strategy. With immense daring he left the western road, through Carlisle and Lancashire, open to Charles and the Scots army and they duly marched down it, heading for London. It was known in the south that the Scots had crossed the border and the nation rallied against the invasion. In spite of royalist talk of the English being held in subjection, only waiting for their deliverance, 'the King's expectation of the people's coming in to him was strangely frustrate' and the Scots army dwindled in the course of the march.[19] By the time they reached Worcester Cromwell was ready for them. His army had marched south at great speed, following the eastern road through Yorkshire, parallel with the Scots, and by the time he cut off the King's road from Worcester to London he had the massive support of Fairfax and Fleetwood with their armies, as well as that of Lambert and Harrison.

When news reached Westminster early in September of Cromwell's great victory at Worcester, just a year after Dunbar, and of Charles defeated and on the run, it seemed that the Royalists were finally overthrown. Whitelocke was one of Parliament's four Commissioners sent to greet the Lord General on his triumphant journey home. They met him a few miles beyond Aylesbury, and after delivering Parliament's congratulations they all went hawking, with falcons provided by Richard Winwood. They spent the night in Aylesbury and Cromwell regaled them with stories of the battle. To each of the Commissioners he made a present of a splendid horse and also a pair of Scottish prisoners, captured at Worcester; these could profitably be sold into slavery, since there was traffic in white as well as in black skins, for work on the plantations. Whitelocke showed his opinion of this horrific gift by granting his prisoners their freedom, and arranging a pass for them to return to Scotland.

Cromwell entered London accompanied by the four Commissioners and was greeted by the Speaker, the Lord President of the Council, Members of Parliament, the Lord Mayor, Sheriffs and Aldermen as well as by enormous crowds. There were volleys of shot and cries of acclamation for the hero who had saved them from invasion and from King Charles's son; he was humble in his response 'and in his discourses about the business of Scotland and of Worcester he would seldom mention anything of himself, but the gallantry of the officers and soldiers'. The next day he invited Whitelocke to his house and in the following months they spent a good deal of time together. The leader's friendship was flattering but could also be embarrassing. When a relative, a Mrs. Cromwell from Slough, was concerned in a Chancery dispute Whitelocke was expected to be helpful. He explained that he would not act against his conscience or his oath to please anyone and Cromwell appeared to accept this answer, but it was reported later that he 'expressed a dislike of it, and expected more compliance . . . to his desires'.

On 10 December 1651 a few Members of Parliament and army officers were summoned to meet at the house of Thomas Widdrington, the Speaker. With Charles I dead and his son defeated at Worcester, Cromwell wished to discuss a settlement of the nation. Whitelocke recorded part of the debate in which he himself put to the meeting that they must decide between 'an absolute republic or . . . any mixture of monarchy'. He and other lawyers favoured mixed monarchical government, which at that date could have implied government by a king and commons rather than by king, lords and commons. The late King's third son, Prince Henry, Duke of Gloucester, was named as a possible sovereign since, unlike his brothers, he had been too young to take up arms against the Commonwealth. Most of the soldiers spoke in favour of a republic. Cromwell spoke as if he liked the notion of mixed monarchy, although he put off debating the choice of a king; Whitelocke suspected that he 'discovered by this meeting the inclinations of the persons that spake, for which he fished, and made use of what he then discerned'.

Chancery work was notoriously profitable. Even though Whitelocke rejected bribes and 'gratifications', he had done well for himself since the end of the war and had been steadily investing in land. He had consolidated his riverside home by adding Greenlands to Fawley Court and Phyllis Court. After finding £6,500 for this purchase he was not planning to buy more land but Lord Lovelace, an impoverished Royalist, implored him to buy Blunsden, a large estate near Swindon. Lovelace had originally been assessed as a delinquent, in 1646, for a fine of over £18,000 but at the end of 1651 this was reduced to a little over £7,000.[20] A week or two later he came to Whitelocke with his pitiful story of being deep in debt and in danger of imprisonment. If he could sell his land and pay the principle of £9,000 his creditors would waive the interest of £3,000; otherwise his estate would be seized and 'torn to pieces'. Whitelocke doubted the legality of such a sale since the property was entailed to the heir who was still a minor. Lord Lovelace brushed aside this objection with a solemn undertaking that his son, when he came of age, would confirm the transaction.[21] Against his better judgement, and partly because he was approached by William Willoughby, Whitelocke agreed to buy the place for £10,000, which allowed Lovelace £1,000 clear after settling his debts. It is likely that this ill-fated purchase was made from Mary's money with a view to providing a legacy for her son Samuel.

Whitelocke's claim that Cromwell enjoyed his company and treated him with great respect was probably accurate; he was quick to detect the slightest lack of courtesy shown to him by those in high places. In Parliament, too, his experience and judgement were valued. He was consulted over foreign affairs. He negotiated with the Agent of the Hanse towns, and prepared terms for the surrender of Barbados by his brother-in-law Lord Willoughby, who had governed the island on behalf of the exiled Charles II.[22] He also drafted the Bill for the Union of Scotland and England which followed the defeat of the Scots army at Worcester. During the summer of 1652 he was offered the post of Chief Commissioner for Civil Affairs, one of the most important civil appointments in Ireland, with a strong financial inducement.

He suspected that this had been engineered by John L'Isle to get him out of the country and that Cromwell might have been a party to it, not finding him sufficiently yielding, particularly in Chancery matters. He excused himself on grounds of health.

Mary was expecting another child. A few days before her son Carleton was born she accompanied Bulstrode on a visit to Martin Abbey. This was the home of her first husband's father with whom she had, by that time, come to terms over the legacy. There they met her former physician Dr. Thomas Winston. The old man gave an account of the injustices he had suffered during the troubled years. He had left England, under licence from the House of Lords, daunted it seems by the Levellers 'in an age when it was a crime to be rich', and had lived for a time in France. He returned to find that, although he had never actively opposed Parliament, his estate had been sequestrated and he had been deprived of his appointment and lodgings as a professor at Gresham College. Whitelocke decided to investigate. The next day, after verifying with the Clerk to the Committee of Sequestrations that Parliament had nothing against the Doctor, he made out an order for Winston's lands and appointment to be restored.[23] Dr. Winston was deeply touched and a few days later called to ask a favour: 'You have many children and a great family, which cannot be without some . . . sickness among them. I have an affection for you and some knowledge of my profession, and my suit is that I may be the physician to your family, and I shall constantly visit you and take the best care I can of yourself and of your lady and children, and of the meanest servant in your house.' The offer was accepted and on his first visit the Doctor was paid a fee which he called his 'retainer'; after that he refused any further payments saying tartly 'What, take a fee of thirteen children? I will not! I have lesser need of money than you' – which Whitelocke admitted was 'most true'.[24]

With the anguish and achievement of the wars behind them the army felt insecure. Officers and men viewed the politicians in the Rump, who had remained in power with army support, as corrupt self-seekers. In August 1652 they presented Parliament with a petition for various reforms. Cromwell sympathized, but Whitelocke criticized them for 'petitioning with their swords in their hands'. The sense of high purpose which had inspired men in wartime had worn thin; the danger seemed to be past and the Commonwealth lacked any objective that could unify its people. There was fear of anarchy. As far back as November 1649 Whitelocke had noted 'men took strange liberty to calumniate all in authority and to clamour if they had not what themselves thought fit respecting themselves and their private interest and concerns, much more than the rules of right and justice and the law itself'.[25]

One afternoon in November 1652 he was walking in St. James's Park, after a busy day in Westminster, when Cromwell beckoned to him and greeted him with even more respect than usual. As they strolled round the park together Cromwell said cordially, 'I know your kindness to me, your old friend, . . . I can trust you with my life and the most secret matters relating to our business.' He went on to observe that God had given them victory against their enemies but there was now such a division among themselves that he saw a danger of losing what they had won, through 'jarrings, animosities . . . and private janglings'. They both considered that the army's services to the Commonwealth had been undervalued and touched on the danger of mutiny. Cromwell referred to some of the short-comings of Members of Parliament, their refusal to resign and give way to a newly-elected House, their insolence, the scandalous lives some of them led and the fact that they were no longer accountable to anybody; Whitelocke was hostile to any hint that the army might dislodge them by force; the officers were appointed by Parliament and were its servants. 'Suddenly and unexpectedly Cromwell brake forth in this expression: "What if a man should take upon him to be King?" '[26] Whitelocke answered smoothly that such a remedy would be worse than the disease; the royal title could add nothing to Cromwell's stature; he already wielded as much power as any king; he would on the other hand lose the support of the army and the City, whose members had chosen a republican form of government; they might not welcome the choice between a Stuart and a Cromwell for king. Cromwell asked what alternative there was. Whitelocke evaded the question but eventually replied by asking another question: 'What if Your Excellency should bring in him that hath the legal right to be King, upon such con-ditions as you shall think?' The youthful Charles II, 'the King of the Scots', was in such a weak position since the battle of Worcester that Whitelocke believed he would accept any reasonable terms on which to be restored to the throne. Cromwell seemed to take the proposal in good part. At the end of a long discussion he said that the subject called for deep thought and he would arrange for further talks. With that he broke away abruptly and something in his bearing suggested that he was displeased. Although White-locke noted that Cromwell continued to consult him about affairs of state and behaved 'very fair to me outwardly', after that talk the former friendliness was lacking and within six months Whitelocke found himself out of politics.

It was a trying winter. The army's animosity against Parliament continued to foment and in the first week of April 1653 Whitelocke recorded, after a talk with Cromwell, 'I still found him in distaste with Parliament and hastening their dissolving'. On 19 April Cromwell summoned him to a conference to discuss dissolution. The remnant of that Parliament which more than a decade earlier had legislated that it could only be dissolved by its own decision, this 'Rump' of a once great Parliament, had no intention of ending its own life, although Whitelocke wrote that for his part he was tired of serving in it.[27] Sir Henry Vane the younger with his republican supporters had promoted a Bill which had already reached its second reading. This aimed at filling vacancies by means of elections, while allowing Members who were already entrenched to keep their seats and giving them power to reject newly-elected Members who did not meet with their approval. The Bill was anathema to the army, and some officers at the meeting clamoured to expel Parliament by force. Ironically, it was Cromwell who rebuked them. A more moderate proposal by the army recommended that Parliament should dissolve itself, giving way to a provisional Council of Forty consisting of Members of Parliament and army officers, who would govern until a new Parliament could be elected. It was left to Whitelocke and the Speaker, Sir Thomas Widdrington, to argue the merits of a parliamentary Bill for dissolution, to be followed by new elections. There were serious difficulties in that Royalists were certain to be returned; moreover, provision had to be made for an interim government. The debate raised problems and demanded decisions for which there was no constitutional precedent.

The conference went on far into the night and Whitelocke 'came home weary and troubled'. The army disliked legal and constitutional arguments, and he believed he was placing himself and the family in jeopardy by insisting on such procedures. A further meeting had been called for the following morning and he went early to Cromwell's lodgings, hoping to see him alone, but was dismayed to find Colonel Ingoldsby and one or two others there before him. While they were talking news arrived that Parliament was already sitting. Ingoldsby, Whitelocke and others set off for the House where they found that, far from debating a Bill for dissolution, Members were preparing for the third reading of Vane's hated Bill. Ingoldsby hurried back to inform Cromwell, who descended on the Commons accompanied by his musketeers.[28] Some of them he placed at the doors of the House and in the lobby while others, according to Whitelocke, filed into the chamber with him. Whitelocke's account of this disturbing scene is compressed, impressionistic and probably less accurate than that of some other eye-witnesses. He had slept very little the previous night, had been hurrying from place to place in the morning and was deeply worried; he was in no condition to give an exact report. Others recalled that Cromwell sat silent taking stock of the situation and then started speaking, at first calmly; Whitelocke's account left this out and went straight to the fury with which Cromwell ordered the Speaker to leave his chair; it told how he then turned on Members of the House, abusing some as whoremasters (here he turned his eyes on Henry Marten and Sir Peter Wentworth), others as drunkards, corrupt, a scandal to the Gospel they professed, or as unjust. According to one report Whitelocke was the target of this last accusation. Widdrington remained in the Speaker's chair until Colonel Harrison took him by the arm. Members stood up to protest but did not draw their swords. Finally, Cromwell dissolved Parliament and they 'tamely departed', while their master pointed at the mace and ordered one of the musketeers to 'take away that fool's bauble'.

'Thus' Whitelocke wrote bitterly 'was this great Parliament, which had done so great things, . . . routed by those whom they had set up and that took commissions and authority from them; nor could they in the least justify any action they had done, or one drop of blood they had spilt, but by this authority. Yet now the servants rose against their masters.'[29] He was right. The officers had received their commissions from the Long Parliament. But Parliament had forgotten that it owed its life to the army.

Chapter Seven

Ambassador Extraordinary

Suddenly, after more than twelve years, Whitelocke found himself out of touch with the policy-makers, cut off from the secrets of Westminster and passed over, in July 1653, when Cromwell summoned the Barebones Parliament. Even his office as a Commissioner of the Great Seal was in doubt.

On 12 June he went to his parish church in Chelsea but there was no joy for him there for the parson, Dr. Samuel Wilkinson, preached the sermon. Whitelocke found him 'a dull, proud, scandalous man and a dry, pitiful preacher'. It set him studying a text from Malachi, 'The priest's lips should keep knowledge. . . .'[1] 'I was very much retired and alone in my house at Chelsea, and those former seeming friends who used almost daily to frequent me, when I was in a capacity to do them service, now that they saw me left out . . . deserted me and I was left alone.'[2] He was out of favour even as a lawyer; his wealthy client Elias Ashmole consulted the stars as to whether he should engage my Lord Whitelocke in a case against Sir Humphrey Forster of Aldermaston, but it looks as if the stars said no.[3]

When Whitelocke took his wife to stay at Cotton End, in the middle of August, some of his former friends in Bedfordshire slighted him, but at least he was his own master again and could look forward to the autumn's hawking. He spent some time 'meditating upon the high flying of the hawks and the persecution of the poor innocent partridges'.[4] This was a political metaphor, not unlike the twentieth century concept of 'hawks and doves'. Occasionally he felt uneasy about blood sports and deplored the fact that some rich men made hunting their main concern in life, but he silenced his conscience with the proviso that the huntsman must avoid needless cruelty.[5] With time on his hands he meditated on several other subjects, including the creation. He reflected, with poetic insight, on the words 'the spirit of God moved upon the face of the waters.' The Hebrew word, translated as 'moved', implied 'such a waving and fluttering as eagles and other birds use over their young, cherishing and stirring them up'.[6] His thoughts on the creation of the heavens led him to consider astronomical questions concerning the relative size of the earth, the sun and the moon as these were understood by his contemporaries. Mary meantime was having a rest from the children, and preparing for yet another confinement.

Into this placid, rural scene the news from London crashed like a cannon ball. The letter from his secretary, Daniel Earle, dated 23 August 1653, opened quite harmlessly:

I have been this morning to Chelsea, where I found my little masters and mistresses and all your family in good health.

It went on,

When I waited on Sir Charles Wolseley, he was pleased to tell me that you were named by the Council of State to go Ambassador into Sweden, and that my Lord General had undertaken to write to your lordship about it. I presume ere this you have heard from him.[7]

Whitelocke had not heard. He must have felt some quickening of the blood at the prospect of returning to a post of such distinction, but he was mystified. Viscount L'Isle, the eldest son of the Earl of Leicester, had been nominated earlier that year for the Swedish embassy and had received the first payment towards his expenses.[8]

Although Whitelocke told himself that he was happier riding in the English countryside than listening to flatterers in Whitehall or travelling abroad, he could not put the matter out of his mind. 'The letter was often read and paraphrased upon and several meanings of it collected.' Mary's comments were accompanied by floods of tears but she was a shrewd woman and her advice, as her husband acknowledged, was worth heeding. They tried to guess why Philip L'Isle had turned down the appointment, and they inevitably recalled the dreadful fate of Dorislaus and Ascham who had taken the appointments Whitelocke had declined. He was highly suspicious, yet as he had been made politically impotent he could see no reason why the Council of State or Cromwell should wish to send him overseas; he concluded that he was looked on as 'no friend to their affairs having opposed them in the business of breaking the Parliament and in several other matters, as contrary to right and law', and concluded that 'he being in their judgements fit for the employment it would be a handsome way to be rid of him by sending him into Sweden, thereby to remove an obstacle of their designs.'[9]

As time went on with no official confirmation they began to tell themselves it was a false alarm. All the same, the Whitelockes could no longer feel at peace in the country. Early on the morning of 3 September they set off for London, taking the road through Haynes and on to Luton, a small town 'pleasantly and healthfully situated in an open country about it but not much frequented with trading'. They stopped at St. Albans for a rest then travelled on to Barnet, Highgate and home in one day to Chelsea.[10] Whitelocke was still in bed next morning, recovering from his long journey, when the letter he dreaded arrived. Cromwell and Gilbert Pickering had been instructed to write and Cromwell had drafted the letter himself.

For the right honourable the Lord Whitelocke, one of the Commissioners of the Seal, these
My Lord,
    The Council of State, having thoughts of putting your lordship to the trouble of being Extraordinary Ambassador to the Queen of Swethland, did think fit not to impose that service upon you without first knowing your own freedom thereunto, wherefore they were pleased to command our services in making this address to your lordship; and hereby we can assure you of a very large confidence in your honour and abilities for this employment.
To which we begging your answer do rest
    My lord
        Your honourable servants
            O. Cromwell
            Gil. Pickering.[11]
September 2 1653.

Again the family analysed it line by line, reading a good deal into the words 'not to impose that service' and 'confidence in your honour and abilities'; Whitelocke decided that the only way he could find out what lay behind the proposal was by confronting Cromwell. Before he could do so he had a visit from Lord L'Isle's brother, Colonel Algernon Sydney, who tried to talk him into accepting the mission. Sydney's explanation that L'Isle had resigned because, with his poor health, he could not face the rigours of the winter journey was hardly reassuring.[12]

    At the interview with Cromwell Whitelocke used every argument he could muster against going, from the inauspicious time of year and his wife's pregnancy to his ignorance of court ceremonial on which the young Queen Christina set great store. Bluff and genial, Cromwell brushed aside all excuses:

The Council have pitched upon you unanimously as the fittest man in the nation for this service. We know your abilities, . . . we know you have languages and have travelled and understand the interest of Christendom; and I have known you in the army to endure hardships and to be healthful and strong and of mettle, discretion and parts most fit for this employment. You are so indeed. Really, no man is so fit for it as you are. We know you to be a gentleman of a good family, related to persons of honour, and your present office of Commissioner of the Seal will make you the more acceptable to her.

In spite of these compliments Whitelocke refused to commit himself. He would think it over and give his reply in a fortnight's time. Cromwell was taken aback: 'I pray, my Lord Whitelocke, do not think of so long a time but let me entreat you to accept of the employment and to return your answer within a few days to me.'[13]

The family was vocal but divided. James, an adventurous young Colonel, just turned twenty-two, was eager to accompany his father and made light of the danger; his half-sister, Frances, did everything in her power to dissuade her father from going, even writing to old William Cooke for his support.[14] Mary, although a Puritan, imputed the most unscrupulous motives to Cromwell:

... He means no good to you but would be rid of you. ... He would take this occasion to lay you aside that you might be no hindrance to his further designs.

Her husband asked soothingly,

What further designs can he have? He exercises more power than any King of England ever had, or claimed.

Mary was adamant:

His ambition is higher than we can imagine, and you have often declared yourself for the law and rights of the people; which, if they stand in his way, he will lay them or you or anything aside. ... Nor would he shed many tears if you miscarry in the journey.

Not so many as you have shed for fear I should go. Yet he can shed tears, sometimes.[15]

It would be a grave decision to leave his wife in charge of most of her ten step-children and two sons of her own, with another child on the way, and to give up a legal practice for hazardous promotion which might well cost him his life. Before making up his mind he went to Fawley and put the problem to William Cooke, who responded with his usual cheerfulness:

Why Sir, many honest gentlemen before now have bint sent overseas and yet have returned well home again, and so I hope will you. ...

But my wife much fears the danger. ...

There will be dangers everywhere.

But more apparent on this journey.

Cooke answered shrewdly,

I cannot tell that, for I have heard that our great man (I mean my Lord General) would have you to go; and if it be so and yet you will stay at home I doubt there may be as much danger for you to stay as to go. . . .

I am not under his command. What can he do to me?

Cooke was derisive,

What can he do? What can he not do! Don't we all see he does what he list? We poor countrymen are forced to obey him to our cost. And if he have a mind to punish us or you, it is an old proverb that it is an easy thing to find a staff to beat a dog.[16]

In principle Whitelocke agreed, yet at the next interview with Cromwell he again asked to be released from the appointment. At this, the General's tone changed and there was a hint of intimidation:

I hope you will show a little regard to me. . . . If you should decline it, as I hope you will not, the Commonwealth would suffer extremely by it; your own profession perhaps might suffer. . . . Indeed you cannot be excused.

Whitelocke changed his ground. He suggested that once he was out of the country his financial needs might be forgotten. Cromwell answered with a vivid phrase:

I . . . will stick as close to you as your skin is to your flesh. You shall want nothing, either for your honour and equipage or for power and trust to be reposed in you . . . I will make it my business to see it done.[17]

With this assurance, Whitelocke thought it wise to accept and Cromwell appeared to be delighted. Parliament then proceeded to debate the matter. A Member objected that, although Whitelocke's other qualifications were suitable, the House did not know whether he was a Godly man. Another replied sharply that since 'Godliness was now in fashion' some men made a show of piety for their own ends; Godliness was to be judged by its fruits and those who knew Whitelocke were satisfied on that score; in any case, it was better for a Godly man to look into his own heart than to judge a man he did not even know.

Parliament was still smarting from their earlier blunder in sending a callow youth with letters to Queen Christina; unaccustomed to Scandinavian toasts he had disgraced himself in front of the hard drinkers.[18] The Committee for Foreign Affairs ordered Whitelocke and his company to refuse to pledge any toasts whatever during their stay in Sweden. Whitelocke fretted against such precise instructions. He was even more irritated when, in spite of Cromwell's promises, the Finance Committee voted him only £1,000 a month; it was no more than they had promised to Lord L'Isle to travel in summer, when food was cheap and fuel bills low. He wrote asking for £1,500 a month and received (through the carelessness of a clerk, he supposed) two identical replies stating that the Council would not go beyond £1,000 a month but that they would supply the ceremonial coach, horses and liveries. Whitelocke envisaged embarrassment abroad as the servant of 'such narrow-hearted masters'; he wondered whether, even at that late date, he could extricate himself but quickly realized that this too would be dangerous. In the end he appealed to Cromwell, at whose intervention the Committee voted a single extra payment of £500. The General, he thought, could easily have agreed to an additional £500 a month, 'for what Cromwell and his private junta thought fit to be done was generally confirmed without objection.'

Since the King's execution the Council of State, often dominated by Cromwell, had directed foreign policy. They had a variety of motives for sending an Ambassador Extraordinary to Sweden. Cromwell still cherished the fantasy of creating a league of protestant countries; Europe offered little ground for such a hope, most alliances and wars being based on economic and territorial interests and ambitions rather than on ideological ones; nearer home catholic Spain had recognized the Commonwealth, while Protestant and republican Holland had been at war with Britain since May 1652.[19] Like other Protestants of his generation Cromwell had seen King Gustavus Adolphus as the hero of their cause; for them Queen Christina took on something of her father's aura. At the same time there were disturbing rumours that Sweden might join with other states in support of Charles Stuart; Christina was certainly corresponding with him. Denmark had allied herself with Holland and had closed the Sound, the entry to the Baltic, to English shipping for the duration of the war. This was a grave loss to English merchants and to the English dockyards.[20] A treaty with Sweden could adjust the balance and lessen the effects of losing the Baltic trade, for Sweden could export direct to England from her rapidly growing port of Gothenburg. The outline for the treaty envisaged a friendly alliance, free trade and navigation between the two nations and an undertaking not to harbour or befriend each other's enemies.

No sailing date had been fixed but arrangements seemed to be moving

ahead. The Council of State ordered that their blue damask coach should
be delivered to Daniel Earle for the use of the Lord Ambassador Whitelocke
and they placed at his disposal a set of rich hangings known as 'the naked
boys'. Sir William Fleetwood wrote enclosing a letter of introduction to his
brother, Sir George Fleetwood, in Stockholm (not to be confused with
Whitelocke's former rival for Mary's hand, Colonel George Fleetwood, the
M.P. and regicide). Sir William advised the Ambassador-designate to provide himself with 'furs and hot waters and warm clothes, and a stronger body
than I fear your lordship hath at present'.[21] Gentlemen in many parts of the
country wrote asking for a job or recommending a son, a friend, a servant
for the Swedish mission. In spite of Whitelocke's misgivings, the embassy
carried considerable prestige.

He set up a small committee to scrutinize applicants. He was trying to
ensure that no hired assassin infiltrated his company. Parliament's intelligence
service was efficiently organized by his friend John Thurloe who kept him
informed about the latest plots; royalist agents were putting it about that
when they had 'taken off' Cromwell and Lambert they would need to
dispose of Whitelocke and a few others who might attempt to seize power;
one agent was gleeful about Whitelocke being sent to Sweden and forecast
grimly 'before he comes to his journey's end he may meet with divers good
friends'.[22]

About the middle of October Whitelocke was dining with Samuel
Wilson, when his fellow guests started speculating as to whether the embassy
would be postponed until the spring of 1654. Whitelocke hoped, from
Parliament's silence, that this was the case. Sir Charles Wolseley and another
member of the Council of State offered to move a resolution to this effect,
but Whitelocke thought it wiser to let it stand over; in spite of this, his well-
meaning friends insisted on raising the matter. The Council of State promptly
told their Ambassador that he must be off within three weeks.

This time he moved fast. He made a new Will and sealed documents for
the sale of his lands 'to prevent controversies after his death'.[23] He arranged
for Bartholomew Hall and George Cokain to deal with his correspondence
but made it clear that while he was away Mary would be in command. Even
Cokain, her chaplain, had to promise to obey her. Old William Cooke
travelled to London with his grandson and other servants to deliver cartloads
of wheat, apples, butter and other provisions for his master to take with him.
Cooke refused to stay the night in town and on the way home, trudging
down a hill in the dark, he stumbled and fell. The others lifted him into the

cart and there he died. Whitelocke wrote 'I have a great loss of him . . . and
I know no man alive whom I can trust more, or speak so freely as I could
to him.'[24]

Two merchant ships were hired, the *Fortune* to carry baggage and provisions and the *Adventure* to be equipped as floating stables. The frigates
Phoenix and *Elizabeth* were placed at his service, and their Captains had
orders from Admiral Blake and Admiral George Moncke to take their
instructions from the Ambassador, a compliment which was not lost on
Whitelocke. No goods were to go aboard any of the ships unless stamped
with his badge of three falcons, to give diplomatic immunity, and no one
was to embark without a pass from the Appointments Committee.

A farewell banquet was arranged in his honour at Grocers' Hall, attended
by Cromwell and hundreds of other guests; Members of Parliament and
colleagues in Chancery sent him respectful messages and the congregation
at George Cokain's church, Pancras, in Soper Lane offered prayers for his
safety, but it was clear from their tragic tone that the chance of his ever
returning was reckoned to be very slender.

With great reluctance Whitelocke handed over the keys of the Royal
Library to the appropriate committee, before he left the country. In spite of
his preoccupation with the journey he still found time to work at his Latin
and French, and for some weeks he had been studying in the great library
which his friend Sir Thomas Cotton had inherited from his father Sir Robert.
There he perused thirty folio volumes relating to negotiations and treaties
between England and the Netherlands, and three large volumes of transactions between England, Denmark and Sweden.[25] His customary meditations on the scriptures centred at this time on two themes, ambassadors and
women. He rejected as a joke Sir Henry Wotton's cynical definition of an
ambassador as 'a wise man sent abroad to tell lies for the Commonwealth's
sake.'[26] Nor would he agree that an ambassador should claim immunity for
actions which would be unlawful in another citizen. His desultory meditations
on women were presumably prompted by the prospect of negotiating with
the famous and capricious young Queen. He reflected on some women's
coyness; how they said 'no' when they meant 'yes'. He may have been
thinking back to his courtship of Frances, to her undisguised love and simple
acceptance of his proposal. Some of the widows he had encountered since
her death annoyed him with their pretences. He disliked women 'who will
be sick if the servant do but put on his hat before them' and who indulge
in 'scornful and dissembling pranks'.[27] Mary was not like that. Although

she was over-wrought her manner was direct and her judgement sound;
he could still write with feeling 'surely of all human blessings and comforts
a good wife is one of the greatest.'[28]

He was determined to speak to Christina on equal terms and to dispel
the legend that leaders of the Commonwealth were ignorant and uncouth.
Like the young Queen he was widely read. He had been in charge of the
Royal Library; he possessed a large library of his own, and had studied in the
Cotton Library as well as in that of his friend John Selden. His jottings,
whether on constitutional, religious, philosophical or legal subjects, reflect
an extensive knowledge of classical and contemporary writings, as well as of
legal records. His company was to include other men of culture. The sailing
list which he submitted to the Council of State was impressive, with its
preponderance of linguists and musicians. It included two chaplains, Charles
de la Marche from Guernsey, who was widely travelled and spoke perfect
French, and Nathaniel Ingelo, a Fellow of Eton, who knew Latin, Greek,
Hebrew and Italian; being an accomplished musician Ingelo was appointed
master of the Ambassador's music. Dr. Daniel Whistler was engaged to look
after the company's health. He had been selected by Dr. Winston who
decided regretfully that, at eighty, he could not himself attempt the journey.
Whistler had been a naval doctor in the war against the Dutch and was a
skilful physician as well as a surgeon; he had applied for release from his
naval service and this had been granted by an order of the Council of State.
Whitelocke's secretary, Daniel Earle, spoke French and understood Latin;
the assistant secretary, William Swift, wrote a very good hand and had a gift
for accurate reporting. There were twelve gentlemen who were to sit at
the Ambassador's table, including his sons James and William, as well as
gentlemen of the bedchamber and gentlemen 'chiefly for music'; his steward
John Walker, a barrister-at-law, had some knowledge of French and German
(or 'high Dutch'); there was a gentleman of the horse and a clerk of the
stable besides servants, lackeys, a barber and an apothecary; there were
eight of Cromwell's infantrymen and two trumpeters, Edward Simpson
being 'one of the best trumpets in England'; there were two butlers, two
head cooks and two coachmen; Aurelius Newman, one of the postilions,
also had the high Dutch. There were grooms and porters and Sebastian
Corall 'an honest old fellow, the sculleryman' and finally three washer-
women who, besides their laundry duties, were engaged to make broth if
anybody was ill. The list comprised about a hundred names.[29]

Whitelocke called them together. He told them he would care for all who served him as if they were his own family and would share in whatever dangers and hardships they might have to face. If any of them felt daunted or was unwilling to accept strict discipline it was not too late to resign. Nobody did so but a further two hundred applications were received.

On the last Sunday in October 1653 Cromwell invited Whitelocke to dinner at the Cockpit in Spring Gardens. Early in their conversation Whitelocke thanked his host for a noble present he had received of a sword and spurs inlaid with gold; Cromwell begged him not to speak of so poor a gift. When the appropriate courtesies had been exchanged Whitelocke said he would like to ask certain favours:

One of my suits is that if, in my absence, my wife or friends shall have occasion to attend Your Excellency on my behalf, that they may have the favour of access to you and Your Excellency's assistance.

The reply was reassuring:

They shall at any time be welcome to me, and I shall give order for their admittance and my best furtherance in any matter which shall concern you.

Whitelocke then asked that his bills of exchange should be paid promptly:

A failure therein, especially in a foreign country, is a tender thing.

Again Cromwell answered readily:

I will take particular care for answering your bills speedily. Nay, I will say more to you. I know your allowance is but small, I wish it had been more, yet if I live I will see that you shall not be the loser by this employment. . . .

Like Machiavelli, Whitelocke realized that the absent are always wrong:

I shall do the utmost in my capacity to serve you, but must expect to have my actions traduced and scandalized; but I hope Your Excellency will give no credit to whisperings, or officious words, or letters of pickthanks behind my back.

I shall not easily give belief to such backbiters. I hate them.

It may be that Your Excellency will hear that I am great with some Cavaliers when I am abroad and that I make much of them, and truly that may well be. I love a civility to all . . . and perhaps may use it more than ordinary when I am abroad and to those of the King's party, and by them I may be the better enabled to secure myself and to understand their designs, which will be no disadvantage to your affairs.

I think such a carriage towards them will be prudent . . . and it will never occasion in me, nor I hope in any other sober man, the least jealousy of your faithfulness.[30]

Whitelocke's parting from his family was intensely painful. Mary and the children clung to him weeping; she begged him not to leave her but to wait until their child was born so that she could go with him. Her entreaties ended in a hysterical outburst and friends had to drag him away. They accompanied him to the state barge waiting at Tower Wharf, in which he was rowed downstream to the *Phoenix*, at anchor off Gravesend. Two of his ships had not yet appeared so he slipped away after dark for a last good-bye to Mary. He could not bear to leave her in distress and she was so touched by his thoughtfulness that she managed to talk calmly, holding back her tears until he left her the next day. He kept his escapade a secret 'that the Council might not have notice of it' and he and Daniel Earle got back to Gravesend by three o'clock in the afternoon, to find that the master of the *Adventure* had decided not to take on his cargo until the following day. Whitelocke decided otherwise and stood by while more than thirty struggling horses were hoisted aboard, including the valuable gelding which Cromwell had given him after the battle of Worcester; he noted approvingly the care which Mr. Stapleton, master of the horse, showed for the animals' comfort.[31] Besides saddle horses there were eight large black coach horses, six to draw the crimson-lined ceremonial coach and two as reserves. Correspondingly, there were eight bays for the blue-lined travelling coach. The coachmen, postilions, grooms, lackeys and stable boys sailed with the horses.

The small fleet consisted of the two frigates, commanded by Captain Foster and Captain Mennes, a private man-of-war, commanded by Captain Welch, two merchant ships and a ketch to carry messages. The Ambassador sent for the officers of the six ships and gave them their sailing orders. He promised that his instructions would be given 'with love and kindness as to my countrymen, friends and fellow-seamen' and added 'I shall hope for . . . obedience to this way of command, which I have observed most suitable to the disposition of free Englishmen.' He admitted his lack of nautical experience and said he would be glad to learn from the humblest sailor aboard, but he let them know that it was not his first time at sea. Prayers were to be said morning and evening on deck or in the steerage according to the weather; smoking would only be permitted behind the mainmast where a tub of water must be set, into which they would empty their pipes. The seamen crowding round responded to these comradely words by throwing their caps in the air and shouting.[32]

On Sunday 6 November 1653, committing themselves to the protection of God, they weighed anchor and hoisted sail. Next evening when they reached the Nore buoy, at the mouth of the Thames, the wind 'chopped about to the north' and Whitelocke decided that the ships should lie at anchor until morning. In the middle of the night he was woken by a knock-ing on the cabin door. His first thought was of danger, then that the journey was to be postponed. In fact two waterman, hired by brother Wilson and George Cokain, had rowed downstream with letters telling him that Mary had given birth to a son (later christened Bigley) and that the child and his mother were well.[33] 'A hard time to be hurried away from her,' Whitelocke reflected, adding however that the news 'did exceedingly comfort him'. He wrote a letter for the watermen to take back and this done 'the wind instantly came about again, very fair to proceed in his voyage' and with some mis-givings, 'they bid adieu to the coast of England, their most dear and native country.'

Out at sea next day the weather was stormy and the inequality between the ships began to be felt, but Whitelocke would not allow them to sail singly for fear of encountering Dutch ships; he kept his convoy in close formation, the *Phoenix* in the lead, followed by the two merchant ships, with the *Elizabeth* in fourth place. The man-of-war protected them to port and the ketch to starboard. He tried having a tow-rope fixed from his frigate to the cumbersome *Adventure*, the floating stables, but during the night the cable snapped with a terrific crack, waking everyone aboard and no doubt causing consternation among the horses.

The following day two or three sail appeared on the horizon and were recognized, no doubt by the cut of their sails, as Dutch fishing boats. The *Phoenix* set off in pursuit of the enemy and the order was given to 'fire the chase pieces at them when they came within distance, but for a warning only'. Whitelocke demanded that the Dutch captains strike sail meaning, presumably, that they should strike their topsails, the usual salute from a foreign vessel to an English warship in waters claimed by England. He wished moreover to enquire of them what hostile men-of-war were lurking on the seas between him and the Sound; the matter of fishing rights was also in his mind, as the subsequent cross-examination indicates. Large fleets of Dutch herring busses were in the habit of fishing in the North Sea and off the English coast, and most of them tried to avoid paying the licence required by England. One of the Dutch skippers was ordered to receive a boarding party and seemed ready to obey, until suddenly he made all sail and got away. Captain Foster was very angry and asked leave to go in pursuit, but with a huntsman's admiration for a crafty fox Whitelocke told him to keep his temper. Instead they made after another vessel. Her master evidently refused to salute until bullets were shot through the ship's 'tackle' (probably the rigging), when he was forced to surrender. He was brought aboard the *Phoenix* and many of Whitelocke's gentlemen and members of the crew crowded into the cabin to hear the interrogation. The skipper was a fisherman from Flushing with a wife and seven children. Whitelocke asked aggressively:

What right have you to come upon the seas of our Commonwealth to fish?

The skipper replied, reasonably enough:

I know not who have the domination of the sea, except those that have the strongest fleet. I have been a fisherman these thirty years and never yet asked leave to fish on these seas.

Indeed, a good fleet is . . . a strong argument of the dominion of the sea. But though you never asked leave to fish on these seas yet your predecessors have often done it at Scarborough and other places. . . .

I know not what my predecessors have done, but my father and grandfather before me were fishermen upon these seas, and I never heard them speak of asking leave to fish.[34]

Whitelocke liked a man who dared give a straight answer. In any case he had in mind something more important than fishing rights, so he answered mildly:

It may be so, yet that hath been done.

I must not contradict you.

Thou may'st speak freely.

No, I thank you. I know to whom I speak.

Whitelocke was surprised

Dost thou know me?

I think you are the English Ambassador going for Sweden.

. . . What do they say of my being sent Ambassador to Sweden?

Our lords do not like it but their subjects think you do wisely to get the Swedes to friend you.

We must seek for new friends when our old friends forsake us and make war upon us, as your lords do.

We poor men give our lords no thanks for having a war with England. I'm sure we are sufferers by it.

Why then is the war continued?

Because 'tis the pleasure of our lords, but they are sufficiently cursed for it.

But God tells you you must not speak evil of your rulers.

The fisherman retorted:

And God says our rulers must not do evil, if they would not be cursed!

God will punish them for evil.

Here the skipper scored a point, saying boldly:

And man too. I am sure you have done it in England, to purpose.

And you did it in the Netherlands, when you revolted from your King.

Extricating himself from this controversial topic the Dutchman replied with finality:

Well, I shall not talk of these things. But I may tink!

Not for the first time Whitelocke, with a keen ear for speech, wrote the word phonetically. He enquired next what the Dutch people thought of the English Ambassador:

We hear that he is a very honest gentleman and a fit man for such a business, and one that loves peace and is likely to do his duty.

The object of this flattery responded with humour:

I see now you know to whom you speak.

I should say the same behind your back!

The skipper claimed that he had never fought against the English and that he heartily disliked the war:

We are neighbours and both of us now are Commonwealths, and we should love and stick close to one another.

That would be the best way for both. But dost thou not say this to please me, or is it the opinion of thy neighbours?

The reply was blunt and uncompromising:

I do not speak it to please you . . . and five for one are of this opinion.

After further interrogation Whitelocke told the skipper that because he had shown he loved England he should have his ship back. The poor man was incredulous, but once he knew the Ambassador was serious he observed:

Your men have taken a world of my goods from me when they boarded me; if I might have them too?

Whitelocke ordered Captain Foster to see that the skipper's goods were restored to him. 'Then the poor skipper, who was before in a great sweat and fright and the tears trickling down his cheeks, stretching over the table took Whitelocke by the hand and shook it heartily, often praying to God to bless him.'[35] Whitelocke sent for wine and while they drank together he asked the skipper to tell the Dutch lords what had taken place, and to assure them that the English Ambassador wished for a good peace. The skipper returned to his ship in high spirits and sent back a present of a cheese and a large bottle of brandy; Whitelocke, knowing the man's need, returned them with 'hearty thanks to the skipper for his love'. The story of the interrogation was told and retold in Holland and later came back to Whitelocke through Lagerfeldt, the Swedish agent in London, who heard it on a journey to Uppsala.

During the next week Whitelocke wrote, with the effortless superiority of a good sailor, that only he and three or four others 'held well'; later he had to admit that even he succumbed after a supper of eggs, 'which is bad diet at sea'. He went round the frigate visiting his servants and received reports from the other vessels, some of whose passengers wished they had never left home. He made friends with the ship's company, 'being much on the decks and drolling with them . . . affording them now and then a dowse in the neck or a kick in jest, seeing them play, and then giving them some of his own tobacco, wine and strong waters.'[36] To some extent he was swept along on the revolutionary faith that England was moving towards a more brotherly and happier pattern of life, but his appreciation of his fellow men sprang as much from an impulsive nature as from any scriptural or political doctrine. As far back as the 1630s he had shown this in his respect for William Cooke's advice and in his dealing with the French mariners. He recognized, with the surprise common to formally educated men, that some of his humblest servants could preach as good a sermon as that of a university man.

This gave him pleasure. He was by nature unassuming and to some extent egalitarian although, when occasion demanded, he could enjoy an exalted sense of his own importance and carry it off in style.

It was suggested that the *Phoenix* might sail ahead, leaving the other ships to follow as best they could; the idea commended itself to the frigate's sea-sick passengers, but Whitelocke would not leave the others to the mercy of the weather and the enemy so they sailed on together at the speed of the slowest vessel. There were signs of unrest aboard. One of Whitelocke's gentlemen had a string of complaints. The *Phoenix* rolled and tossed; the food (which he said was bad anyway) landed in the passengers' laps; the water was undrinkable, the crew incompetent and he objected to sea-water coming over the top of his boots. His only consolation was that things were as bad for the Ambassador. Whitelocke could do nothing to remedy these conditions so he was thankful that most of his company joked about their discomfort.

Nine days after sailing from Gravesend they reached the craggy coast of Norway, made more terrible by seamen's tales of witches and of giant fish that snatched men off the decks. Whitelocke was inclined to be sceptical, preferring a rational explanation for disasters. At noon on 15 November the *Phoenix* sailed into Göteborg (Gothenburg) harbour followed by the other ships. Gustavus Adolphus had built the town and offered inducements to enterprising merchants, not only Swedes but also Dutchmen, Scots and others, to develop it. His object was to avoid the toll which Denmark imposed on goods from the Baltic coming through the narrow Sound between Elsinore and Helsingborg.[37] By 1653 Göteborg was already a prosperous, cosmopolitan port.

The Englishmen's arrival caught the city fathers unprepared; the Governor suggested that the Ambassador should come ashore the next day, so that he could be accorded the formal civic welcome, but Whitelocke and his companions had already been too long at sea and disembarked at once. Determination not to tolerate the smallest affront to the Commonwealth made Whitelocke unusually truculent. He wanted to know why he was only accorded a two-gun salute from the castle but was mollified by the assurance that this was their custom, in order to save gunpowder. He was irritated when harbour regulations left him and the company stranded for the first night without their luggage. He objected to having a guard stationed outside his lodgings after dark, until he learned that this too was customary. His lodging was a poorly-furnished inn which he thought compared unfavourably with those in England; he rejected the Swedish bedding which consisted of two feather mattresses, and slept under rugs and blankets in his own field-bed. He refused unfamiliar food, preferring to eat the provisions supplied by William Cooke and Mary.

By the following day the officials had brushed their uniforms and prepared their speeches. Assessing the Ambassador at his own valuation they addressed him in Latin and showed what even he felt was a proper respect for his country, referring to it as the 'free Commonwealth of England'. In his first letter to the Council of State he claimed with satisfaction that the use of this title implied recognition of the new regime. He was handsomely entertained during his stay in Göteborg and returned the hospitality; the Swedes had not expected him to be accompanied by skilled musicians, for according to the Dutch news sheets, singing and music were abhorred in puritan England. Nor were they prepared for his domineering attitude over England's rights. His men had captured a Dutch vessel and he entered into a protracted dispute with Vice-Admiral Thysen, a Dutch official and servant of the Queen. Nothing less than a humble petition which recognized the Commonwealth and its Ambassador would move Whitelocke to restore the ship. Thysen and the skipper resisted making such a concession to their country's enemy, but eventually 'their stomachs came down and their great master, profit, prevailed'.

The Queen had left Stockholm because of the plague, and sent word that she would receive the Ambassador in Uppsala. On the eve of his departure, at the end of November, an order went out to the peasants, or boors, for a hundred saddle horses and as many small wagons to be brought to his lodging at daybreak. These were to take the company on the first stage of the journey. Whitelocke was impressed by the discipline of the Swedish peasants who could be relied on to carry out such an order at a day's notice. The wagons, only large enough to take a trunk each, were drawn by one horse or two oxen and many of them were driven by women; the saddle horses were typical of the Swedish breed, being small, thickset and hardy. The bits were of rams' horn, the bridles of rope and the stirrups of twisted twigs. The wooden saddles were unpadded, with nothing between them and the person of the unfortunate rider.

The amazing procession set off from Göteborg with an escort of officials including Vice-Admiral Thysen. Whitelocke reckoned that some two thousand citizens turned out for the spectacle and twelve hundred garrison soldiers. This time the guns were fired regardless of wasting gunpowder.

Musket volleys too were fired in salute at uncomfortably close range and 'some complimental bullets came very near', but Whitelocke supposed that they were not directed at him. About a mile outside the town the officials turned back except for the Recorder of Göteborg who, with one or two other Swedish gentlemen, travelled with the party to arrange accommodation on their journey of some 320 miles. It was not easy to find quarters, often in remote hamlets, for the Ambassador and a hundred servants with horses, wagons and coaches, but during the previous decade a number of diplomats, scholars and other visitors from Europe had taken the same route. Their money was welcome and the sight of foreigners in the villages was no longer a gaping matter, particularly since many of the villagers had recently returned from the Thirty Years War. There were small inns to accommodate travellers and large, low-roofed farm buildings, granaries and stables; some had the cold, silver-grey appearance of unpainted wood but more of them were painted a deep reddish brown with Falun rödfärg, a by-product from the copper mines not far from Uppsala.[38]

When the officials turned back Whitelocke dismounted and joined two of his company in the travelling coach, with its blue velvet lining and silver tassels, the colours he had adopted twenty years earlier for the royal masque. The chaplain, Nathaniel Ingelo, was too ill and Whitelocke's relative, Colonel Potley, too stout to ride on horseback. Potley was well known in Swedish circles and spoke the language, having given distinguished service to King Gustavus Adolphus. He had an interest in accompanying the party as he wished to enquire about the payment of his state pension. The ceremonial crimson-lined coach travelled empty under a protective covering. For practical reasons the quartermaster, cooks and butlers were placed at the head of the procession.[39]

The first day's journey over stony, ice-covered roads was typical of many which followed. On the first night they stayed in the village of Lerum where 'the meat was not good, the beer worse' and 'their best refreshment was lusty fires and their own cheerfulness.' The Ambassador slept in his field-bed with most of the company lying on straw. Two evenings later, during supper at Shifda,[40] one of his people warned him that the 'beef was of a rotten cow that died in a ditch', but as there was nothing else to be had Whitelocke told his servant to keep the information to himself, and 'to those that knew it not it went down savoury'; he even sampled it himself 'and made mirth of it' but another evening a plate of beef 'suspected of kin to the last' made him very ill.

One Swedish stage equalled about seven English miles, and at each stage the luggage had to be transferred into other wagons and the riders onto fresh horses; being December there were only about six hours of daylight and the slowest vehicles sometimes managed no more than two miles a day, but where the roads were better the procession covered up to thirty-five miles. The hire charges for one stage were about threepence a horse and ninepence a wagon, so one day's journey of fourteen miles cost ten pounds in hire charges alone.

The first casualty on this hazardous journey was one of Whitelocke's pages, young Henry Elsynge, who fell over indoors 'by chance or play' and broke his arm; Dr. Whistler set it in splints and Henry joined the distinguished travellers in the coach.[41] The next accident occurred when the Doctor's servant fell off his horse and broke a leg; Whitelocke offered to leave him behind with two companions at the small cathedral town of Skara, but the injured man preferred to endure a journey of over two hundred miles in an improvised litter slung between two horses. Another day, one of the gentlemen was kicked by a horse and it was feared his skull might be cracked, but the wound was treated with ointments from Whitelocke's medicine chest and, after joining the passengers for a time in the already crowded coach, he recovered. The horses had their share of misfortunes, those from England proving less sure-footed than the Swedish ones. The worst mishap was when one of the coach horses broke its neck and 'never ate again'. Although many of the company had suffered hardship in the Civil War, Whitelocke believed the conditions they endured on this journey were even worse. Most of them accepted the discomfort cheerfully; once only he recorded 'a kind of mutiny' when one of the gentlemen started making trouble about bad accommodation and hard saddles; Whitelocke persuaded him to travel in the coach for a time while he himself mounted the Swedish horse, with its wooden saddle, and rode with his people 'drolling and partaking with them in their hardships, which', he thought, 'gave more satisfaction than severity at such a time would have done.'

In spite of the rigorous checking of passes when the company embarked, a 'proper lusty fellow' had appeared who could not be accounted for; he had made himself useful looking after the horses when the grooms were sea-sick, but there was a strong suspicion that he had been planted by the Royalists. Characteristically, Whitelocke promoted the horse-boy to serve his eldest son, telling James to watch the lad closely and to treat him with the greatest kindness. The company became convinced, from casual remarks, that their suspicions were well founded and before the end of the journey the stranger ran away. Royalists in England had boasted that the Ambassador would be fortunate indeed if he escaped the fate of Dorislaus and Ascham, for there were agents 'in Sweden already (two of them have been used to such sport) that . . . have designed to kill him and if they miss, there are those that will go over in the ships with him that may do Whitelocke that friendly office.' John Thurloe sent this disturbing news in a letter but, in spite of wondering which members of the company might be hired assassins, Whitelocke continued to treat them all as his 'family'.

In Köping he was told that officials refused to arrange accommodation because the English Parliament, made up of tailors and cobblers, had killed the King. When Whitelocke warned his Swedish escort that he would not budge until his Parliament was vindicated, the Mayor and Sheriff were summoned to explain themselves. The Ambassador kept them waiting and by the time he deigned to admit them they were both in tears, 'half-drunk for sorrow'. The Sheriff protested that he had only remarked 'What lies do the Holland gazettes tell us when they say the Parliament are a company of tailors and cobblers, when you see what gallant fellows they are by their Ambassador!' For himself, he 'loved and honoured the Parliament of England and London with all his heart'. The Mayor went one better, claiming that 'he had read Milton's book and liked it, and had it at home.' He was no doubt referring to *The Defence of the English People* written in 1651 in reply to Salmasius' work *The Defence of the King*. Honour being satisfied, Whitelocke ordered drinks and the contrite officials became overwhelmingly friendly. In another town his steward and others were locked up by the landlord until they bought their freedom; Whitelocke threatened to stop where he was until a complaint had been sent to Christina and the innkeeper punished, but he was pacified by an assurance that the local magistrates had already dealt severely with the offender.

In general he got on well with the Swedish people and noted admiringly how honest they were in spite of their poverty; sometimes the coaches and wagons had to be left out all night but the luggage was never pilfered, and when a trunk of money broke open spilling half-crowns all over the road every coin was handed back; the only thing he lost on the whole journey was a large jar of tobacco.

At intervals letters from England caught up with him. Mary wrote that she spent most of her time crying and would gladly take the place of his humblest servant only to be with him. Thurloe sent a key to the code which the

Council would use for secret despatches; Whitelocke was astonished at the incompetence of officials in Westminster who, instead of handing this to him before he left London, entrusted it to a messenger.

Twenty days after leaving Göteborg he arrived in Uppsala; he could have been there sooner but he had travelled faster than Christina expected and she sent word asking him to wait a few days at Enköping until preparations were completed for his reception. On the appointed day he was greeted outside the city by two Senators, representing the Queen, and by Monsieur Vanderlin, the Master of Ceremonies, attired, Whitelocke frowningly recorded, 'in a careless garb'. Large crowds turned out to stare at the English Ambassador as he drove to the residence which the Queen had placed at his disposal. It was a handsome three-storey brick house built by a rich merchant and alderman, Claes Eden, in Stora Torget, the great square;[42] Whitelocke later described it as the finest residence in the city apart from the Castle. The Senators and Master of Ceremonies led him upstairs through a reception room carpeted with cloth-of-gold, and into his bedroom which had bed-hangings of blue velvet and a carpet of crimson velvet, both embroidered in gold. The furnishings had been provided by the Queen who was clearly conscious of the deference due to an Ambassador from England, even if her Senators were not. The Master of Ceremonies was 'of so slight a carriage' that Whitelocke did not take much notice of him, nor was he impressed by the Senators, one of whom turned out to be Vanderlin's brother. After escorting the Ambassador to his bedroom they withdrew, saying they must report his arrival to the Queen.

Before long Vanderlin came back to expostulate that Whitelocke had not shown a proper respect for the Senators; he had failed to see them to their coaches and had been sparing in giving them their title of 'Excellency'. Whitelocke listened to a string of complaints then answered with composure that he was tired after his journey. Because he was lame he had more difficulty than most people in climbing stairs. He did not wish to be found lacking in respect and if, in his ignorance, he was at fault he would always be glad to be put right by so learned an exponent of good manners as the Master of Ceremonies. As to the shortcomings with which he was charged, he assured Vanderlin that these had not been due to any oversight on his part. The Senators had been negligent in giving him his title and had slighted him by allowing their lackeys to push past him at his residence. He was no stranger to correct behaviour nor was this his first experience of a royal court. Naturally he was obliged to protect his honour and that of his nation.

The Master of Ceremonies seemed taken aback by this straight answer and replied lamely that he hoped there would be a good understanding between Whitelocke and the Court. For his part he would be glad to be of service.

Ironically, the only envoy at Court who sent a message of greeting was the Spanish Catholic, Don Antonio Pimentel de Prado. Apart from this Whitelocke's arrival was ignored. The Ambassador Extraordinary was beginning to take stock of the situation. Before he had finished with the Swedish Court the prestige of the new Commonwealth was to be greatly enhanced.[43]

Chapter Eight

Christina

Like many intelligent men of his day Whitelocke believed in astrology. He justified his credulity on the grounds that his friend William Lilly was usually right in his prognostications. In 1647 Lilly had dedicated *Christian Astrology Modestly Treated of in Three Books* to him, and he referred to Whitelocke as his patron.[1] Yet, although it was widely practised, astrology, for various reasons, was being subjected to scrutiny. Stenius, who held the chair of astronomy at Uppsala, had written a courageous work entitled *The Uncertainty and Vanity of Astrological Predictions* but had been condemned for his scepticism, whereas Forsius, the self-styled Astronomer-Royal of Sweden, had been in trouble for asserting that the stars determined men's actions, which allowed no scope for free will.[2]

In spite of the unresolved status of the stars, it is said that King Gustavus Adolphus consulted the court astrologer in 1626 and received the assurance he wanted, that the child to be born of Queen Maria Eleonora would be a son. When an ugly, hairy infant was delivered and uttered a deep-throated yell, the midwives shouted for joy and announced the birth of a prince. On closer inspection they discovered their mistake. They would not shock the Queen with the bad news until she was stronger, for she was an unstable, hysterical character, and at first nobody dared tell the King, who was known for his uncontrollable temper. In the end his sister, Princess Catherine, picked up the baby and showed him what she lacked the courage to tell. Instead of falling into a rage, he took the child in his arms and welcomed her.[3] During the few remaining years of his life he treated Christina like a son, and gave instructions that if he died she was to receive a prince's education.

The protestant hero of the Thirty Years War had seemed to possess a charmed life, but in 1630 he had a sense of foreboding. Before returning to the war he summoned the Estates of the Realm, lords, prelates, townsmen and peasants, and stood before them holding his four-year-old daughter. At his request they gave their solemn assurance that Christina should succeed him on the throne.

At the battle of Lützen in November 1632 the King, according to report, had his left arm shattered, was shot in the back, dragged with one foot in the stirrup face downward through the mud and was finally shot through the head. His body was plundered of all but his shirt and left on the battlefield in a thick mist, exposed to pounding hooves. If the remains which were brought back to Sweden were those of the 'Lion of the North', they must have been unrecognizable. His widow Maria Eleanora, *'toujours plaintive'*, wished to have his coffin in her bedroom, and insisted on having his heart embalmed and hung in a casket at her bedside.

Christina was rescued from these morbid surroundings and placed in the charge of tutors appointed by her father. She grew up despising her mother, caring little for clothes or cleanliness and holding feminine accomplishments in contempt. Belonging to a more sceptical generation than her father's she took the view that 'You must know enough about medicine and astrology not to be fooled by doctors or astrologers; you cannot foresee or avoid your destiny but you can accept it.' She accepted her destiny as a ruling prince and astonished Europe by the brilliance of her performance. By the age of twenty-seven she was famous for her love of learning, for her political acumen and for her odd, mannish ways.

Whitelocke's impression at his first audience, two days before Christmas, confirmed the legend. The Queen was sitting on a crimson velvet chair at the end of the room; she was wearing a grey skirt, a long jacket like a man's and a black scarf tied round her neck, such as soldiers wore. She was very pale and when she stood up he was surprised to notice that she was quite short, but she carried herself nobly. When he took off his hat she responded by pulling off her fur-lined cap, as if she were a man. While she was simply dressed, Whitelocke and his followers would have done credit to any prince in Europe. His servants' liveries were of grey cloth, trimmed with blue velvet or satin, thick with silver and gold lace. Whitelocke wore a black suit of very fine English cloth, plain except for its diamond buttons, and his hat band was also of diamonds. The outfit had cost him about a thousand pounds.

After presenting letters from Parliament he addressed the Queen in English, which his chaplain M. de la Marche translated into French. He saluted her on behalf of Parliament, pointing out that the Commonwealth of England was not encouraged to send ambassadors abroad after the barbarous treatment accorded to them in some countries, but his government had no fear of any such reception in Sweden. He promised not to bore her with long speeches, his dealings would be honest and straightforward and he would neither paint a glowing picture of his own country nor 'draw black lines upon any, though our adversaries'. He referred, as diplomats will, to common bonds between their two countries and, in a burst of unrepublican zeal, drew a parallel between the happy condition of Christina's reign and 'those blessed days of our virgin Queen Elizabeth' under whom the people of England had enjoyed security and justice. Nor, he added pointedly, need the pattern have changed for the Kings who followed 'but through their own ill-government'. That put the Stuarts in their place while letting it be known that he was not hostile to monarchy as such. He knew that Sweden nursed a grudge against the memory of Charles I for ignoring the great Chancellor Oxenstierna's eldest son, when he came on a mission to England. Whitelocke spoke of defending freedom and Protestantism. He could not know that the Queen had been receiving instruction from two young Jesuits sent to her from Rome.[4] He turned next to the horrors of civil war, but assured her that anyone visiting England would hardly see a trace of it. He concluded with hopes for even closer friendship and an alliance between their countries.

While he was speaking the Queen came close to him and his gentlemen had the impression that she was trying to daunt him, but he was not afraid of women and noted afterwards with amusement, 'those who have been conversant in the late great affairs in England are not so soon as others appalled with the presence of a young lady and her servants.' After he had finished speaking Christina stood quite still for a time, then replied in Swedish welcoming him to her country. Mr. Lagerfeldt, whom Whitelocke had known in London, translated her address sentence by sentence. The formalities over, Whitelocke and the Queen talked together in French; he introduced his two sons and sixteen of his gentlemen, all of whom asked to have the honour of kissing her hand. Four years of republican rule had not taken away the appetite for royal patronage.

Whitelocke returned to his lodging in good spirits and two Senators paid him the compliment of supping with him. They refrained from proposing his health, explaining that this was not from lack of respect but because they understood that he objected to the practice. In view of the instructions from the Council of State this was correct. At supper on their first evening the Master of Ceremonies had pestered him about it, proposing first a health to the Commonwealth of England; when the Ambassador declined the toast he was told, imperiously, that he could not refuse to drink to his masters and the Commonwealth; Whitelocke replied that, on the contrary, if his masters were present they too would refuse. In spite of this, Vanderlin raised his huge glass again, this time to General Cromwell. Whitelocke refused to join him and the Master of Ceremonies asked contemptuously whether the English thought it wrong to drink. Whitelocke answered that he did not condemn anyone for drinking a health nor should

anyone criticize him if he chose to abstain. After further unpleasant ex-
changes the Master of Ceremonies told the English company to practise
their 'country fashions' at home; abroad they should observe the customs
of the country they were visiting. 'The dispute concluded in a silent discontent during the rest of the suppertime.' News of the incident had travelled
round the Court and the Queen instructed Vanderlin not to annoy her guests
in future, after which he became 'more courteous and quiet and free from
drinking healths'.

Whitelocke possessed the sharp gifts of a diplomat. He had a flair for
discerning who was exerting pressure behind the scenes, whether prompted
by considerations of purse, prestige or politics; for judging which faction
to play off against another, when to cultivate and when to annihilate an
opponent, the time to outwit him with skill or cunning and the time to
baffle him with a show of bland ignorance. Over Christmas he set to work

. . . to inform himself of the Queen's disposition and inclination to his superiors, of
what principles she was as to the affairs of England, wherein lay her dissatisfaction
and objections, what ways were more likely to remove them, upon whose judgement
she did most rely, what manner of conversation and discourse was most pleasing to
her, what power she had as Queen and how restrained by any laws, councils or interest
of great men; who were most trusted by her, whose counsel most followed, what
ambassadors and foreign ministers were now in her Court, what their business was,
how far prosecuted, how likely to succeed, what relation of them to England, how
their masters were affected to our Commonwealth and what repute they had in
this Court.

He knew what to expect at a foreign Court and was not dismayed by
conduct which his government might have condemned as dissolute. He did,
however, criticize the widespread drunkenness and lack of Sunday observance. He was at pains to cultivate the acquaintance of the Queen's favourites.
Count Klaus Tott, a 'handsome young courtier of good parts and mettle
and much of the French mode', volunteered the information that he was the
first gentleman of the bed-chamber, and it did not take long to discover
that the Queen had honoured Don Antonio Pimentel de Prado by arranging
a suite of rooms for him in the Castle, close to her own apartments. The
'Journal' expresses nothing but approval that her favours were so wisely
placed.

Whitelocke's immediate problem was how to arrange an informal meeting
with the Queen. On Christmas Eve, Pimentel came to call. Though only
an Envoy, he was flattered at Court with the courtesy title of Ambassador

and Whitelocke was careful to address him as Excellency. After the requisite compliments had been exchanged the Spaniard came to the point:

What course do you intend to take for procuring your audiences?

Knowing that the proper channels were often the ones to avoid, Whitelocke answered innocently:

The Master of the Ceremonies adviseth that I must go by way of memoir to the Secretary of State.

Pimentel was glad to show that he knew the short cuts.

With submission to him to whose office it doth belong, I apprehend that way to be . . . not so agreeable as to desire private audiences from the Queen herself.

Did your Excellency use that way?

I took that course in all my business, and it succeeded well and was best liked by the Queen . . . I am confident that if your Excellency desire to have a private audience tomorrow, though Christmas Day, the Queen will give it you.

In puritan eyes the feast of the nativity was a popish invention unwarranted by holy scriptures but, knowing that the reformed church in Sweden still observed it, Whitelocke declined the suggestion and, instead, a private audience was arranged for 26 December.

He started with an advantage. The Queen was interested in him as a scholar who could offer a new intellectual stimulus. The scholars she collected round her or with whom she corresponded included some of the most learned men in Europe. Her major achievement, four years before Whitelocke's visit, had been to coax Descartes away from his over-heated house in Holland, where he had worked under the patronage of Prince Rupert's sister, Princess Elizabeth. Descartes had agreed to stay in Stockholm and enliven the winter months for Christina with philosophical disquisitions and ideas for founding a Swedish academy of learning. It never occurred to the young woman in her mid-twenties that sessions in the icy library of her palace in the early hours of the morning might not suit an aging philosopher. In the new year of 1650 Descartes had contracted inflammation of the lungs and within a few weeks he was dead. Europe's scholars were shocked. Princess Elizabeth took it very badly, and Christina was deeply distressed. After escaping into another frenzied bout of culture, with twenty learned men invited to her Court together, she broke down and was obliged to rest from her studies.

By 1653 she was fit again and ready for a fresh experience. The scholarly Englishman was quite old, in his late forties, but he was attractive and had style and he could satisfy her curiosity about Oliver Cromwell. She soon discovered that the Ambassador was astute, subtle and a match for her intelligence. He impressed her with his learning, admonished her like a daughter and could turn in a moment to flattery and gallantries, or to drolling. Christina for her part was sturdy in mind as in body, resilient, independent and quite unsentimental. She could hunt all day and dance all night. It was said that she possessed the qualities to lead an army, a notion which greatly pleased her. Yet she could also present herself as a fascinating, pleasure-loving young woman whose attraction sprang not from her appearance so much as from her intellect and her dazzling vitality.

At the first private audience her attention darted from one subject to the next. Whitelocke was to find this characteristic tiresome when it came to negotiating. She promised to consider forming an alliance with England but since Sweden was at peace with her neighbours she thought it might be better to leave things as they were. She asked for details of Whitelocke's power to act and, on scrutinizing them, remarked that his authority was very full. Before he could bring her back to the treaty she was off again on a new theme, praising Cromwell as 'one of the gallantest men in the world'. Was it true, she asked, that officers in Parliament's army prayed and preached impromptu, with their soldiers? Did Whitelocke do so? And General Cromwell? He assured her that they had both done so in the Wars. When she questioned him about the struggle against the King he corrected her unfavourable impression of Parliament and 'she seemed much satisfied therewith, saying that she never had been truly and clearly informed of those affairs until now.' For over two hours no one came near them and throughout the interview they stood or walked up and down; by the end Whitelocke's leg was troubling him and he returned to his lodgings in considerable pain. This was reported to Christina who arranged that in future two stools were always provided. She had learned something from Descartes's untimely death.

Three days later another private audience was arranged. Whitelocke considered that it was time the Queen learned something of England's power so he produced an inventory of Parliament's navy with details of tonnage, ordnance and ammunition. Christina was impressed and admitted she had thought only the Dutch had a fleet of such size and strength. She was beginning to see some value in the proposed treaty and observed, thoughtfully,

'Some of these ships of yours would do good service to open the Sound.' Although Sweden's shipping was exempt, the Danes and the Dutch were imposing tolls on ships of other nations, passing through the Sound, to the detriment of Sweden's overseas trade. She asked

What way do you think fit to be taken, to make free the passage thereof?

As she was now interested Whitelocke held back:

That must needs be better known to your Majesty, who is a neighbour to the place and much concerned in it, than to me who am a stranger.

I desire your opinion of it.

I do not think it convenient to permit the Dane and the Dutch to lay what exactions they please upon all the people of the world who have occasion to pass that way.

It cannot be taken out of their hands but by force.

At this the Queen drew her stool closer and asked quietly:

Do you think that the Commonwealth of England will give assistance in that business?

Madam, I think they will upon such just and honourable terms as may be agreed.

Par Dieu! this is worthy the consideration of both nations . . . I do extremely like the business.

She asked the Ambassador not to disclose their conversation to anybody except Cromwell; not even to her own ministers. It was his first taste of her passion for secrecy and intrigue. She asked abruptly:

Have you not heard in England that I was to marry the King of Scots?

If the Queen hoped that Whitelocke would be taken aback she was disappointed. He replied easily:

It hath been reported so in England, and that letters have passed between Your Majesty and him for that purpose, and that Your Majesty had a good affection for the King of Scots.

She was at pains to allay the rumour.

I confess that letters have passed between us, but this I assure you that I will not marry that King. He is a young man and in a condition sad enough. Though I respect him very much yet I shall never marry him.

With this encouragement Whitelocke suggested that she should sever relations with Charles. Christina was intrigued to know how this disciplined, courteous man would behave if she confronted him with English Royalists. His reply was firm.

I hope that in reason and in right of friendship with our Commonwealth, I may prevail with Your Majesty not to entertain any such minister or message.

At the end of a long and friendly interview he handed her the draft treaty. She asked for a few days in which to study the proposals but the next day, when Whitelocke was writing a report for the Council of State, she summoned him to yet another private audience. It was clear that she had been talking to Pimentel, for she now proposed that the alliance should include the King of Spain. Whitelocke hedged. This placed him in an embarrassing position since one of the aims of his mission was to move towards a protestant alliance. The Queen waived all his objections aside; she pointed out that Europe's 'papists have not equal liberty with others as they ought to have'. She enquired imperiously what religion was professed in England and in his reply Whitelocke made a sly comment on her manner.

In regard Your Majesty doth me the honour to catechize me, I shall answer you very freely. We profess the true, reformed protestant Christian religion. We believe in God the Father, our creator, in God the Son, Jesus Christ our redeemer, and in God the Holy Ghost, our comforter. Three persons and one God.

The Queen said she had heard there were many sects in England. Sensing criticism, Whitelocke answered:

. . . Difference of opinion in ceremonies or some matters of worship and discipline, it is incident to men as much as differences of countenances or of diet. . . . The late troubles occasioned people to take a greater liberty in all things, particularly in matters of religion, than formerly and there it is esteemed the highest tyranny of all others to tyrannize over men's judgements and consciences.

To the authoritarian young Queen this seemed a rash attitude towards dissent.[5] She turned to another subject. Her curiosity had been aroused about Whitelocke's correspondence with Cromwell and she had naïvely offered to despatch his mail with her own. This had naturally been refused. Now, she had the audacity to ask whether he wrote in cipher. Whitelocke cheerfully dismissed such an idea, indicating that codes were easy to crack, but he volunteered that he used a special kind of invisible ink which he mixed himself. The conversation was interrupted as an intruder by the name of Lyon entered, and the interview ended in a mood of high good humour:

What huge dog is this?

It is an English mastiff, which I brought with me, and it seems is broke loose and followed me even to this place.

Is he gentle and well-conditioned?

The more courage they have the more gentle they are. This is both. Your Majesty may stroke him.

I have heard of the fierceness of these dogs. This is very gentle.

They are very gentle unless provoked, and of a generous kind; no creature hath more mettle or faithfulness than they have.

Is it your dog?

I cannot tell. Some of my people told me that one Mr. Peter sent it for a present to the Queen.

Who is that Mr. Peter?[6]

A minister, and great servant to the Parliament.

That Mr. Peter sent me a letter.

He is a great admirer of Your Majesty. But to presume to send a letter – or a dog for a present to a Queen – I thought above him and not fit to be offered to Your Majesty.

I have many letters from private persons. His letter – and the dog – do belong to me and are my goods, and I will have them!

Your Majesty commands in chief and all ought to obey you; and so will I, not only as to the letter – and the dog – but likewise as to another part of his present, a great English cheese of his country making.

I do kindly accept them from him, and see that you send my goods to me.

I will not fail to obey Your Majesty.

And so they parted, he says, 'in much drollery'. Returning to his letters, Whitelocke dictated to two secretaries while writing a third letter by hand; even so he was obliged to sit up most of the night to finish his correspondence. He was summoned next day for another talk with the Queen. In the course of it she questioned him about prominent English men and women including the Duke of Buckingham and the Earl of Arundel, as well as John Selden and the Countess of Kent, whose names were commonly linked. She was impressed to find that he knew many of those she named, and was connected with men of rank.

Taking stock, he had reason to feel satisfied with his progress. He reported to his masters at Westminster that between Christmas and 31 December he had attended no fewer than four private audiences. He refrained from mentioning that one topic which the Queen seldom discussed was the treaty.

New Year's day, 1 January, fell on a Sunday in 1654, and after the morning sermon Whitelocke addressed the members of his household. He reminded them that, because of the moral claims made by the Commonwealth, people delighted in accusing the English of 'the worst of vices'. It had come to his ears that some of his followers were lazy. Idleness could lead to debauchery. He thought it strange that anybody should be bored when there were plenty of books and the Bible was not prohibited reading. He had warned them, before leaving England, that undisciplined behaviour would be punished by dismissal. He repeated the threat, adding, 'Such disorders as I hear of, and some of you know that you have fallen into, I must not, I cannot, I will not bear.' Besides this, some of them had allowed themselves to be drawn into discussing controversial issues which were not their concern. This too must stop. Finally, they were to decline invitations to the court ball that evening since it was Sunday. Most of them would be aware, he said, of what such a festivity would lead to, even in England. 'You all know I prohibit not honest, lawful recreations, but where sin accompanies them I shall bear my testimony against them. Such I account this ball on this day.' The moral sanctions established under the Commonwealth acted as a brake, reinforced by the terrifying prospect of dismissal in a foreign land; moreover, during the long Swedish evenings Whitelocke kept his household occupied at home with dancing, music, and debates in Latin.

Another ball was arranged at the Castle. This time, as it was on a weekday, Whitelocke accepted the invitation and allowed his gentlemen to do so. He sat all evening next to the Queen except when she was dancing which, he noted admiringly, she did 'with more life and spirit than the rest of the ladies, or than any he had seen'. During his stay in Uppsala she set a number of traps for him, as if to gauge his integrity and also to see whether she could outwit him or disturb his gentlemanly composure. Among the older men whom she might have trusted Descartes was dead and Chanut, the French Ambassador, had left her Court. When speaking of Chancellor Oxenstierna, who nourished himself by recalling his position during her father's lifetime, she was noticeably cool, if not disloyal. To the annoyance of several men at Court she was beginning to confide in the English Ambassador. There was mischief and flirtation in the tests she set him but her purpose was serious.

Earlier on the day of the ball she had sent for him and opened a long interview with another cross-examination. She had enquired about Cromwell's origins and about his wife and children; she had compared his rise to power with that of her ancestor Gustavus I, founder of the House of Vasa, recalling that his victories in battle had been rewarded with the kingship.

I believe that your General will be King of England in conclusion.

Hugh Peter had said as much after the battle of Worcester, and although at that time it had not been Cromwell's intention, he had later confronted Whitelocke with the question 'What if a man should take upon him to be King?' In spite of this, the Ambassador assured the Queen that England was a Commonwealth and that Cromwell already had power enough. She brushed this aside saying that it was in the nature of men to crave for more power; 'I find no such nature in my General,' Whitelocke insisted, but Christina retorted that ambition could be concealed. Next, directing the inquisition at her companion, she asked:

How many wives have you had?

I have had three wives.

Have you had children by all of them?

Yes, by every one of them.

Par Dieu, vous êtes incorrigible!

He replied urbanely:

Madam, I have been a true servant to your sex.

In the questioning which followed, on all manner of subjects, he had the impression that the Queen knew the answers and was only checking whether he told her the truth. Eventually he took the initiative, telling the Queen that she was wrong to countenance dancing and debauchery on Sundays.

She accepted his criticism meekly 'and much more to the like effect'. After that, he noted, there were no more dances at Court on the Lord's day.

She was glad to turn the conversation to the question of freeing the Sound, and asked thoughtfully:

How many ships do you think the Parliament will lend me for this design?

I believe they will send a considerable number of ships upon this or any other design to be undertaken by them.

. . . I do not desire above twenty or thirty English ships, and some money.

The Ambassador affected to be taken aback:

. . . I suppose you will not expect ships and money too, from others to do your work?

The Queen was imperious:

I am in great want of money and England hath money enough.

They have enough for their occasions.

And some to spare, which I have not.

To avoid reaching an impasse with this demanding young woman White-locke remarked tactfully that she could not be accused of wasting her revenue on clothes. He said nothing about her extravagance on books, pictures and cultural pursuits, her gifts to favourites or the poor state of the Swedish economy; in case his words were misconstrued he added, 'Your wearing plain clothes makes them rich.' Christina ignored the compliment and said abruptly that her Chancellor, Axel Oxenstierna, would soon be in Uppsala and that he was a very able and honest man who understood the business of the Sound. Whitelocke took the hint and refrained from pressing the question of a treaty until he could meet the Chancellor.

Officials impressed on him that at this Court it was customary for an Ambassador to pay the first call on the Chancellor, who had become the elder statesman of Christendom, but this Whitelocke refused to do. When the Queen expostulated he told her plainly that he must not be guided by other men's behaviour, nor would he do anything to reflect upon the honour of his nation. The Queen admired audacity and told Oxenstierna to concede the point. The old man had served under three monarchs and been Chancel-lor and principal minister of state since Gustavus Adolphus came to the throne in 1611. His relationship with Christina was an uneasy one. During her minority he had dominated her life. When she grew up she had recognized that she must either defer to him for the rest of his days or show that she was the sovereign. She had made the position quite clear when she insisted on bringing the Thirty Years War to an end, in defiance of her Chancellor and many of the generals.

At private audiences Whitelocke and Christina talked together in French. He had compiled a phrase book with some of his constitutional arguments set out in English, French and Latin. It also included sentences for use when Senators and other visitors came to see him, translations of such homely remarks as 'I myself am a bad carver . . . I desire you therefore to carve yourself any meat which you like, and I am sorry that there is no better cheese.' He knew that Chancellor Oxenstierna resented France's influence in Europe and objected to French being spoken at the Swedish Court, so he prepared to talk to the old man in Latin, with the opening gambit, 'Will Your Excellency be pleased to rest yourself in a bedroom here below, rather than to be put to the trouble of going up so many stairs as lead to the better rooms above?'[7] His aged guest agreed to talk in a room on the ground floor and asked for his chair to be turned away from the fire as the light hurt his eyes. He was over seventy and Whitelocke's first impression was of a sober, solemn character but it was soon obvious that Oxenstierna had an abrasive humour and was given to indulging in what he himself called the talkativeness of old age. The Chancellor asked searching questions about the English revolution and enquired about Cromwell's age and health, family background and character. It was a style of interrogation to which Whitelocke was becoming accustomed.

Two days after this interview the Queen announced that she was going into the country for about a week. She assured the Ambassador that she did not wish to delay his business and that while she was away the Chancellor would confer about the treaty. It was obvious, in spite of their denials, that Christina and Oxenstierna were delaying the negotiations until they knew the outcome of peace talks between the English and the Dutch. A peace treaty would release the English navy for Christina's plans. It would also save Sweden from the loss of trade which must result from becoming England's ally against the Dutch and the Danes.

At the next meeting the Chancellor asked questions about the stability of the regime in England. If one parliament could be dissolved and another constituted what foundation would that be for a treaty? Whitelocke answered that the government of England remained fundamentally the same as it had

been under a king. Foreign treaties, matters of peace and war, raising money
and law-making had all been 'the proper business of Parliaments in the time
of our kings (so admitted by the best and most successful of them) . . . and
so it is still.' Personalities might change but government commitments continued as an obligation on subsequent parliaments and also, he stressed, on
the people. The Chancellor asked whether, since the abolition of monarchy,
the nature of the government was 'aristocratical' or 'democratical'. Whitelocke replied that it was 'clearly democratical'.[8] Next came the awkward
questions 'Do you hold kingly government to be unlawful?' Whitelocke
replied cautiously, 'Every government which the people chooseth is certainly lawful, whether kingly or other, and that to be accounted best which
they, by their representatives, do make choice of as best for them.' The
Chancellor asked what Whitelocke desired from the Swedish government.
The reply was swift and uncompromising. 'I desire nothing from you. I come
not to you in a precarious way, *non ut cliens, sed ut amicus*. My business is to
make you an offer . . . which is worthy acceptance by any prince in Europe,
the friendship of the Commonwealth of England.' The value the Ambassador
set on his country was taking effect. The old statesman responded with
amused appreciation, and before the end of the interview Whitelocke had
secured for himself the title of 'son by adoption', an honour which the
Chancellor had extended to certain men of distinction.

On 13 January 1654 Whitelocke learned, with dismay, that in mid-
December Cromwell had assumed the title of Lord Protector. It was galling
to receive such momentous news from a Swedish source. He saw only too
plainly that if the new government repudiated him, he and his servants
could be stranded without funds. He wondered what treatment he could
expect from the Queen and, putting a bold face on it, he sent to ask for an
audience. Before the servant came back Count Tott arrived with the Queen's
congratulations on the 'good news from England'. Whitelocke called during
the afternoon and was shown into Christina's bedroom. She was enthusiastic
about Cromwell's action: '*Par Dieu!* I bear the same respect and more to
your General, and to you, than I did before . . . I had rather have to do with
one than with many.' Privately, Whitelocke saw the Protectorate as illegal
and as a threat to the Commonwealth. Yet although he criticized the coup
he never believed that Cromwell acted from motives of ambition.

Letters from England arrived the same evening, with an embarrassed
account from John Thurloe of the changes at Westminster.[9] New credentials
for Whitelocke to hand to the Queen were signed *Vester bonus amicus*

Olivarius P. These replaced the earlier ones, signed by the Speaker of the House of Commons. There was also an exuberant letter from the journalist Marchmont Needham, who at that time in his changeable career was supporting Cromwell:

We have a new world formed, like the old, out of chaos, by the prudence and industry of that excellent person who may most meritoriously challenge the style and title of Lord Protector.

It is Your Excellency's honour that you now represent the person of so great a captain, and the glory of our nation to have such a governor. I would choose much rather to serve him upon any terms than be a favourite to any of those golden things that are dropped, at adventure, into the world with crowns upon their heads.

He ended by observing how fortunate the Protector was in having such an Ambassador to report the news to the royal virgin.[10]

Officials and members of the Court reflected the Queen's enthusiasm. England seemed to be coming into line with the authoritarian patterns recognized by the princes of Christendom, and away from the revolutionary thinking of Anabaptists and Levellers. On the other hand, some excitable members of the Ambassador's household were in a state of panic, and begged him to dissociate himself from the new regime. Under the Treason Act of 1649 anyone attempting to alter the style of government or promoting an individual as chief magistrate of England was guilty of high treason, besides which most Englishmen over the age of eighteen had pledged themselves to be 'true and faithful to the Commonwealth of England as it is now established, without a king'. Whitelocke's companions were anxious to know how he could justify serving the Protector. He was ready with a constitutional answer: 'If a government be altered and another power in possession of it, all private men are bound to submit to the present powers.' He could not be accused of complicity with the 'violent and unjust actions' at Westminster but he maintained that he must not neglect any lawful business undertaken for his country's benefit.[11] In spite of these brave words, the coup gave substance to his earlier misgivings about being sent abroad. It was known that he would disapprove of any unconstitutional attempt to solve the country's problems. The sudden eagerness shown by the Council of State in October to pack him off to Sweden suggested that the Protectorate was already envisaged by that date, and perhaps even in August when he was first named. It was significant that the oath had been administered to Cromwell by the remaining Commissioners of the Great Seal.

Oxenstierna made the most of the situation as a new excuse for delay:

... There hath been a great alteration among you, pulling down one and setting up another, abolishing kingship, ... resolving yourselves into a republic and now again setting up another monarchy; which uncertainty in your government may occasion some doubt how the treaties made with you may be observed.

Whitelocke again insisted that treaties were made on behalf of the people of England, who did not alter when there was a new government. Changing his tactics, the Chancellor asked how Parliament justified their action in not deposing or quietly assassinating King Charles, but putting him on public trial before the world. Whitelocke had submitted to probing questions from the Queen but was not prepared to be brow-beaten by the Chancellor. He answered inexorably:

I suppose you do not expect from me here, where I am under the protection of a sovereign Queen, a justification of that proceeding? I had no hand in it and those who had, by authority of the Parliament, I believe held it more justifiable to proceed in an open trial than by secret means to take his life away. Their reasons and grounds for the action concerneth themselves, and is not my present business.

It was at once a skilful and a loyal answer from a man who had dissociated himself from the proceedings. Oxenstierna answered more affably:

It was ... rather minatory to all princes of the world. Yet I must confess, it was more honourable to proceed in an open, avowed way than by underhand dealing to have cut him off.

Whitelocke took advantage of this concession to deliver an ultimatum.

If you are not satisfied with our government, that it is such as you may safely proceed in the treaty with me, my stay here is to small purpose.

The Chancellor knew better than to allow the negotiations to flounder while the Queen was away, so he replied that he was indeed satisfied, especially since the Protector's power was limited by law. Using a soldier's metaphor, he added:

There remains nothing for him now to do but to get him a back and breast of steel ... I mean the confirmation of his being Protector, to be made by your Parliament, which will be his best and greatest strength.

He was right. But this formal endorsement by Parliament, which might have established the legality of the regime in the nation's mind, was never achieved.

When Lagerfeldt, the Chancellor's secretary, called after a further un-satisfactory meeting, Whitelocke 'seemed, in a careless way, not so much to mind the business as he had done before'. He remarked casually that as he had discharged his duty it did not matter if he returned to England without a treaty. Lagerfeldt was worried. He asked why the Ambassador should feel any doubt. When Whitelocke referred to endless delays and obstacles Lagerfeldt pleaded that the Chancellor was an old man, 'not so nimble in business as he had been', but that he was eager to reach agreement.

On 21 January Whitelocke called to congratulate the Queen on her safe return and to report on the negotiations. Suddenly, she drew her stool close to his, saying she had something to confide in him which would surprise him, but that he must respect her confidence as she had not spoken of it to anybody else. She told him that she had thoughts of abdicating. He was completely taken aback and asked what had prompted such an idea. She replied lightly that as a woman she was not well fitted to govern; that the glory and power were outweighed by the cares of government; that she would find contentment in retiring from public life and that her cousin, Charles Gustavus (the Heir Apparent and Crown Prince) would succeed her. Whitelocke was immediately suspicious that she was being ousted. This she denied, but he still tried to dissuade her.

With your Majesty's leave, I shall tell you a story of an old English gentleman who had an active young man to his son, that persuaded the father to give up the manage-ment of the estate to the son, who could make greater advantage by it than his father did. He consented. Writings were prepared and friends met to see the agreement executed to quit all to the son, reserving only a pension to the father. Whilst this was doing the father, as is much used, was taking tobacco in the better room, the parlour, where his rheum caused him to spit much, which offended the son, and because there was much company he desired his father to take the tobacco in the kitchen and to spit there, which he obeyed. All things being ready the son calls his father to come and seal the writings. The father said his mind was changed. The son wondered at it and asking the reason the wise old man said because he was resolved to spit in the parlour as long as he lived. And so, I hope, will a wise young lady.

The Queen took his fatherly advice in good part.

Your story is very apt to our purpose and the application proper – to keep the crown upon my head as long as I live. But to be quit of it, rather than to keep it, I shall think to be to spit in the parlour.

Whitelocke kept this conversation to himself but during the next month officials told him (in the strictest confidence) that the Queen was planning to abdicate, and he responded with incredulity. Gradually the secret leaked out and became yet another excuse for postponing the treaty. The weeks which followed were frustrating. It was rumoured that the Chancellor was jealous of Cromwell's achieving something he himself had once attempted without success; he was consequently 'no friend to Cromwell the Protector'. More significant was his hostility to the article which would prevent Sweden from shipping goods to Holland, while that country was at war with England. The proposed embargo irritated the Chancellor to such an extent that Whitelocke spoke about it to the Queen.

Perhaps he and his sons may have some shares in merchants' ships, which may occasion their extraordinary care in matters of that nature?

She replied:

That is very true; but I will be judge at last, and you shall not be unnecessarily delayed.

By the beginning of February Whitelocke realized the inadequacy of his allowance. Gratuities were heavy, he was buying thirty loads of firewood a day and providing food not only for his own large household but also for a number of senators, grandees and hangers-on. He heard with displeasure that when Mary appealed on his behalf to members of the Council they kept her waiting. Only Sir Charles Wolseley had been unfailingly kind and courteous. Whitelocke wrote boldly reminding Cromwell of his promise and coolly asking for settlement of two thousand pounds which he had already overspent. Demands on his generosity continued. Lagerfeldt told him how greatly Her Majesty admired English horses and Whitelocke 'understood this Swedish language, and the English of it to be to get some of his horses for the Queen'. He made her a present of three fine saddle horses, with which she was delighted, but her acquisitive nature was not satisfied until he also sent her a mare.

She found time for everything except the treaty. She paid Whitelocke the compliment of being his Valentine and he gallantly wore her name in his hat and made her a gift of a large English looking-glass. When she was ill he sent James to enquire about her health. She sent back word that she was sick of no other disease than that the Ambassador had not visited her for three days. He called next day to present her with an English-French grammar, especially written for her because she wished to study English. The

Queen asked Dr. Whistler, who accompanied Whitelocke, whether physicians understood the science of medicine or treated their patients by guesswork; also whether good philosophers were likely to be good Christians. She was impressed by the Doctor's answers and by the information he gave her concerning William Harvey's treatise on the circulation of the blood, published in 1628. She was a capricious creature, a mixture of spoilt child and scholar.

She sent Whitelocke an invitation to attend the audience for the Envoy from Moscow, but this had to be postponed because the Russian had not been notified until ten o'clock in the morning, by which time he was too drunk to appear before the Queen. The same evening Whitelocke attended a musical soirée given by a group of Italian eunuchs and other singers.

The Queen was in a very good humour, and taking Whitelocke by the hand she led him to a lady in the room whom they called *la belle Comtesse* . . . the wife of Graf Jacob de la Gardie. The Queen said to Whitelocke 'Discourse with this lady, my bedfellow, and tell me if her inside be not as beautiful as her outside.'

This frank introduction to the beautiful Ebba Sparre did not seem to shock Whitelocke, who wrote in his 'Journal' that the lady possessed great modesty, virtue and wit.[12] The Queen playfully pulled off the Countess's gloves, giving one to Whitelocke for a favour and tearing the other in pieces which she distributed to Count Tott, Pimentel and two of the Italians. To compensate the Countess, Whitelocke sent her a gift of twelve pairs of white gloves, brought from England.

Although the Queen was friendly, even affectionate, there were hostile influences at work. The Archbishop of Uppsala asked challenging questions about the King's death and the new regime. Whitelocke retaliated by criticizing the profanation of the Lord's day and the widespread drunkenness he had observed in Sweden. His views on both subjects were well known in Uppsala, so it was with all the offensiveness of gentlemen whose pleasures are under attack that a crowd of army officers and their servants assembled one evening – one *Sunday* evening – in the great square outside his house. Kneeling in a circle as if for prayer they proceeded to imbibe huge quantities of wine and to pledge toasts, with 'drums and trumpets and roaring at every drinking of the health'.[13] The Ambassador loftily 'took no notice of it, but pitied their condition and was grieved for them'.

Letters from England warned him of new assassination threats. On the night of 21 February, a crowd of Royalists and drunkards gathered outside his house, with drawn swords, yelling 'Come out ye English dogs. Ye king-killers. Base rogues!' Whitelocke's people clamoured to unbar the door and 'have a crash with them', but their master ordered them not to attack unless the door were broken down, and then to give no quarter. However, after making a lot of noise the rioters withdrew.

News from England was depressing. Mary wrote to warn her husband that a member of his household was sending reports on him to Cromwell. This confirmed a suspicion which he and Daniel Earle had already discussed. Mary added that Cromwell had spoken slightingly of the mission, yet by the same post the Protector sent a cordial letter in which he stressed again the importance of the treaty.

Enemies at Court muttered that a country so unstable as England was unfit to sign a treaty, especially since it was rumoured that Charles Stuart would soon overthrow the rebel government and punish the ring-leaders. It was whispered, too, that Whitelocke was afraid to return to his own country. Malicious stories seemed to originate with van Beuningen, the unpopular Dutch representative, whose letters were intercepted by Thurloe's agents and sent to Whitelocke for comment. A courtier told the Queen that the Dutchman 'did not hold up his head so high as before, nor was his gait so light and frisking as it was before the coming of the English Ambassador, who had hereby much improved the Holland Resident'.[14] In letters to his government van Beuningen complained about the length of the English-man's audiences. He need not have been alarmed. Whitelocke was in fact obliged to spend much of his time in light-hearted banter or scholarly dis-cussions with the Queen while he fretted to complete the negotiations; when eventually it dawned on him that the uncertainty was worrying the Dutch, and making them eager for an early settlement with England, he no longer pressed for a speedy completion. Interviews with the Queen went well enough, when he could persuade her to discuss the articles, although he complained in a letter to Thurloe, 'When I speak with the Queen she seems to be satisfied, and then some of the grandees seek to persuade her to a contrary opinion, and to keep me from her and lay objections in the way.' Thurloe wrote with his unfailing cordiality: 'The particular account your Excellency gives of your negotiations is very acceptable here, as is also your dextrous management thereof.'

Among the personal letters was an affectionate, respectful one from the aged John Selden:

. . . There is nothing happens here that can be worthy of your knowledge but you meet it doubtless long before I could send it (indeed, I think long before I know it) so that I cannot present you with any English news. My still keeping in from the open cold air makes me a mere winter stranger in my own country.

The best news I have heard since I had the honour to see you, and that which brought me with it an ample store of gladness, was the assurance of Your Excellency's safety which a false rumour, with great confidence, had utterly destroyed here. There is none living can with more hearty affection wish all happiness to you and good success in your great employment there, and a safe and timely return, than doth most really

    Your Excellency's most obliged and most humble servant
Whitefriars   J. Selden[15]
February 10.1653[4]

Selden was referring to a persistent rumour that Whitelocke had been stabbed to death. Friends kept the report from Mary until someone burst in with the news that her husband was after all alive, at which she broke down in the general excitement and relief.

    Whitelocke also received a long letter from Jonathan Pickes a humourless and devout member of George Cokain's congregation:

My Lord
    . . . My soul and many more have been set a-praising God on your behalf for that noble Christian testimony and dislike of that wicked custom of cup-health pledging, whereas a Christian's health is God and his cup salvation. And blessed be the Lord that did give you to dislike the ball of pleasure, and that the Lord of that day was so precious. Go on nobly for the Lord. Give your testimony against the wicked customs of a strange country or dying world . . . the Lord fill your sails with his gales, make you holily successful and give you to see your land and relations full of heavenly fruition, is the humble and hearty desire of one of the least sons of Zion, ready to serve the Lord in you or yours.
    Jonathan Pickes[16]

It was fortunate that Mr. Pickes knew nothing of the vanities of music, dancing and, worst of all, acting which Whitelocke permitted in his house, or of his attendance at weekday balls and his frivolity on St. Valentine's day.

    Friends and enemies alike were curious about Cromwell's policy in building up the English navy. Whitelocke (who was himself in the dark about these plans) was perversely enigmatic, glad that Oxenstierna and van Beuningen should remain 'amused' – or bemused – as to Parliament's intentions at sea. The monotony at Court was broken by a light-hearted interview with the Queen, in which she told Whitelocke that she planned, after abdicating, to go to Pomerania. Not for the first time he advised her to make careful provision for her revenue and to guard against treacherous servants. They were back on the earlier footing and she told him charmingly, 'I could freely trust yourself with any of my concernments; and if you will come to me into Pomerland you shall be as welcome as any man living, and we will be merry together!' Whitelocke replied teasingly, 'I humbly thank Your Majesty for your great favour to your servant – who hath a wife, and children enough to people a province in Pomerland; and I shall bring them *all* thither to do Your Majesty service.' It was hardly what she meant, but she assured him that they would be very welcome.

Vanderlin had by that time learned to proceed carefully with the English Ambassador, while still looking for opportunities to put him in his place. When Whitelocke accepted an invitation to a court masque, arranged in his honour, Vanderlin asked tentatively:

What would Your Excellency expect in matter of precedence, as in case you should meet with any other Ambassador at the masque?

I shall expect that which belongs to me as Ambassador from the Commonwealth of England, Scotland, and Ireland; and I know no other Ambassador now in this Court besides myself – except the Ambassador of the King of Denmark who, I suppose, hath no thoughts of precedence before the English Ambassador; who is resolved not to give it him if he should expect it.

Refusing to give in, the Master suggested slyly:

It may be insisted on that he of Denmark is an Ambassador of an anointed King, and you are only Ambassador to the Protector – a new name, and not *sacré*.

. . . I understand no difference of power between King and Protector, anointed or not anointed. . . . The nation of England hath ever been determined superior to that of Denmark . . . I must not suffer any diminution of that honour . . . to please any whatsoever.

Vanderlin tried again.

I shall propose an expedient to you, that you may take your places as you come. He who comes first the first place, and he who comes last the lower place.

The reply was uncompromising.

I shall hardly take a place below the Danish Ambassador, though I come into the room after him.

But when you come into the room and find the Danish Ambassador set you cannot help it, though he have the upper place.

I shall endeavour to help it.

Aghast at such presumption Vanderlin could only say anxiously:

I presume you will not use force in the Queen's presence?

Master it is impossible for me, if it were in the presence of all the Queens and Kings in Christendom, to forbear to use any means to hinder the dishonour of my nation.

In the end Vanderlin conceded heavily,

... The Danish Ambassador must be uninvited again, for I perceive that you two must not meet.

The masque that evening was an elaborate affair, and the reception lasted from eight o'clock at night until two in the morning.

Two days later, on 10 April 1654, Axel Oxenstierna took the opportunity of giving Whitelocke some unsolicited advice to pass on to Cromwell. The Protector, he said, should curb dangerous opinions on religion, provide money and employment for his soldiers and watch for royalist plots or treachery within his own party. He should also

... let the people see that he intends not to rule them with an iron sceptre nor to govern them by an army, but to give them such a liberty and enjoyment of the benefit of their laws that the continuance of his government may become their interest, and that they may have no cause to desire a change. Else, though they must bear the yoke for a time yet, as soon as they meet with an opportunity, they will shake it off again.

These liberal observations were in line with Whitelocke's own view so he replied warmly:

... Your Excellency hath rightly stated the disposition of my countrymen, who love peace and liberty and will hardly brook slavery longer than they are forced to it by necessity, and the best way to govern them is to let them enjoy their laws and rights.

Most of the articles in the treaty had been agreed, but negotiations came to a standstill when the Queen and the Chancellor abruptly left Uppsala. It was hinted that Christina had no intention of returning. Although he was anxious, Whitelocke firmly maintained that she would be back within ten days, for she had told him so and she never broke her word to him.

In the dull days that followed he visited Uppsala University but was not

impressed, for his jaundiced mood made everything Swedish seem inferior
to its counterpart in England. The professors were underpaid and did not
give of their best; there were no residential colleges; discipline was lax and
there were only enough students to fill a single college at Oxford; the
library was no larger than his own at Fawley. Even the river Sale, from
which Uppsala derived its name, was only half the width of the Thames at
Henley.

He used his enforced leisure to arrange for a mining expert to come to
England in an advisory capacity and to enquire about the purchase of falcons.
Before he left Uppsala he was to receive a letter on that subject from George
Cokain, which reflected the sad lack of honour between sportsmen.

Your old servant Abel is much courted by His Highness to be his falconer-in-chief.
But he will not accept it except Your Excellency had been here to give him your
explicit leave to serve His Highness, and told me, without stuttering, he would not
serve the greatest prince in the world, except Your Excellency were present to make
the bargain that he might wait upon you, with a cast of hawks, at the beginning of
September every year into Bedfordshire. . . . Certainly it is a noble profession that
inspires him with such a spirit.

Although the Lord Protector was not above filching the Lord Ambassador's
falconer-in-chief, in other ways he showed himself a good friend. Whitelocke
held the office of *Custos Rotulorum*, the chief Justice of the Peace in Buckinghamshire, and, when the Clerk of the Peace died, local Justices hurried to
London to press for a new appointment. Cromwell, recognizing that it was
for Whitelocke to fill the vacancy, insisted that the appointment should
be left until the Ambassador's return.[17] In another letter Cokain wrote
anxiously, 'I could wish that you would make what haste you can home for
I am informed, by a special hand, that there is great labouring to make a
Chancellor whilst you are absent, and to take that opportunity to put you
by, whom I believe they doubt to be too much a Christian and an Englishman to trust in their service.' Thurloe, too, referred in a postscript to rumours that Whitelocke was to be removed from the Seal but added, 'His
Highness commanded me to assure you that there are no such intentions but
much the contrary, whereof your Excellency will have real demonstrations.'

Whitelocke was still waiting for the Queen's return when he heard from
Thurloe that the Dutch peace treaty was, at last, ready for signature. He was
bewildered to read that, as a result, new instructions would be sent to him
in the next letter. He could not imagine what that meant. A letter from

Mary warned him of a report that 'if he should do anything too suddenly, without good warrant, it might cost him his life.' It was an alarming predicament. He was too far away to consult his superiors and too near agreement to draw back. If the treaty with Sweden were not signed before Christina's abdication he envisaged further postponement until after the coronation. He kept his thoughts to himself and decided to complete the negotiations, even at the risk of their not being ratified.

At about nine o'clock on 23 April the Queen returned to Uppsala. It was a relief that she had kept her word, even though Whitelocke deplored her travelling on the Lord's day. She sent for him the next day and assured him that the articles could be signed on the Tuesday. She also raised the question of his giving her a set of coach horses which she wanted for her journeys after the abdication. He suggested that she should have the eight black horses from the state coach; he planned to present the bays to the new King. He gave her, as well, a beautifully printed English Bible, saying that it would help her to learn English besides bringing comfort and contentment to her soul. She protested, 'I doubt you have an ill opinion of me that you so earnestly persuade me to this, as if you thought me too backward in it.' He answered simply, 'I only give my humble advice to Your Majesty, out of my own experience of the great comfort, wisdom and true pleasure which is to be met with in this book, and nowhere else.' Whitelocke thought she was more responsive than usual to this advice. Perhaps the turmoil in her life made her so. She could not tell him that she was preparing to give up not only the crown but also the protestant faith.

She said nothing more about her promise to sign the treaty, but Count Erik Oxenstierna volunteered that there was no reason why it should not be signed as soon as his father came back. In spite of this, on the following day Whitelocke and Count Erik had an acid exchange about the delay at the end of which Whitelocke, in exasperation, announced that England's peace treaty with Holland contained a clause preventing either party from forming a new alliance, without reference to the other. Consequently, as soon as he heard that the treaty was signed, he would lose his authority to sign a treaty with Sweden. Count Erik was taken aback. 'This is indeed a material point, and I am much startled at it. I shall go and see if my father be come to town . . . doubtless the business may be finished tomorrow.'

It looked as if this had clinched the matter but when Whitelocke sent a message, asking the Chancellor when he might call, Oxenstierna's reply was evasive and 'a little different from the ordinary rules of civility'. Next day the old Chancellor protested that he was tired after his journey and it appeared that the Queen had again left the city; Whitelocke 'perceived that their little design was, notwithstanding all he had endeavoured, that before they would sign the articles they desired to see this week's letters.' When an appointment was finally made on 28 April 1654, he went to the Chancellor's lodging accompanied by his son James and Daniel Earle. The Chancellor insisted that ratification in England should be under the Great Seal of the Commonwealth, not that of the Protector, and promised that ratification on their part should be under the Great Seal of Sweden. The Anglo-Swedish treaty for amity, commerce and free navigation was then signed 'after a long and intricate (it might be said vexatious) transaction of this great affair, for near five months together'. The Whitelocke treaty has never been revoked.

Cromwell sent his portrait to Christina. Conscious perhaps that this was an odd gift from a regicide to a monarch, he despatched a reassuring Latin verse composed by Andrew Marvell. Its last lines have been translated:

> To you this shade its reverent forehead bends,
> My looks not always stern to royal friends

or more elegantly by Voltaire:

> *Regardez sans pâlir cette image fidèle:*
> *Mon front n'est pas toujours l'épouvant des rois.*

According to a newsletter, addressed to Edward Hyde and headed London May 20 1653, Christina had already sent her portrait to Cromwell, months before Whitelocke's embassy was even mooted. The author of the letter had observed derisively: 'The General's lady looks on the portrait of the Queen of Sweden, lately presented to him, and says with a sigh "If I were gone, that were she that must be the woman".'[18]

Chapter Nine

Abdication

Everybody at Court, including van Beuningen, showed a new respect for the English Ambassador. Even the Master of Ceremonies unbent so far as to be 'frolic at dinner'.

Cromwell wrote a friendly letter to say that, as posts took a month in each direction, he would leave it to the Ambassador to come home when he thought fit. It only remained to make the customary presentations. Whitelocke was forestalled in this by Christina who decided to make him a gift of some copper; this was considered by some Ambassadors to be more acceptable than diamonds or jewelry for, although it was costly to transport, it was easy to sell. It was no longer forbidden for an English official to accept gifts of this nature, but Whitelocke was sensitive to any hint of corruption so in accepting the copper, valued at £2,500, he felt easier for knowing that gratuities to the Queen's servants would cost him at least £3,000. No one could charge him with profiting from the mission and lavish hospitality ran him into further expense. At an audience with the Queen, he took her by surprise when he asked

Will your Majesty be pleased on Monday next to go into England?

Hardly so soon! Yet perhaps I may one day see England; but what is your meaning in this?

Madam, Monday next is the first day of May, a great day in England; we call it May-day. . . . If you will do me the honour that, after the custom of England, I may wait on you on May-day and have a little treatment for you after the manner of England, this I call going into England, and shall take as a very great favour from Your Majesty.[1]

It was an odd day for a Puritan to choose. May-day had been popular in mediaeval and Tudor England as a day for crowning the May Queen, for dancing, riding hobby-horses and for much eating and drinking. In 1583, Stubbes, the puritan pamphleteer, had written of the 'gadding to the woods, groves, hills and mountains' which followed; he had heard it reported 'that of forty, threescore or a hundred maids going to the wood overnight, there have scarcely the third part of them returned home again undefiled.'[2] The pagan festival was naturally frowned on by Puritans, and the heathen maypole had been banned; in spite of this, boyhood memories or love of tradition or Whitelocke's idea of entertaining royalty prevailed.

On a cold May-day the Queen and a group of courtiers arrived at the
Ambassador's house. He had provided a spread that might have been set
before a Tudor monarch. There was meat and poultry served with English
sauces, ox-tongue and potted venison, cakes, creams and custards as well as
tarts and tansies.[3] There was good salt butter, brought from England in
November and soaked in milk overnight, so that it tasted like fresh. For
dessert there were English apples and *Bon Chrétien* pears which had been
stored through the winter. A dry white wine and a claret were served and
there was also home-brewed ale. Christina was in excellent form and,
according to her servants, ate more at that meal than she would normally
eat in three or four days at her own table; best of all, her conversation 'was
all of mirth and drollery'.

Vanderlin called a few days later to enquire whether Whitelocke and his
company would care to attend the meeting of the *Riksdag* at which the
abdication would be announced. It was to be held in the Castle hall and he
offered to arrange seats in the gallery at the back, from which the English
party could watch unseen. The old question arose as to who should take the
upper seat if the Danish Ambassador also accepted. Whitelocke was obliged
to be civil, since Denmark was no longer an enemy, but that did not imply
that he would make the slightest concession on matters of precedence. To
avoid embarrassment he asked Vanderlin to call him early, ensuring that he
arrived first, since he could not permit the Dane to sit above him.

On 10 May, the very eve of her ordeal before the four Estates of the
Realm, the Queen invited Whitelocke and his sons to a wedding. Vanderlin
called for them between ten and eleven o'clock at night, in one of the royal
coaches. The ceremony was conducted in the great hall of the Castle by one
of the Queen's chaplains. When it was over the bridegroom took the Queen
by the hand and paraded her round the hall. Whitelocke followed with the
bride. Then it was his turn to escort Christina at the head of the torch-light
procession. She was in high spirits, and when the dancing began she put him
to a final, teasing test by asking him to be her partner. He tried to extricate
himself:

Madam, I am fearful that I shall dishonour Your Majesty, as well as shame myself,
by dancing with you.

I will try whether you can dance!

I assure Your Majesty I cannot, in any measure worthy to have you by the hand.

I esteem you worthy, and therefore make choice of you to dance with me.

He replied like a courtier:

I shall not so much undervalue Your Majesty's judgement as not to obey you herein, and wish I could remember as much of this as when I was a young man.

At the end of the dance the Queen suddenly exclaimed '*Par Dieu!* these Hollanders are lying fellows.' Whitelocke asked what could have brought the Dutch to her mind at such a moment and she replied:

The Hollanders reported to me, a great while since, that all the *noblesse* of England were of the King's party, and none but mechanics of the Parliament party and not a gentleman among them. Now, I thought to try you and to shame you if you could not dance. But I see that you are a gentleman and have been bred a gentleman, and that makes me say the Hollanders are lying fellows.

He agreed that the greater part of the nobility and gentry had supported the King but assured her that there were also many gentlemen on Parliament's side; he himself could claim an ancient lineage. She answered:

. . .You have all the qualities of a gentleman, and I believe that you were excellent in your music and dancing in your younger days.

I was bred up in the qualities of a gentleman, and in my youth was accounted not inferior to others in the practice of them, but it is so long since I used this of dancing, especially after we learned to march, that had it not been to obey Your Majesty I should hardly have been drawn to discover my deficiencies.

The Queen replied charmingly:

. . . I take it as a favour that you were willing to lay aside your gravity and play the courtier upon my request, which I see you can do so well when you please.

In spite of the momentous day ahead of her Christina showed no sign of dismissing her weary guests, who included the newly-married couple. Whitelocke knew her well enough to take a liberty. In the early hours of the morning he observed laconically to one of the Senators that the Queen was a great tyrant. The Senator was shocked and repeated the words to the Queen who marched over to demand an explanation. Unabashed, Whitelocke told her gravely 'I see Your Majesty, even now, exercising an act of tyranny.' She asked what she had had done wrong and he replied 'Madam, it is this. Here is a couple of handsome, gallant young persons, newly married, and it cannot but be imagined that they have their longings, as well as others who are made of flesh and blood, to partake of those enjoyments and pleasures which they expect. And yet, Madam, from these you have restrained the bride and bridegroom, till it is now two o'clock in the morning.' This made the Queen laugh and, promising to reform, she stopped the dancing but still insisted on the company sitting down to a banquet. As soon as that was over she sent them home. Many of the guests, and especially the bridegroom, said how grateful they were for Whitelocke's timely joke.[4]

Dawn was breaking when the Ambassador was driven back to his lodging and he can only have snatched two or three hours' sleep before Vanderlin called him for the meeting of the Estates. Not that he need have hurried, for the Danish Ambassador had contracted a diplomatic illness. The meeting had been postponed until nine o'clock in the morning, allowing the servants an extra hour in which to remove all trace of the night's revels. In the hand-to-mouth manner of Christina's Court her officials had removed the rich curtains from the walls of Whitelocke's lodgings and hung them in the great hall, which was laid out with rows of benches covered in red cloth.

At the appointed hour members of the four Estates of the *Riksdag* entered. The eighty representatives of the peasants, the boors, trooped in behind their marshal; they were followed by the townsmen, then came the nobility and finally the bishops and clergy, each Estate with its own leader. When the Queen's guard, the officials, the members of the Council and the Senators had taken their place the Queen herself entered and sat on the silver chair of state, under a canopy of crimson velvet. There was an embarrassed pause. She beckoned to her Chancellor who went over and whispered something. Later Whitelocke learned from the Queen that, without warning, Oxenstierna refused to announce the abdication because he had promised her father he would keep the crown on her head. The Queen sat thinking for a few moments. Then, as she later explained to Whitelocke, 'I plucked up my spirits the best I could, and spake to them on the sudden as you heard. . . . You see I did adventure upon it, remembering that they were my subjects and I their Queen.' In her short, impromptu speech she reminded her parliament, the *Riksdag* that her desire to resign was not new. She had proposed it on an earlier occasion and they had talked her out of it. She spoke of her cousin, the Prince of Sweden, whose name they had accepted as her lawful successor. She thanked her people for their loyalty during her reign, and informed them, quaintly, that she had come to ask consent to a resolution from which they could not dissuade her. Then she sat down. After a moment the Archbishop of Uppsala approached and begged her, in a long and loyal speech, not to abdicate; when he had finished he bowed three times, kissed her hand and withdrew. The marshal of the nobility went through a similar routine and after him the marshal of the burgesses. Then it was the turn of the countryman, a thick-set, roughly dressed man wearing heavy, nailed shoes who spoke, Whitelocke thought, with deeper feeling than any of the others.[5]

O Lord God, Madam, what do you mean to do? It troubles us to hear you speak of forsaking those that love you so well as we do. Can you be better than you are? You are Queen of all these countries and if you leave this large kingdom, where will you get such another? If you should do it (as I hope you won't for all this) both you and we shall have cause, when it is too late, to be sorry for it. Therefore my fellows and I pray you to think better on't, and to keep your crown on your head. . . . Continue in your gears, good Madam, and be the fore-horse as long as you live, and we will help you the best we can to bear the burden.[6]

Your father was an honest gentleman and a good King, and very stirring in the world. We obeyed him and loved him as long as he lived. And you are his own child and have governed us very well, and we love you with all our hearts (and the Prince is an honest gentleman, and when his time comes we shall be ready to do our duties to him as we do to you); but as long as you live we are not willing to part with you, and therefore I pray Madam do not you part with us.

When the boor had ended his speech he waddled up to the Queen without any ceremony, took her by the hand and shaked it heartily, and kissed it two or three times. Then turning his back to her, he pulled out of his pocket a foul handkerchief and wiped the tears from his eyes, and . . . returned back to his own place again.

An official then read aloud the formal proposal and the Queen withdrew, without replying to the objections or allowing opportunity for debate. The representatives filed out of the hall and Whitelocke returned to his lodging.

His final audience was to take place on the following day. After that he could still see the Queen privately but must not appear at any public function. Instead of the black suit he had worn at the first audience he put on a plain, musk-coloured suit with points and ribbons of gold; the buttons were of enamelled gold, each one set with a ruby. This time the speeches on both sides were short but very cordial. Later he called on the Queen's cousin, who was shortly to be crowned Charles X of Sweden. Charles was the son of Christina's aunt, Princess Catherine of Sweden, and of Count Palatine John Casimir. Whitelocke was received with an unusual show of courtesy. He was greatly flattered when the Prince paid him the exceptional compliment of returning the call.

The exchange of presents was already in full spate. Besides the copper, the Queen sent Whitelocke her portrait in miniature, set in a locket of enamelled gold encrusted with diamonds, and asked him to wear it for her sake. His sons James and William were each given a gold chain with a medallion of the Queen's head. The principal officers of his household received similar gifts but Stapleton, the Master of the Horse, and Walker, the Steward, complained because their chains had three links, while Potley's and Beake's had four. Whitelocke deplored the evil effects of gold but tried to smooth over the ill feeling by explaining that Potley had served under the Queen's father, while Beake had been a commander of the guard under Cromwell. He also pointed out that none of them had any claim whatever on the Queen's generosity. Stapleton, who had already shown an awkward side to his character, threatened to return his chain. When reports of the grievances reached Vanderlin he protested upon his soul and honour that he had nothing to do with the allocation; the Queen herself had studied the list of names and marked those to whom particular gifts were to be made. Whitelocke told him not to worry; in a large family it was difficult to satisfy everybody.

Vanderlin's unusually circumspect behaviour suggested that he was already calculating the value of his own prize. In awarding it Whitelocke permitted himself a piece of good-natured malice. He despatched Daniel Earle to deliver a fine beaver hat and an expensive pair of English gloves. Vanderlin's face fell. Other ambassadors, he said, had treated him more handsomely. Earle ignored the reproach and asked him to try the gloves for size, and when Vanderlin pulled them on he found them filled with forty golden coins, worth twenty shillings apiece. A similar prank was played on Secretary Canterstein, who had done much of the clerical work for the treaty, when he was given a silver inkstand.[7]

Gifts of ribbons, gloves, stockings and in one case a hanging clock were made to ladies at Court. Oxenstierna received a hogshead of Canary wine and a quiet English nag with a finely-wrought saddle. Wrangell, Tott and other prominent courtiers were each given an English gelding. The Prince sent Whitelocke a miniature of himself in a gold enamelled jewel set with diamonds, and Whitelocke presented him with the bay coach horses and also the spirited gelding which Cromwell had given him after the battle of Worcester.

On the morning of 20 May 1654, the Ambassador and his company set off on the first lap of the journey home. The Queen lent him coach horses, and an official provided the other horses but forgot to order saddles. The riders were obliged to improvise with straw and cushions for an uncomfortable forty-mile journey to Stockholm, where they arrived the same evening. During his few days' stay in the capital Whitelocke spent some time in the company of Vice-Admiral Wrangell, who showed him some of Sweden's warships and invited him to attend the launching of a man-of-war, standing on a steep slipway, and to name her. The Ambassador suggested calling her the *Wrangell* but the Vice-Admiral would not hear of it, 'possibly to avoid the envy of it at Court'; correspondingly, Whitelocke would not agree to them taking his own name, 'lest it might argue too much height in himself'; nor would he agree to the *Cromwell* or the *Protector* since she only carried thirty guns. He noticed that her ordnance was marked with a hawk, like those on his family arms, so as the ship was 'swifter of sail than ordinary' he named her the *Falcon*.

He was impatient to be off, but was still waiting for a favourable wind when a packet of letters arrived from England. Thurloe wrote about the proclamation of peace with Holland and the festivities which had followed. His brother-in-law, Samuel Wilson, deplored the effects of peace which would put an end to capturing enemy vessels: 'Our trade, some report, is almost at an end in the Prize Office; others say it will begin elsewhere; the effect of all only God knows. I wish amongst all that Spanish wines may sell well, for I am full of that commodity.'[8] Another relative, Colonel Thomas Bulstrode, wrote about the Protectorate, saying that supporters of the Commonwealth were so bewildered by the turn of events that many of them wished themselves with Whitelocke in far-away Sweden. To Englishmen's minds Sweden was in the antipodes. At some time during the Swedish mission Andrew Marvell wrote a long letter in Latin verse to Whitelocke's chaplain, Nathaniel Ingelo, hoping that he was adequately protected with furs, and demanding news about the kind of men and places he had seen – if indeed there were any men or places where he was. There was a flattering letter from Edward Eltonhead and one with news of lawyers, judges and other friends from Bartholomew Hall. Old Dr. Winston wrote reassuringly that whoever had frightened Whitelocke with news that Mary had a tumour on her breast was quite wrong; it was only a pimple and it had soon responded to treatment. Finally, there was a tender letter from Mary in which, as usual, she referred to her step-sons as if they were her own:

London the 3 April 1654
My dear heart,
    Having opportunity I could not forbear writing to you by the ship. I have in the
Golden Hawk, by Mr. Dickenson, sent you a pair of silk stockins for your pages etc.
Pray remember my love to my two sons and tell them I have sent them a small token,
each of them a pair of silk stockins. I am very much troubled that I have not received
any letters from you, this post, for the post is not come as yet. The Lord send I may
hear good news of you from day to day. . . . Truly now every day seems as a year
before I hear of your return. . . . I can assure you I never did so much instruct other
women to love and prize their husbands as when I was a widow; and now, in your
absence, if they do at any time fall out with their own husbands then I tell them, many
times with tears, if their husbands were in Sweden they would prize them more than
now. . . .
    This you may be sure of, you have my love and heart. . . .
        Your loving wife
        Mary Whitelocke[9]

    According to Whitelocke, Wrangell and George Fleetwood left Stock-
holm for Uppsala before the end of May, to be present at the abdication and
coronation, and Wrangell returned late on the day of this double ceremony
to give an eye-witness account.[10] Whitelocke viewed the abdication with
particular interest. He may have wondered whether the late King of England
could not have been pensioned off and allowed to keep his head without the
crown.
    Christina, he learned, had come before the *Riksdag* wearing her crown and
purple robes. A table had been set with five large cushions, on one of which
lay the sword of state, on another the sceptre, on a third the orb and on a
fourth the keys. The fifth cushion was bare. When she had finished a speech,
in which she wished her cousin success, she called on her servants to remove
the crown from her head. No one stirred. She called on Count Tott and
another courtier to do so but they refused. She urged them once again and
this time they removed the crown and laid it on the fifth cushion. Had she
wished the ceremony to run smoothly (remembering the earlier incident
with her Chancellor) she would have arranged the ritual beforehand. As it
was, her taste for high drama, sharpened perhaps by an erotic pleasure,
moved her to play out the harrowing scene in which her favourite eventually
took the crown from her head, while others stripped her of her robes. Her
manner throughout showed the utmost composure.
    Her motives for abdicating remain obscure. The simple explanation that,

as a woman, she felt herself unfit to rule is unconvincing.[11] She did not suffer from the feminine weaknesses she despised in others, nor did she lack authority and self-assurance. Once she had made up her mind to change her faith her resignation was inescapable, but teasing questions persist as to what lay behind it all; as to how far she experienced an intellectual or emotional conversion; as to whether she was looking for greater freedom for rational speculation in the Roman Church than she found in the narrow Lutheran Church of her day; as to whether she was chiefly prompted by a desire to follow cultural pursuits in European centres of learning; as to whether her abdication was in part a capricious act. Whitelocke did not attempt to explain her actions. He was a good judge of men and women, his admiration for Christina never diminished, and years later he pointed to the young Queen as one among several examples of women's fitness to govern a kingdom.

Large crowds lined the waterfront on 31 May 1654 when the Ambassador and his company left Stockholm by boat for Dalarö, the small historic port in Stockholm's archipelago. Next morning the party boarded the *Amaranth*, a new man-of-war which the Queen had placed at Whitelocke's disposal for the voyage across the Baltic.[12] The imagery of the amaranth, the flower that never fades, appealed to Christina as the falcon did to Whitelocke; perhaps too she found pleasure in the arcadian innocence of the shepherdess, Amarante, a part she had played in one of the court masques, and there may have been an association of ideas with Don Antonio Pimentel de Prado's native town of Amarante. Not only was her new warship named *Amaranth*; in 1653 she had founded the Order of Amaranth, and Whitelocke's knighthood was of that Swedish Order.[13]

After eight stormy days at sea the Ambassador and his company were thankful to land at Travemunde, near Lübeck, where a large crowd had gathered to watch their arrival. They were welcomed by the Governor of the fort, a tall man with an impressive white beard. He led them to his house and, with every show of hospitality, entertained them on strong beer, calling for flagon after flagon until Whitelocke began to feel anxious about certain members of his company. Colonel Potley, who was acting as interpreter, whispered that the Governor expected to be paid for the drinks. At that the Ambassador called for his bill, and hastily escaped from the 'honourable alehouse'. In Lübeck refreshments at the civic reception, though sparse, were provided free of charge. Again the streets were lined with

8 Christina in 1645. Drawing by P. Holsteyn

9 Don Antonio Pimentel de Prado, Spanish envoy and a favourite of Christina's. Engraving by Frederik Bouttats

Excellentissimus Dominus. Dⁿᵘˢ ANTONIVS PIMENTEL DE PRADO. Eques auratu' ordinis S Iacobi, ad Regem Christianissimum pro pace legatus etc.

C. Woulier pinxit   Fred. bouttats exc Antverpiæ 1649

10 Uppsala from the south, showing the Edenberg House,
where Whitelocke lived from 1653–4, on the right.
Woodcut from O. Rudbeck's *Atlantica*

11 Uppsala castle. Woodcut from the same source

people, most of them women, and the town musicians turned out to play English tunes, for which they too expected payment. Two days later the travellers pushed on towards Hamburg, stopping for a night in wretched lodgings which they were told had been plundered during the wars and had not yet been repaired. Two beds were provided, and these 'were made only of straw and fleas mingled together'. Whitelocke insisted on having fresh straw put down. He decided to sleep in one of the coaches, with his sons and some of the servants on the floor close by; the rest settled down in the large barn, which they shared with horses, cows, sheep and pigs. Nobody felt like undressing and they were glad to be away by four o'clock next morning.

They jolted over the rough roads in the Ambassador's two coaches and twelve hired wagons, each of which carried up to eight passengers. The servants were armed with pistols, guns and swords in case of attack. In a light-hearted moment one of them shot a stork, but Whitelocke warned them that this could cause grave offence for in Holstein, the Netherlands and the Hanseatic towns, storks were prized as birds which only lived in a land 'where the people are free, as in the Low Countries'.[14]

He was met by members of the powerful English colony of Merchant Adventurers, who arrived in twenty-two coaches. They invited him to stay at the English House during his visit to Hamburg. Lines of onlookers stretched for a mile outside the gates, while inside the city musketeers had to clear a way through the streets. After he had settled into the English House Whitelocke was visited by city officials, bringing what they described modestly as something for the kitchen and something for the cellar; the gifts consisted of two large fresh salmon, two sheep, two lambs, a calf, four sturgeon, hogsheads of beer, of Spanish and Rhenish wine and of claret. The English colony insisted on entertaining the party to supper that night, although the travellers 'had more mind to sleep than to eat'.

Whitelocke used his short stay to see something of the city's fortifications and to attend a session of the *Diet*. On the fourth evening a lavish reception was arranged by the English Resident, at which Whitelocke met a number of Senators and Burgomasters. He was impressed to find that, in cosmopolitan Hamburg, they all spoke French or Latin or both languages. He ate little and only drank a glass of Spanish wine, followed by a glass of small beer. This was handed to him by a stranger whom he never saw again. He was dubious about the colour and taste of the beer and when he went back to his lodgings he developed pains in his stomach like sharp dagger strokes, followed by attacks of vomiting. He was immediately treated by Dr.

Whistler for suspected poisoning, and within two hours was able to doze off; by the next evening he was on the way to recovery.[15] Several offers of help from physicians in Hamburg were courteously refused, for royalist agents came in many guises.

Whitelocke was impatient to sail for home. After one or two mishaps on the way he reached the frigate sent for his use by Parliament; she was lying at anchor off Glückstadt, near the mouth of the Elbe. The sailing was delayed by gales and then by fog, which demoralized some of the ship's company. Two of them were heard, when drunk, threatening to blow up the ship and cut the Protector's throat and the throats of ten thousand of his party. By the time they were brought before Whitelocke the sailors had sobered up. They begged to be forgiven, swearing that they felt no ill will towards Cromwell or the regime. They were cross-examined separately and absolutely denied that they knew of any plot against the Lord Protector or the State.

In spite of the rough seas the Governor of Holstein, Count Ranzau, a servant of the King of Denmark, paid a formal visit to the frigate and was joined by the Dutch Agent, who was equally anxious to pay his respects. Both guests stayed for dinner. The food was served on a silver dinner service supplied by the English government and the visitors kept picking up their plates to inspect them. After the meal Count Ranzau commented on Whitelocke's golden tobacco-box with three falcons engraved on it; this set them talking about the sport and the Count promised to send Whitelocke some hawks from Iceland, where he said they raised the best in the world.

A session with a self-important official tended to bring on Whitelocke's teasing mood so, when Ranzau left, he gave the order to fire a salute of only one gun. Governor Ranzau declared, on his way to the shore, that his King had been insulted and he himself slighted. After an interval Whitelocke threw convention aside and ordered that his frigate, the *President*, should fire all her guns; the *Elizabeth* followed suit and the fortress answered with all guns. The deafening compliment continued until the Count stepped ashore, overwhelmingly satisfied, handing out liberal gratuities to the sailors and two pieces of silver-gilt plate to the officers. He later despatched a boat-load of supplies including carp, hare, deer, partridge and wild boar to Whitelocke, who was astonished that anybody should send such a present on the strength of one meal. He underestimated the flattering effects of the gun salute.

On 28 June the wind veered to the west-south-west and the small fleet set sail, to a salute from the fort. Whitelocke reflected that some people might think these gun salutes extravagant, but he believed they provided 'a kind of sea language' for the sailors which kept up their spirits. There was evident friction between the Captains. Mennes was disgruntled because the Ambassador was not sailing in the *Elizabeth* but Whitelocke had no choice, since the *President* had been sent specifically to bring him home. Out at sea on the first day the *Elizabeth* lagged behind as if she were a stranger and on the second day, contrary to instructions, she raced ahead of the other ships. That afternoon the wind changed and soon they were enveloped in a heavy mist. Towards evening, Whitelocke summoned Captain Parkes and his officers on deck and asked why their sails were fully spread, although they could not see a ship's length ahead. They answered that they must take advantage of a favourable wind. When he asked if they knew their direction they admitted they were not sure. The Ambassador pointed out tactfully that, in such weather, no sailor could be certain of his course and that there was a risk of running aground on the English or even the Dutch coast. He advised them to take in sail until day-light. The officers argued that they had sea-room enough but his commonsense made him order Captain Parkes to furl all sail except the mainsail, which was to be reefed. Parkes disputed the order until Whitelocke told him sharply that it would be given to a sub-ordinate. Next, he made the Captain take soundings. It was ten o'clock at night and they found a depth of eighteen fathoms. A few minutes later it was fifteen and before a quarter past ten, only eight. The laconic officers were alarmed and tried to tack about when suddenly the frigate pranced like a huge horse, throwing several of the gentlemen flat on the decks. The frigate had run aground on a sand-bank. Panic ensued and Whitelocke realized that he must retain command. 'In this frightful confusion God gave him extra-ordinary fixedness and assistance, a temper and constancy of spirit beyond what was usual with him.' It was a significant self-appraisal. Except in a crisis he was an uncoercive leader.

He ordered the master gunner to fire distress signals, but the gunner forgot to 'unbrace' (or run out) the guns and might have shattered the side of a smaller ship; as it was he shot away the main-sheet. No answering shot came to them through the mist. They hoisted a light on the top-gallant but there was no one to see it. In an attempt to rock the ship free Whitelocke directed everyone to crowd to port then to starboard, to the stern and then into the bows, but the frigate was stuck fast. He ordered the seamen to launch a small boat and some of his company urged him to escape in it, but he refused. Apart from the dishonour of abandoning his ship he knew that 'a life knows

no ceremony'. So many of the company would try to crowd in with him
that the little boat would sink. Instead he ordered Captain Parkes, accompanied by one or two sailors, to take soundings; they found there was deep
water to leeward and hearing this the ship's master recommended throwing
the cargo overboard. Whitelocke made up his mind that the ordnance should
be jettisoned first.

Officers spread alarm by declaring that when the tide rose the frigate
would undoubtedly be dashed to pieces. Heartrending cries were coming
from all parts of the ship. Men who had boasted their courage the loudest
were among the most hysterical. Imminent death gave point to each man's
actions. One was preparing to escape on a plank, others clung to the mast.
Back on the quarter-deck Parkes announced heroically that he had spent his
life there, and there he would die. Daniel Earle was intent on saving his
master's jewels. Whitelocke slipped into his pocket a portrait of Mary set
in a golden tablet; apart from its meaning for him it might serve to identify
his body and could be sold to defray the cost of burial. His personal concern
was to save his books and manuscripts. At forty-eight he felt he had lived a
full life but he grieved to think that James and William must die.

He was up on deck when the boatswain, with a directness that belongs to
the frontiers of death, told him he was wrong to have the guns thrown overboard:

If it be done, we are all destroyed.

What reason have you to be of this opinion? Must we not lighten the ship, and can
we do it better than to begin with the ordnance?

. . . You can but drop them close to the ship's side, and where the water is shallow they
will lie up against the sides of the ship and fret it, and with the working of the sea
make her to spring leaks presently.

This was irrefutable and Whitelocke agreed to delay the order. The boatswain said confidently that they would be saved from death and when
Whitelocke asked whether he really saw any hope of escape the seaman said
no, but that God had put it into his heart to say this. He seemed to believe it,
too, for he sauntered up and down quite unconcerned. Nathaniel Ingelo
found Whitelocke sitting on deck and remarked on his composure; he asked
permission to call the company together in the Ambassador's cabin to
prepare them for death. At that moment a sailor rushed up, shouting so
incoherently that Whitelocke thought the ship was going down.

My Lord. My Lord. My Lord!

What's the matter, mariner?

She wags. She wags!

Which way doth she wag?

To leeward.

I pray God that be true and it is the best news that ever I heard in my life.

My Lord, upon my life the ship did wag. I saw her move.

Whitelocke told Mr. Ingelo to wait, as the style of their prayers might need be changed; then he turned back to the sailor.

Fellow-seaman, show me where thou sawest her move.

My Lord here, at the head of the frigate I saw her move – and she moves now – now she moves – you may see it.

My old eyes cannot discern it.

I see it plain, and so do others.

Within fifteen minutes the *President* was afloat. The sailors wished to hoist sail but Whitelocke insisted that they lie at anchor until daylight. There was endless speculation as to how they had escaped and everyone propounded his own theory. Whitelocke stayed up talking for the rest of the night and promised a bottle of sack to the first sailor aloft at dawn who reported seeing land. Many of them claimed the prize next day and he tried to reward them all.

They were off the Norfolk coast and after daybreak they sailed gently past Yarmouth, Orfordness and Harwich. Eventually they sighted the *Elizabeth*, overtook her and fetched Captain Mennes aboard. Whitelocke was unusually stern and charged him with disobeying orders from the outset and failing to come to their rescue when they fired distress signals. Mennes spoke up for himself, pointing out sturdily that although the *President* was the swifter ship, the *Elizabeth* had kept up with her and they had only lost contact in the mist. He swore he had no idea that the Ambassador's frigate was in trouble; certainly he had heard cannon fire but he thought it was a fog signal. When the mist came down he had sailed out to sea, fearing to run aground, and expected the other frigate to do the same. That, he suggested respectfully, was the correct course. Here Parkes intervened to criticize his brother officer, but Whitelocke was convinced by the argument that Mennes had displayed the better seamanship.

The voyage was nearly over and he had no taste for disputes 'so they proceeded together lovingly and friendly' and when they lay at anchor that night, near the mouth of the Thames, Captain Mennes brought his ship alongside the *President* and entertained the company with fireworks.

They returned on 1 July 1654 to the rigours of an English summer, 'cold, wet and windy as if it had still been winter.' It was three o'clock in the morning when they embarked at Gravesend in the small craft waiting to take them to Westminster, where they stepped ashore to a tremendous welcome from a crowd of Whitelocke's friends. The Protector was not among them. He had gone to Hampton Court. Whitelocke went home to Chelsea where, although Daniel Earle had hurried ahead to break the good news, Mary greeted him by bursting into tears. Sudden joy, he noted, had the same effect on her as fear or grief. He may have contrasted her in his mind with the resolute young woman in Uppsala, who had given up the crown without a trace of emotion. The Lord Protector learned from Captain Beake of the Ambassador's return; he expressed great joy and sent word that he would like to see his old friend in Whitehall on the following Monday. When Whitelocke duly presented himself at nine o'clock in the morning, he was greeted 'with great demonstration of affection' and the two men talked privately for about an hour.

So many visitors called at his Chelsea home next day that he had no time to prepare a report for the Council and the day after he was busy again, having invited his whole company, with other friends, for a marathon thanksgiving. Hugh Peter, who had served for a short time under Gustavus Adolphus and had sent the dog and the cheese to Christina, was the first to address them. Nathaniel Ingelo led them in prayer. George Downing from Harvard, who had been an army chaplain in a parliamentary regiment, gave a dissertation on a passage from the scriptures.[16] Mr. Stapleton, who had sometimes been troublesome as Gentleman of the Horse, 'prayed very well and spake pertinently and feelingly'. After a psalm it was George Cokain's turn and Whitelocke wound up by thanking his friends for their prayers, his companions for their diligence and courage, and God for his protection. He then took his guests into another room where Mary had prepared a huge spread, set out as he used to have food served in Sweden, to show his friends how they had lived. This, he noted with a twinge of regret, was 'farewell to those pomps and vanities'. It was not quite true, for early next morning he went to Thurloe's lodgings in Whitehall where he was joined by most of his company; dressed in their official suits and liveries they accompanied him in procession, as they had done in Sweden, for his audience with Cromwell and the Council. It was galling after that to be kept waiting for an hour and a half. When he was admitted Whitelocke gave an account of his journey, of his stay at Court with its long negotiations, and of the final exchange of gifts. Cromwell welcomed him back in the name of the Council, thanked him very cordially for his services and said he wished to speak to the rest of the company. He received them with great courtesy, praising them for their conduct abroad and for the care they had taken of the Ambassador. 'He gave . . . assurance of his affection to them when any occasion should be offered for their good or preferment. They withdrew, full of hopes every one of them to be made great men – but few of them attained any favour.'

From about that time a note of disillusionment crept into Whitelocke's comments. An idealized vision of England as a country offering freedom of conscience and protection under the common law, as a land in which the will of the people prevailed, had been sharpened while he was abroad describing it in these terms and defending Parliament's record. When he returned to political reality the dream began to fade. He was increasingly conscious of intolerance and injustice, of high-handed politicians and of men's ingratitude.

Samuel Wilson was obsequiously helpful. He collected Whitelocke's arrears of salary and saw his consignments of copper and timber through the customs; the copper was sold to the State for ordnance at its market rate of £2,500. The Swedish boards were sent by barge to provide wainscoting and a new floor in the hall at Fawley Court. Whitelocke wrote 'they were extraordinary good boards, and those of the floor were about two inches thick. There they are and there may they long continue, for the use of me and my children.'[17]

He settled down to his old work again and to the pleasant routine of visiting Henry Elsynge who, after resigning as Clerk to Parliament at the time of the King's trial, had retired to Hounslow. Whitelocke thought highly of him and regretted that the talents of such an able lawyer and author on constitutional subjects should be neglected. The other guest at dinner was usually John Selden, who did most of the talking, and the three of them enjoyed 'great cheer and greater learning'. At about that time Whitelocke began to think of turning from the stress of politics, to the greater safety and contentment of an academic career.

Chapter Ten

The Last Years in Office

The Swedish mission had given Whitelocke new confidence, but it was not easy for him to knuckle down afterwards to the uneasy humdrum of service under the Protector, in a regime which he mutely distrusted. The conviction that he had been pushed into the mission because he would have opposed the Protectorate chafed his mind. He believed that his health had been impaired in the service of his country, and increasing pain from stone in the kidneys made him peevish sometimes, and sharper in judgement than before.

He was approaching his forty-ninth birthday and there were still high appointments to tantalize him for, in spite of ill-health, he had not yet turned that corner in life at which a man's ambition falters, as he feels himself drawn towards home and rest. His work as First Keeper of the Great Seal was familiar but irksome, and he noted irritably his colleagues' displays of 'trouble and crossness'.[1]

The City Fathers of Bristol were another cause of annoyance. Some time earlier they had persuaded him to accept appointment as their Recorder, but before he left for Sweden they had written inviting him to resign, for even when he was in England he seldom visited them. Without the Recorder a new mayor and aldermen could not be sworn and they had difficulty over appointing new justices; the City Charter did not provide for the appointment of a deputy recorder. Whitelocke's sharp rejoinder to their letter in 1653 had caused them to ask him to retain his post.[2] Towards the end of August 1654 he was invited to Bristol, for a banquet in celebration of his safe return, but seven months later the Mayor and Aldermen ventured to suggest that if, with his many commitments, he felt it necessary to give up the work they must reluctantly consent. That time he was to reply that he had raised objections to being appointed; if they thought his resignation desirable he would tender it. The City Council accepted with alacrity, forgetting even to thank him for past services.

It seems that he was still in Bristol, after the banquet, when he heard that Christina was planning to visit England. Since her abdication she had visited Hamburg and the Spanish Netherlands and, according to a letter she wrote from Antwerp to Ebba Sparre, *la belle comtesse*, she had been occupied with pleasure, talking, play-going and laughter; 'everyone' she wrote 'should live happily, eating drinking and singing.'[3] When she was satiated her thoughts had turned towards London and a meeting with the mysterious Oliver Cromwell. If, on the journey home, Whitelocke indulged in dreams of a state visit involving him in scenes of splendour, such visions were soon dispelled. Cromwell was implacably hostile to the proposal, on the grounds that the royal lady's way of life would set a bad example. So what could have been a highly entertaining encounter never took place. Perhaps it was as well for Mrs. Cromwell's peace of mind.

The first Parliament of the Protectorate assembled on 3 September 1654; with a choice of three seats, Whitelocke decided to represent Buckinghamshire. When Cromwell gave his report and policy outline to the new Parliament he selected a motley herd of scapegoats – Presbyterians, Fifth Monarchy men, Jesuits and Levellers – and criticized the spirit in the nation which demanded 'overturn, overturn, overturn.' He commended the treaty with Sweden, negotiated by 'the endeavours of an honourable person here present'. He referred to plans for the reform of Chancery and other Courts of Law. He apologized for being tedious but assured Parliament that, by supporting his efforts to bring stability, they could 'put the topstone to the work and make the nation happy'.[4] Some days later Whitelocke gave the House his report of the mission, regaling them with side-lights on the character of the Swedish people. At Lord Broghill's instigation a payment of £2,000 was voted in appreciation of the Ambassador's services; Whitelocke calculated that he had incurred £1,500 beyond his allowance, so the money voted left only £500 as a fee for nearly a year's work.

Parliament quickly settled down to challenging the newly-framed constitution. This was not putting the topstone on the building and it was not for this that Cromwell had summoned them. He promptly required Members to sign a pledge of loyalty to himself and to the Commonwealth, with an undertaking not to attempt to alter the form of government. Ninety Members refused to sign this Recognition and were barred from the House; the rest, including Whitelocke, conformed and then proceeded to find fault with the Instrument of Government and debate ways of blunting it. Doubts as to the legality of the new regime were expressed in Whitelocke's notes. 'What the law is in relation to a protector is not in our law books, and how the laws can limit an officer or chief magistrate who is not known, or ever mentioned by those laws, is hard to be understood.'[5]

Whitelocke noticed that his own influence was growing and that 'Oliver was displeased at it.' (He only adopted the familiar form of address when *he* was displeased with *Oliver*.) His attitude towards Cromwell's parliaments was curiously detached; he told them how they stood in law and referred to 'your books' as if dissociating himself from an assembly whose legality was in doubt. He made enemies. Some were plainly jealous. Others disliked his moderation, belief in the common law and, not least, his habit of pointing out inaccuracies; in an earlier parliament he had corrected William Prynne, when that distinguished lawyer misquoted documents, and the affront was never forgiven.

By January 1655 the Protector was fidgeting to be rid of Parliament. Whitelocke advised him not to dissolve it until the full five months laid down in the Instrument of Government had expired.[6] Cromwell, following the lunar month, dissolved it on 22 January which according to Whitelocke 'caused much discontent in the Parliament . . . but he valued it not, esteeming himself above those things.'[7] As a realist, Whitelocke thought it 'unseasonable, now that it was done, to allege anything against it' and instead 'gave his best advice what way was fit to be done for contenting of the people'. Even under an unlawful regime the administration of justice must be carried on if a country is to be saved from collapse, and Whitelocke believed that tyranny was preferable to anarchy.[8] In any case he was in no mood for a fight. His eldest daughter, Frances, who had been his companion after her mother's death, had just died of smallpox. Mary tried to console him, and a few months later when her first girl was born she named her after the wife and the daughter her husband had lost.

John Selden died soon afterwards. Whitelocke described him as a man with no love for the clergy and a true supporter of Parliament; 'a man of prodigious learning and of a great mind. He was my particular and very affectionate friend. . . . He was as hospitable and generous as any man, and as good company to those whom he liked, as ever I conversed with. He was to me as a father and director of me in my studies. . . . I lost a great friend by his death.'[9]

For several weeks after Parliament's dissolution the Protector and his Council were busy examining conspirators. These included the Republican, John Wildman, who had been excluded from the first protectorate Parliament for refusing to subscribe to the Recognition. He was captured in the act of dictating an incitement to take up arms against 'the tyrant Oliver Cromwell Esq.'. A copy of the document was laid before Whitelocke who recorded, in the privacy of his 'Diary', that Wildman's views on liberty and justice contained 'much of reason and truth'.[10] It must have been known that Whitelocke was out of sympathy with the Protector, for at that highly critical time the conspirators sent word to him, the first Lord Commissioner of the Seal, offering the command of three thousand horse if he would place Windsor Castle at their disposal.[11] He may have been sceptical as to the existence of this cavalry, but whatever his thoughts he kept the treasonable offer a secret. The revolutionaries, like others before them, misconstrued his criticism of the regime. His tidy, unwasteful mind was set on consolidating and moderating. He had little taste for further change.

At the end of April 1655 he was summoned, with the other Commissioners of the Seal, before a committee of the Council. The Chairman informed them that an ordinance had been drawn up to modify the slow and costly proceedings in the High Court of Chancery, a court which was unpopular with everybody except the lawyers. The Protector, they were told, was confident that they would execute the ordinance under Seal, since it was for the public good. Whitelocke answered cautiously that he and his colleagues had not been consulted; they would comply as far as they could but they were men under oath; he asked for time to study the document. Lenthall, the Master of the Rolls, who had been Speaker of the House of Commons, in the Long Parliament, vehemently opposed the ordinance until the chairman silenced him with a warning not to oppose His Highness' wishes.

The threat to their income was surpassed by the insult to their profession. For the Keepers of the Seal not to be consulted on Chancery reform was intolerable. Some of the proposals were inept and impracticable. After discussing the matter among themselves Widdrington, Lenthall and Whitelocke agreed to oppose the Protector's wishes, while John L'Isle decided to conform. The three distinguished lawyers rejected several of the proposals as unworkable – although some of them were later adopted – and pointed out that it would be contrary to their oath to seal as a law a measure only passed as an ordinance by Cromwell and his Council. This, Whitelocke reflected, would be 'too much countenancing of an illegal authority, and a betrayal of the rights of the people of England'.[12] 'The people of England' had come into prominence after the King's execution; they had featured in at least two bills drafted by Whitelocke in 1649.[13] In Sweden he had quoted the people as the sovereign power in his country and he defiantly continued to invoke their rights and authority, even under the Protectorate. They were his pretext for demanding frequent parliaments and opposing government by the Protector and his Council. Not wishing however to be purged as traitors the three lawyers wrote explaining that, after examining their consciences and seeking God's guidance, they found they could not execute the ordinance under seal.

Cromwell was not prepared to argue about trifles. He summoned them, telling them to bring the Seal. They knew what that meant. He informed them that while he regretted their decision, he thought none the worse of them for it; but the business was urgent and he must find men who could carry out his instructions.[14] John L'Isle complied and carried on his duties as Commissioner with an offensive air of superiority, while Lenthall, who had protested the loudest, 'wheeled about and . . . deserted those to whom he had engaged to adhere'. Mary did not try to influence her husband although she had reason to hope he would remain in office. There was a risk of losing the Chelsea house, which they had made their London home, and there were fourteen children to consider, four of them her own. Various supposed friends pressed Whitelocke to compromise and withdraw the offending letter. When he declined their manner changed, 'such is the dirty course of worldlings'.

He was not entirely sorry to be out of office, and busied himself during June improving the house and grounds at Fawley and attending to family business. At about that time impoverished Royalists were beginning to suffer decimation of their incomes or new sequestration of their land, virtually without appeal, at the hands of the hated major-generals who had been appointed by Cromwell to command the militia in eleven regions. Lord Willoughby was in an even worse plight than most, being imprisoned in the Tower under suspicion of treason. Although Whitelocke was advised not to meddle, since he was out of favour himself, he approached the Protector on his brother-in-law's behalf, and to good effect.

He was not to remain out of work for long. At the beginning of July he wrote, 'The Protector being good natured and sensible of his harsh proceeding against Widdrington and me, for keeping to that liberty of conscience which himself held to be everyone's right and that none ought to suffer for it, . . . he put in Sir Thomas Widdrington and me to be Commissioners of the Treasury.'[15] Like their fellow Commissioners, William Sydenham and young Edward Montagu (the future Admiral who would bring Charles II back to England), they received a salary of £1,000 each. Whitelocke was heartened by the friendly atmosphere at the Treasury and impressed by its efficiency; he recorded with pride that all receipts and payments were accounted for weekly, down to the last penny.

In the summer of 1655 he, Montagu and Walter Strickland drove to Tower Wharf, in one of Cromwell's coaches, to welcome the Swedish Ambassador, Christer Bonde. Strickland, like Whitelocke, was a former

Ambassador; Montagu, though less well known at that time, was a close friend of Cromwell's. A torch-light procession, with a hundred coaches and scores of outriders, escorted the Ambassador to his temporary residence in Westminster where Whitelocke stayed for supper. After a few days as a guest of Parliament, Bonde moved to Dorset House where he paid his own expenses; Whitelocke recalled with satisfaction that, throughout his stay in Uppsala, he had been granted free lodging.

For some months his time was divided between treasury business, the Swedish Ambassador and consultations with Cromwell. At the end of October he wrote:

The Protector often advised with me in his greatest affairs and I was faithful in my advice to him though sometimes it was less pleasing to him than the counsel of some others who, for their private ends, would flatter him and seldom differ from him in judgement, whereof he grew at last sensible. He seldom omitted to advise with me about his foreign affairs . . . and did much follow my counsel therein, and I did often press him to have frequent parliaments – against which he wanted not the counsel of others.[16]

In November Whitelocke was appointed to the important Committee for Trade and Navigation.

He spent what spare time he had with his family, travelling between London and Fawley and paying an occasional visit to Hertfordshire to see old Henry Dixon, his late sister's father-in-law. When he took his young daughter Mary to stay with Mr. and Mrs. Dixon at Braughing, near Pucke-ridge, old Dixon impetuously gave her some silver apostle spoons, without consulting his wife. That lady waited, tight-lipped, until breakfast time when she observed that she would need the spoons for the milk; Mary fetched them, and never saw them again. Dixon died a few months later and his widow was indignant that young Willoughby Whitelocke was to inherit her husband's house and land in Wandsworth, and that after her death the Hertfordshire estate would pass to him. The Wandsworth legacy was part of a settlement under which Whitelocke paid Dixon nearly £400 and agreed, as executor, to find £300 in legacies after the old man's death. He felt that, as usual, Dixon had struck a hard bargain; but it provided an inheritance for another of the boys and that was a matter of concern. A battered notebook, its corners apparently rubbed from being carried in his pocket, contains his view of the subject a few years later:

My dear children

God having blessed me with sixteen of you . . . I have made, and shall endeavour to make, a competent provision for you of temporal things which, though it be not so much as I hoped for or as others in my condition have done, yet I shall say to you (as your grandfather said to me upon the like occasion) be not troubled that I leave you less estate than those in my employment have commonly left their children, but be contented with it and . . . consider how many as good or better than ourselves have less. . . .

> Your truly loving father
> Bulstrode Whitelocke[17]

The eldest son by each wife was to be heir to an estate. Fawley Court would go to James and Phyllis Court to William. Chilton Lodge in Wiltshire was later willed to Samuel; this was a large house bought with Mary's money after the Restoration.[18] The girls could expect dowries of £1,500 each, while provision was gradually being made for the younger sons. In return for Whitelocke paying some mortgages on behalf of William Lilly, the astrologer promised to settle his property in Hersham and Walton on young Bulstrode.[19] In October 1655 that son received another substantial legacy, through an unexpected bequest from Dr. Thomas Winston. A double inheritance for one child at the expense of another was unjust so the parents decided, quite reasonably, that the old doctor had probably intended to help one of Mary's boys but had muddled the names. Accordingly they diverted the legacy to three-year-old Carleton, since Dr. Winston had been particularly fond of him. The scrivener who drafted the death-bed Will had saved it from being destroyed by the Earl of Portland; the Earl proceeded to contest it but eventually Whitelocke made a cash settlement to secure the inheritance for Carleton.[20] It consisted of lands in Northamptonshire, and the reversion of Blunt's Hall in Essex.

At about that time, perhaps with his other sons in mind, Whitelocke claimed his land in Ireland, having 'adventured' £400 during the Civil War. After 1653 Adventurers were entitled to draw for their Irish lands in lotteries conducted at Grocers' Hall; Whitelocke received 666 Irish acres of fertile land in Rathconrath, Westmeath; he also acquired some land in Kildare. An Irish acre was equivalent to 1.6 English acres so it was a substantial estate but the income, at two or three shillings an acre, can only have been worth about £100 a year.[21]

The irascible Swedish Ambassador was costing Whitelocke a good deal in time, money and patience. He complained, as other Ambassadors did, that it was difficult to gain access to the Protector, and that even when an audience was granted he was kept waiting for an hour. Whitelocke spoke to Cromwell 'freely and plainly' about this insult and the Protector promised not to allow it to happen again; he agreed that Whitelocke should invite Bonde to dinner and blame the discourtesy on to incompetent officials. When Bonde said he would like to see an Englishman's country home Whitelocke and Mary took him to stay with Sir Humphrey Forster at Aldermaston Court. The Ambassador travelled incognito and was able to enjoy a few days' hawking, hunting, fishing and playing cards. Whitelocke lent his own coach with six horses, as well as saddle horses for the servants, but his out-of-pocket expenses were not refunded. Perhaps Cromwell only approved unofficially; Whitelocke was a Commissioner at the Treasury and public servants were forbidden to make social contact with foreign diplomats.

Lord Say and Sele, Montagu and Whitelocke were eventually appointed to negotiate the new treaty with Sweden. England wished to strengthen the protestant trade bloc, but Bonde was dismayed at the proposal that the Low Countries might also be included. He was provoked, too, by the fortnight's delay while the articles were translated into Latin, complaining that they were 'sent . . . to one Mr. Milton, a blind man, to do this business.'[22] The treaty was signed in the summer of 1656, after which Bonde was lavishly entertained at Hampton Court. Suddenly, he became noticeably cooler towards Whitelocke, who was not a member of the Council, was clearly out of favour, and was not even invited to see him off at Gravesend. Although Cromwell was sometimes insensitive to people's feelings, the various snubs do not appear to have stemmed from him: George Fleetwood volunteered the information that Whitelocke had been kept off the Council by enemies who had two grudges against him. Their first complaint was that the Uppsala treaty inhibited English merchants from profiting out of the war with Spain.[23] Whitelocke reminded Fleetwood that the terms had been approved by Parliament and the Council itself; it was unfair to criticize him in the light of subsequent events. The second objection went deeper. The Council resented being told by a lawyer what they could or could not do according to law and precedent.[24] To this Whitelocke replied that lawyers had, in the past, been a curb on tyrants. It seemed that the new men in power rejected this help, preferring to surround themselves with soldiers. He hoped they would not have cause to regret their choice.[25] Since the appointment of the major-generals the previous year, with their moral and financial as well as military powers, the soldiers were increasingly regarded as the oppressors.

Elections for the Protector's Second Parliament were held in the summer of 1656, before Ambassador Bonde left England. This time Whitelocke was summoned to appear at the George, in Aylesbury, and was again returned to represent Buckinghamshire.[26] The Council, in collusion with the army, illegally excluded about one-third of the newly-elected Members of Parliament, apparently because of these Members' opposition to military rule. Whitelocke, although he was allowed to take his seat, believed that Cromwell and the Council thought him 'too much in public favour', which might explain why they humiliated him. In spite of this he was kept busy in the new Parliament, which assembled in September. Throughout the session Cromwell consulted him on foreign affairs, entrusted him with drafting the Bill for union with Scotland and appointed him to promote another Bill, for the registration of births, marriages and burials. Whitelocke also concerned himself in hotly-debated legislation to limit new building in and around London.[27] In spite of his suspicion of Roman Catholics, he insisted that recusants ought not to be at the mercy of arbitrary judgement but should be subject to legally defined rules, and he boldly opposed the Militia Bill, with its sanction for Cromwell's major-generals to raise money by indiscriminate decimation of the income of Royalists.

In spite of his unpopularity with the Council and the army, he was appointed, in October 1656, to the parliamentary committee which was to consider the case of James Naylor. That fanatical Quaker had already been rebuked for his excesses by George Fox; but the conviction that he was called to be a 'sign', a reminder of Christ's second coming, had compelled him to overcome his fears and ride into Bristol on a donkey, while adoring women strewed their clothes before him, chanting hosannahs as if he were the Messiah. His offence was all the more heinous because he looked like the popular image of Jesus Christ. The very mention of Naylor aroused that primitive ferocity which is generated by an assault on property or on accepted standards or beliefs. Before they had even heard the committee's report, or examined the charge of 'horrid blasphemy', rigid Presbyterians and military men had thought up Naylor's punishment. Under Mosaic law blasphemers were stoned to death. This sentence appealed to Major-General Downing. The toleration clause in the Instrument of Government was not, one Member said, intended to bolster up blasphemers. Another declared that if Naylor's antics were an example of liberty of conscience he begged God to deliver

12 Edward Hyde, Earl of Clarendon. After G. Soest

13 Believed to be George Cokain. Portrait by unknown artist in Harecourt United Reformed Church, London

14 George Moncke, 1st Duke of Albemarle

15 Archbishop Sheldon

him from such liberty; the Lord Jesus had been abused and trampled on and Members could not wait to vindicate God's honour.

With considerable courage Sir Gilbert Pickering and Sir William Strickland reminded Parliament that they must not condemn a man before hearing the evidence and the Lord President, Henry Lawrence, recalled that the apostles who asked for fire to be called from heaven were rebuked by their master; he went so far as to ask 'Is not God in every horse, in every stone, in every creature?' adding 'I do not believe that James Naylor thinks himself to be the only Christ, but that Christ is in him in the highest measure. This', he added quaintly, 'is sad.' The Master of the Rolls, on the other hand, had never heard of such a horrid sin in all his life, and strong men said that to hear of the blasphemy made their hearts tremble and their ears tingle. To the mortification of the rigid men, the lawyers, supported by the more merciful men, told them they could not, under the law as it stood, condemn Naylor to death. Downing and his friends had to content themselves with sentencing him to stand for two hours in the pillory at Westminster, to be whipped to the Old Exchange and be pilloried there for another two hours. Two days later he was to be branded with the letter B, for blasphemer, on his brow and to have his tongue bored with a hot iron. He was to be sent back to Bristol for further humiliation and whipping and then to be returned to London for imprisonment in Bridewell deprived of pen, paper, ink, and of any charity towards his maintenance.

Naylor had not been allowed to defend himself, no witnesses had been called, and when Cromwell asked by what right Parliament had judged the case they were at a loss for an answer. Whitelocke's main contribution to the debate was to cast doubt on the argument that God's will or God's law required a blasphemer's death, but he did not exert his usual tolerant influence. Perhaps his relations with the City of Bristol made him reticent. He regretted that the case had not been left to the Law Courts, deplored the amount of time Parliament had spent on the case and commented in his 'Diary' that Naylor was 'too fiercely persecuted by some rigid men'. The prisoner put his persecutors to shame. Without being told the charge against him he was called into Parliament to be informed of his punishment. He said simply that God had given him a body and would, he hoped, give him the spirit to endure the sentence. As he left the chamber he added 'the Lord lay not these things to your charge.' Thomas Burton, while abhorring the blasphemy, admitted that Naylor bore his punishment with fortitude and charity, even embracing the man who inflicted it.[28] It was not until

Whitelocke became Lord President of the Council that Naylor was eventually released.

In January 1657 Whitelocke was appointed to act as Speaker while Thomas Widdrington was away ill. In his orderly, systematic way he steered the House through their business with unaccustomed speed, keeping Members to the point in debate. His claim that he received a great deal of favourable comment was confirmed by Thomas Burton. When Widdrington heard this, and realized that his colleague, with the consent of the House, was pocketing the five pounds a head from applicants for naturalization, he got up from his sick bed and hurried back to work. With Lord Broghill, L'Isle and others, Whitelocke was active in preparing proposals that Cromwell should assume the Crown, and he was appointed Chairman of the committee which drew up the Humble Petition and Advice. This was a reversal of his attitude in 1652; but the circumstances had changed radically and he saw little to choose between a protector and a king, except that the constitution was built around a king and parliament. Cromwell agreed that he should assume the royal title, until pressure from the army and a growing conviction that he would be betraying the ideals of those who had fought with him compelled him to change his mind.[29]

Apart from this, the spring and early summer of 1657 passed pleasantly for Whitelocke. On instructions from Parliament he was working on a new translation of the Bible, helped by a group of scholars who met regularly at his home in Chelsea. This was work he enjoyed. The Authorized Version of 1611 had its faults but was still, in his view, the best translation in the world.[30] Parliament meantime was occupied with preparations for the Protector's installation, which took place on 26 June in Westminster Hall. It was a diluted version of the coronation, presented before the Lord Mayor of London, the Judges and Members of Parliament; Whitelocke was one of the principal officers at the ceremony, which was staged with considerable pomp. It coincided with the adjournment of Cromwell's second Parliament.

From that summer until the Protector's death, a year later, Whitelocke was back in favour. This change in Cromwell could have been a result of the proposals on kingship, but Whitelocke preferred to think that the Protector was finding the men close to him were too amenable, and was beginning to value disinterested advice. Whitelocke was the younger man by six years but even before the Civil War he had a good income and considerable standing as a lawyer. In the early years of their acquaintance there had been a trace of that aggressive uneasiness in Cromwell's attitude which a man in authority, even a genius, feels towards a subordinate with wider social and worldly experience than his own. In the last year of his life this wariness vanished and the Protector's manner became easy and affectionate. Whitelocke still criticized him for lack of gratitude, for discarding men who had served their turn, but consistently denied that Cromwell's actions were motivated by ambition. He and Lord Broghill and Thurloe were frequent visitors at Hampton Court.[31] They played bowls together, wrote verses 'according to each one's fancy' and talked endlessly; smoking was frowned on by strict Puritans but the servants knew to bring pipes, tobacco and a candle for Whitelocke, and Cromwell sometimes had a pipe himself. Then, after relaxing with them and 'laying aside his greatness', he would consult his friends on affairs of state.

Cromwell was obsessed with well-grounded fears of assassination. When Christina sent an Italian servant to deliver a letter he was reluctant to receive it, since Italians were notorious poisoners; Whitelocke told him that Christina would be offended if her messenger were turned away and suggested handling the communication himself. This made Cromwell laugh but he accepted the offer. They both read the letter without comment and for once Whitelocke refrained from recording its contents; it was apparently Christina's attempt to justify the gruesome execution (or murder) of her Chamberlain, Monaldeschi, on 10 November 1657, in the library at Fontainebleau.[32]

James Whitelocke, meanwhile, had been writing home from Paris, pestering his father for some horses. He was a feckless young man. When he was not asking for horses he wrote for money to pay his debts, yet soon after he returned to England he was knighted by the Protector. The title was probably intended as a compliment to his father, who never received an English knighthood but was designated Sir Bulstrode after Christina made him a Knight of the Order of Amaranth.[33] There had been talk of arranging a marriage between young Sir James and some lady of his father's choosing; James's eye lighted, however, on a gay young widow from Trumpington, near Cambridge. Mary Pilchard was encumbered by two children but was good looking and possessed a small fortune. James first confided his intentions in his uncle, Richard Bennet, and it was at a reception given by Bennet that Whitelocke met his future daughter-in-law. He thought her arrogant and ostentatious. Probably no woman would have been good enough for his eldest son, but at least he recognized that he could not stop the marriage. He made a settlement on James of £300 a year while the bride's father, Mr. Pyke, raised a marriage portion of £2,000; there was also money from the

Pilchard estate. After the wedding, James wrote ecstatically from Cambridge, 'This is a place where we shall never want company till we want means.' It did not occur to him that an income of £1,200 a year could ever run dry, so he was soon in debt again, and some years later sold the £300 annuity to keep his creditors at bay.

It was an expensive year for Whitelocke. His daughter Mary married George Nevill of Sheffield Park near Horsted Keynes, a member of Lord Abergavenny's family. Nevill's father had been a Gentleman of King Charles's Bedchamber; his widowed mother made an excuse not to attend the wedding in Chelsea and Whitelocke realized later that, unlike her son, she was a Roman Catholic. Another daughter, Anne, married George Hill, a young merchant whose father, Alderman Hill, gave a misleading impression as to his son's prospects. The next year, Cecilia married Samuel Harvey which cost her father a third dowry of £1,500. Sam proved to be a conscientious young man but his father, Colonel Edmund Harvey, was no asset to the family. Already, as a Colonel of Horse in Essex's army, there had been charges against him of extortion and murder yet he had prospered and, on the deprivation of Bishop Juxon in September 1647, he had bought the Bishop of London's residence, 'the Manor of Fulham, and divers lands, parcel of the Manor' for £7,617.2.10d.[34] In spite of his discreditable record in Parliament's service he was appointed one of the Commissioners to try King Charles, but he dissented from the verdict. Soon after the King's execution Cromwell made Harvey Collector of Customs and Navy Commissioner and, early in November 1655, was entertained by him at the Manor of Fulham. Perhaps the sumptuous dinner set Cromwell thinking. On 13 November the House of Commons ordered an examination of Harvey's accounts which (according to a later report by a Royalist) revealed a deficiency of £56,000. He was sent to the Tower but in February 1656 the embezzlement was charged against his estate and he was released. At the Restoration he was justly spared the fate of the Regicides but was sentenced to life imprisonment.[35] A Royalist described him as 'a little, inconsiderable rat', and Parliamentarians thought no better of him.

Whitelocke often dined with the Protector, who talked to him with great freedom; when Francis Rous, the presbyterian Provost of Eton, died in October 1657, Whitelocke applied for the post which he considered 'quiet and honourable and fit for a scholar' and he thought himself 'not wholly incapable of it'. He had coveted it when Rous was appointed in 1644 but had not, he felt, pushed himself forward enough. Again he was disappointed. The

Protector may not have been as ungrateful as he seemed, and possibly he wished to keep his friend free to guide Richard's clumsy steps in the years ahead. Although Whitelocke felt some resentment it was not in his nature to nurse a grudge. When the rift between Bradshaw and Cromwell widened he rejected advice from friends to side with Bradshaw (who never forgave Cromwell for assuming the title of Protector) and he worked instead for a better understanding between the two of them.

The Protectorate limped on, governing for some months without Parliament; in December 1657 rumours were rife that some congregations, whether from religious conviction or political defiance, intended to celebrate Christmas. This was forbidden by Ordinance, on the grounds that there was no scriptural warrant for the festival. Whitelocke took no notice of Christmas beyond keeping up the country custom of entertaining neighbours, tenants and labourers at the end of the year; yet he had opposed the Ordinance, believing that men should worship as they thought fit; unlike his colleagues he saw no justification for banning the Prayer Book under a regime which still boasted respect for freedom of conscience. He failed, however, to convince the Protector that Christmas observance was harmless, and the soldiers were called out. John Evelyn described how they pushed their muskets against communicants as they went up to the altar to receive the sacrament, then waited awkwardly until the service was over before detaining worshippers for questioning.[36]

The Commons' fanatical attitude towards Naylor had convinced Cromwell that a second parliamentary chamber was needed, to provide a counterbalance.[37] In December 1657, Whitelocke was invited to sit in the newly constituted 'Other House' with the title of Viscount Henley, but doubts as to the Protector's power to bestow titles or misgivings about the future made him decline the honour, on the vague pretext that he 'did not think it convenient for him'. He agreed nevertheless to serve in the new House.

After seven months' adjournment the Commons came back in a belligerent mood. Several of their moderate Members had been lost to the 'Other House'; those who remained resented its existence although earlier they had voted for it. They knew it had been restored to curb their powers. As usual the Protector took their hostility as a personal affront; in spite of Whitelocke's warnings that if he dissolved Parliament he would be in financial straits, Cromwell listened to the 'fierce men and flatterers'.

With customary efficiency, Thurloe's spies reported a number of plots and 'the Protector's party was full of unquietness and alarms'. Whitelocke advised against setting up a special court to deal with conspirators, urging that they should be tried under the normal procedure of the Courts, but Cromwell was 'too much in love with the new way' which he hoped would intimidate his enemies.[38] A special High Court was accordingly set up with Judges, Commissioners of the Great Seal and Commissioners of the Treasury. Whitelocke refused to serve.

A page from a notebook records the birth of his daughter Rebecca on 7 March 1657 [8];[39] she was born in the same year as his first grandchild. This page seems to be all that has survived of the original 'Diary'. In the 1660s he made a fair copy of it and the second volume of the transcript turned into his day-by-day record.

At the beginning of August, after terrible suffering, Cromwell's daughter Elizabeth Claypole died of cancer. Gay, worldly and outspoken, she had been fond of Whitelocke and had enjoyed teasing him; she had objected to his going to Sweden, saying tactlessly that he was being sent in the hope he would never return. A few days after her death Cromwell was taken ill and Whitelocke visited him at Hampton Court and stayed to dinner. The Protector 'discoursed privately . . . about his Great Business and about his own illness'.[40] 'The Great Business' had been the term applied to King Charles's trial and death; here it seems likely that Cromwell talked of his own death and of what must follow. It was their last meeting. On 3 September 1658 'after his many great actions and troubles, he now died quietly in his bed' but Whitelocke added sombrely 'some were of the opinion that he was poisoned'. There was a ferment of speculation as to the succession. When the relevant paper could not be found there were accusations of treachery. Whitelocke, who probably knew as much as anyone about Cromwell's intentions, wrote, 'Being satisfied that the Protector in his life-time, according to the Petition and Advice, had declared his son Richard to be his successor, the Council caused the same to be proclaimed in a solemn manner in London and Westminster.'

Whitelocke was often at Court in the next months and noted that members of the Council 'showed more than ordinary respect' for him, while Richard treated him with deference and turned to him for advice. He showed a fatherly concern for the young Protector who, like Christina of Sweden, was born in 1626, but while she had been educated as a prince Richard had grown up as a sporting, country gentleman. There was nothing in him of the decisive statesman but neither was he the gauche, 'tumble-down Dick' his enemies liked to make out. Whitelocke described an audience

granted to the French Ambassador when 'Richard did carry himself discreetly, and better than was expected'.[41] He always referred to the new
leader by his first name.

For some months, ambitious and disgruntled army officers grappled
among themselves for power. There were three factions: those loyal to the
Protector; the Republicans; and between the two the Wallingford House
group, centred on Charles Fleetwood who (although Cromwell had called
him a milksop) enjoyed a substantial following. Whitelocke, in the meantime, was urging Richard to summon a new Parliament and this assembled
on 27 January 1659; five days earlier he accepted re-appointment by Richard
as Commissioner of the Great Seal. He took his place in the 'Other House'
which was overweighted by army officers. By April, the officers had set
their minds on dissolution and, to that end, Fleetwood and some of his
friends approached their enemies, the civilian Republicans. Whitelocke still
hoped that the Commons, who had found time for angry debates about the
constitution and the 'Other House', would turn to the business of raising
money to settle the army's arrears, and to considering the complaints in the
officers' Humble Representation and Petition. They failed to do so. 'This', he
wrote, 'was the beginning of Richard's fall.' It was hastened by Fleetwood
and Desborough, both of them related to Richard by marriage. When the
inevitable collapse came it brought joy to the army and to the Republicans.
As the price of his deposition, Richard stipulated that his debts must be paid
and that he and his family should be granted an 'honourable subsistence'.[42]

Under pressure, Fleetwood and the General Council of Army Officers took
it on themselves, after a few weeks, to recall the Rump which Cromwell had
expelled in 1653. Remembering the early ideals and achievements of the
Long Parliament, Whitelocke hoped wistfully that it might still restore
freedom and peace. But the Parliament which met in 1640 had been a very
different assembly from the purged Parliament, that contemptible tail-end
which was summoned in 1659. This travesty of a once great assembly
floundered through the summer without policy or leadership, in an atmosphere of suspicion and insecurity. The republican Regicide, Thomas Scott,
detested Whitelocke whose son James had ousted him, in Richard's Parliament, as Member for Aylesbury. Restored to the Commons with the Rump
and appointed to the Council, Scott accused Whitelocke, along with
Anthony Ashley Cooper, of corresponding with Charles Stuart and Edward
Hyde and threatened to charge them before the Council.[43] Ashley Cooper
protested his innocence so vehemently that it 'bred in some the more

suspicion of him'. Fleetwood advised Whitelocke, if he were guilty, not to show his face in the Council and promised that the matter could be hushed up, but Whitelocke denied corresponding with Charles or any of his party and continued to serve.[44] His post as Commissioner of the Seal had ended in May, but his appointment in August as Lord President of the Council indicates that his word was accepted. His health was deteriorating and he was suffering increasing pain from stone in the kidneys. On his appointment as Lord President he moved, with his family, to a house in Scotland Yard to avoid the anguish of the daily coach journey from Chelsea.

In the purged Parliament of 1649 the Speaker had ranked as the chief official in the land; by the summer of 1659 the Lord President seems, in practice, to have assumed that position.[45] When John Lambert was sent north to suppress Sir George Booth's rising in Lancashire and Cheshire, it was to Whitelocke that he sent his despatches. At first there were two or three a day; by the time the army reached Lichfield Lambert was sending reports every two or three hours. When these arrived late at night White-locke sat up in bed reading them and dictating replies; if the news was of special importance he called the Council to meet in the middle of the night. There was widespread fear that the nation would be plunged into another civil war, but on 20 August a messenger brought news that Booth was on the run. In their ecstasy, the House sent Lambert a message of thanks and a jewel worth £1,000. Booth, dressed as a woman, was later captured in Newport Pagnell and committed to the Tower. Appeals on his behalf were made to Whitelocke by men as influential as Lord Say; but it was one thing to obtain release for Sir William Davenant, the poet, traditionally held to be Shakespeare's son, who was more interested in plots for operas than in plots against the government; it was another matter to be approached by an old rival on behalf of a traitor.[46]

Once more, the republican element in Parliament hardened against the soldiers who had won them respite and brushed aside a letter from a group of distinguished officers, including Lambert. One of the requests in the army's Petition and Proposals was for an increase in the number of officers. White-locke was hostile to military rule but thought it inopportune 'to exasperate those who had so lately done so great service to the Commonwealth, by denying them a matter not of great consequence'. He looked for a workable relationship. Haselrig and his republican supporters, with less sense of political reality, were meantime sponsoring an Act to make the raising of money without consent of Parliament high treason; after achieving this they proceeded to dismiss nearly a dozen high-ranking officers, including Desborough and Lambert himself. Conceited and pragmatic, Lambert knew how to deal with civilians. On 13 October 1659 some of his soldiers filed into Palace Yard; others took up positions at the approaches to Parliament and inside Westminster Hall; soldiers lined the streets and when Lenthall appeared they stopped his coach and sent him home ensuring, by the simple device of removing the Speaker, that the House was unable to function. Members of the Council of State were summoned to meet the officers. At the end of a long debate it was agreed that, in order to save bloodshed, Parliament should be dissolved and a new one summoned; during the interim the Council of Officers would maintain law and order. At the end of this chaotic day Whitelocke went home to Scotland Yard and told his servants to lock the doors and close the shutters. He was concerned to protect Mary and their week-old son, Stephen, from noisy demonstrations which he expected during the night. Apart from the woman who waited on his wife he sent everybody to bed, with orders to extinguish all fires and candles. He himself sat up all night. A little before daybreak he heard the soldiers clattering back to their quarters; in their exuberance they fired countless rounds of ammunition but his house, being in darkness, escaped their attentions and Mary slept undisturbed.

For several weeks the officers were intensely active. They appointed Charles Fleetwood Commander-in-Chief and John Lambert Major-General of the Forces in England and Scotland. Whitelocke was deeply troubled by the growth of military rule, and even more so when he learned, on 21 October, that he had been named to join the Committee of Safety, most of whose members were army officers. The Committee's purpose, he was told, was to preserve peace and direct the affairs of the Commonwealth until a new style of government could be devised; Fleetwood and Desborough urged him to serve as he would counterbalance extreme republicans, including young Harry Vane. He had little time to reflect for he was required to attend a meeting the following day. Mary feared reprisals against him if he collaborated with the soldiers but James and (which was more significant) George Cokain, supported by other friends, pressed him to accept the appointment in the interest of law and liberty since the officers, left to themselves, were likely to govern by the sword. There being no alternative government Whitelocke, by his own account, decided uneasily to join the Committee with the object of trying to keep its activities within the law. He was greeted next day by members of the Committee with every sign of respect. The

Republican and Regicide Edmund Ludlow put a different construction on Whitelocke's decision, accusing him, with three or four other civilians, of making a deal with the Wallingford House group by offering to raise £100,000 for the army, on condition their own privileges were safeguarded and the advice of Harry Vane was disregarded. According to Ludlow, this secret understanding virtually destroyed any hope of legal or ecclesiastical reform.[47] A few days after joining the Committee of Safety Whitelocke was re-appointed Keeper of the Great Seal.

Fear of civil war continued and commissions were signed for raising forces. Both Vane and Whitelocke were given command of a regiment of horse. It was recognized that powerful Presbyterians in the City of London were a threat to the Commonwealth. To counter this, Whitelocke, Fleetwood and Desborough were sent to address the Lord Mayor, Aldermen and Common Council of London at a meeting in Guildhall on 8 November 1659. Whitelocke informed them bluntly that letters had been intercepted which proved that General George Moncke had been behind several of the risings and had friends in the City ready to support him; he warned the audience of the need for constant vigilance against the 'old enemy', who would readily reduce the country to 'slavery under tyranny'.[48]

George Moncke, in Scotland, refused to support the Army Council. Whitelocke claimed to be one of the first to recognize and warn the nation of the General's design to restore the King. The warning was ignored. Lambert was, however, sent north to check Moncke and his army, if they should march on England, but he met three of the General's Commissioners in York and accepted their talk of peaceful intentions. Whitelocke insisted that Moncke was prevaricating and that Lambert must be ordered to advance. Again his advice was ignored. Moncke, meanwhile, informed a meeting in Scotland of 'a call from God and men to march into England to settle the peace there' and on 28 November there were 'letters of Moncke's march from Edinburgh towards England, with bag and baggage'. His army reached Berwick on 5 December but did not cross the Tweed until 1 January 1660. Whitelocke evidently wished to anticipate this move and was prepared to face civil war rather than unconditional monarchy. He urged Fleetwood, the Commander-in-Chief, to attack.

In spite of the crisis, the General Council of Officers managed to agree on seven basic articles of government. There should be no king, no protector, no house of lords, no imposition on conscience; the army should remain in being, the legislative and executive powers should be in separate hands and

Parliament should be elected by the people. A small working group was set up to devise a new constitution but only Whitelocke and John Wildman committed anything to paper. There was something in the draft which Whitelocke did not wish his enemies to see; a few weeks later he was alarmed in case Wildman had given him away, but the Colonel kept his own counsel.[49] It is a matter of conjecture whether, in the scheme he devised with Wildman, Whitelocke may himself have figured as the nation's first magistrate and leader or whether they named a king.

He sealed a proclamation for the Rump to be reconvened on 4 January 1660. When the General Council of Officers tried to lay down conditions of eligibility Whitelocke reminded them that he was under oath, and could not seal writs to summon Members of Parliament on terms dictated by the army. Nettled by this, one of the officers asserted that in time of emergency the Great Seal should not be entrusted to a lawyer but to a man who had risked his life for the Commonwealth. The Colonel had chosen the wrong target. Whitelocke replied:

The gentleman who so much disparaged lawyers would do well to call in mind the services performed by Ireton, Jones, Reynolds and others in the profession, during the war. As for myself, I have been exposed to such perils in the service of the State, particularly in my Embassy to Sweden, as would have appalled this much-speaking Colonel.

Fleetwood, Lambert and other officers supported Whitelocke and silenced their colleague.

By mid-December Whitelocke admitted to himself that restoration was inevitable. 'The King's party was very, very active and every man was guided by his own fancy and interest.' Lord Francis Willoughby, a Royalist though formerly a Parliament man, visited him on 22 December. He was accompanied by Charles Fleetwood's royalist brother, Sir William, by Major-General Richard Browne, who had fought for Parliament but had for months been plotting for the King, by Alderman John Robinson, who was also a Royalist, and a Mr. Loe. They confirmed Whitelocke's suspicion that Moncke was plotting to restore Charles II unconditionally, and that those who had governed since 1649 would be at the King's mercy. They proposed that Charles Fleetwood should be persuaded either to crush Moncke, or to anticipate him by sending a negotiator to Breda who would safeguard the principles for which Parliament had fought, and the lives and property of those who had been in control during the Interregnum. They feared that if the King were not restored on agreed terms the prospect would be grim for men in Whitelocke's position since 'the King and his party . . . were sufficiently enraged against them, and in need of repairing their broken fortunes.'

On their advice Whitelocke went to the Commander-in-Chief with the alternative proposals. Fleetwood was attentive. Would Whitelocke be prepared to join him on the battlefield or else sail for the Netherlands and on to Breda? Whitelocke said he would do either. Fleetwood decided to send him to the King and told him to be off the same evening or early next day; his experience in treating with Charles I and with Christina, his standing as the leading Parliamentarian and not least his possession of the Great Seal made Whitelocke the obvious choice.

As he left the room he ran into Desborough, Vane and Berry who had been waiting in the anteroom. On seeing them Fleetwood told him to wait. Fifteen minutes later, after consulting them, he came out much distressed crying, 'I cannot do it. I cannot do it.' His friends had reminded him of a promise not to approach Charles without Lambert's consent. Whitelocke stressed the urgency but Fleetwood, with stubborn weakness, could only wail, 'I cannot do it without him.' Whitelocke retorted, 'You will ruin yourself and your friends,' but the Commander-in-Chief answered feebly, 'I cannot help it.'

It had been worth the attempt. Had Fleetwood held to his resolution the Restoration might have been based on a limited constitutional monarchy, such as Whitelocke had envisaged for some years, and both men's place in history would have been greatly enhanced.[50] The presence of three Republicans in an anteroom tipped the balance. It was the end of Whitelocke's political career.

Chapter Eleven

'Bonfires and Joys'

By the turn of the year, the former Lord President of the Council was on the run. After the fateful encounter with Fleetwood he had resisted pressure from Ingoldsby and another Colonel to act on his own and deliver the Great Seal into the King's hands.[1] It would have been treachery to those he worked with, but it might have brought him fame and a dukedom. Instead he busied himself sealing writs for the new Parliament, which assembled on 26 December 1659. Lenthall, who was reinstated as Speaker, urged him to take his seat as proof that, although he had collaborated with the officers, he still accepted Parliament's authority.[2] In spite of assurances that he would be made welcome, Whitelocke was doubtful and his fears were confirmed when he called on his republican friend, Sir Arthur Haselrig, who gave him a very cool reception; other friends in the Commons were equally reserved, while his enemy, Thomas Scott, wanted him hanged as a traitor with the Great Seal round his neck.

In fear for his life he decided to disappear and on 30 December, a bitter snowy night, he strapped on a sword-belt with a great basket-hilted sword, wrapped himself in a voluminous grey cloak and rode from Bishopsgate Street towards Hertfordshire, accompanied by a manservant of brother Wilson's. Two miles out of London he turned into a gateway and pulled on an enormous grey wig to complete the disguise. His companion, who had not been long in Wilson's service, was afraid the new master was planning a robbery but Whitelocke spoke reassuringly as they rode northward through the snow. They stopped at an inn for the night, probably at Waltham Cross or Cheshunt, then hung about until dusk next day before jogging on towards Hunsdon House, near Stanstead Abbots, where they arrived after dark. This former palace of Henry VIII, in which the royal children Mary, Elizabeth and Edward once lived, had belonged, since 1653, to Colonel William Willoughby.[3] That staunch Royalist did not at first recognize his brother-in-law. When he did, he took the fugitive upstairs to a secluded suite of rooms consisting of a small dining-room, a bedroom leading off it and an inner room for the servant.[4] For the next ten days William and Anne Willoughby took it in turns to sit with their guest at meal times and for part of the day. They had been his support when Frances died and, although they had frowned on his third marriage, they were still trusted friends. They kept his identity a secret from the servants and children and told his man to refer to him by an assumed name; only the eldest son,

George, 'said that he knew but would take no notice'. It was ironical that a distinguished Parliamentarian should take refuge from Parliament among Royalists, but it did not denote any change of allegiance.

Mary stayed on with the Wilsons in London. She kept her husband informed of events at Westminster, addressing her letters to Colonel Willoughby. On her husband's instructions she locked the Great Seal, the stamp of government authority, in a portable desk and delivered it into the Speaker's hands. Lenthall commended Whitelocke's good sense in surrendering it and promised that this would be remembered in his favour. Perhaps he was aware of the temptation to divert it to Flanders. Having disposed of the Seal, Mary went home and burned those of her husband's papers which she considered incriminating. Later, he wrote in the 'Diary' that her action made his record less perfect, 'but she did [it] in pure love'.[5] In the meantime Vane, Lambert, Desborough and other members of the Committee of Safety, had been sent home ignominiously and were under house arrest. Whitelocke's timely disappearance had saved him from a similar fate.

After some days in hiding, he heard that Parliament was to review the case of Members of the Rump against whom objections had been raised. This brought him back to London where he spent a few hours with the family but, as he still thought it wise to keep out of sight, Mary took him by night to an apothecary's house on Tower Hill where he could take refuge. She settled him into the small, smoke-grimed room, then walked home alone through the deserted streets of the city. Two nights later she trudged back through the dirt and the dark with an apron full of provisions. The tearful girl who had clung round her husband before he sailed for Sweden had grown into a resourceful and resolute woman. Whitelocke had soon had enough of lonely discomfort. One night he turned up at the Wilsons without warning and never went back to his hide-out.

His political and financial predicament was by this time common knowledge; when Sir Ralph Verney planned to buy the deer from Fawley for his own park he wrote to Winwood 'if it be known at Henley that the deer are sold, my Lord Whitelocke being now under a little cloud, they will endeavour to share with his Lordship, therefore the sooner and the privater the business be done, the better.'[6]

Several times Parliament fixed a date for hearing Whitelocke's case then postponed it to give way to more pressing business. He was saved, unexpectedly, from enemies in the House by the arrival of his new arch-enemy. In spite of letters from General Moncke to the Commons, in which he admitted that he had prevaricated with Fleetwood but promised to deal faithfully with them, Whitelocke consistently declared that Moncke had no intention of submitting to the men at Westminster. By the time the General started marching south his unspoken aim was widely recognized, and when he entered London on 3 February 1660 he was acclaimed like a hero. His arrival prevented Whitelocke's case being heard, and within a week the nation's new idol was demanding that the Rump should readmit the secluded (or excluded) Members, without trial or investigation. This was to be followed by early dissolution leading to the election of a *free Parliament*. The magic words were bandied about suffused with patriotism and promise of prosperity. Free Parliament meant the King's restoration.

The air was full of excited confusion. Church bells rang; bonfires blazed in the streets; Cavaliers flocked into London boasting that the King would soon be in England. Much that Parliament had enacted was reversed. Members were freed from their oath of allegiance; traitors to the Commonwealth were released; a loan was raised to settle the English soldiers' arrears of pay; above all, money started to flow again in the City. George Moncke, promoter and patron of all these delights, was proclaimed General of the Forces of England, Scotland and Ireland.

Parliament dissolved itself in March and Whitelocke decided not to stand again. He left London, lived for short spells at Fawley and with the Wilsons at a house in Greenwich, was 'very careful of his words and actions and stayed not long in one place'. Loyalties were changing overnight. Sir Harbottle Grimston, a Presbyterian and formerly a Parliament man, declared himself a supporter of Charles II and was appointed Speaker of the House of Commons in the Convention Parliament; Colonel Alexander Popham, who had served under Cromwell, raised a troop of horsemen to pay homage at the Restoration; Luke Robinson 'formerly a most fierce man against the King' recanted in a tearful speech which went on for an hour and a half.[7] Whitelocke, making few concessions to the times, was in constant fear of arrest. Charles Stuart was corresponding with the freely elected House of Commons and on 8 May he was proclaimed King, at which 'the bells rang, the great guns and small shot gave many volleys and the City was full of bonfires and joys.'[8]

Three days later Whitelocke was walking down a road in Greenwich, when he met a well-dressed man with a large feather in his hat and a sword by his side. This unmistakable Cavalier greeted him by name. Alert for trouble Whitelocke said he did not know the stranger, who introduced himself as Colonel Napper and said he had reason to remember Whitelocke from earlier kindnesses, having once been his servant. It was Thomas Napper who had been apprenticed to him as a clerk in 1633; Napper to whom he had written from France about two little coats for James; Napper who left his service to better himself with Attorney General Bankes. He had subsequently fought for Charles II, commanded a regiment in the French army and, as it later appeared, changed his name to the more high-sounding Nappier. He volunteered that he could arrange an introduction to 'the King of England who would now shortly be restored to his right'. Whitelocke welcomed the offer and some days later thought it prudent to write a note to the Speaker of the House of Commons, his old friend Harbottle Grimston, at whose first wedding he had played the coachman:

Sir

I had waited on you, but that I am in great extremity troubled with the tormenting disease of the stone, and therefore ask your pardon for presenting my humble thanks to you for your favour, and my suit unto you by these lines, which is that if any gentlemen have made application to you (as I am told some have) that their names may be entered with you as persons desiring to lay hold on His Majesty's gracious pardon within the 40 days prescribed, I desire that my name, and the name of my son James, may likewise be entered among the rest, as humbly praying to be admitted to lay hold on His Majesty's gracious pardon within the time limited.

    I entreat the continuance of your favour to
        Your ancient friend and most faithful servant
            B. Whitelocke.[9]

May 22
1660

The Bill of General Pardon Indemnity and Oblivion had been introduced on 9 May. It was to cover everyone in the kingdom except those whom Parliament specifically excluded under two categories: those who were to be hanged as traitors and those permanently excluded from office-holding. There was no need for Whitelocke to apply on behalf of the younger boys, but James had attained the rank of Colonel in Cromwell's army, while he himself had fought for Parliament and the ambassadorship carried the rank of General; he had also held office as Governor of a garrison, Governor of Windsor Castle, Keeper of the Great Seal and Lord President of the Council. As a Judge in Chancery he had inevitably made enemies and he knew that he was vulnerable.

Before the end of the month Charles landed near Dover. Evelyn and

Pepys gave exuberant descriptions of the procession through London. Whitelocke's account was flat and factual. He was like a widow at a wedding; recalling as he must have done the part he himself had played in earlier ceremonies he could only feel 'full of trouble in the midst of this jollity'.

It was a time for settling old scores. In the Commons Sir Ralph Assheton, a Presbyterian from Lancashire against whom Whitelocke had once made an alimony order, demanded persistently that the man who once sat in judgement on him should be excluded from the General Pardon; but malice can grow tedious, and those who knew the facts took to chanting 'alimony, alimony' when Assheton stood up to speak, which 'shamed and stopped his mouth'. The Presbyterian, William Prynne, was already encouraging the Commons to extend the death sentence beyond the Regicides; he busily thumbed through parliamentary records in search of damaging evidence against Whitelocke, who claimed that for his part he 'never did half so much against the King as Prynne had done'.[10] Prynne's animus may have dated back to the days when he lost his ears while young Whitelocke, at Court, arranged the music for a royal masque, but Whitelocke believed it stemmed from his having corrected Prynne's inaccuracies in Parliament.[11] Embittered, courageous and truculent, Prynne could not bear to be crossed. As a Parliamentarian he had claimed at one time that the people could lawfully depose an erring king, but he had deplored the execution of Charles I, and had, in good faith, advanced the cause of restoration. Consequently he was in favour with the King and was once more serving in Parliament. Friends advised Whitelocke to propitiate this dangerous enemy but he 'could not bring his heart to it'. Mary had no such false pride and as she and Rowland Wilson had once befriended Prynne, when he was in trouble with Archbishop Laud, she went to Lincoln's Inn to plead with him. After a long delay she was admitted to his study. Prynne embarked at once on a tirade against her husband, threatening to have him excluded from the pardon, 'testifying his . . . malice and bloody mind' and treating her 'more like a kitchen-maid than a gentlewoman'. She left in such distress that she nearly collapsed on the way home.

Whitelocke had received a letter from the city of Oxford asking him not to take it amiss if they acknowledged the Earl of Berkshire as their High Steward, since that nobleman had never resigned; this was a loss to pride and to pocket.[12] Sir Heneage Finch, whom Whitelocke had previously helped, was appointed Solicitor-General on 6 June, and 'now to curry favour' demanded Whitelocke's exclusion from the Act of Pardon, until Colonel

Willoughby suggested that Parliament might also hang some of Finch's friends.[13] Because of the imminent danger Whitelocke prepared a defence of his actions during the previous twenty years under the title 'The Case of Bulstrode Whitelocke, Knight' and handed copies of it to friends in both Houses of Parliament. The defence stressed that he had tried to prevent the Civil War and had, at personal risk, negotiated as a Commissioner for several peace treaties; he referred irrelevantly to Fawley Court being sacked by royalist soldiers which had cost him £10,000; he had been riding the circuit when Parliament first nominated him as a Commissioner of the Great Seal during the lifetime of Charles I; the appointment had been unsolicited and he had accepted it reluctantly, at financial loss to himself, resigning it later when required to execute as law an Ordinance not promoted by Parliament; he had refused to take part in the King's trial or in other political trials on capital charges (he ignored the part he had played in Strafford's trial); he had not participated in sequestration nor in excluding any Member from Parliament; he had gone as Ambassador to Sweden under pressure from Cromwell; Christina had testified that he spoke with courtesy of Charles Stuart and other adversaries, while Cromwell suspected him of favouring some form of monarchy. He had been out of the country when the protectorate was announced; on his return he had submitted to policies which he could not alter. He restated his reasons for joining the Committee of Safety, adding that he had warned the army officers that he was likely to oppose some of their designs. In 1659 he had again accepted the Great Seal, to ensure its lawful use. He made the surprising claim that, without breach of trust, he had been of service in connection with the Restoration and that Lord Francis Willoughby and Sir Humphrey Bennet could vouch for this. (It seems, from a Commons debate, that he had sent over £500 to the King.) He also circulated a shorter document, signed by prominent Royalists whom he had helped during the Interregnum, in which they appealed for him to be included in the General Pardon. He was fighting for his life and to save the family from destitution.

His most formidable enemy was George Moncke. Between 1656 and 1659 the General had written thanking him for various services and expressing, in fulsome terms, indebtedness and lasting friendship.[14] He had probably assumed that Whitelocke, a useful ally and Keeper of the Great Seal, would support him but finding he was wrong he turned vindictive. Whitelocke wrote him a humble letter and later demanded an explanation for the change of attitude. Moncke indicated that he had not forgiven his former friend for publicly warning the City of London of the plan to bring in King Charles.[15] This foresight could have 'spoiled all the business'. Since Moncke was already glorying in the fulfilment of the design which Royalist agents had put before him eighteen months earlier, and as he was shortly to be created Duke of Albemarle it seemed unnecessary for him to be so angry. Conceding that they had worked for different ends Whitelocke appealed to his generosity, saying that a man of honour did not trample on a former enemy or seek to ruin him, but Moncke 'churlishly went away' and continued to press for Whitelocke's exclusion from the General Pardon. William Willoughby astonished his brother-in-law by expressing pleasure at this news; he explained that Moncke had become so overbearing and so eager to look after his friends that many Members of Parliament opposed him on principle. Willoughby proceeded to canvass votes for Whitelocke from Moncke's new opponents.

Two lists were being compiled of men to be excluded from the General Pardon. If Whitelocke's name appeared on the first he would be hanged with the Regicides, his estate would be confiscated and Mary and the children would be left destitute. If it appeared on the second he would be subject to such fines as Parliament might impose and be debarred from ever again holding office. During June he learned that his name had escaped the first list in the Lower House but he was still in danger from the Upper House, where Lord Francis Willoughby seemed to be almost alone in supporting him. Young Lord Falkland, who had once come to him in tears begging for an appointment, was urging the Lords to vote for the execution of his father's old friend. Other Members were eager to punish the man who, in his official capacity, had signed warrants for their committal or that of their relatives, as traitors. Their Lordships must have remembered too that it was Whitelocke who, in 1649, drafted the Bill for abolishing the Upper Chamber. The majority of them were returning to power impoverished by years of decimation, sequestration and often exile. Whitelocke was at their mercy.

The Lady Mary Howard, whom he had committed to prison for supporting Booth's rebellion, intended to make the most of the new turn of events. Whitelocke called to discuss her grievance with her father, the Earl of Berkshire. The Earl opened the interview by deriding Members of Cromwell's 'Other House' as common working men; Whitelocke observed mildly that they had included members of old English families, but he added that this was not what he had come to discuss. Berkshire conceded that some of Cromwell's Lords were indeed gentlemen, and that he was not implying that Whitelocke and his sort were 'mechanic fellows'. Turning to the business of his daughter, he demanded £500 in reparation for her sufferings; if this were not forthcoming he would see to it that Whitelocke was excluded from the General Pardon. It is senseless to argue with a vulture, so the ransom was paid.

Whitelocke was fighting for his dignity as well as for his life. He told William Willoughby that 'he was resolved not to submit himself a guilty person more than others, but rather to stand it out to the utmost'. The Colonel liked him for showing 'so much mettle' and promised to 'do the best he could for him'. Reasoned argument and legal defence were of little use. Extortionate demands had to be met. Whitelocke managed nevertheless to retain some initiative, and nowhere was this more evident than at the audience with Charles II.

Colonel Nappier was as good as his word. He introduced the two men who had been his masters, then left them alone. After Whitelocke had gone through the formality of kneeling to entreat pardon he and the King talked freely for nearly an hour, discussing Swedish and parliamentary business with the easy equality which had characterized the meetings with Christina. When the audience was drawing to a close, Whitelocke told the King that he had in his custody books and manuscripts from the Royal Library which he had saved from plunder; he had deposited them in a trunk in an outer room. Charles sent for it and proceeded to go through the contents item by item, with the relish of a connoisseur. The greatest treasure was the 'Septuagint' or 'Codex Alexandrinus', the manuscript of the Bible in Greek written in the first half of the fifth century. Whitelocke claimed that the only other copy was in the Vatican and that he had been offered £4,000 to sell the 'Alexandrinus' overseas.[16] There were other rare books and some manuscripts of his own which he presented to the King, with a collection of antique coins; the King displayed his skill at reading the inscriptions on the coins but one of the books baffled him. Whitelocke told him it was in His Majesty's mother tongue; Charles objected that it was not in English, to which Whitelocke replied that it was older than that, for it was British; it was in fact a Welsh dictionary. The King smiled saying he was indeed a Briton in origin. Finally, he gave Whitelocke his hand to kiss and is reputed to have closed the meeting with the gracious, if ominous words, 'Mr. Whitelocke go into the country; do not trouble yourself any more about state affairs, and take care of your wife – and your sixteen children.'[17]

Some months later Thomas Nappier called to collect his reward. There had been no hint that he expected to be paid for the introduction, but it had been of value and Whitelocke reckoned £100 would be a generous return. His former clerk was disgusted, having counted on at least £500. In the end Whitelocke gave him £250 which Nappier coldly accepted. It has been alleged that the King imposed an illegal fine of £90,000. Whitelocke's 'Diary' makes no mention of this fantastic figure; he did however agree to pay two years' income from his estates as the price of his pardon, if William Willoughby could purchase it from Parliament. According to another report the King made him a gift of the coronation Bible and Prayer Book; if this is true it may have been in recompense for the manuscripts.[18]

In spite of the audience with the King, Whitelocke still dreaded his name appearing, as Lenthall's did, on the list which would exclude him from ever holding office again. When he heard that, by a margin of fifty votes, his name had escaped both lists he made up his mind to obtain his costly pardon under seal. He was perplexed by the delay in accomplishing this until the Lady Mary Howard's brother, Sir Robert, whom he had helped during the Interregnum, explained that a gift of £250 to the Lord Chancellor was probably needed. Whitelocke was shocked by such an 'unhandsome action in an old and intimate friend', for the Chancellor was his former friend Edward Hyde; but he paid the bribe and received his pardon under seal at a further cost of some £32.[19] Years later when Whitelocke was living in relative poverty the Earl of Clarendon, as Lord Chancellor Hyde became in 1661, sent a message asking him to arrange delivery of a hundred loads of billet. Possibly this was an idiom from their student days, a billet being firewood, something quickly expended. Whatever the usage, Whitelocke understood well enough that he was required to send a present of a hundred pounds.[20]

Early in October 1660 the family moved to a pleasant brick house with a garden in Coleman Street. Mary thought the fresh air of Moorfields would be good for the children, and she and her husband may have been attracted by the prospect of joining John Goodwin's Independent congregation.[21] They could not foresee the bad name the street was to earn. In any case this might not have deterred them, for Whitelocke was paying scant regard to his own safety. Deciding to build up a new legal practice he engaged as his clerk a man named Joseph Nanson, who had served the notorious republican Sir Arthur Haselrig; he appointed as the children's tutor a Mr. Chancey, just returned from the free-thinking climate of New England; his clients included dissenters, men petitioning for pardon and political prisoners.

Such associates could only bring him under suspicion. Parliamentarians who failed to turn with the tide learned what it was like to be a vanquished people, outside the protection of the law.

Early in November Whitelocke wrote to Lord Willoughby with the engaging buoyancy of a man who has nothing to lose:

Dear Brother

. . . When I had the honour to attend His Majesty, he was pleased to receive my submission with very gracious respect (much more than I have received from some of his subjects), and freely to give me his pardon. This called to my memory our story of King William I, who by force conquered the bodies of some of the English, but gave pardon to all that submitted and employment equal with the Normans. Our King hath conquered the hearts and affections of his people. I am sure he hath mine. . . .

I entreat your advice. I have spent much time in collecting matters relating to government of this kingdom, and somewhat of others. . . . I know the King cannot have leisure to read many books, yet such matters as these are not improper for a prince's view, and if I thought my pains . . . might be useful and acceptable to His Majesty where, with little trouble, he might inform himself . . . and see at once much reading digested and contracted on this subject, I should willingly prepare and present these fruits of my labours to him. I have imparted this to none but yourself, and if you judge it worthy the proposal you will take your opportunity and let me know His Majesty's pleasure, that I may go in hand with it, and none to know where His Majesty hath these things but himself and you. . . .

Your most obliged faithful servant and brother
10 Nov. 1660   B. Whitelocke.[22]

Lord Willoughby was not responsive, but Whitelocke was undeterred and his compilation of 'Notes upon the King's Writ for choosing Members of Parliament' was eventually commended by Clarendon and accepted by the King, despite its cheekily democratic text from the Book of Proverbs: 'In the multitude of counsellors there is safety.'[23]

Money troubles continued to haunt Whitelocke in petty ways as well as in large ones. Dr. Samuel Wilkinson, the parson of his former parish in Chelsea, had for years placed a pew at the family's disposal, free of charge, while they occupied Buckingham's house, but realizing that Whitelocke was under a cloud Wilkinson sent him an account for three years' pew rent, amounting to eighteen pounds.[24] James, who had fled to France to escape his creditors, wrote home for money. Worst of all, in November 1660 Lord Chancellor Hyde wrote to say that he had met Gilbert Sheldon, the new Bishop of London, at a play in the Middle Temple and Sheldon had spoken about reclaiming the Manor of Fulham.[25] This was occupied by young Samuel Harvey who had married Whitelocke's daughter Cecilia; the Bishop hoped there would be no unpleasantness over getting them out. Whitelocke had always realized the hazard of buying forfeited lands and had avoided doing so himself, but had not objected to the Manor being settled on the young couple, by Sam's father, Colonel Edmund Harvey. The Colonel, with his unfortunate record, was serving a life sentence passed on him in October.

Whitelocke recognized that the claim could not be resisted and took his son-in-law to see Bishop Sheldon, warning him to be very circumspect. He assured the Bishop that Sam had had no part in purchasing the Manor and undertook that the property would be handed over on demand. Sheldon seemed so genial that Whitelocke told him Cecilia was expecting her first baby, and as she was a nervous girl he hoped she might be allowed to remain at the Manor until after the child was born. He particularly asked the Bishop not to send in soldiers to evict the family. Sheldon agreed affably to both requests.

On the Sunday before Christmas a party of soldiers burst into Fulham Manor to take possession for the Bishop. Cursing and swearing, they proceeded to ransack the house, breaking open chests and trunks and helping themselves to bed linen, clothing, money and family plate. They even went off with the baby linen. Cecilia and Sam were destitute. Although Whitelocke gave them a home Sam's spirit was broken and within eighteen months he and his wife and their child were dead. 'All their blood', Whitelocke was to write with unaccustomed bitterness, 'lies at the door of that Bishop.'

Chapter Twelve

Pardon – and Oblivion

Against the slander of a quizzical look, a casual word, or a deprecating silence there is no defence. Whitelocke was beginning to experience the power of that unwritten black-list, which bars a man from work whenever his name comes up. In January 1661, months after his pardon had been sealed, he and John Thurloe went to Charterhouse near Smithfield to attend a Governors' meeting.[1] They were drawn aside however by two recently appointed Governors, the Earls of Manchester and Northumberland, who explained that when the list of Governors had come up for review by the Council, the King had announced that Whitelocke and Thurloe 'were not fit men to be there'. Whitelocke asked whether His Majesty had made any specific charge against him. The cryptic answer 'No, but this was too much' told him what he already knew, that he was living at the wrong address.

The trouble had started a few weeks earlier. At the beginning of January he and Mary had been spending a few days at Fawley, without the family, when news reached them of riots in Coleman Street. Alarmed for the children's safety Mary set off for London riding behind her chaplain, Mr. Hartcliff, but on the way the minister took fright and left her to finish the journey by stage coach, accompanied only by a manservant. They reached Coleman Street the same night, and found the children scared but unhurt. Soldiers had searched the house for arms and confiscated two finely-wrought foreign guns. Mary returned to Fawley with an account of the troubles which her husband dismissed as 'the mad freak of Venner and his little party'. It cannot have taken him entirely by surprise. Four years earlier Thomas Venner of Coleman Street, a vintner by trade, had plotted with other Fifth Monarchy Men against Cromwell, the 'Bastard of Ashdod'. Since the Restoration some of them had turned to Whitelocke for legal advice, although he was not in sympathy with their bloodthirsty campaign to establish the kingdom of God, their great Fifth Monarchy, by the sword. On 6 January Venner had been rousing himself and the congregation with his exhortations at a conventicle in Coleman Street and they had come out of the meeting alight with apocalyptic zeal. Calculations based on the Book of Daniel and Revelation convinced them that the reign of King Jesus was at hand. Stationing themselves at St. Paul's, they asked passers by whom they were for. When one man answered that he was for King Charles, they told him they were for King Jesus and shot him through the heart. About fifty of them terrorized the City on 6 and 9 January until 700 horsemen were

sent in; Venner was captured, tried at the Old Bailey, then hanged and
quartered outside the Coleman Street meeting house on 19 January.[2]

On returning to London Whitelocke was astonished to learn that enemies
had accused him to the King of living in Coleman Street in order to advise
the conspirators. Both the Lord Chancellor and the Attorney General
(Whitelocke's old friend, Geoffrey Palmer) told him he had better move out
of the district. Their words sounded more like a command than a piece of
friendly advice. It was a few days after these conversations and three days
after Venner's execution, that Whitelocke learned of the King's attempt to
force him off the governing body at Charterhouse. Defying the warnings,
he continued to live in Coleman Street for another eighteen months and
went on advising dissenters. He did not resign from Charterhouse; when
some of the Governors asked why not, Clarendon for once spoke up for
him, but it does not appear that Whitelocke attended any more meetings.
Professionally he never recovered.

With no regular salary he was in difficulties raising money to meet fines
and 'gratifications'. He was cheated over the sale of timber to a crown
official, who happened to be related to George Moncke, the newly-created
Duke of Albemarle. Lord Lovelace revoked his earlier promise, which he
had signed under seal, and announced that his son would not, after all,
surrender his rights in Blunsden, the estate which Whitelocke had bought
for £10,000 in 1652 in response to an urgent appeal from Lovelace. It was
agreed to refer the dispute to arbitration and Whitelocke's relative Adrian
May, a staunch Royalist, acting on his behalf recommended a further payment of £2,000, in return for which Lovelace must induce his heir to confirm the sale; Lovelace affected to be so indignant that he would have nothing
more to do with arbitration. He offered to have the purchase confirmed in
return for a payment of £5,000. Clarendon commented fatuously that 'It
was very unjust and that he would rather have lived upon bread and water
than have dealt so.' His own estate at Pyrton, near Swindon, happened to be
'next hedge' to Blunsden, and he only waited for Whitelocke to establish
the title before stepping in to buy the place himself. Whitelocke and Mary
were reluctant to sell but 'it was thought not safe to deny the Chancellor';[3]
Clarendon paid £13,000 of which, according to the 'Diary', Lovelace
appropriated £6,000. Blunsden had evidently been bought with Mary's
money, for her relatives humiliated Whitelocke by insisting that receipts
from its sale must be held in trust by Samuel Wilson.

When George Villiers, second Duke of Buckingham, reclaimed his great house in Chelsea negotiations were again one-sided. The Duke had escaped to the continent during the Interregnum and, when the opportunity arose, had promised that whatever his kinsman spent on the house would be repaid when he 'came into his own again'.[4] In the event, the Duke's agent brushed aside Whitelocke's claim for £2,000 and paid only half that sum.

There were mounting troubles within the family. Mary, who had shown great fortitude while her husband was in danger, found it hard to bear the nibbling poverty which eroded her children's inheritance. James kept up a steady demand for money. Hester became infatuated with a dissolute young man, married him without her father's consent and went to live in Barbados. Anne died of 'spotted fever' and Whitelocke, in his sorrow, longed to escape from meeting people. A few years later, in 1665, there was to be a further shock; his son-in-law George Nevill was out hunting one day and stopped at a tavern in Croydon. A group of drunkards picked a quarrel with his servants and, as he came down the stairs to intervene, one of them stabbed him in the stomach. He was brought to London in a litter and, because his father had been in the service of Charles I, the Queen Mother, Henrietta Maria, sent her own physician and surgeon to tend him; but in spite of their care he died, leaving his widow Mary with five young children and a load of debt. Thirty years later their son George succeeded to the title of Lord Bergavenny, or Abergavenny. Among Whitelocke's youngest children, Sam and Bigley contracted smallpox and Stephen injured a hip-bone; two bone-setters and a surgeon disagreed on its diagnosis and it remained for the famous Irish 'stroker', Valentine Greatraks, to effect a cure.[5] Mr. Chancey, the children's tutor, gave Carleton a blow on the head with a heavy book and the boy started suffering from bouts of nose-bleeding, which were not finally staunched until someone applied stinging nettles to his nostrils. Whitelocke dismissed Chancey and in his place appointed a Mr. James Pearson, who became a valued friend to the family.

Measures against nonconformists had begun with the Corporation Act of 1661, the first of the four oppressive statutes which came to be known as the Clarendon Code although the Chancellor did not initiate them. Between May 1661 and April 1662 Whitelocke made repeated representations to Clarendon concerning liberty of conscience for nonconformists, or 'fanatics', in general and for Independents in particular. The King took for granted a rigid interpretation of right worship and doctrine within the Anglican Church, but was looking for a formula by which he could legalize liberty of conscience outside the Church. Ostensibly, this was for the benefit of nonconformists but his true intention was to ease the pressure on Roman Catholics. Clarendon, for his part, favoured broadening the Church of England to embrace a greater diversity of view.[6] In March 1662 he invited Whitelocke to bring Thomas Goodwin, Thomas Mallory and another nonconformist to meet him. Dr. Goodwin had at one time led an independent congregation or 'gathered Church' at St. Dunstan's-in-the-East, he had been President of Magdalen College, Oxford, from 1650 until the Restoration, and had attended Cromwell on his deathbed. Mallory had also once been the pastor at St. Dunstan's-in-the-East and at St. Nicholas' Church, Deptford and was by that time at St. Michael's, Crooked Lane, but refusing to conform to the Act of Uniformity, with its deadline on 24 August 1662, he was shortly to be ejected. The interview seemed highly encouraging.

The Chancellor . . . caused chairs to be brought and them to sit down and discoursed very freely about liberty of conscience, and professed himself a great friend to it and that he would bring the King to assure it to them, and gave them so many good words that they thought their desires in this point to be accomplished; and after about an hour's discourse with them, in all courtesy and freedom, he dismissed them; and proved afterwards the greatest enemy that could be to them and their desires.[7]

Whitelocke's harsh judgement was misdirected; it was neither the King nor his Chancellor but Parliament who, by their legislation, hounded dissenters out of public life, compelled them to worship in secret and sent many to jail.

On 7 May 1662 Whitelocke was summoned by Clarendon to an interview with the one man he bitterly disliked, Gilbert Sheldon, Bishop of London. His temper was not improved by the Bishop keeping him waiting. The Chancellor opened the proceedings, saying he was sorry to learn that Whitelocke was 'head of the fanatics in the City'. This was a lawyer's probe; if he was referring to Venner's fanatics, as distinct from nonconformists generally, he knew that the charge was unjust. Whitelocke replied blandly that he would be glad if it were true. 'With a show of anger', Clarendon asked why. The fanatics, Whitelocke replied, were a powerful group and if he were their leader he could do the King a service by keeping them in order. Sheldon broke in to say petulantly:

You gave counsel to the parishioners of Coleman Street against me, and that a commission for a vestry, granted by me, you said was against law.

The reply was smooth to the point of insolence.

I confess I did so, and I am of the same opinion still. . . . My Lord Chancellor knows it to be the liberty of our profession to be of counsel against any – against the King himself, who will not take it amiss for any lawyer to be of counsel against him.[8] By the grace and favour of the King I have the same liberty with others of my profession and with other English gentlemen.

The Chancellor interjected:

You told your clients that the Bishop's commission was against law, in disparagement of the Bishop and his power.

I told my clients my opinion in law, when they asked it and gave me my fee, and I humbly appeal to your Lordship whether my opinion were not according to law.

Whitelocke proceeded to elaborate a point of democratic procedure. Sheldon had granted a commission to certain members of the Coleman Street parish of St. Helen's, men he could rely on to constitute themselves as a vestry or parish council; the action was illegal since these vestrymen should have been elected by the parishioners. Whitelocke was warming to his subject.

Another reason why I thought it not good was because part of the business of the vestry is to nominate scavengers, constables, and other civil officers, and to look after the rates for the poor, and other civil matters which pertain not to the jurisdiction of the Bishop; and therefore for his commission to constitute such a vestry was against law.

Knowing that the former Keeper of the Seal could annihilate the Bishop in a legal contest, Clarendon intervened:

My Lord of London, Whitelocke is a shrewd fellow. We were best to let him alone. That which he saith hath some weight.

The Bishop could not take a hint.

He needed not to have set the parishioners to oppose me.

This time the reply was devastatingly gracious:

Neither did I. But if I had been worthy to have advised your Lordship, you should not have been put upon such a question as this is, nor upon anything but what will be justified by law.

The two legal experts had been indulging in the ancient sport of bishop-baiting. Whitelocke admitted in his 'Diary' that he had been 'more sharp than ordinary, remembering the great injury done to his children by the Bishop'. Later that month his daughter Cecilia, who had been ejected from

the Manor at Fulham, was to die at his home in Coleman Street; Sam and the
infant were already dead. With unusual anger Whitelocke wrote of the
'barbarous dealings of the Bishop of London'.[9]

In his own time he moved from Coleman Street to Chancery Lane but
not liking it there he moved again, to a house in Fleet Street which had a
short-cut to his modest quarters in the Middle Temple. He had been obliged
to surrender his spacious chambers to the Attorney General.

His immense legal knowledge could not be entirely ignored by those in
power. On 13 March 1663 he received a message from the King, inviting
him to set down his views on the royal prerogative in ecclesiastical matters.
In February the Commons had condemned Charles's proposed Declaration
of Indulgence as 'establishing schism by law'. Its effect would have been to
soften the impact of the Act of Uniformity on dissenters and Roman Catholics. In response to the King's request Whitelocke worked for twelve days
to produce a small manuscript volume, 'The King's Right to grant Indulgence
in Matters of Religion asserted by B. W. Kt.'[10] In it he quoted innumerable
precedents for the King, as head of the Church, extending toleration to his
subjects. He mustered practical, moral and historical arguments in favour of
freedom of conscience. He pointed to England's neighbours, in the Netherlands, who experienced more peace for having granted such indulgence. He
quoted from the Sermon on the Mount 'the rule of doing as we would be
done by' and claimed that dissenters outnumbered the Anglicans who were
trying to repress them; (Bishop Sheldon took the opposite view). Kings in
the past had discovered that they could not control men's hearts as they
could their bodies, that 'religion could not be forced, that truth could not
be joined with violence neither justice with cruelty . . . there is nothing so free
and voluntary as religion.' He wrote dryly 'Those meek spirits who would
have the blood of dissenters fancy impossibilities when they fancy an extir-
pation by that means.' Persecution only strengthened those who were
oppressed, as was seen with the Huguenots in France. He used the financial
arguments which men resort to when giving evidence to the authorities:
dissenters were necessary to the economy; they were in general 'sober,
industrious trading men, either merchants or artificers, both which are
useful and necessary members of a state, and perhaps', he added on a radical
note, 'more than debauched drones who are born to consume provisions,
not to increase the public wealth.' They were likely to banish themselves,
taking their skills to lands which allowed liberty of conscience. He argued
that a man in power might as reasonably ruin another because he differed

from him in conscience, as because he differed in countenance or stature. Judgement belonged to God and 'it would be happy if some, in our time, would . . . leave the works of God to be done by God.' With good sense and charm, he presented the case for legalized spiritual freedom. It was a per- missive policy not at all to Parliament's liking.

The approach from the King raised Whitelocke's hopes of obtaining an appointment in London. Harbottle Grimston, who had been made Master of the Rolls, asked him one day why a man with his qualifications remained out of office when Clarendon could easily find him a post.[11] Whitelocke was reticent in answering but it came out that Grimston had already spoken about him to the Chancellor, who had dismissed the subject on the grounds that Whitelocke was too friendly with John Wildman. It was a curious allegation. The two men were never close friends. They dined together sometimes, when Wildman was out of prison, and in later years they both welcomed George Cokain to their Wiltshire homes, as a visiting preacher, but Whitelocke never shared Wildman's appetite for intrigue. Ironically, the republican Major was appointed to the Government Post Office after the Restoration, serving until he was imprisoned for conspiracy in 1662; Whitelocke, who never plotted against the regime, remained out of office because, replying to a question from Clarendon, he had once spoken well of Wildman. There was talk of his being appointed a legal adviser to the King but nothing came of that; more than once he hurried to London for a post which never materialized. After nearly twenty years at Westminster he could not escape a devouring sense of loss.

He resorted to intense, self-imposed activity: writing, studying, making hectic journeys between London and Wiltshire often twice in a month. The Lodge at Chilton Foliat near Hungerford, bought with the money Brother Wilson was holding for Mary, had once belonged to Thomas Sutton, the benefactor of Charterhouse. Whitelocke made it serve as an outlet for his burning energy. He supervised the construction of a gate at the bottom of the south walk, then a trout pond and a kitchen garden, before embarking on costly improvements to the house. When the plague was raging in London he thought it wise to retreat with Mary to the country, taking with them their dependent children.

On 3 September 1666 news reached him of the Great Fire of London. He set off for Littlecote to ask Colonel Alexander Popham for more details but was accosted on the way by the local magistrate, Sir Seymour Pyle, who as usual had been drinking. Pyle volunteered that 60,000 Frenchmen, Dutchmen and Presbyterians had been under arms in London at the time the fire broke out. The King's forces had been called out, had killed half that number and taken many prisoners, including dissenting ministers of religion. He hinted that other dissenters would soon be arrested and, glaring at his neighbour's servant, declared that loyal Englishmen would kill every Frenchman on sight; Whitelocke hastily explained that his man was German. He decided to humour the magistrate and went home with him hoping, as he wrote idiomatically, 'to get as much as he could out of him'. Later that day James Pearson, the tutor, went over to Littlecote for more news. He was assured by Colonel Popham that the army had not been called out and that there had been no fighting, although 'several foreigners had indeed been murdered'.[12] The Dutch war had been going on for two years, at great cost to the English, and early in 1666 the French had allied themselves with the enemy; consequently, they and the Dutch became the immediate scapegoats for London's disaster. Popham dismissed Pyle's threat that dissenters were to be rounded up, as an invention inspired by 'too much wine and too little grace', a view which the magistrate evidently shared, for when he was sober he sent an apology.

In spite of Popham's reassuring words the Whitelockes stayed at home. There were alarming rumours that fires would be started all over the country, and at Chilton and Hungerford a watch was kept against incendiaries. Mr. Pearson set off for London to find out what was happening but after he left a letter arrived reporting that young Bulstrode, a boy of nineteen, had salvaged two loads of his father's possessions, apart from which their Fleet Street home and its entire contents, including valuable manuscripts, had been destroyed.[13] The fire cost Whitelocke about £1,000. On his next visit to London he had no choice but to stay with the Wilsons, who received him with grudging hospitality. His Temple chambers had just escaped the fire and he dined there frugally, distressed, when a friend called, not to be able to offer him a meal. Samuel Wilson and Bartholomew Hall refused to lend him any money, yet he had not long returned to Chilton Lodge before Father Hall turned up with several sons, a daughter-in-law, three men-servants, two maid-servants and five horses. At the end of their stay Hall gave twenty shillings to the servants and the same to the children, but offered nothing towards the housekeeping. When Brother Wilson came he was equally inconsiderate, whereas old friends like the Winwoods and John Wildman would arrive bringing with them a fat doe, and neighbours made timely gifts of venison or trout when guests were expected at the Lodge.

After several attempts Whitelocke succeeded in disposing of the great house at Newton St. Loe, near Bath, which his widowed daughter, Mary Nevill, had inherited.[14] Hopes of raising money for himself by selling Greenlands, his property adjoining Fawley Court, were frustrated by viewers who showed a great interest but failed to complete the purchase; one of them went so far as to start chopping down the trees, until Whitelocke put a stop to that and made some ready money by selling the timber himself. Incessant poverty put a strain on everybody's temper. In May 1667 he wrote of unkind words at home, of James grumbling about money and of friends he had helped in the past despising and deserting him; tenants defaulted or died insolvent and creditors harassed him. He was supporting the seven youngest children on a negligible income from his legal practice, an uncertain one from his estates and on what was left of Mary's fortune; he was incurring more than he could afford in wages to pay bricklayers and builders, for he was afraid to leave the completion of Chilton Lodge to Sam, the heir to this property. Mary's first-born was not the careful and devout son she had expected in answer to prayer. Like most of her children he was infected by the worldliness of the 1660s.

At the end of August 1667 Colonel Popham broke the news that Clarendon had been ordered by the King to surrender the Great Seal. Whitelocke recorded the Chancellor's fall without comment.

The anguish he suffered from stone was increased by travelling. As he was still determined to get about he had a special sedan chair constructed, on the principle of a horse litter; its swaying motion was preferable to the jolting of coach wheels, especially on cobblestones. In March 1668, while staying in London, he was humiliated by the arrival of two sergeants to arrest him for debt, at the instigation of James's wife. The action was based on a fraudulent affidavit which stated that he had guaranteed his eldest son's debts up to the sum of £200. Instead of contesting it Whitelocke paid the debt, congratulating himself that Mary was not with him. Sixteen months later James wrote from France complaining of the poverty in which his wife and children were living and asking for a hundred pounds. His father scraped together seventy but it seems that Mary had stood enough, for the next time her stepson turned up at Chilton Lodge he was smartly packed off to London in the flying coach, with only a few unspecified gifts, and when he sent a friend to plead his case the go-between met with a firm refusal; Whitelocke referred to his own poverty and to some undertaking he had given, presumably to Mary. Even so, a few months later he was 'put to

straits' for forty pounds to hold off James's creditors. He could not say 'No'
to the son who had been the compensation for his marriage to Rebecca, and
for over forty years the spoilt child never scrupled to exploit his father's
weakness.

Mary's eldest boys, Sam and Carleton, were to take their degrees at Oxford
before entering the Middle Temple. Mr. Pearson took them to the University and stayed a few days to see them settled at Edmund Hall, under the
presidency of Dr. Tully. Three weeks later their mother made an appointment with a Dr. Elliot in Oxford, which provided a pretext for going to
see her sons; but the consultation was no frivolous excuse. One doctor had
pronounced that she was pregnant again, another had diagnosed cancer
while a third insisted that this was incorrect. She went to drink the waters
at Bath and later at Astrop Spa near Banbury, accompanied by Mr. Pearson
and by her daughter Frances, who was known to the family as 'Frank'.[15]
At Astrop they met a Mrs. Carter whose son took a liking for Frank and
soon afterwards he came to stay near the Lodge; Frank announced flatly that
she did not love him, which made her parents suspect that she was listening
to bad advice; they never forced their children into marriage but it was not
easy in their impoverished state to find partners for them all. Frank may
already have turned her eyes in the direction of Francis Pyle, the magistrate's
son; later she had her own way and married him but it turned out badly for
her. After several fruitless attempts to find a wife for Sam he was eventually
married to Elizabeth Gough from Vernham, in Hampshire. This was a
happier marriage than his sister's, but his parents were dismayed to find that
the daughter-in-law of their choice was preoccupied with fashion, that she
wore black patches and colour on her face and that she wanted to live in
London and go to the playhouse.

Throughout Mary's protracted illness, which included an attack of St.
Anthony's fire, the burning, itching erysipelas, Whitelocke 'left not his wife's
company and bed'. But illness, anxiety and poverty continued to cause
'domestic troubles', 'discontents' and 'unkindness at home'. Whitelocke
ruefully quoted a line from the *Satires* of Juvenal: '*res angusta domi*', cramping
poverty at home.[16] He had spent two fortunes and was seldom out of debt.
When he sold one of the tenant farms at Chilton, Mary was displeased,
feeling that Sam was cheated of part of his inheritance. He tried to econo-
mize, but the style in which he had lived for the greater part of his life made
it difficult. He could not grasp the fact that a second-hand glass-windowed
coach, lined with crimson velvet, was only a bargain to a man who could

afford £26. He bought it, and was at his wits' end to pay the boys' university fees. He was annoyed by their extravagance at college and perhaps somebody hinted that in this respect they took after their father, for there was a note of self-justification in one of his sermons to the family, 'Upon the New Buildings at Chilton Lodge 1667'. Supported by classical and biblical quotations he conceded that ambitious men often ruined themselves by too much building; that the Italians had a curse for an enemy, 'may the plague of building possess him!', but a God-fearing man showed charity by employing his poor, industrious neighbours on work of this nature. It was a better form of charity than handing out money to beggars. (So much for anyone who thought he wasted money on building.) He went on to show that a home was a place for offering hospitality, not to 'grandees' so much as to poor strangers. (This was no doubt directed at Mary, who was expected to feed impoverished scholars like the German, Dr. John Campius, when he turned up, ostensibly to read Hebrew with his host, and made a long stay.)

On his next visit to London, Whitelocke was heartened by receiving an urgent message from a very old friend. In September 1660 Lord Broghill had been created Earl of Orrery, in recognition of his help in securing Ireland's loyalty for the King and inviting Charles to land at Cork, but during the next decade he had made enemies in Ireland. One of them was James, Duke of Ormonde, the Lord Lieutenant of Ireland. There were stories of Orrery's corrupt administration, as Lord President of Munster, and on 25 November 1669 he was accused in the House of Commons of 'raising of moneys, by his own authority, upon His Majesty's subjects; defrauding the King's subjects of their estates'. It was alleged that the money raised was for bribing hungry courtiers to come to his aid. He was also charged with plotting 'to stir up the people to rebellion' and of uttering a threat that if the King would not support him he had 50,000 swords to compel him.[17] On a division in the Commons it was resolved that he should be impeached for high treason, having conspired to levy war. The Earl consulted his old friend, who prepared a statement to the effect that there was insufficient evidence to justify the charge. Orrery told him admiringly that he was 'a bold fellow to deliver his opinion under his hand, contrary to what the House of Commons had voted'. Whitelocke replied that 'those who were out of the House might not take notice of the votes of the House, and he had delivered his opinion according to what he thought was the law.'[18] It did him good to feel that his judgement influenced the outcome but in fact the Commons were lukewarm about the impeachment, which some suspected was concocted by the Earl's enemies, and when, on 11 December, the King prorogued Parliament for two months they discreetly dropped the charge.[19]

As usual the Whitelockes spent Christmas at Chilton but they returned to London in January 1670 to stay with Samuel Wilson. They brought provisions from the country and several loads of fuel to use in their own apartments. Whitelocke was taken aback to see the Wilsons piling these logs onto their fires and even storing some away, on top of which Brother Wilson expected forty shillings a week from his relatives for rent. Funds were desperately low. Mary was pressing for money to settle household accounts and her husband could see little hope of raising it. He was walking to the Middle Temple one day, brooding on his predicament, when a clerk came over to inform him that Sir William Drake's Will had just been read and that it included a legacy to Whitelocke of £20. This windfall from an old client enabled him to stay in London for several weeks and he began to emerge from obscurity. Lord Orrery consulted him frequently and tried to find work for him; the Earl's sister, Lady Ranelagh, treated him with the respect accorded to him in the old days; he had long discussions with Lord Willoughby, Dr. Owen and others who shared Lady Ranelagh's concern for liberty of conscience.[20] He was also consulted about the scandal of the day, the divorce proceedings initiated by Lord Ross, whose wife had failed to provide him with an heir but had nevertheless given birth to a son. Dr. Owen was writing a paper on the religious aspect of the divorce and the King sent a message by Lord Willoughby, asking Whitelocke to write on its legal implications. Charles sat in the gallery of the House of Lords throughout the proceedings. He had a personal interest in the outcome. His faithful wife, Catherine of Braganza, had failed to give the nation an heir to the throne. Whitelocke's comments were evidently favourable to the divorce, for the King 'liked them exceeding well'.[21] The succession was of direct concern to Charles's brother James, and the King with his sardonic humour may have watched the divorce proceedings in order to make James uneasy.

When Whitelocke left London in the summer of 1670 it was for the last time. He had planned to go back for the Michaelmas term but the government was increasingly nervous of plots and insurrection, and a new proclamation prohibited men who had taken up arms for the Commonwealth from entering London without licence.

There were numerous family problems to keep him busy at Chilton Lodge. Young Bigley had been engaged by a French merchant 'for a month or two upon trial', but was dismissed for disorderly behaviour. His parents took trouble in finding him a new master and eventually signed an indenture with Thomas Earle, a Bristol merchant, who demanded £200 as well as the boy's clothes during apprenticeship. 'Somewhat high terms for Bristol', they thought, but Earle had a good name which was more than could be said for Bigley. The children had begun to scatter. Bigley was sent to Malaga, near Gibraltar; James continued to cross the Channel when creditors threatened; young Bulstrode was studying medicine in Leyden. Willoughby was learning the wine trade in the Canary Islands, working for Sam Wilson, whom he found a hard master. He resigned, and his parents thought of sending him to New England or to work for his uncle Lord William Willoughby: instead, their son took a post as a shipping agent or 'marine factor' in Turkey, with glittering prospects of £500 a year and all found. He started confidently at £100 but a few months later he was dead.

Whitelocke's own health had deteriorated, after a fall when mounting his horse, and he was hardly expected to live through the winter of 1670–71. The crisis came when he passed sharp stones and large clots of blood. The violent pain and loss of blood caused him to faint. 'His wife was very tender and careful of him, and Mr. Pearson took much pains about him. His children were affectionate. His wife's maid Betty was very careful, and his other servants ready to do anything for him.' Confronted by death he was surprised to find that he was not so much afraid as he expected. In January 1671 Dr. Whistler, who had accompanied him to Sweden, called in Dr. Elliot for a consultation. They reported that if there were no improvement in the next two days the patient would die. After breaking this news Whistler went to stay with friends, telling the family to send for him if he were needed, 'but it was thought that he went away because he was unwilling to see Whitelocke die'. Whistler was by that time a man of consequence, a friend of Sir Christopher Wren, and of John Evelyn who found him polished and witty, 'the most facetious man in nature', while Pepys described him as 'good company and a very ingenious man'. In spite of having a successful London practice to look after, he still found time to make the two-day journey to Chilton Lodge. When next he called he found some improvement, but Whitelocke's legs began to swell alarmingly from dropsy; under Whistler's direction Mr. Pearson applied fomentations to prevent the onset of gangrene, and again the patient recovered. Mary gratefully offered the doctor a fee of ten pounds which he accepted, unlike Dr. Winston in the old days.[22]

Whitelocke worried less about his health than about money troubles and the inadequacy of his legacies to Mary's children. The older boys meantime hurt him by their disregard for his wishes; he tried to deal with them 'meekly but as a father', reflecting that the love of children for their parents does not match the love of parents for their children. His sons made it plain that he was old and his opinions did not count any more.

He escaped from insults and disappointments to the contentment of study and writing. In the last fifteen years of his life his clarity of mind, scholarship and literary output were prodigious. He had prepared, in his own hand-writing, the six-volume 'Notes Upon the King's Writ for choosing Members of Parliament' and 'The King's Right to grant Indulgence in Matters of Religion', and presented both works to Charles II; he made the fair copy of 'A Journal of the Swedish Embassy' and transcribed, with additional comments, his earlier 'Diary' which he then kept up to date. He completed his largest single work 'The Annals of his own Life Dedicated to his Children', memoirs which he had started in 1655.[23] He wrote letters, sermons, legal, political and historical treatises. An undated manuscript with the title 'Whitelocke's History of the Parliament of England and of Some Resemblances to the Jewish and Other Courts' has two Latin tags in his handwriting on a fly-leaf which indicate, by their bitter disillusionment, that they belong to this post-Restoration period.[24] In the last five years of his life he embarked on a massive 'History of Persecution' which incorporated a store of information from many countries of Europe; the manuscript ends abruptly at the bottom of a page, in the middle of a sentence about the first Duke of Buckingham; the account of persecution during Whitelocke's adult life has been torn out but the paging and headings in the table of contents refute the opinion that this section was never written. It is likely that Mary destroyed the most important chapters, after his death. What survives reflects his life-long hatred of intolerance and cruelty.[25]

In June 1671 Prince Rupert sent an urgent message asking him to outline the rights of the Constable of Windsor Castle, an office to which the Prince had been appointed in 1668 but which was not working out to his satisfaction. Rupert's secretary wrote that, 'the King desired satisfaction before he granted a thing to the Prince and . . . the Prince was confident that if the King read Whitelocke's opinion, in his own hand, that he would be satisfied in it and grant the Prince what he denied, and therefore he requested Whitelocke to send him his opinion.'[26] It was not to his predecessor Lord Mordaunt, a loyal Cavalier, that Rupert turned for advice but to the old Parliamentarian who had governed the Castle under Cromwell. That was not altogether surprising, since Mordaunt had resigned the post after the Commons threatened him with impeachment. The three years' delay, before the Prince consulted Whitelocke, suggests a gradual hardening in the King's attitude against his cousin. Early in the 1670s it became obvious that Rupert was allying himself increasingly with the 'country party', the Whig party in its infancy, and in particular with its leader Lord Ashley, the former Anthony Ashley Cooper. This small, ambitious, gifted man, although he was not at that time so unpopular at Court as he later became, was stamped by Charles with the malicious nick-name 'Little Sincerity'.

Rupert's enquiry evoked a detailed reply which ended discouragingly: 'the office of Constable of Windsor Castle is of very great antiquity, honour, power and pleasure, but of very little profit.' Perhaps the incident stirred Whitelocke to consider whether, instead of addressing himself to future generations, he could write for his contemporaries and make some money; a few months later he wrote to Prince Rupert's friend and his own former acquaintance, Lord Ashley, who was shortly to be created first Earl of Shaftesbury. The draft is dated Feb 22 71 [72]

My Lord
I understand by Mr. Rumsey that I am exceedingly engaged to Your Lordship for your favour to your old servant which I hope never to forfeit. . . . In discourse with him I declared my thoughts of writing the History of England, which is not so well written as those of other countries . . . but held it not fit for me to engage in this business without His Majesty's command and encouragement, which Your Lordship knows hath been given by Princes on the like occasions.

The frowns of the world and particular injuries have brought me and my numerous family into greater straits than I am willing to mention. If it be agreeable to Your Lordship's judgement. . . to move His Majesty herein and to grant me some allowance (what he pleaseth will content me) for my pains and necessary charge herein, I shall thereupon lay aside the practice of my profession to apply myself wholly to this work, so as I hope may be pleasing to His Majesty and for the good of future times.

I should have waited on Your Lordship if I had been able, but the extreme violence of my distemper of the stone confines me to my house and study, where yet I hope to live to serve His Majesty. . . .[27]

To publish a work of that nature he needed sanction from the Secretary of State, but there is no evidence that Ashley used his good offices to give any help or encouragement. It is difficult to date Whitelocke's History of England which was published in 1709 with a biographical introduction by William Penn. It is however tempting to suppose that he had the draft in his desk, before he wrote to Ashley, based on the 'Abridgment of the Whole History of England' which he started when he was nineteen.[28]

In July 1671 the Wilsons and the Cokains came to stay at the Lodge. They had travelled from London with Mr. Pearson and two of Whitelocke's sons. In order to share out expenses on the journey, Samuel Wilson and George Cokain jokingly set up 'a committee to order the housekeeping' which 'put Brother Wilson into his element'. The committee continued to function while they were at Chilton, so for once Mary received something towards the cost of her guests, their servants and the horses. 'Brother Wilson was fearful that he should taste no venison at the Lodge' but disaster was averted. A servant arrived from Littlecote bringing a fat buck, and as Richard Winwood also sent a side and shoulder of venison Wilson was able to take some back with him to London.

In October Mary travelled to London by coach, Mr. Pearson, Carleton and Frances accompanying her on horseback. She expected that the Wilsons or the Cokains would return her hospitality and was dismayed when even George Cokain made some excuse, and arranged a room for her at the Dolphin on Ludgate Hill. 'Such are friends in time of declining.'[29] Whitelocke was not well and was left at home, forlorn, with less than five shillings to last until Mary's return. To add to his troubles, workmen repairing the stable roof uncovered dry rot in rafters which had clearly been put in by the previous occupant 'only for a present show, intending to sell it'.

Whitelocke's youngest children found life at home very quiet. Their father was old enough to be their grandfather and had become too shaky even to take them hunting. There was the occasional wedding in the family and an outing in 1672 when 'the young people went to Chilton Church to see the funeral of the Lady Popham and to hear the sermon'. Occasionally the boys broke loose and went off to an all-night harvest feast with dancing and 'disorders'. The world Whitelocke had known was gone. His married children made frequent trips to London only for pleasure; he thought it an unnecessary expense and was always happy when they were safely home. William wrote an unpleasant letter saying that his father was liable to arrest for a debt of £600; Whitelocke could not imagine what this meant but it caused him great anxiety. William also sent word that he had sold the woodland at Phyllis Court for £2,000; his father had not been consulted and felt 'over-reached by his own child'. Irritation and discontent smouldered. Two days before Christmas 1672 there was a dispute in which the family again blamed him for wasting money on the Lodge; he replied that it would be

well if he were dead and he thought bitterly that it would be no loss if the
new buildings came down. That night there was a violent storm in which
two sheets of lead were ripped off the roof and fell with a clatter into the
courtyard. With a self-reproach uncommon in his writings he reflected that
God seemed to rebuke him. He made up his mind in future to 'take heed of
such indiscreet thoughts'.

The new year brought no relief. It was good to have the older children
come and stay but it was costly and he was beginning to find that he liked it
best when he and Mary were alone. He, who had always been proud of his
large family, thought to himself that smaller ones meant fewer troubles. He
continued to entertain visiting preachers. George Cokain in his mid-fifties
still commanded such a following that when he preached at the Lodge some
three hundred neighbours came to hear him and the Rector, Dr. Grindall
Sheafe, planted a spy in the congregation; William Penn, in his late twenties,
who had been in and out of prison for his convictions, sometimes came to
hear Whitelocke preach at conventicles; when the young Quaker himself
'preached admirably' in Whitelocke's study, the Rector appeared in person
and interrupted the service. Years later Penn wrote the introduction to a
small volume containing three of Whitelocke's sermons, on the text 'Quench
not the Spirit', which was published in 1711. With their emphasis on the
spirit of God in man and on the variety of God's manifestations, the sermons
might well have been written by a Quaker.

New anxiety was generated when young Francis Pyle discovered that his
wife had signed a financial document before their marriage. Whitelocke
explained patiently that Frank had only promised to give Carleton and
Rebecca £200 each in the event of her being left a widow; in that case she
would be entitled to do as she pleased with her own money, and the undertaking was just, since her brother's and sister's estates would be more modest
than her own. Pyle, however, thought he had somehow been cheated and
threatened to charge Cokain and Whitelocke with treason. Under the
Conventicle Act of 1664 and the sterner measure of 1670 they were both
vulnerable, though not as traitors.

In all the family's fortunes and misfortunes James Pearson could be relied
on to help. He not only taught the children, he nursed them, dosed them,
preached to them and dashed up to London to fetch a marriage licence for
one of them; it was he who signed the application for a licence to use Chilton
Lodge as a preaching place, when the King managed for a time to suspend
the Conventicle and Five Mile Acts; he kept creditors at bay and helped

Mary to support her husband through the physical indignities which illness imposed on a touchy, frail old man. When Rebecca – Beck – was sixteen years old and was taken ill Pearson, who had been training as a physician, sat up with her for two nights until she was out of danger. After she recovered, he decided to take her to London calling her, 'in frolic', his wife. Her parents were not at all displeased and when it appeared that he wished to marry her they gave their consent; to their annoyance Beck's brothers and sisters talked her out of marrying a man old enough to be her father, though young enough to be their father's son.

In his seventieth year Whitelocke was still advising one or two clients each week and he was still busy writing, but he was living from day to day and no longer planning for the future. During the previous two years the 'Diary' entries had become short and laconic; by 1675 they had dwindled to three or four shaky words a day and the cool, third person references to himself were giving way to 'I' and 'me'. Instead of the carefully ruled sepia line down the centre of each page this was drawn in a wavering freehand. The first weeks of July tell of fees from clients, visits from friends and of intense pain. The entry written on 21 July 1675 refers almost illegibly to his illness, then trails away. The opposite page, already divided into two columns, is blank.

His death remains obscure. The Bishop of Salisbury's transcript, in the Wiltshire archives, has an entry concerning 'Sir Bulstrid Whitlock' in which *buried* has been altered to *died* 27 August 1675, but this is contradicted by the Fawley parish register which records that he was buried on 6 August that year. Mark Noble in his *Life of Cromwell* gave the date of death as 27 July, six days after the last entry in the 'Diary'. More authoritatively Elias Ashmole, a wealthy acquaintance, noted on 28 July 1675 'Sir Bolstrode Whitlock died 6 H. A.M.'. William Penn, who wrote that his old friend died at Chilton Foliat, confirmed the date as 28 July adding that Whitelocke was buried in the south transept of Fawley church, but that his 'great modesty would not permit the erecting of any memorial, epitaph or inscription'.[30] Whitelocke's bravura and love of display had slipped from him as he approached death. In his last Will, dated 17 May 1675 and proved in November 1676, he expressed a wish to be buried at Fawley 'without any pomp or much charge . . . if it may be without inconvenience to my dear wife'. Earlier he had written that he wished to lie in the family vault beside his wife Frances. In 1860, on the other hand, Professor R. H. Whitelocke wrote that the whole world had been led to suppose that the body was in the vault at Fawley 'and the error was only discovered in 1830'.[31] The Professor's assumptions were sometimes inaccurate and he gave no indication as to the nature or reliability of the discovery in 1830; if he was right it is curious that when George Whitelocke, from Ireland, was buried in the family vault in 1831 his relatives should have put up a tablet listing the seventeen White-lockes buried there, including Sir Bulstrode 'who was patron of this church buried 6 Aug 1675'. Taking this in conjunction with the church register, Penn's recollection and Mary's magnanimous nature, the evidence points to his having been buried beside Frances, in accordance with his wishes.

Whitelocke achieved three distinguished careers, first as a writer, historian and chronicler of his times, second as a Parliamentarian and third as a lawyer.

Until recently his writing on legal, political and religious subjects attracted little attention from modern historians. Thomas Carlyle wrote him off as 'Dry-as-dust' and Sir Charles Firth, in the *Dictionary of National Biography*, dismissed his work as greatly over-estimated by whig writers; since then he has often been ignored or ranked as a plodding lawyer, but Firth's remark is a reminder of the regard in which Whitelocke was once held by men of whiggish and liberal outlook. The list of his works published between 1682 and 1855, including second and third editions, is considerable; his views were probably more acceptable to the Whigs than they had been to his contem-poraries and his influence on political thinking greater after his death than during the Interregnum or the immediate post-Restoration years. Tory writers of the eighteenth century abused him. Whig writers praised him. In the end, most of the liberal and constitutional views he had advocated came to be accepted as a commonplace. This was followed by a contemptuous reaction against him. His belief that women should share in government took longer than his other views to find acceptance. His sense of history, matched by a feeling for the future, prompted him to help save Oxford's treasures from plunder, the College of Heralds from abolition, the four Inns of Court from being commandeered and the Royal Library from dispersal and sale overseas. It moved him to hoard up papers of all kinds, from important documents and personal letters to scraps which would have made another man's pipe-spills. His History of England up to 1625 was principally sig-nificant because of the paucity of such records. From his student years on-wards he recorded compulsively the great happenings of his day, side by side with trivial ones. This constituted his most important historical work.

His interpretation of events may be challenged, his statements are sometimes inaccurate, but the 'Diary', the 'Annals' and *A Journal of the Swedish
Embassy* together provide an unparalleled account of a man's public and
private life in England and Sweden, covering nearly three-quarters of the
seventeenth century.

As a Parliamentarian, in the years between 1641 and 1660, he drafted
historic bills and served on numerous parliamentary committees, often as
chairman, an indication that he was acceptable to men of differing views.
He was regularly consulted on high policy, both domestic and foreign.
Before the King's execution he believed in mixed monarchy, shared between
a constitutionally bound King and a powerful Parliament. After January
1649 he brought himself to believe in a sovereign House of Commons
expressing the will of the people, and at some date between the Swedish
mission and the Restoration he went so far as to express antimonarchical
sentiments, which were later expurgated from the manuscript by his son
Carleton. For Whitelocke, as for Cromwell and many Independents, there
was nothing sacrosanct about any particular form of government.[32] The
style of government was acceptable if it was what the people chose, and for
him 'the people' were not merely his wealthy friends, landed gentry, lawyers
and merchants; they included Toucher Carter, along with the shopkeepers
and bargemen of Marlow who had sent him to Westminster in 1641, and
men like William Cooke who could barely write a letter but whose judgement he could trust. Despite this, Whitelocke cherished a sneaking regard for
money, rank and title, although this did not extend to princes of the Church.
He and his father had climbed the political and social ladder fast and he liked
what he saw from the top. He has been called a political trimmer. A man
with a wife and seventeen children does not lightly throw over a good job,
but historians who, even to-day, refer to him as a time-server do him less
than justice. He recognized that if the lawyers and members of the government walk out in the wake of a military revolt, the soldiers will certainly
march in to rule with military courts and the sword. He sometimes served
with misgiving but when he could not square his conscience he dissented;
he resigned sooner than use the Great Seal for what he considered unlawful
purposes, and refused to take part in the trials of Archbishop Laud and King
Charles. He was suspicious of party groupings which, like many of his
generation, he considered factious; even when he aligned himself with
Pym or Essex or Cromwell, he withheld his unqualified support. As Ambassador he planned his tactics like a chessplayer, enjoying every move; his

mission to Sweden enhanced England's prestige abroad; Edward Hyde admitted to a friend that Whitelocke was the first ambassador from the rebels who dared show his face at a foreign Court, and that he had done so to good effect.

Whatever his political aspirations, and he was not without ambition, he was in all his thinking essentially a lawyer, immersed in the new ideas of the seventeenth century, some of which he had absorbed from his father, from John Selden and from the great Edward Coke. The law was the defence against tyrants whether they came in the guise of Kings, Lords or Members of Parliament, Protectors, Divines or army officers. All men, including the King, must be subject to it. He believed in liberty of conscience under the law's protection. He was fond of saying that men could no more be expected to believe or to worship alike, than all to have the same faces or the same taste in food.

He was an individualist, at his best working on his own in Sweden or following a lonely path, after 1660, in defence of nonconformity. It is as difficult to find an appropriate religious label for him as to find a political one. At times he was called an Erastian, a disciple of Selden, and (after meeting Mary and her chaplain) an Independent; several Independent congregations prayed fervently for his safe return from Sweden. After the Restoration he openly helped the Independents while his own outlook, in the last years of his life, has been justly described as approaching that of a Quaker. Had he been the turn-coat that some historians imply he would have conformed to Anglicanism after 1660, discarding his friendship with dissenters and with dangerous companions like John Wildman.

The high opinion he had of his own abilities may be judged as monumental complacency or as natural exuberance. Whichever it was, he seldom over-rated his gifts. Under the arduous conditions of the Swedish mission he showed his power to command on a basis of comradeship, while presenting himself to the Court at Uppsala as a formidable negotiator. So long as England, in his person, received the respect due to her he had the self-assurance to unbend and exercise his undoubted charm, which was not the least of the weapons in his armoury. He was not equal, it has been said, to the tasks which confronted him. This was true after Cromwell's death, when the nation was near to anarchy. Only a man of stamina and magnetism could have dominated at once the men entrenched in Parliament and those in the army. Whitelocke was by then over fifty and suffering acute pain. Had the vacuum occurred earlier he might have filled it and have won support, through his influence with different groups, for humane and tolerant policies. In 1653 Royalists had ranked him among the handful of men who must be 'taken off' once they had disposed of Cromwell. Six years later, as Lord President of the Council, he may have seen himself as the nation's leader but by then it was too late.

His writings reveal a complex character, by nature artistic and emotional, by training astute and reserved. He could be cautious to the point of indecision, or confident and ebullient to the point of vanity. He was full of curiosity, interested in trifles, fond of money, devoted to his wives and a man of prodigious learning. In his variety of talents and interests he was a renaissance man, while he anticipated by a century that love of nature which the romantics adopted as their own discovery. In one of the last sermons he preached to the family he quoted words which reflect the principle which had sustained him for half a century, 'Whatever happens is best — if I make it so.' They express his wry and invincible view of life:

They that have taken away my goods, and have banished me into the woods, cannot hinder the earth from putting forth the flowers, nor the trees from yielding their fruit, nor the birds from singing among the branches. No, nor me from entertaining myself with all these pleasures. At least, from being contented.[33]

Postscript

A Needle in an Irish Haystack

What became of Whitelocke's possessions? The family portraits? The miniature framed in diamonds, given to him by Queen Christina? Above all, what became of the manuscripts? His last Will reads as follows:

In the name of God Amen. This is the last Will and Testament of me Bulstrode Whitelocke Kt. made the 17 day of May in the year of our Lord God 1675 I being then in good memory for which I praise the Lord and for all his mercies and deliverances vouchsafed to me, and I still desire to trust in him, and to forget the hard usages of me, and the injustice to me by some men. . . . I desire that my body may be buried without any pomp or much charge in the burying place of my family in Fawley Church in Bucks if it may be without inconvenience to my dear wife Dame Mary Whitelocke whom I make executrix of this my Will.

I am sorry that I am not able to make so good and full a provision of worldly estate for my dear wife and my children by her, unprovided for, as the great estate she brought to me, and our mutual love might require, but I have been disabled therein by worldly changes and injuries, and what remains of worldly estate both real and personal in my power I have settled upon my son Carleton Whitelocke my beloved friends Mr. George Cokain Mr. James Pearson and Mr. William Pendlebury with a declaration of their trust for the payment of my debts, and making some provision for my children yet unprovided for which I pray them to observe, and whereby my wife is to have such of the goods as she shall think fit to make choice of. And I desire that she may dispose of all my manuscript books of my own handwriting as she shall think fit. And that my son Carleton may have £50 per annum during the joint lives of him and my kind friend Mr. William Lilly. And that my son Bigley may have £20 per annum for his life and my daughter Hester £20 per annum for her life. And that all my children and grandchildren and my trustees and my brother and sister Wilson and Mrs. Cokain and my old friend Mr. Bartholomew Hall and Mr. Thomas Butler may have each of them a ring of 20s price. And I desire that after my debts upon mortgage shall be paid then in the next place all such debts of mine for which any of my trustees or Mr. Thomas Butler do or shall stand engaged as surety or sureties for me may be paid and also all charges by reason of the Trust. I charge all my children to be dutiful and respectful to my wife and loving to one another. And I commend them all to the blessing of our most gracious God, whom I counsel them to follow fully in all things, and I bless his name for all my mercies and afflictions which have been and still are very great and wearisome but I hope all of them in love to me.

Signed Sealed and published
as my last Will in the presence of
JOHN HUNT [signed]
the mark of   B. WHITELOCKE [signed]
George + Sharpe

I have not as yet uncovered Mary's Will or that of her second son, Carleton, who was twenty-three years old when his father died. Working backwards from those items which I have been able to trace, it is clear that most of the heirlooms went to Carleton and remained in the hands of his descendants until May 1946. There were exceptions. I have been told that Christina's miniature was taken to Jamaica by one of the family, after a runaway marriage early in the nineteenth century, and incidentally that there was at one time a Bulstrode House on the island. There are still Whitelockes living in Jamaica. It appears that the wife of the runaway marriage, needing money to send her cleverest son to study in Edinburgh, sold the heirloom at Sotheby's in the middle of the nineteenth century. I have not succeeded in tracing the present owner and the miniature was not among those shown at the Council of Europe's Christina Exhibition in 1966. Some family portraits went to Whitelocke's granddaughter Elizabeth, who married William Wiseman, and these are in the possession of Wiseman-Clarke descendants. A portrait of Queen Christina, and probably some of Whitelocke's portraits, as well as an armorial window, were owned by Bulstrode's second son, Sir William Whitelocke (the father of Elizabeth Wiseman). They remained at Phyllis Court after the house passed to Gislingham Cooper who married Sir William's granddaughter, Ann, and they were still there when the property was sold to Sambrook Freeman, of Fawley Court, in 1768. In 1784 George Whitelocke, a grandson of Carleton Whitelocke and son of John Carleton, called at Fawley on a visit from Ireland. Phyllis Court had by that time passed into the hands of Sambrook Freeman's nephew, Strickland Freeman. When George Whitelocke paid another visit in the following year he found the old house was being demolished. Its owner gave him the armorial glass from the dining parlour and the portrait of Queen Christina and possibly other family portraits, which went to the Irish branch of the family at that time if not earlier.

The manuscripts had an equally chequered history. On 27 May 1712 Philip Stubs (or Stubbs), the first chaplain of Greenwich Hospital, subsequently Archdeacon of St. Albans and a keen antiquarian, wrote to the Archdeacon of Colchester, Dr. Humfrey Wanley:

Dear Sir,
    After many traverses, Mrs. Whitlocke hath at length brought up all Sir Bulstrode's Autographa for sale, consisting of 25 MSS, most of them in Folio: she asks 100 Guineas; I know not what she may take, 'cause she hath another chap in view who may raise the Market. She protests he hath not seen them, nor shall he till I have made

my option: you'll signify so much to my Lord (with my humblest duty) that I have his last orders in the affair. As to my own part I have such a notion of their value, of his Diary, Swedish Embassy, Political Schemes and Comments on all the Texts in O & N Testaments relating to Government, etc. that had I so much money to spare as will compass them, I would take them off her hands myself, and rejoice under the purchase: I see you, God willing, tomorrow
            and am
        Yours humbly
        PS.
Royal Hospital Greenwich
May 22. 1712.

Dear Sir,
    I have had a lurking fever about me these 4 or 5 days so that I could neither discourse over F. Aymon's or Mrs. Whitlocke's affair: I am with you, God willing, this evening, or tomorrow morning or both.
        Yours
        PS.*
Sion, May 27. 1712

'My Lord' in the first letter presumably refers to Robert Harley, first Earl of Oxford, who had started making purchases in 1705 for what was to become the great Harleian library. In 1708 Humfrey Wanley had begun to compile the catalogue and this great collection was, for some years, in his charge. Father Jean Aymon, referred to in the second letter, was a French renegade priest and such an eager collector that he had filched manuscripts from the Royal Library in Paris and found it necessary to escape to Holland. I have not yet succeeded in identifying the Mrs. Whitelocke who offered the manuscripts for sale. It could not have been Whitelocke's widow Mary, for she died in 1684. It seems likely that it was Carleton's second wife and widow, also named Mary. Carleton had been connected with the manuscripts. He had edited what he called the *Essays Ecclesiastical and Civil*, which were selections published in 1706. He also wrote on the title page of 'The History of Whitelocke's Embassy from England to Sweden' that he had edited those two massive manuscript volumes; but they have never been published. Clearly Mrs. Whitelocke sold the manuscripts but the question is, to whom? In the second half of the eighteenth century Dr. Morton, a

* B.M. Portland Loan 29/257
756E

physician and scholar and the first under-librarian of the British Museum, began collecting Whitelocke's manuscripts and gave several volumes to the Museum. These and later acquisitions carry indications that they had belonged variously to the Duke of Chandos and Thomas Carew of Crocombe, Somerset, to Thomas Rodd, J. B. Marsh, T. Thorpe, Dr. Routh, Isaac Reed and Sir George Savile. Whitelocke manuscripts are also included in the Stowe, Malet, Ayscough and Egerton Collections in the British Museum. At dates which I cannot ascertain, a mass of Whitelocke papers, the two-volume 'Diary', and most of the volumes of the 'Annals', were acquired respectively by ancestors of Lord Bath, Lord Bute and Lord de la Warr, the 'Annals' being subsequently purchased from Sotheby's by the British Museum. So much for the dispersal of the most important collections of Whitelocke's work.

While I was writing the first draft of *The Improbable Puritan*, I discovered that the first volume of the 'Annals of his own Life', covering the first twenty-nine years of Whitelocke's life, had been separated from the others since the early eighteenth century, or perhaps even farther back. This teased me quite a bit, and I began to think I ought to try and find that missing manuscript. Dr. Morton had borrowed it from Sir Bulstrode's grandson, Major John Carleton Whitelocke of Priorswood, Co. Dublin, in the eighteenth century. I later found that, believing mistakenly that it had been given to him, Morton wrote his name on the title page. The manuscript was also known to Dr. Charles Burney, the music historian and father of Fanny. It was borrowed by Professor R. H. Whitelocke in the middle of the nineteenth century and was referred to, obscurely, in the Third Report of the *Historical Manuscripts Commission*, 1872.

In 1965 I wrote to all the Whitelockes in the telephone books for Berkshire, Buckinghamshire and Oxfordshire. This followed my discovery, from the Parish Register at Fawley, that the last burial of a member of the family, that of Mr. Hugh Anthony Bulstrode Whitelocke, had taken place as recently as 1946. One of the replies I received was from his widow, Madeleine Whitelocke. We met. She invited me to her home and allowed me to study a Bulstrode Whitelocke manuscript volume as well as family trees and papers. One letter stopped me in my tracks. It was written from Dublin in the 1930s and was signed Percy G. Whitelocke-Lloyd. It claimed that he owned the 'Diary' of Bulstrode Whitelocke, and that of Judge James Whitelocke. I knew it couldn't be the 'Diary', since Lord Bute's family had owned that for at least 150 years. It must be the missing volume of the 'Annals'.

But Percy Whitelocke-Lloyd had died and so had his wife, Leila. The only surviving member of the family in Ireland was a sister, Miss Winifred, living in Co. Waterford. So I wrote to her, but she replied that she had never heard of any manuscripts in the family. A few months later she wrote to say that if I could go across to Dublin she would arrange for her solicitors to let me inspect the family files and deed boxes. I went over in the last week of October 1965, with just one week for the search, and was joined there by Mrs. Wyatt. On the Monday morning, we went to the solicitors' office in Merrion Square. They were most kind to us. The papers yielded some interesting information but no clue as to the whereabouts of the manuscript. We called on the widow's solicitor and then on the Press Secretary to the Archbishop of Ireland, to whom I had received an introduction from an English nun. After listening to the story of my search he said that if I would write a letter he would send it to all the Irish newspapers, and ask a columnist to interview me at the hotel, and he was as good as his word. On the Tuesday morning I hired a mini car and we drove some 200 miles to Co. Waterford to visit Miss Winifred. Next day we asked in Cappoquin how to get to her house. 'You go back on the Dungarvan Road.' 'The lady should do nothing of the sort. She should go the way we went that Sunday afternoon, past the old ruined graveyard . . .' and so on. We eventually found the house and Miss Winifred came down the stairs in profile, looking uncannily like the portrait of her ancestor in St. John's College, Oxford, with the distinctive family nose. She took one look at a photograph of the portrait and said 'but, he's just like us!' We knew by that time that the family heirlooms had been sold by auction at the Mansion House, Dublin, in 1946, at a sale which went on for several days, but Miss Winifred had kept back one item. Leaning against the wall was the stained glass window with Whitelocke's armorial bearings. The College of Arms Report indicates that this was probably made early in the 1630s. Miss Winifred asked me to arrange for it to go back to Fawley as a memorial to her ancestor, in the Church where many of her forbears from Ireland were buried in the eighteenth, nineteenth and twentieth centuries. I already knew that Mr. John Piper lived in the village. His son transported the glass back to the studio and in 1972 Mr. Piper arranged for it to be framed and placed in the Church.

We drove on from Co. Waterford another 200 miles through the rain and, after several adventures, called next day on the Lady Abbess at Kylemore Abbey, the great Benedictine Convent in a remote part of Connemara. I had telephoned her and there in the drawing room, ready for our visit, were a portrait of Bulstrode Whitelocke and one of his father Judge James Whitelocke. These had been given to the nuns by Percy and Leila Whitelocke-Lloyd. The Lady Abbess invited us to lunch and afterwards we talked and laughed, and presently I plucked up courage and said 'I don't want to be presumptuous, Mother Abbess, but it seems rather odd to keep portraits of two puritan gentlemen in the nuns' enclosure, because you can't explain them to the visitors.' I told her that, before leaving England, I had been in touch with the Director of the National Portrait Gallery, Mr. David Piper, and that the Gallery would probably like to buy them. She agreed at once, saying that with the money they would make a memorial to Percy and Leila, and some months later they were purchased by the Gallery.

We spent that night at Athlone. We still had no trace of the manuscripts and there was only Friday left and half of Saturday. Friday started with a puncture (our second) and I had to buy a new inner tube. That set me back by an hour and a half and thirty-nine shillings. We telephoned the Press Secretary to the Archbishop, but his number was out of order. Back in Dublin, we went to see him. He was out. We decided to call on the Whitelocke-Lloyds' parish priest in Clontarf. At the Presbytery the housekeeper said 'I'm sorry, the Father is away on a fortnight's holiday. Would you like to see the senior curate?' I said I'd love to see the senior curate. He couldn't help us himself but he sent us to a priest in another part of Dublin, who had known the family. The second priest told us he had never heard of any manuscripts but he gave us some useful advice: to go back to the widow's solicitors and ask three questions: who were the executors to her Will, who were the auctioneers who sold her estate and what was the address of a family friend, whose name he gave us? We followed this up immediately and learned that there had only been one executor, that he could have told us everything, but he died in June. We were given the address of the auctioneers in O'Connell Street, and three addresses for the family friend. By that time we were in the Friday rush hour. I tried to negotiate the car into a parking space in the middle of O'Connell Street but the attendant said crossly 'Move on, lady, move on, can't you see the lights are red?' so on I went, over the red lights. I stopped at the number we'd been given. But the auctioneers had moved. When I telephoned them from the hotel they said, categorically, that there had been no books and no manuscripts in the sale.

All we had left on the list was the old family friend. I telephoned his two home numbers but there was no reply. Late that evening I tried his place of work and a secretary answered. 'Yes. He will be in Saturday morning. Maybe he'll see you if you come about 11.15.' I drove to the house in another Georgian Square at 11.15 and a big car came in alongside the mini. A big man got out, went up the steps and let himself in with a latchkey. I went up the steps and rang the bell. The big man opened the door. I was there without any introduction so I told him my name, said I was writing a book about Bulstrode Whitelocke and that I believed he had known the White-locke-Lloyds. He invited us in. I didn't like to start with the only question that mattered, so I asked if he knew what had become of Whitelocke's ring with the three falcons on it, or of the family tree. Suddenly he said 'This is absolutely fascinating. I've got the original diaries of Bulstrode Whitelocke and of his father.' Then the hunt really began. He looked through drawers and bookshelves. They weren't there. He telephoned his son, an antique dealer, at their new home in Co. Dublin. 'Are they in the tall-boy in my bedroom?' They weren't. He turned to us and said he hoped they hadn't been stolen. So did we. He had to keep an appointment but he invited us to come to lunch at 12.45 at his Dublin home, which he was on the point of selling. We returned to the hotel in a state of euphoria. By the time I had paid the bill I was down to my last ten shillings, but with the whole of Dublin to choose from, the house where we were going to lunch was round the corner from the garage from which we had hired the mini. I ran in and said 'I believe you pay for repairs?' 'Yes.' I said 'I've had two flat tyres this week.' 'Oh I'm sorry, I don't pay for punctures.' 'But I had to buy a new inner tube.' Her face lit up and she said 'In that case I'll pay you the whole of the bill.' She gave me thirty-nine shillings, and I was back in the money again.

We arrived for our lunch appointment at a quarter to one. Now, I knew the size and shape of the volume I was looking for, but I realized that the binding would be different from its companion volumes in the British Museum. Our host's son started pulling out old books. I said 'No. No. No.' Then suddenly I said 'That looks more like it.' He answered 'It's only a transcript.' 'But could I see it, please?' He handed it over. I opened it and said 'This is not a transcript. It's the first volume of Bulstrode Whitelocke's autobiography in his own handwriting.' Then, out came Judge James's 'Liber Famelicus', with portions scored out for the Camden Society edition; next came a 'Diary' for September 1653, when Whitelocke was preparing to go to Sweden, and finally a little volume of sermons preached by White-locke in conventicles, during the last years of his life. Our host allowed me to borrow them and, after he had consulted the National Library of Ireland, he authorized me to arrange for their purchase by the British Museum.

Three years later I attended an international conference in Dublin. When it was over, I set off to revisit and photograph the places connected with the last phase of this treasure hunt. As I turned into the road where we had finally run the manuscripts to earth my heart gave a jump. The house had gone. The builders were on the site, with their concrete mixer, scaffolding and crane. If we had postponed our visit, we might never have found that needle in an Irish haystack.

Principal Manuscript Sources

with Notes

THE MARQUESS OF BUTE'S COLLECTION
MS. 196 D.13 '1605–1675'. The Diary of Bulstrode Whitelocke. Vol. i 1605–1659, Vol. ii 1659–1675.

THE MARQUESS OF BATH'S COLLECTION
Bulstrode Whitelocke's Collected Papers. 30 folio vols. also Index and Calendar; 9 parcels. Muniments Room, Longleat.
MS. 124 'Book of Expenses attending Sir Bulstrode Whitelocke's Embassy to Sweden'.
MS. 124a 'Journal of the Swedish Embassy'.
The original version. Incomplete. Library, Longleat.

BRITISH MUSEUM
(1) *Judge James Whitelocke:*
Stowe MS. 569 fol. 35. 'Of the Antiquity, Use and Ceremony of lawful Combats in England' 1601.
Attributed in the Stowe Catalogue to James Whitelocke.

Stowe MSS. 297 fols. 35 and 298 (2). 'Arguments against Impositions' by James Whitelocke M.P. for Woodstock.
The compilation of these arguments is attributed to Henry Yelverton.

Add. MS. 53725. 'Liber Famelicus'. Autobiography, incompletely published by the Camden Society, 1858.

(2) *Bulstrode Whitelocke:*
Add. MSS. 15622 and 15623. 'Whitelocke's Treatise on Parliament'. Vol. i autograph MS., vol. ii in another hand.
Fols. 102–102b, at the end of vol. ii, refer to the Petition and Advice offered to the Lord Protector by 'the last Parliament', indicating that this MS. was completed in 1657.

Add. MSS. 4749–4754. 'Whitelocke's Notes upon the King's Writ for choosing Members of Parliament 13. Car. 2'. Written by Whitelocke for Charles II, details are given in the 'Diary'. Dr. Morton edited the Notes for publication in 1766.

Add. MS. 53728. 'Lectures upon Particular Occasions by a Father to his family'. 'Upon the new Buildings at Chilton Lodge 1667'.
A companion volume of Whitelocke's sermons, *Quench not the Spirit*, was published by William Penn with his own introduction, 1711.

Add. MS. 21099. 'The King's Right to Grant Indulgence in Matters of Religion'.
Small volume on toleration of dissenters, written March 1662–3 at the request of
Charles II.

Add. MS. 4993. 'Whitelocke's Treatise of Government'.
In another hand. Some chapters correspond with chapters in Add. MSS. 37341 and
37342. Chapter 15 refers to Writs of Summons issued December 1658 in the name
of Richard, Lord Protector of the Commonwealth 'to this present Parliament
1658 [9]'.

Stowe MS. 333. 'History of the Parliament of England and some Resemblances of
the Jewish and other Councils'.
Incomplete. Several chapters overlap with Add. MSS. 4993 and 37341. Two
Latin tags on the fly-leaf are so bitter as to suggest that Whitelocke wrote them, if
not the MS., after the Restoration.

Add. MSS. 37341 and 37342. 'Whitelocke's Annals of his own Life Dedicated to
his Children'.
Written in retirement, but based on earlier work started at the age of 50. Whitelocke
explains in the Preface why he inserts this 2-volume 'History of the Parliament
of England', in effect a treatise on government, at the beginning of his 'Annals'.
Numbers 1 and 2 on fore-edge do not correspond with those on the volumes of
'Annals' which concern his own life.

Add. MS. 53726. 'The Annals of his own Life Dedicated to his Children'.
Marked 1 on fore-edge, this volume runs from Whitelocke's birth in August 1605
to August 1634. In his autobiographical writing the years used in the headings run
from about 1 August, the month of his birth, to 31 July. This has sometimes led
to confusion for the unwary. The Preface in Add. MS. 4992 belongs to this manuscript, as Whitelocke's paging shows. Dr. Morton presented 4992 to the British
Museum between 1770 and 1780; he also borrowed, and thought he had been
given, the volume now numbered Add. MS. 53726. It seems likely that while it
was in his possession the Preface fell out of the borrowed manuscript and was
bound into the other. 53726 was the 'missing manuscript', the search for which is
described in the Postscript to this book.

Add. MS. 37343. 'Annals'. August 1634 to 1645, marked 2 on fore-edge.

Add. MS. 37344. 'Annals'. August 1645 to 1649, marked 3 on fore-edge.

Add. MS. 37345. 'Annals'. August 1649 to 1653, marked 4 on fore-edge.

Add. MS. 4992. 'Annals'. July 1653 to April 1656, marked 6 on fore-edge.

Although the years run continuously in the 'Annals' there is no volume marked 5. Whitelocke wrote two volumes, listed below and bound as 'Annals', which cover the period of the Swedish embassy, 1653–54. The last volume of the 'Annals', from 1656–1660, is missing. The only clue to its having been written is in the printed *Memorials*, based on the 'Annals', which finish at the Restoration.

Add. MSS. 37346 and 37347. 'The History of Whitelocke's Ambassy from England to Sweden'.
Bound as 'Annals', numbered 1 and 2 on fore-edge. Vol. i September 1653–February 1653[4]. Vol. ii March to June 1654. Written after Whitelocke's return from Sweden but before the Restoration. Passages favourable to Cromwell or hostile to monarchy heavily deleted by Carleton Whitelocke. Material in some chapters overlaps with that in the works on parliament and government.

Add. MSS. 4991 A and 4991 B. 'The History of Whitelocke's Ambassy from England to Sweden with notes thereupon and touching the Government, Public Councils and Persons in those and in other Countries'.
Transcript from 37346 and 37347. Formerly in 4 vols. Vol. i marked 1 and 2 on fore-edge, vol. ii marked 3 and upside down 4.

Add. MS. 4995. 'Papers relating to Whitelocke's Swedish Embassy'.
Mainly transcripts.

Add. MS. 4902. 'A Journal of the Swedish Ambassy in the Years 1653 and 1654 impartially written by the Ambassador'.
Whitelocke's most carefully written account of the embassy, probably intended for publication. It was eventually edited by Dr. Charles Morton and published 1772. A new edition, prepared by Henry Reeve, appeared 1855. Morton acquired the manuscript from Sir Bulstrode's grandson, John Carleton Whitelocke, of Priorswood, Co. Dublin. The printed editions contain some errors of transcription and omissions.

Add. MS. 31984. 'Whitelocke's History of the Forty-Eighth Year of his Age . . . dedicated to his Children'.
1 to 31 August 1653. Aug. on fore-edge.

Egerton MS. 997. 'Whitelocke's History of the year 1653'. The misleading title page refers to 'Passages in August 1653'.
The MS. covers September to 30 November 1653. Small notebook, corners rubbed away as if from being carried in Whitelocke's pocket. Opens with a draft for the preface to the 'Journal'.

Add. MS. 53727. 'September 1653'.
Supplements the other versions of Whitelocke's preparations for the embassy.

Add. MS. 4994. 'Passages in November 1653'.
1 to 12 November 1653.
Entry on fore-edge indecipherable, owing to rebinding.

Egerton MS. 1048 fol. 160 Draft of the 'Commission of Bulstrode Whitelocke as
Ambassador Extraordinary to Queen Christina of Sweden, 21 Oct 1653'. Latin
and English.

Stowe MS. 189 fols. 59–59b. Bulstrode Whitelocke's 'Commission to treat with
the Queen of Sweden 1653' in Latin.

UNIVERSITY LIBRARY, LUND
Whitelocke's pocket Phrase Book for use in Sweden, with sentences in Latin,
French and English.

UNIVERSITY LIBRARY, CAMBRIDGE
MS. Dd 12. 20–22. A Parliamentary Diary for 1626. Attributed to Bulstrode
Whitelocke.
His signature is on the inside cover and a marginal note on fol. 30 '*Me B.W. Absente*'.

MS. Mm 6. 57 fols. 92–94.
Copy of a document from Charles II to Sir Bulstrode Whitelocke granting, or
confirming, and defining Whitelocke's entitlement to lands in Ireland.

WINDSOR CASTLE
'Windsor Castle Governors' Book 1668–1671', pp. 1–7.
'Certain Particulars Relating to the Office of Constable of Windsor' collected by
Sir Bulstrode Whitlock' (*sic*).
Transcript of Whitelocke's report to Prince Rupert 1671.

MRS. M.A. HAWKSLEY
Sundry letters and papers of Sir William Whitelocke.

MRS. MADELEINE WHITELOCKE
'August 1653'
Diary notes and meditations during the month in which Whitelocke heard he had
been nominated as ambassador.

Bibliography

ARCKENHOLTZ, J., *Mémoires concernant Christine reine de Suède* (Amsterdam and Leipzig 1751–60)

ASHMOLE, Elias, *Elias Ashmole 1617–1692* His Autobiographical and Historical Notes, his Correspondence, and Other Contemporary Sources Relating to his Life and Work (ed. C. H. Johnsten) (O.U.P. 1966)

AUBREY, John, *Brief Lives* (ed. Oliver Lawson Dick) (Peregrine Books 1962)

BLUNT, Reginald, *Historical Handbook to Chelsea* (Lamley & Co. 1900)

BOWEN, C. D., *The Lion and the Throne* (Hamish Hamilton 1957)

BRYANT, Arthur, *King Charles II* (Collins 1960)

BUCHAN, John, *Oliver Cromwell* (Hodder and Stoughton 1935)

BURNE, Alfred H. and YOUNG, Peter, *The Great Civil War* (Eyre and Spottiswoode 1959)

CAMPBELL, John, Lord, *Lives of the Lord Chancellors and Keepers* (John Murray, 1856–7)

CARLYLE, Thomas, *Oliver Cromwell's Letters & Speeches* (Ward, Lock, Bowden and Co. 1892)

CHRISTINA, Queen, *Drottning Kristina, Maximer les Sentiments Heroïques* (ed. Sven Stolpe, Bonniers, Stockholm 1959)

COKAYNE GIBBS, Herbert, *The Parish Registers of Hunsdon, Co. Hertford, 1546–1837* (The St. Catherine Press 1915)

CURTIS, M. H., *Oxford and Cambridge in Transition 1558–1642* (O.U.P. 1959)

DAVIES, Godfrey, *The Early Stuarts 1603–1660* (O.U.P. 1952)

DAVIES, Godfrey, *The Restoration of Charles II* (O.U.P. 1955)

DAVIES, Randall, *Chelsea Old Church* (Duckworth and Co. 1904)

D'OYLY BAYLEY, William, *Account of the House of D'Oyly* (John Bowyer Nichols and Sons 1848)

FIRTH, C. H., *Last Years of the Protectorate* (Longman, Green and Co. 1909)

FIRTH, C. H., *Cromwell's Army* (University Paperbacks, Methuen 1967)

FIRTH, C. H., *Oliver Cromwell* (G. P. Putnam's Sons 1900)

FIRTH, C. H. and RAIT, R. S. (eds.), *Acts and Ordinances of the Interregnum* (London 1911)

GARDINER, S. R., *History of England 1603–42* (Longman, Green and Co. 1877)

GARDINER, S. R., *Constitutional Documents of the Puritan Revolution* (O.U.P. 1962)

GILLESPIE, George, *Notes of Debates and Proceedings of the Assembly of Divines* (ed. David Meek, Edinburgh 1846)

GREY, Anchitell, *Debates of the House of Commons From the Year 1667 to the Year 1694* (London 1769)

GOUGH NICHOLS, J. and J. BRUCE, (eds.) *Wills from Doctors' Commons* (Camden Society 1863)

HALLER, William, *Liberty and Reformation in the Puritan Revolution* (2nd ed. paperback, Columbia University Press 1963)

HARRIS WILLSON, David, *King James VI and I* (Jonathan Cape paperback 1966)

HARWOOD, T. E., *Windsor Old and New* (Printed for the Author 1929)

HEXTER, J. H., 'The Problem of the Presbyterian Independents' *Reappraisals in History* (London 1961)

HILL, Christopher, *Puritanism and Revolution* (Mercury Books 1962)

HILL, Christopher, *God's Englishman* (Weidenfeld and Nicolson 1970)

HOLLES, Denzil, *Memoirs of Denzil Lord Holles Baron of Ifield in Sussex from the Year 1641 to 1648* (1699)

HYDE, Edward, Earl of Clarendon, *The Life of Edward, Earl of Clarendon* (O.U.P. 1857)

HYDE, Edward, Earl of Clarendon, *The History of the Great Rebellion* (ed. W. D. Macray) (O.U.P. 1888)

JONES, J. R., *Britain and Europe in the Seventeenth Century* (Edward Arnold 1966)

KEELER, M. F., *The Long Parliament 1640–41* (The American Philosophical Society, Philadelphia 1954)

LAMONT, William M., *Marginal Prynne* (Routledge and Kegan Paul 1963)

LEFKOWITZ, Murray, *Trois Masques à la Cour de Charles Ier D'Angleterre* (Centre National de la Recherche Scientifique 1970)

LUDLOW, Edmund, *The Memoirs of Edmund Ludlow* (ed. C. H. Firth) (O.U.P. 1894)

MARSH, J. B., *The Story of Harcourt* (Strahan and Co. 1871)

MARVELL, Andrew, *The Poems and Letters of Andrew Marvell* (ed. H. M. Margoliouth, O.U.P. 1927)

MOORE, James, *Memorials of Charterhouse* (London 1844)

MUNK, William, *The Roll of the Royal College of Physicians of London* (Longman, Green, Longman and Roberts 1861)

NOBLE, T. C., *Memorials of Temple Bar* (Diprose and Bateman 1870)

OGG, David, *England in the Reign of Charles II* (O.U.P. 1934)

PENNINGTON, D. H., *Seventeenth-century Europe* (Longman 1970)

PEPYS, Samuel, *The Diary of Samuel Pepys* (ed. Robert Latham and William Matthews) (Bell 1971–)

POWELL, Anthony, *John Aubrey and his friends* (Mercury Books 1963)

PRENDERGAST, J. P., *The Cromwellian Settlement of Ireland*, 2nd edition (Dublin 1875)

PROTHERO, G. W., *Select Statutes and Other Constitutional Documents*, 4th edition (O.U.P. 1913)

ROBERTS, Clayton, *The Growth of Responsible Government in Stuart England* (C.U.P. 1966)

ROBERTS, Michael, *Essays in Swedish History* (Weidenfeld and Nicolson 1967)

ROBERTS, Michael, *Gustavus Adolphus: a History of Sweden 1611–1632* (Longman, Green and Co. 1953)

SHAW, W. A., *History of the English Church* (Longman, Green and Co. 1900)

STOLPE, Sven, *Christina of Sweden* (Burns and Oates 1966)

STUBBES, Phillip, *Anatomy of the Abuses in England in Shakespeare's Youth* (Trübner and Co. 1877–9)

TANNER, J. R., *English Constitutional Conflicts of the Seventeenth Century* (C.U.P. 1961)

TREVELYAN, G. M., *England under the Stuarts* (Penguin Books 1960)

TREVOR-ROPER, H. R., *Archbishop Laud 1573–1645* (Macmillan and Co. 1962)

UNDERDOWN, David, *Pride's Purge* (O.U.P. 1971)

UNDERDOWN, David, 'The Independents Reconsidered' *Journal of British Studies*, iii (1964)

VERNEY, *Memoirs of the Verney Family* (Longman, Green and Co. 1907)

WESTON, C. C., *English Constitutional Theory and the House of Lords 1556–1832* (Routledge and Kegan Paul 1965)

WEDGWOOD, C. V., *Thomas Wentworth* (paperback, Jonathan Cape 1964)

WEDGWOOD, C. V., *The King's Peace* (Collins 1955)

WEDGWOOD, C. V., *The King's War* (Collins 1958)

WEDGWOOD, C. V., *The Trial of Charles I* (Collins 1964)

WHITELOCKE, Bulstrode, *Essays Ecclesiastical and Civil* (London 1706)

WHITELOCKE, James, *Liber Famelicus* (ed. John Bruce) (Camden Society 1858)

WHITELOCKE, R. H., *Memoirs, Biographical and Historical, of Bulstrode Whitelocke* (Routledge, Warne and Routledge 1860)

WILLEY, Basil, *The Seventeenth-century Background* (Penguin Books in association with Chatto and Windus 1962)

YULE, George, 'Independents and Revolutionaries' *The Journal of British Studies* May 1968, vol. vii No. 2.

YULE, George, *The Independents in the English Civil War* (C.U.P. 1958)

Abbreviations

A & O	*Acts and Ordinances of the Interregnum* by C. H. Firth and R. S. Rait
Annals	'The Annals of his own Life Dedicated to his Children'
Add. MSS.	British Museum Additional Manuscripts
B.I.H.R.	*Bulletin of the Institute of Historical Research*
C.S.P.	*Calendar of State Papers*
C.U.L.	Cambridge University Library
C.U.P.	Cambridge University Press
D.N.B.	*Dictionary of National Biography*
Eg. MSS.	British Museum Egerton Manuscripts
E.H.R.	*English Historical Review*
G.E.C.	*The Complete Peerage* by G. E. Cokayne
H.M.S.O.	Her Majesty's Stationery Office
J.M.H.	*Journal of Modern History*
Journal	*Journal of the Swedish Embassy* by Ambassador Bulstrode Whitelocke
L.C.C.	London County Council
Liber	*Liber Famelicus* by James Whitelocke
Longleat	Longleat Whitelocke Papers
Memorials	*Memorials of the English Affairs* etc. by Bulstrode Whitelocke
O.U.P.	Oxford University Press
S. P. Dom.	State Papers, Domestic
Stowe MSS.	British Museum Stowe Manuscripts
V.C.H.	*Victoria County History*

Reference Notes

PREFACE
1. Thomas Carlyle *Oliver Cromwell's Letters and Speeches* (Ward, Lock, Bowden and Co. 1892) p. 469.
2. William M. Lamont *Marginal Prynne* (Routledge and Kegan Paul 1963) p. 1.
3. Add. MSS. 37346 and 37347.

CHAPTER 1: 'The Best School in Christendom'
1. '*Sans culottes*', 'Bolshies', 'Commies' and 'Terrorists' are among the abusive names which conjure up visions of uncouth behaviour. As a scandalized Victorian lady said to the author's grandfather: 'Mr. Cayford, you cannot be a gentleman *and* a radical.'
2. *V.C.H. Berks.*, Vol. iv, pp. 4, 5. Bulstrode Whitelocke referred in his 'Diary', 14 December 1670, to a letter from the minister of Aldworth concerning the monuments of the Whitelocke ancestors in his church. See also Nikolaus Pevsner, *Berkshire*, The Buildings of England Series (Penguin Books 1966) pp. 63–4.
3. Sir James Whitelocke, *Liber Famelicus* (ed. John Bruce) (Camden Society 1858) p. 3.
4. James Whitelocke, *Liber*, pp. 4 and 5.
5. James Whitelocke, *Liber*, p. 6. James recorded that in February 1606–7 his mother Joan who 'had her senses and memory to the last gasp. . . went away . . . with old age, as a candle that goeth out'; she was uncertain as to her exact age but she and her relatives 'reckoned her near four score'.
6. James Whitelocke, *Liber*, p. 6.
7. The fifth earl, who was married to the daughter of Sir Philip Sidney, died in 1612. He was succeeded by his brother Francis, who was in turn succeeded in 1632 by another brother, George. In 1634 this seventh earl tried to prevent his niece, Frances Willoughby, from marrying a commoner – Bulstrode Whitelocke.
8. James Whitelocke, *Liber*, pp. 7–11. Edmund died at Newhall, near Chelmsford.
9. James Whitelocke, *Liber*, pp. 11–12. Drake's widow, Elizabeth, received a substantial bequest while the bulk of the estate went to his brother, Thomas Drake. *Wills from Doctors' Commons* (ed. J. Gough Nichols and J. Bruce) (Camden Society 1863) pp. 72–9.
10. James Whitelocke, *Liber*, pp. 12–13; M. H. Curtis, *Oxford and Cambridge in Transition 1558–1642* (O.U.P. 1959) pp. 59 and 77–8.
11. Add. MS. 37343 fol. 201b. Bulstrode quoted this after his father's death.

12. James Whitelocke, *Liber*, p. 9.
13. Sidelights on John Croke's encounters with Edward Coke are given by C. D. Bowen, *The Lion and the Throne* (Hamish Hamilton 1957).
14. The house was in the parish of St. Dunstan in the West. Sir George's father lived at The Sign of the Chariot in Fleet Street and it may have been the same house but it has not been possible to locate it.
15. T. C. Noble, *Memorials of Temple Bar* (Diprose and Bateman 1870) p. 83.
16. Add. MS. 53726 fol. 3. This volume of 'The Annals of his Life', covering the first twenty-nine years of his life, was paginated by Whitelocke and starts at page 25. The Preface and Dedication to his Children, which covers twenty-four pages and is bound into the beginning of Add. MS. 4992, clearly belongs here. The entry in the parish register, now in Guildhall, London, spells the name Bulstred Whitelock.
17. Add. MS. 53726 fol. 3. 'Shaffling broth' seems to have been a peasant recipe. Elizabeth had to ask what it was.
18. 'Diary' 1607–8. Since the 'Diary' is neither paginated nor foliated references are given throughout by date.
19. James Whitelocke, *Liber*, p. 47. James noted that unlike many judges of the day Coke did not accept bribes and counsel was not expected to make annual gifts of money and plate in order to win favour for clients. *Liber*, p. 50. C. D. Bowen, *The Lion*, p. 254 *passim*, gives a detailed account of Coke's struggle with King James and of the legal principles he expounded, which deeply influenced James Whitelocke and his son.
20. G. W. Prothero, *Select Statutes and Other Constitutional Documents* 4th edition (O.U.P. 1913) pp. 351–3. James Whitelocke's argument foreshadowed his son's contention, nearly thirty years later, that control of the militia lay neither with the King alone nor with Parliament alone, but with the King and Parliament acting together. This was his version of the theory of 'mixed government', according to which monarchy, aristocracy, and democracy each acted as a counterweight to the other. This classical concept had been in vogue in the sixteenth century and came into prominence again through Charles I's answer to Parliament's Nineteen Propositions in 1642; it was talked about by lawyers during the Interregnum and again after the Restoration. Bulstrode Whitelocke expanded the argument in more than one of his manuscripts on government. Different versions of the theory of mixed monarchy are described by C. C. Weston, *English Constitutional Theory and the House of Lords 1556–1832* (Routledge and Kegan Paul 1965) and more briefly in 'The Theory of Mixed Monarchy in the Reign of Charles I' (*E.H.R.* July 1961).
21. James Whitelocke, *Liber*, pp. 34–40.
22. James Whitelocke, *Liber*, p. 48; also G. M. Trevelyan, *England under the Stuarts* (Penguin Books 1960) pp. 114–15.

23. *V.C.H. County of Buckingham*, vol. iii, p. 40, gives the date as 1617. Bulstrode and his father give the earlier date which is confirmed by the privately owned title deeds and conveyance. During the Interregnum Bulstrode added Greenlands, the estate adjoining Fawley Court on the Hambleden side.

24. The Thames was a working river with barges gliding along the foot of the hills 'to carry their burdens of wood and corn to . . . London'. B. M. Egerton 997 fols. 22b–23. Whitelocke's stretch of the river bank is the setting for Henley Royal Regatta.

25. Parsons later studied medicine at Padua and became Principal of Hart Hall, Oxford.

26. Add. MS. 37343 fol. 11b.

27. In the seventeenth century riding to beagles seems to have been usual, instead of following on foot. There are references to King James I and his courtiers on horseback with beagles.

28. Hydrotherapy has long been practised in Germany. This version of the hot water compress appears to have been effective.

29. Clarendon, *The Life of Edward, Earl of Clarendon* (O.U.P. 1857) vol. i, p. 29.

30. Add. MS. 53726 fol. 11.

31. Their well-to-do neighbour was a Deputy Lieutenant for Oxfordshire and Justice of Oyer and Terminer. William D'Oyly Bayley, *Account of the House of D'Oyly* (John Bowyer Nichols and Sons 1848) p. 28.

32. The *Memorials*, published seven years after his death, ignored the fact that Whitelocke was a member of this Parliament.

33. Political parties in any modern sense are commonly stated to have been unknown before 1700; the word 'party' is used advisedly since Whitelocke used it freely to describe shifting groups of politicians whose leaders were anxious to win adherents.

34. Add. MS. 53726 fol. 16b.

35. Details of Clement Coke's and Samuel Turner's protests are given by S. R. Gardiner, *History of England 1603–42* (Longman, Green and Co. 1877) vol. vi, p. 76. His account from manuscript sources tallies with Whitelocke's but is more specific about Dr. Turner. A parliamentary diary for 1626, C.U.L. Dd. 12.20–22, is attributed to Whitelocke. The cramped handwriting, even allowing for it being written on his knee, gives rise to doubts as to whether it is an autograph MS. in spite of an entry on fol. 30 '*me B. W. absente*'. An account of this diary was given by W. A. J. Archbold (*E.H.R.* 1902) vol. xvii, pp. 730–7.

36. Dr. Turner is identified by Clayton Roberts, *The Growth of Responsible Government in Stuart England* (C.U.P. 1966) p. 56, as a physician, Samuel Turner, 'better known for diverting noble lords at Court than for advocating popular causes'. It was the same Dr. Turner whom Whitelocke later encountered with the King in Oxford. See also *D.N.B.*

37. G. Roberts, *The History of Lyme Regis* (1823) p. 35.
38. Add. MS. 53726 fol. 35.
39. According to modern measurements the distance from London to Land's End is 51 miles farther than Whitelocke believed it to be.

CHAPTER II: Rebecca

1. Add. MS. 53726 fols. 32b–33.
2. Add. MS. 53726 fol. 45b.
3. Add. MS. 53726 fol. 50b.
4. Add. MS. 53726 fol. 54b.
5. 'Diary' 1630.
6. Add. MS. 53726 fols. 55–55b.
7. Longleat Whitelocke Papers vol. v. fol. 153.
8. 'Diary' 1630–31.
9. 'Diary' 1610–11.
10. Add. MS. 53726 fol. 55b.
11. Longleat, vol. v. fol. 180.
12. Longleat, parcel 6 (folder).
13. Longleat, parcel 6 (folder). Some years later Bulstrode Whitelocke sent one of his finest singers from Fawley to York for the King's entertainment, at the request of Sir Arthur Ingram. Add. MS. 53726 fol. 85b.
14. Six years later Williams infuriated the Archbishop by his pamphlet *Holy Table: Name and Thing*. Fawley was in the diocese of Lincoln, for until 1837 the See stretched from the Humber to the Thames.
15. Add. MS. 53726 fol. 65b. II Kings 9 v. 20 . . .'the driving is like the driving of Jehu the son of Nimshi; for he driveth furiously.'
16. Add. MS. 53726 fol. 67.
17. Longleat, parcel 6 (folder). Letter to his sister Elizabeth Mostyn.
18. Add. MS. 53726 fol. 68b. Bull was in his service for forty years.
19. The text of the Deed of Gift and of the Will are given in Add. MS. 53726 fols. 69b–70. *Liber Famelicus* was one of the four Whitelocke manuscripts which the author discovered in Ireland in 1965. On the title page are written the Judge's purchases of land – Fawley Court £9,000, Phyllis Court £1,200, as well as smaller acquisitions, which brought the total to £11,020.15.4d. These do not appear in the printed version. The published *Memorials* gives an emaciated account of the Judge's death, paraphrased by its editor and parading, like much else in the *Memorials*, as Whitelocke's exact words.
20. Longleat, vol. v. fol. 235.

21. Longleat, vol. v. fols. 227 and 240. These are Judge Whitelocke's propositions for the marriage settlement and the discharge, signed and sealed by the bride and bridegroom.

22. The shorter version in the 'Diary' uses these words. Set out 'dialogue-wise' in the 'Annals', Add. MS. 53726 fol. 74b, Laud advised him to work hard but added 'you need not sweat so much as others at it'.

23. Whitelocke referred to him as Archbishop of Canterbury at this meeting in September 1632; Laud had been appointed Chancellor of Oxford in 1629 but was not made Archbishop until August 1633.

24. Longleat, vol. v. fol. 246b.

25. Longleat, vol. vi. fol. 29. Receipts for the work are dated 12 October 1633. Add. MS. 53726 fols. 79b and 88–9. I am indebted to Mr. John Piper for pointing out that, on the architectural evidence, the transept in which the tomb is now housed cannot be the one built by Whitelocke. The earlier one may have been larger, covering the area of the present south transept and extending eastward. It is likely that the monument itself was originally erected in that eastern section. Access to the new 'aisle', as Whitelocke called it, was probably through the, now blocked-up, rounded doorway in the chancel. This can be seen in an early picture of the interior of the Church, and can still be discerned from the outside.

26. Add. MS. 53726 fols. 96–96b gives the notation of the Coranto in Whitelocke's handwriting.

27. It is strange that twenty years later neither Pepys nor Whitelocke referred to the other in his journal, yet they must have met through their connection with Edward Montagu, who was Whitelocke's colleague and Pepys's master; in at least one letter, Pepys referred respectfully to 'my lord Whitelocke'. Bodleian Library Carte Ms. 73. fol. 170. 5 December 1657.

28. Longleat, parcel 2. Nos. 17, 18. Correspondence with Nicholas Lanier. Lanier put the blame on one Dr. Adson, a member of the King's music. Murray Lefkowitz pp. 38 footnote 4bis and 59–60 *Trois Masques à la Cour de Charles Ier D'Angleterre* (Centre National de la Recherche Scientifique 1970) Lefkowitz points out that Nicholas Lanier's complaint arose because Whitelocke planned to replace the King's musicians, at the second performance, by twelve City musicians employed at the Blackfriars and Cockpit theatres. On pp. 27–109 Lefkowitz gives a richly detailed account of the masque from different sources but principally from the Whitelocke papers at Longleat and the *Memorials*. The book contains reproductions of some of Inigo Jones's costume designs and stage sets with Shirley's libretto and what survives of the music. Faced by conflicting evidence M. Lefkowitz argues convincingly that *The Triumph of Peace* was presented on Monday 3 February 1634 instead of on Candlemas (2 February) as Whitelocke recorded. In identifying Whitelocke's manuscripts, giving their location and suggesting their relationship to the printed *Memorials* M. Lefkowitz has followed

the partly inaccurate and out of date information given in the *Historical Manu-scripts Commission* 3rd Report, and has clearly drawn some of his information from the unreliable, published versions. It follows that his most valuable findings are those based on his study of the Longleat and other manuscripts.

29. Longleat. Parcel 2 contains bills and receipts and Whitelocke's stage plots for placing the musicians.

30. Add. MS. 53726 fols. 95–95b.

31. 'Diary' 1633–34. Add. MS. 53726 fol. 99.

32. Add. MS. 53726 fol. 100.

33. 'Diary' 1633–4. Other claims of this nature, made in the 'Diary', are usually substantiated by the original letters among the Longleat papers. Correspondence with Richelieu is missing but may have been destroyed with other Whitelocke documents in 1642, 1660 or 1666.

34. Letters from and to Whitelocke in Paris: Longleat, vol. vi. B.W. first letter to Cely fol. 93; to Bartlett fol. 88; Hyde to B.W. fol. 61; B.W. second letter to Cely fol. 99; B.W. to Napper fol. 97; B.W. to Elizabeth Mostyn fol. 119.

CHAPTER III: Frances

1. Add. MS. 37343 fol. 1. It was characteristic of the humility which underlay his conceit that he chose to record a discussion in which he was politely rebuked by a servant; even at the height of his power Whitelocke could cheerfully accept advice or criticism from anyone, except his superiors. In the 'Annals', unlike his other works, he wrote in the first person, although in the 'Diary' and even in his carefully revised 'Journal of the Swedish Embassy', he occasionally broke into the first person, usually in moments of stress.

2. In the original, the idiomatic contraction is spelt 'Ile'. Later in the conversation Whitelocke writes 'Thats true.'

3. Add. MS. 37343 fols. 1–2b.

4. The dowager Countess of Sunderland, formerly Elizabeth Manners, was a daughter of John Manners, 4th Earl of Rutland. By her marriage and that of her youngest sister the families of Manners, Scrope and Willoughby were brought together.

5. Add. MS. 37343 fol. 2b.

6. Add. MS. 53727 p. 38. Nearly twenty years later he described this first impression to his eldest daughter. Whitelocke paginated instead of foliating his manuscripts; the page number is given because, at the time of writing, this volume has not been foliated.

7. Add. MS. 37343 fol. 5b.

8. Longleat, vol. vi. fol. 129. Mrs. Thynne's cousin, the Duchess of Buckingham, was the daughter of Frances Manners, 6th Earl of Rutland; see note 4.

9. Add. MS. 37343 fol. 5b.

10. 'Diary' 1634. This information throws light on the two earliest portraits, plates 1 and 3, which show Whitelocke before and after he fell in love with Frances.

11. Add. MS. 37343 fol. 8.

12. This account is taken from the 'Diary'. There were only four trusty stalwarts according to Add. MS. 37343 fol. 8b.

13. Kitson could hardly refuse since the living of Fawley was in Whitelocke's gift, but he was in danger of invoking the displeasure of his Archbishop for marrying a commoner to a nobleman's daughter, without official consent.

14. Add. MS. 37343 fol. 9b.

15. The word 'cousin' was often used loosely. Pembroke's first wife was Susan de Vere, daughter of Edward, Earl of Oxford whose sister, Mary de Vere, was the mother of Robert, Earl of Lyndsey (Lord Willoughby de Eresby).

16. Add. MS. 37343 fol. 11.

17. Longleat, vol. vi. fol. 157.

18. 'Diary' July 1635.

19. Longleat, vol. vi. fol. 200.

20. Edward Hyde, Earl of Clarendon, *The History of the Rebellion* (ed. W. D. Mackay) (O.U.P. 1888) vol. i, p. 85.

21. H. R. Trevor-Roper, *Archbishop Laud 1573–1645* (Macmillan and Co. 1962) pp. 301–2.

22. Longleat, vol. vii. fol. 79.

23. William became a successful lawyer, treasurer of the Middle Temple and a prominent Whig.

24. G.E.C.

25. Add. MS. 37343 fol. 5b. She 'played very well herself upon the stump and lute'. Shortly before the Civil War Lady Sunderland wrote teasingly to Whitelocke 'We want your company to sing mass songs – if you dare.' Longleat, vol. viii. fol. 229 20 June 1642.

26. 'Diary' 1640.

27. Add. MS. 37343 fol. 148b.

28. Add. MS. 37343 fol. 198. The 'public good' was an emotive term like 'democracy' or 'freedom' to-day. Milton later used it with a touch of satire in *Samson Agonistes*.

29. Add. MS. 37343 fol. 198b.

30. Longleat, parcel 1, item 1.

31. Add. MS. 37343 fols. 208–212b. An interesting analysis is given by Mary Reno Frear in 'The Election at Great Marlow in 1640' (*J.M.H.* XIV No. 4) pp. 437–45.

32. Ironically, one of the seventy-six who had resisted the King was the former Thomas Wentworth, who had later become King Charles's friend and counsellor, the hated Earl of Strafford.

33. James Whitelocke, *Liber*, Introduction p. xv.

34. Add. MS. 37343 fols. 214b–215.

35. Add. MS. 37343 fol. 216.

36. C. V. Wedgwood, *Thomas Wentworth* (Paperback, Jonathan Cape 1964) p. 347 *passim.*

37. This was a private meeting. Rushworth, who recorded the public proceedings, makes no mention of it.

38. Whitelocke repeatedly referred to article 23 as article 24. The five articles 23 to 27 were taken together, which may have caused this confusion.

39. Wedgwood, *Wentworth*, p. 352. Add. MS. 37343 fols. 221–2.

40. Add. MS. 37343 fol. 226b. 'Diary' 1640–1. The House of Commons frequently employed Whitelocke for drafting bills. His parliamentary work had already become so heavy that he had moved to a house in Dean's Yard, Westminster, to avoid a journey every day. Add. MS. 37343 fol. 217b.

41. Whitelocke may not have written in these terms at the time, but it was in character for him to express admiration for a courageous enemy.

42. Add. MS. 37343 fol. 218.

43. Add. MS. 37343 fol. 229.

44. Add. MS. 37344 fol. 296b.

45. The portraits in question are plates 1 and 3. A third and later portrait, plate 4, which is probably a copy, has a small, commonplace nose instead of the distinctive family beak.

CHAPTER IV: 'A Spirit of Division and Contradiction'

1. Add. MS. 37343 fol. 229.

2. Godfrey Davies, *The Early Stuarts 1603–1660* (O.U.P. 1952) pp. 100–17 and C. V. Wedgwood, *The King's Peace* (Collins 1955) Ch. 6, *passim.*

3. Add. MS. 37343 fol. 232b.

4. The voting figures are taken from C. V. Wedgwood, *The King's War* (Collins 1958) p. 29. Whitelocke's account is given in Add. MS. 37343 fol. 234b. See also Sir Simonds D'Ewes *Journal* (ed. W. H. Coates) (Yale University Press and O.U.P. 1942) pp. 183–7.

5. Add. MS. 37343 fols. 234b–235.

6. Add. MS. 37343 fol. 238b.

7. Add. MS. 37343 fols. 241b–242b.

8. J. P. Prendergast, *The Cromwellian Settlement of Ireland* (Longmans 1870) pp. 72, 403–42. Add. MS. 37343 fols. 243b and 244.

9. Add. MS. 37343 fols. 249–249b.

10. 'Diary' 1638 [39].

11. The full significance of the Answer is developed in C. C. Weston's study, *English Constitutional Theory and the House of Lords 1556–1832* (Routledge and Kegan Paul 1965).

12. Add. MS. 37343 fols. 251b–252b.

13. Add. MS. 37343 fols. 247b–248.

14. Add. MS. 37343 fol. 247b.

15. An engraved map in the London Museum, dated 1559, shows the earlier use of these fields. See *Moorfields in 1559* (H.M.S.O. 1963). Add. MS. 37343 fol. 279b.

16. Add. MS. 37343 fol. 254b.

17. Add. MS. 37343 fol. 255. Whitelocke's contempt for the Earl of Berkshire was surpassed by that of Clarendon, who assessed the Earl's influence and reputation as 'less than anything but his understanding'.

18. Add. MS. 37343 fol. 253b. Whitelocke does not say whether the gaps in his mouth were filled by transplants of teeth from some of his servants, but this was not an unusual procedure.

19. Years later, Whitelocke wrote generously of Lord Say's fine qualities, but deplored this error of judgement based on 'pique'.

20. Sir Ralph Winwood, *Memorials* 1725, vol. iii, pp. 460–1. King James's favourite, Robert Carr, Earl of Somerset, was later found guilty with Frances of the murder of Sir Thomas Overbury.

21. Add. MS. 37343 fols. 259–60.

22. The account of what led to the battle of Brentford, and part of the description of what followed are taken from the royalist version given by Hyde in *The History of the Great Rebellion* vol. vi, sections 134–7. The rest is from Add. MS. 37343 fol. 260. Whitelocke seems at first sight to have given the date on which he approached the Council wrongly as 13 November, but in fact the figure has been altered by someone from 12 to 13, perhaps to shift the blame onto the King.

23. Alfred H. Burne and Peter Young, *The Great Civil War* (Eyre and Spottiswoode 1959) pp. 32–3 gives a full account of the close of the Edgehill campaign.

24. Wedgwood, *The King's War*, pp. 161, 162, 168, 184.

25. Littleton had left Parliament for the King, sending the Great Seal before him, shortly before the outbreak of the Civil War.

26. Add. MS. 37343 fol. 265. 'Country' was frequently used to denote a 'county'.

27. Add. MS. 37343 fols. 265b–266.

28. Add. MS. 37343 fol. 267.

29. Whitelocke could not know that letters between Charles and Henrietta Maria

indicated that the King had no more intention than Pym had of reaching a settlement.

30. Add. MS. 37343 fols. 286b and 239b.
31. M. F. Keeler, *The Long Parliament, 1640-41* (The American Philosophical Society, Philadelphia, 1954), pp. 159-60.
32. Add. MS. 37343 fol. 280.
33. Add. MS. 37343 fol. 276.
34. The amendment was proposed by Henry Vane who was sent to negotiate with the Scots. W. A. Shaw, *History of the English Church* (Longmans Green 1900) vol. i, p. 143. S. R. Gardiner, *Constitutional Documents of the Puritan Revolution* (O.U.P. 1962), p. 268.
35. Add. MS. 37343 fol. 272b.
36. Add. MS. 37344 fol. 12b.
37. Add. MS. 37343 fol. 11b.
38. Add. MS. 37343 fols. 77b and 131 indicate Whitelocke's Erastian outlook in the 1630s, as a defence against the 'spiritual men'. See also William Haller, *Liberty and Reformation in the Puritan Revolution* (2nd edition, paperback, Columbia University Press 1963), pp. 106-7.
39. George Gillespie, *Notes of Debates and Proceedings of the Assembly of Divines* (ed. David Meek, Edinburgh 1846), p. 27.
40. *Essays Ecclesiastical and Civil* 1709. The published work in Whitelocke's name was adapted from Add. MS. 37343 fols. 51-131 and other MSS. The story from the *Talmud*, which appears in Carleton Whitelocke's edition of his father's work was a favourite of Whitelocke's. In 1663 Whitelocke repeated some of his own arguments from the 1630s when preparing 'The King's Right to Grant Indulgence in Matters of Religion' (Add. MS. 21099) at the request of Charles II. In it he reaffirmed the Erastian view that a secular power should have the final word in church affairs; more important, he made out a detailed case based on precedent for the King, as head of the Church, granting freedom of conscience to nonconformists.

CHAPTER V: Matters of Life and Death

1. Add. MS. 37343 fols. 277-8.
2. Ian Roy, 'The Libraries of Edward, 2nd Viscount Conway and Others: an Inventory of Valuation of 1643' (B.I.H.R. May 1968).
3. Add. MS. 37343 fol. 286b and 'Diary' 8 June 1660. According to Anthony Wood, *Fasti Oxonienses* (ed. P. Bliss, London 1813-20), ii, 63-4, Whitelocke had been a friend of Lane's but when, after the Restoration, the former Lord Keeper's

son asked for the return of the books and papers, Whitelocke denied all knowledge of his former friend. This sounds unlikely, in view of Whitelocke's friendly references to Lane and the categorical statement in the 'Diary' that he returned Lane's property. It is difficult to discern any motive for him writing this if it were untrue, nor would it be in character.

4. 'Diary' 1642–3.
5. Add. MS. 37343 fols. 290–290b. The spelling in the letter has been modernized in line with the author's transcription of Whitelocke's own spelling, but Cooke's personal idiosyncrasies have been retained. The Bell still stands, at the corner of Bell Street in Henley.
6. 'Diary' 1643–4.
7. David Underdown, *Pride's Purge* (O.U.P. 1971), pp. 72 and 213 aptly describes Whitelocke as belonging to the middle group, but on the fringe of the peace party.
8. Add. MS. 37343 fols. 280b, 281 and 282.
9. Add. MS. 37343 fols. 292–3. His words found an echo eight years later in Milton's 'Sonnet to Cromwell':
     . . . Peace hath her victories
     No less renowned than war.
10. Add. MS. 37343 fol. 331b.
11. Add. MS. 37343 fol. 340b.
12. Add. MS. 37343 fols. 335–335b. Whitelocke's *Memorials* (O.U.P. 1853), vol. i, p. 340 states that, when asked for a copy, the King said 'What is that to you who are but to carry what I said, and if I will send the song of Robin Hood and Little John you must carry it.' This is an addition made by the editor, based perhaps on hearsay.
13. Enemies in Parliament like Denzil Holles maintained that Cromwell was an arrant coward. *Memoirs of Denzil Lord Holles Baron of Ifield in Sussex*, from the Year 1641, to 1648 (1699), p. 17.
14. Add. MS. 37343 fols. 343b–346; *The Quarrel between the Earl of Manchester and Oliver Cromwell* (Camden Society 1875); *Camden Miscellany* No. 8 (1883) contains 'A Letter from the Earl of Manchester to the House of Lords on the conduct of Cromwell' Dec [?] 1644.
15. Add. MS. 37343 fols. 358b–359b.
16. John Lord Campbell, *Lives of the Lord Chancellors and Keepers* (John Murray, 1856–7), vol. iii, p. 336, and Clarendon, *The Great Rebellion*, vol. viii, section 248.
17. This is evident in his talk with Dr. Samuel Turner in Oxford, and in his defence of Parliament's policy, even on the question of the King's execution, when challenged about it in Sweden. It is significant that he transcribed most of the relevant episodes *after* the Restoration, when his integrity as a Parliamentarian could only do him harm.
18. Add. MS. 37343 fols. 340–340b.

19. Holles, *Memoirs*, pp. 39–41.
20. It was a tradition in the family to give the mother's maiden name to one of the boys – as Bulstrode, Willoughby and Carleton.
21. 'Diary' Sept. 1645.
22. Add. MS. 37344 fols. 6b–8b *passim* and 12–12b.
23. Add. MS. 37344 fols. 45b, 67b, 70b–71, 99b.
24. Not all soldiers were like that nor all women. At Little Rollright, near Oxford, Whitelocke's sister Cecilia Dixon was in bed recovering from a confinement when a party of Parliament's soldiers were billeted on the house. The soldiers were dissatisfied with their quarters and compelled her to get up and look after them, as a result of which she was taken ill and died.
25. This was some measure of his love for Frances. The journey may be compared with that of a man commuting twice a week by car between Exeter and London, only Whitelocke's journey was colder and joltier.
26. Underdown, *Pride's Purge*, p. 59 *passim*, shows in detail how Holles and his group recognized the connection between the war policy and the threat of social revolution, and the political responses which followed.
27. Add. MS. 37344. fol. 135b.
28. Longleat, parcel 6 (folder).
29. Add. MS. 37344 fol. 163.
30. 'Diary' 5 July 1648.
31. Add. MS. 37344 fols. 229b and 231.
32. Add. MS. 37344 fol. 237b. 'Stales' is used in this context to mean decoys.
33. Details of Manor Lodge (or Manor House) are given by T. E. Harwood in *Windsor Old and New* (Printed for the Author, London 1929), pp. 174–5, and a MS. *Repairs of the Lodges in Windsor Great Park 1687* in the Library, Windsor Castle.
34. The United Provinces were themselves republican, but they had not executed their Prince and remained on friendly terms with many crowned heads of Europe, while the States General recognized Charles II as King.
35. Add. MS. 37344 fol. 293b. This is perhaps the oldest example of a letter written by general practitioners to a specialist.
36. In modern medical terms Frances' symptoms suggest that she was suffering from Pyelitis or Pyelonephritis, quite common in the fifth month of pregnancy. The onset is accompanied by fever, headaches, abdominal pain and convulsions, all of which Whitelocke describes. Biographical notes on the team of royalist doctors who attended Frances are given by William Munk, *The Roll of the Royal College of Physicians of London* (Longman, Green, Longman and Roberts, 1861), vol. i. Dr. Chamberlain was the author of a paper entitled *The Accomplished Midwife*; his collection of midwifery instruments, including the famous 'Chamberlain forceps', was discovered in 1815.

CHAPTER VI: 'The Business of the Widow Wilson'

1. G. Davies, *The Early Stuarts* (O.U.P. 1952), p. 164.
   Add. MS. 37344 fols. 275 and 276b.

2. Add. MS. 37344 fol. 323.

3. Jerome Zankey, or Sankey, at that time sub-warden of All Souls, Oxford, became Commander of Parliament's cavalry in Ireland and was knighted there by Henry Cromwell. J. Foster *Alumni Oxoniensis 1500–1714* (Parker and Co., Oxford 1892).

4. A few months after Zankey sailed for Ireland he and his young pupil, James Whitelocke, were among those appointed trustees of Trinity College, Dublin. This was under the Act for the Better Advancement of the Gospel and Learning in Ireland, 8 March 1649–50, Whitelocke having reported on the Act from the committee. The manors and lands formerly held by the Archbishop of Dublin were to be vested in the trustees. Firth and Rait, *A and O*, vol. ii, pp. 355–6. It seems likely that Cromwell engineered this academic honour to please the boy's father. As a soldier James did well in his own right, and was made a colonel before the battle of Worcester. Add. MS. 37345 fol. 147b.

5. John Lord Campbell, *Lives of the Lord Chancellors and Keepers*, vol. iii, pp. 356–7. Campbell states that these Orders were the basis of ones subsequently adopted by Lord Clarendon, and still of authority in the 1850s.

6. Add. MS. 37345 fols. 28–31.

7. Whitelocke's own account of these proceedings, recollected later in the 'Annals', is inaccurate in detail; it does not, however, exaggerate the important part he played in saving the collection. These books and manuscripts later formed the nucleus of the Royal Library which George II presented to the British Museum in 1757. A full account of the resolutions by the Commons and the Council of State concerning the care of the library, during the Interregnum, is given in *Catalogue of Western Manuscripts in the Old Royal and King's Collections in the British Museum* (G. F. Warner and J. P. Gilson, printed for the Trustees of the British Museum, Longman, Green and Co. 1921), pp. xxi–xxiv.

8. Add. MS. 37345 fol. 18b.

9. I Timothy, 5. There were several ladies of the same name but this was apparently Margaret whose husband, Sir George Hungerford, a general in Parliament's army, had died in 1648. Anthony Powell, *John Aubrey and his friends* (Mercury Books 1963), footnote p. 126.

10. Underdown, *Pride's Purge*, p. 261.

11. 'Diary' March 1649 [50]. Add. MS. 37345 fol. 54 gives a more detailed and even more alarming account, with a suggestion that royalist agitators staged the demonstration, knowing that the streets would be thronged for the procession. Rowland Wilson, a member of the Vintners' Company, had been in partnership with his father, a wealthy merchant, and was said by Whitelocke to be the heir to

£2,000 a year. He had been a loyal Parliament man and Lieutenant-Colonel of a regiment of the London Trained Bands, but had refused to serve as a commissioner for the King's trial.

12. Longleat, vol. x, fol. 149.
13. Longleat, vol. x, fol. 155.
14. Davies, *The Early Stuarts*, pp. 164–5.
15. Extracts from Mary's biography, in its cross-stitch binding, are given in R. H. Whitelocke, *Memoirs, Biographical and Historical, of Bulstrode Whitelocke* (Routledge, Warne and Routledge, 1860), pp. 283–8. It has not been possible to trace the original manuscript which, if it survives, is almost certainly in Eire.
16. The incumbent at the time was Nicholas East, shown in the records as 'intruded'.
17. Add. MS. 37345 fol. 96b. Whitelocke gives 5 September 1650 as the date of his marriage whereas the transcript of the Parish Register (Society of Genealogists) shows it as 11 September. Whitelocke was correct as the next paragraph shows, for news of Dunbar reached London on 7 September.
18. Christopher Hill, *Puritanism and Revolution* (Mercury Books 1962, paperback), Ch. 3 'The Norman Yoke', pp. 50–152.
19. 'Diary' August 1651.
20. G.E.C. and *Calendar for Compositions*.
21. 'Diary' July 1652.
22. Lord Willoughby, who had originally fought for Parliament, turned against them when they failed to make a treaty with the King; his impeachment for high treason followed in 1647 but he was later released and escaped to Holland. Charles Stuart, in exile, appointed him Governor of Barbados in 1650 and the island surrendered to Sir George Ayscue in 1652. G.E.C.
23. Add. MS. 37345 fol. 209.
24. Eg. MS. 997 fols. 61–62b.
25. Add. MS. 37345 fol. 27.
26. Whitelocke recorded this question identically in the 'Annals', Add. MS. 37345 fol. 242, and in the 'Diary' November 1652.
27. Add. MS. 37345 fol. 268.
28. According to other versions it was Harrison who carried the news. Perhaps they both did so.
29. Add. MS. 37345 fols. 270–1.

CHAPTER VII: Ambassador Extraordinary
1. Add. MS. 37345 fols. 375–375b. Whitelocke was living in the Chelsea house which had been the home of that earlier Lord Chancellor, Sir Thomas More;

the Church of St. Luke which he attended (known since 1820 as Chelsea Old Church, and badly damaged in the Second World War) was where More had worshipped and was buried. Information about the house is given in the L.C.C. *Survey of London*, Chelsea, part II, vol. iv (1913) and in Reginald Blunt's *Historical Handbook to Chelsea* (Lamley and Co. 1900) (not entirely reliable); a detailed account of the church, and incidentally of the house, is given in Randall Davies's *Chelsea Old Church* (Duckworth and Co. 1904).

2. Add. MS. 4992 fol. 28.

3. *Elias Ashmole 1617–1692 His Autobiographical and Historical Notes, his Correspondence, and Other Contemporary Sources Relating to his Life and Work* (ed. C. H. Johnsten) (O.U.P. 1966), vol. ii, p. 651.

4. Add. MS. 31984 fols. 144b–145.

5. Add. MS. 37345 fol. 247b.

6. MS. volume 1–21 August 1653, p. 6. owned by Mrs. Madeleine Whitelocke. (The MS. is not foliated.)

7. Longleat, vol. xiii, fol. 181. Only a few lines of the original letter are quoted in the 'Journal'. The quotations in Chapters VII, VIII and IX are to be found in *A Journal of the Swedish Embassy* by Ambassador Bulstrode Whitelocke, new revised edition Henry Reeve (Longman Brown, Green and Longmans 1855) but as there are some vagaries in the transcript, the text of Add. MS. 4902 has been followed. The spelling of 'Oulsey' has been altered, in the present work, to the more usual 'Wolseley'.

8. In the published *Journal* the editor confused Philip Viscount L'Isle with Whitelocke's fellow Lord Commissioner of the Great Seal, John L'Isle. Both men, it seems, wished Whitelocke to go to Sweden.

9. Add. MS. 31984 fols. 144–144b.

10. Add. MS. 53727 p. 43 (at the time of writing, this MS. has not been foliated).

11. Add. MS. 4902 fol. 4b. 'Swethland' was misleadingly transcribed in the printed *Journal* as Swizland.

12. Add. MS. 53727 pp. 53–7.

13. Add. MS. 4902 fols. 5b–6.

14. Longleat, MS. 124a Whitelocke 'Journal' 5 Sep. 1653.

15. Add. MS. 4902 fols. 6–6b. Only a few speeches have been quoted from a long and interesting conversation. It should however be treated with some reservation as it does not appear in Longleat MS. 124a. On the other hand, that manuscript is incomplete.

16. Add. MS. 4902 fol. 8b. The warning in the previous note again applies.

17. Add. MS. 4902 fols. 9b–10.

18. In Scandinavia today toasts are still drunk between each of the numerous courses at a banquet.

19. The economic causes leading to the Anglo–Dutch war are given by Davies, *The*

Early Stuarts, pp. 218–20 and J. R. Jones, *Britain and Europe in the Seventeenth Century* (Edward Arnold 1966), Chapter 4.

20. Michael Roberts, *Essays in Swedish History* (Weidenfeld and Nicolson 1967), p. 148.
21. Longleat, vol. xiii, fol. 242. Sir George Fleetwood had given distinguished service in the Swedish army under Gustavus Adolphus. His younger brother was the parliamentary general, Charles Fleetwood, referred to by Oliver Cromwell as a 'milksop'. His elder brother, Sir William, supported the King. *D.N.B.*
22. It has been suggested that Whitelocke did not take the reports seriously, having been told that Charles II had given orders that he was not to be murdered, but such foolhardy confidence seems incredible and Whitelocke's account of attempted attacks on him does not support the hypothesis.
23. Part of the Will has survived: Longleat, vol. xiv, fol. 166. This was his second, but not his last Will; in it he stated that if he died in England he wished to be buried in the family vault in Fawley church. Before allocating his estate he observed that none of it had been acquired 'by guilt of the State or ruins of others' fortunes'. This was probably intended both to show that his conscience was clear and to assure his heirs that their title to their land was good. 'Guilt of the State' is one of his most critical surviving comments on the Interregnum written before the Restoration. It supports the contention in this book that such criticism of the Interregnum as he expressed after the Restoration was not necessarily an afterthought.
24. Longleat, Whitelocke 'Journal' 26 October 1653.
25. Add. MS. 37346 fol. 45.
26. Add. MS. 37346 fol. 17b. Sir Harry Wotton was Ambassador in Venice and later Provost of Eton. Whitelocke misquoted Sir Henry's actual words which were: 'An ambassador is an honest man sent to lie abroad for the good of his country.'
27. Add. MS. 4994 fols. 8–8b.
28. Add. MS. 4994 fol. 17.
29. Add. MS. 37346 fols. 30b–32 and 4902 fol. 20.
30. Add. MS. 4902 fols. 24–5. This sounds like genuine reporting. It was impolitic of Whitelocke to divulge such tactics when copying his notes after the Restoration.
31. It took nearly eight minutes to hoist each horse aboard. Cars loaded by crane at Tilbury in 1966 took a full three minutes each.
32. Eg. MS. 997 fol. 95b. This pleasing comment is omitted in the shorter version given in the 'Journal'. In the notebook he jotted down the word 'humming' but altered it to 'shouting' in the 'Journal'. 'Humming' was an idiomatic usage.
33. The boy was called after Mary's father, a grocer named Bigley Carleton.
34. Eg. MS. 997 fol. 99. Selden's doctrine of *Mare Clausum* suited Parliament's claims, just as it had suited those of King James and King Charles. The skipper supported, probably unwittingly, the views Grotius had expressed in his *Mare Liberum*.

Whitelocke had studied the English claim; he could not only quote from Selden's *Mare Clausum* but had translated a Latin Eulogy, written by Grotius himself to King James, which rashly described the English monarch's sovereignty over sea as well as land.

35. Eg. MS. 997 fols. 102b-6. This dialogue with the skipper appears in the 'Journal' but the earlier version, quoted in this text, is taken from Whitelocke's pocket book with the rubbed corners, which seems to have been written up from notes taken at the time. His editing of this earlier version for the 'Journal' was skilful. The final text is smoother, less repetitive, clearer and more literary, but the sense is the same except for three small details. The skipper's 'five for one are of this opinion' is stepped up to 'ten for one' which may well have been correct, corresponding (in reverse) to the Dutch idiom, 'he is one in ten.' There are two additions to the later text: Whitelocke adds a short exchange on the subject of English ships and, more important, adds a discussion about toleration in England of different sects. This may have been inserted as propaganda in support of freedom of conscience, based on his talks in Sweden.

36. Add. MS. 4902 fol. 35b.

37. The province of Skåne in the south of Sweden was at that date part of Denmark, which enabled the Danes to command the narrow Sound.

38. This colour is still the traditional one in the Swedish countryside.

39. Eg. MS. 997 fol. 158b.

40. Kullings-Skövde.

41. Henry appears to have been Whitelocke's godson.

42. This stood on the site of the present Town Hall; after its owner, Claes Eden, a rich merchant of German descent, received the title of Edenberg, in May 1654, the house was known by his name. It is described in detail by Whitelocke, Add. MS. 37346 fols. 87-87b, and by Nils Sundquist, antiquarian of Uppsala, in an article *Rådhuset i Uppsala* published in the daily paper, *Uppsala Nya Tidning* (Christmas issue 1943). Mr. Sundquist says it was built of stone. Whitelocke, who lived in it, described it as a brick house.

43. Whitelocke's journey and everything at Court was minutely observed and recorded by him. The endless forests with their strange pungent smell of resin, the huge lakes, rocky open spaces and agricultural land traversed by causeways are still much as he described them three hundred years ago. His details of the great lake he passed were wide of the mark; he called it Meler and editors of the *Journal* added to the muddle by transcribing this as Mälaren, confusing it with the lake on which Stockholm stands. It sounds from his description like Lake Vänern, yet he would not have seen that vast lake from the old road, so it was probably Skagern. He seems to have listened to an exaggerated description of the size of the lakes and the number of islands in them. He named one place Fitzborough instead of Fellingsbro. On such a hard journey, it was easy for the occasional mis-

take to slip into an otherwise accurate account. Retracing his journey in 1966 the author failed to discover the narrow road, over-hung by rocks, with a precipitous fall to the lake below. Swedish scholars and seventeenth-century maps were at first unable to reveal any such cliff face, along which he said his company led their horses. Perhaps in the darkness a dangerous road seemed much worse than it was. Subsequent correspondence with Mr. Thure Elgåsen, an expert on old roads and local history, suggests that it may have been a stretch of the old road high above Lake Skagern, or the north slope of Billingen at Berg or Öglunda. As shown on a modern map, after Göteborg, Whitelocke travelled through Lerum, Alingsős, Kullings-Skövde, Vedum, N. Vånga, Skara, Binneberg, part of the forest of Tiveden, Örebro, Fellingsbro, Köping, Västeras, Enköping and so to Uppsala. The names of the places he visited are given in their Swedish spelling, while other references to places abroad have been Anglicized in the text.

CHAPTER VIII: Christina

1. *Elias Ashmole 1617–1692 His Autobiographical and Historical Notes*, vol. ii, pp. 450–1 note 8.
2. Michael Roberts, *Gustavus Adolphus: A History of Sweden 1611–1632* (Longman, Green and Co. 1953), vol. i, pp. 380, 524 and footnote 2.
3. Christina gave these details in her autobiography and Sven Stolpe, in *Christina of Sweden* (Burns and Oates 1966), pp. 36–7, gives reasons for believing it to be an accurate account. The King's admission that he could not control his temper is quoted by Michael Roberts, *Gustavus Adolphus*, vol. ii, p. 786.
4. The Portuguese Ambassador had visited the Swedish Court, speaking neither Swedish nor French. His confessor had acted as interpreter and, under cover of political discussions, the Queen had interpolated questions on Catholic faith and dogma, the interpreter slipping in replies without his master being any the wiser. At her request Macedo, the confessor, had suddenly left Court to consult the General of the Jesuits in Rome on her behalf.
5. Christina, like many of her contemporaries, regarded Anabaptists as 'violent incendiaries'. Those of Munster were the chief target for abuse since it was reported that their elders claimed to be above the moral law, which gave rise to accusations of scandalous behaviour. Any dissenter who held radical and ega-litarian views was liable to be called an Anabaptist, much as Hitler's opponents were indiscriminately labelled Communists, Catholics, Jews and Freemasons.
6. Hugh Peter, the well-known preacher, had been a chaplain in the new model army. Although not technically a Regicide he was executed for high treason in 1660. Whitelocke spells the name 'Peters' but I have altered it to the more usual 'Peter'.

7. The pocket Phrase Book 1653–4, measuring five inches by just under three, was recently acquired by the University of Lund. I am indebted to the Librarian for permission to study the Xerox copy in the British Museum, R. P. 209. The manuscript is neither paginated nor foliated.

8. Add. MS. 37346 fol. 167. Whitelocke's argument about the people's responsibility is translated into Latin in the phrase book.

9. Thurloe wrote apologetically: 'This change, though somewhat varying from that which seemed the former intentions of this State, yet it hath a very general acceptance, especially among the lawyers, the ministry and the merchants, who conceived themselves most in danger from the temper of the last Parliament.' Add. MS. 37346 fol. 174.

10. Longleat, vol. xv, fol. 1.

11. It might be questioned whether Whitelocke's record of this discussion, in the post-Restoration version of the 'Journal', was accurate; although he was hostile to Cromwell's action it seems curious that he should have criticized the Protector freely to his servants. The relevant pages are missing from the original (Longleat) 'Journal', but Add. MS. 37346, fols. 176b–177b and 181, written evidently before the Restoration, also reflect his sharp criticism of the coup. 'Cromwell who had his commission from the Parliament, who were his masters, had by force turned them out of their authority' *passim*. This account shows that there was a full discussion of the dilemma with members of Whitelocke's household.

12. Sven Stolpe's proposition in *Christina of Sweden*, that this lady-in-waiting (the most beautiful woman in Sweden) only served as a bed-warmer to the Queen, is difficult to credit in relation to a young woman as unconventional and masculine as Christina. The passionate love-letters written by Christina to the Countess, two years later, which Stolpe interprets ingeniously as an example of the Platonic approach of *les Précieuses*, confirm me in my scepticism.

13. The Scandinavian custom was mentioned in *Hamlet* with reference to Claudius's defiant wassails, accompanied by trumpets and kettle drums.

14. Add. MS. 37346 fol. 154b.

15. Add. MS. 4902 fol. 102.

16. Add. MS. 4902 fol. 102b.

17. Add. MS. 37347 fol. 236.

18. It is doubtful whether Christina received the gift, for she left Sweden in the middle of June, but Cromwell's portrait hangs in Gripsholm Castle; Christina's miniature is (or was) at Chequers. It is not clear whether that was the portrait which distressed Mrs. Cromwell, according to the news-letter quoted in C.S.P. Clarendon vol. ii, p. 208, 20/30 May 1653.

CHAPTER IX: Abdication

1. Add. MS. 4902 fol. 132.
2. Phillip Stubbes, *Anatomy of the Abuses in England in Shakespeare's Youth* (ed. F. J. Furnivall) (Trübner and Co. 1877–9), p. 149.
3. A pudding flavoured with tansy juice.
4. This characteristic incident appears briefly in the 'Diary' and in more detail in Add. MS. 37347 fol. 182b. It also appears in the manuscript 'Journal' and in the eighteenth-century edition. It is omitted from the better-known mid-nineteenth-century edition, owing no doubt to Victorian puritanism.
5. It seems probable that Colonel Potley supplied the translation of this eloquent speech which, in its rhythm and directness, is like the language of Juliet Capulet's Nurse.
6. This splendid passage about the fore-horse suggests that the Boors' Marshal was a driver or teamster; 'gears' were harness or traces.
7. Both officials received forty Jacobuses, a golden coin struck in the reign of King James.
8. As a merchant, Samuel Wilson no doubt made cut-price purchases from the privateers. Wilson is thought to have been Mary's sister's husband and perhaps a cousin of her own former husband, Rowland Wilson. J. B. Marsh, *The Story of Harcourt* (Strahan and Co. 1871), p. 43.
9. The letters from England appear in Add. MS. 37347 fols. 233b–237b, except for the letter to Ingelo the date of which is not known. This appears in *The Poems and Letters of Andrew Marvell* (ed. H. M. Margoliouth) (O.U.P. 1927), vol. i, pp. 99–102. W. Hilton Kelliher in 'Marvell's "A letter to Doctor Ingelo" ', *Review of English Studies*, xx (1969), pp. 50–7, makes a persuasive case for his theory that this undated letter may have been the one Whitelocke showed to Christina on 30 March 1654.
10. There is a puzzling factor in Whitelocke's report. The abdication and coronation took place on 6 June 1654 (old style) or 16 June (new style). This account of the ceremony appears in the 'Diary', in Add. MS. 37347 fols. 238b, 240b–241 and in Add. MS. 4902 fols. 163–163b. Whitelocke however gave 30 May as the date, the day before his departure. He quoted the text of his letter, dated 29 May, in which he asked that Fleetwood should be allowed to rejoin him in Uppsala after the ceremony, and he also recorded that Wrangell returned with an eye-witness account late on 30 May. The original 'Journal' (Longleat) includes a transcript of the letter about Fleetwood; it is possible that a page may be missing in the middle of the entry for 30 May (as at other points) but it is remarkable and baffling that even this original version, apparently written during the Swedish mission, gives the date of the abdication and coronation as 30 May.
11. Christina wrote ' . . . Women should never reign, and if there are examples which favour their sex, one should not count on them.' Maxims, no. 356,

Drottning Kristina, *Maximer Les Sentiments Héroïques* (ed. Sven Stolpe) (Bonniers, Stockholm) p. 107. This probably reflects Christina's general contempt for women rather than any lack of confidence in her own ability. It was not long before she was seeking the crown of Naples and that of Poland.

12. There was some risk involved, for Whitelocke wrote 'This ship, the *Amaranth*, had never been at sea, and therefore the more dangerous to adventure in her first voyage'. Add. MS. 4902 fol. 165. No doubt he had in mind the disaster of the warship *Vasa*, which heeled over and sank in Stockholm harbour, at the start of her maiden voyage in 1628. Anders Franzen, *The Warship Vasa* (Royal Printing Office P. A. Norstedt and Sons, Stockholm 1966), p. 10.

13. The *Catalogue* of the Christina Exhibition, Stockholm 1966 (Eleventh Exhibition of the Council of Europe), item 473, gives interesting details. In England Milton referred to the legendary flower from the garden of Eden:

> Immortal Amarant, a flower that once
> In paradise, fast by the tree of life,
> Began to bloom. . . .

Again in line 149 of 'Lycidas' he wrote

> Bid amaranthas all his beauty shed.

In the seventeenth century the unfading flower had great power over the imagination. After the ex-Queen had confirmed it in writing, the College of Heralds, Whitelocke records, recognized his knighthood in 1661, and the title continued to be used on official documents.

14. Add. MS. 37347 fol. 280. Even to-day the stork receives the treatment of a sacred cow, and a farmer finding a stork's nest is overjoyed.

15. The symptoms Whitelocke described suggest arsenical poisoning.

16. According to Pepys this unlikeable man who, with many others, changed his allegiance at the Restoration, was a 'mighty talker'. Hugh Peter had helped to found Harvard College where Downing was one of the first graduates.

17. Add. MS. 4902 fol. 199. Shortly after Whitelocke's death Fawley Court, as he knew it, was pulled down and replaced by what is said to be one of the few private houses designed by Sir Christopher Wren. A tablet on the house states that William of Orange stopped there in 1688, on his journey from Torbay to London to be made King. He was entertained by William Whitelocke, whom he subsequently knighted, in April 1689. (Bulstrode Whitelocke, *D.N.B.* and Le Neve, *Pedigree of Knights*, p. 421.)

CHAPTER X: The Last Years in Office

1. Widdrington, who for some months had been in sole charge of the Seal, may well have resented taking second place on Whitelocke's return.

2. Longleat, vols. xiii fol. 248b and xiv fol. 137, 27 Sept. & 25 Oct. 1653.

3. J. Arckenholtz, *Mémoires concernant Christine reine de Suède* (Amsterdam and Leipzig 1751–60), vol. i p. 474.
4. Thomas Carlyle, *Oliver Cromwell's Letters and Speeches* (Ward, Lock, Bowden and Co. 1892), pp. 530–42.
5. Add. MS. 37346 fol. 181.
6. Add. MS. 4992 fol. 116.
7. 'Diary' 3 February 1654 [5] Whitelocke mistakenly gave this date for the dissolution instead of 22 January.
8. Stowe 333 'Parliament of England' fols. 121 and 126b.
9. Add. MS. 4992 fol. 119.
10. The text of the lengthy declaration is given in Add. MS. 4992 fols. 118–118b. An account of the incident also appears in the 'Diary' 20 Feb. 1654 [5]. To Whitelocke's surprise the Levellers, in collusion with the Royalists, were demanding a freely elected parliament which would lead to restoration of the monarchy. The Levellers claimed that they intended to use the Cavaliers for their own ends and then discard them. Whitelocke was not impressed by the argument.
11. Whitelocke had been Constable of Windsor Castle since 1649.
12. Add. MS. 4992 fol. 125.
13. S. R. Gardiner Nos. 88–91, *Constitutional Documents of the Puritan Revolution* (O.U.P. 1962), pp. 384–91. It is not clear what Whitelocke meant in this context by 'the people'. The term was often used as a synonym for the electorate but the Levellers, who demanded manhood suffrage, used it to cover all grown men.
14. An even more drastic plan had been envisaged by the Barebones Parliament which, on 5 August 1653, resolved 'that the high court of Chancery of England shall be, forthwith, taken away'. Thomas Burton *Diary* vol. i, p. vi. Comments on the ineptness of some of the proposed reforms are given by Whitelocke in the 'Annals' Add. MS. 4992, fols. 123b–125. These are spelt out by Lord John Campbell, *Lives of the Chancellors and Keepers of the Great Seal of England* (John Murray 1857), vol. iii, pp. 364–5.
15. Add. MS. 4992 fol. 126b.
16. Add. MS. 4992 fol. 132b.
17. Eg. MS. 997 fol. 2. Whitelocke's History of the forty-eighth year of his age.
18. This attitude towards James, William and Samuel may provide an answer to the riddle of why Whitelocke wrote three similar (though not identical) accounts of his preparations for the Swedish embassy, a mission which he regarded as the culmination of his career. It was an experience which James and William had shared with their father; Samuel was only two years old at the time.
19. J. G. Nichols and J. Bruce, *Wills from Doctors' Commons* (Camden Society 1863), pp. 131–2. An earlier Will may have left the land to young Bulstrode, but Lilly in his last Will bequeathed his land to his wife for her lifetime and the reversion to Carleton Whitelocke.

20. Add. MS. 4992 fol. 132b. Carleton became a member of the Middle Temple, made two good marriages, died in 1705 and was buried in Sion College. He was, it seems, the most dependable of Mary's sons and inherited the greater part of his parents' effects, including books and some at least of the manuscripts, his father's signet ring and family portraits. His son, John Carleton Whitelocke (who had a commission in Ireland in George I's army) took them to Co. Dublin during the eighteenth century, when he went to live at Priorswood, a Georgian house a few miles north-east of Dublin. The house was demolished in 1968. Carleton prepared several of his father's works for publication: the Introduction to *Essays Ecclesiastical and Civil*, published after Carleton's death, states that he edited it, and two volumes Add. MSS. 37346 and 37347 (although never published) have an inscription on the title page to the same effect.

21. Longleat. Parcel 1, nos. 6, 7 and 40 refer to the Rathconrath and Kildare purchases. His title to both was confirmed by Charles II in 1669 (copy in C.U.L. Mm.6.57 fols. 92–4). In John P. Prendergast, *The Cromwellian Settlement of Ireland*, second edition (1875 Dublin), Whitelocke's purchase is shown as No. 48. A speech of Whitelocke's about the 'adventures' in Ireland 17 Feb. 1641–2 is published in Thomason Tracts E. 200 (30).

22. John Milton was appointed secretary for foreign tongues to the Council of State in 1649. Among the papers at Longleat is one, dated 12 February 1651 [2]. Couched in the immortal language of civil servants, it is addressed to Lord Commissioner Whitelocke by John Milton. An account of Bonde's mission is given by Michael Roberts, *Essays in Swedish History* (Weidenfeld and Nicolson 1967), pp. 145–6.

23. The war had been initiated by Cromwell in 1654 to challenge Spanish claims in the new world and in particular in the West Indies.

24. Thomas Burton's *Diary* (London 1828), vol. i, for the years 1656–9 shows how frequently, in parliamentary debates, Whitelocke advised Members on the legal position.

25. 'Diary' 3 May 1656. Whitelocke gave the absurd figure of 200,000. This may have been a slip in copying from the Instrument of Government which quoted 10,000 horse and dragoons, 20,000 foot, and a *budget* of £200,000 for government expenses and the administration of justice. S. R. Gardiner, *Constitutional Documents*, p. 414.

26. 'Diary' 21 August 1656.

27. 'Diary' 20 June 1657.

28. Burton *Diary*, pp. 10, 24–36, 38–80, 85–92, 96–104, 107–15, 118–26, 128–35, 137–168 *passim*. 'Diary' 6 and 13 December 1656.

29. The Speaker, who put the case to Cromwell, argued that a king and parliament were 'like a building well knit and cemented; if one stone be taken out it loosens the whole.' Charles Firth, *Last Years of the Protectorate* (Longmans Green 1909), vol. i, p. 149.

30. Dr. Walton was at the same time completing his Polyglot Bible. 'Diary' 17 Feb. 1656 [7].

31. Parliament had given this residence to Cromwell after the battle of Worcester.

32. Mazarin wished to cover up the scandal with a story of a private feud between two servants but when Christina openly took responsibility for it, boasting of having no regret 'but innumerable reasons to be pleased', Mazarin condemned her action. *Catalogue* Council of Europe, Christina Exhibition, Stockholm 1965, pp. 295-6.

33. The knighthood was confirmed in writing by Christina and continued to be recognized after the Restoration. 'Diary' 10 Sep. 1661 and 16 Feb 1670.

34. *Collectanea Topographica et Genealogica* (London 1834), vol. i, p. 3.

35. 'Diary' 9 Nov. 1660 and *D.N.B.* and F. E. Hansford, *Our Mannor House at ffulham* (Fulham History Society Publications 1961), p. 7.

36. *The Diary of John Evelyn* (ed. William Bray) (Everyman's Library, J. M. Dent and Sons Ltd. 1952), vol. i, p. 327.

37. This had already been provided for in the Humble Petition and Advice.

38. 'Diary' April 17 1658.

39. Longleat, vol. xii, fol. 56. This item is shown in the admirable Calendar as 1651, owing to a misreading of the final figure. The entry in the surviving 'Diary' is identical with the original page. Apart from the addition of caustic hind-sight observations, the 'Diary' gives the impression of being an exact copy, containing as it does daily trivia side by side with accounts of some great moments in history; in it Whitelocke's frankness about the part he played during the Interregnum does not suggest that he tampered with his earlier entries, after the Restoration.

40. Whitelocke shows the date of his visit as 26 August, which was a Thursday. This conflicts with the accepted account that Cromwell made his last journey to London on Tuesday, 24 August. Whitelocke's visit to Hampton Court was probably a few days earlier; he also made the curious mistake of recording that the Protector died at Hampton Court, whereas he died at Whitehall.

41. Fleetwood commented earlier that Richard had 'much exceeded expectation'. Richard's dignity with the French Ambassador must have struck Whitelocke as the more commendable since France had just rejected an appeal to lend the Protector £50,000. Davies, *Restoration of Charles II* (O.U.P. 1955), pp. 10, 12 and 13.

42. On 4 July Parliament voted that the Protector should be exempt from arrest by creditors, and that his debts, amounting to nearly £30,000, should be paid by the Treasury.

43. Ashley Cooper, later created first Earl of Shaftesbury, came to be known as the first Whig.

44. Whitelocke could have profited by such correspondence after the Restoration. The only hint he gave later that there might have been grounds for Scott's

charge, was a cryptic claim that he had helped the King without any disloyalty to those he was serving. 'Diary' 18 May 1659.

45. Sir Arthur Haselrig would not have recognized Whitelocke as the foremost man in Parliament; early in Richard's Parliament he defied the Protector by telling Chaloner Chute, 'I look upon you as the greatest man in England, the Speaker of the Parliament of England or Commons.' But Chute and the Speakers who succeeded him, Sir Lislebone Long and Thomas Bampfield, were not men of sufficient calibre to play the part for which Haselrig cast them, while Lenthall, as Speaker of the Rump, was old and tired.

46. After the Restoration, however, Whitelocke claimed that he had been of some assistance to Booth.

47. C. H. Firth, *The Memoirs of Edmund Ludlow* (O.U.P. 1894), vol. ii, p. 161. Whitelocke's earlier relations with Vane, at Deptford, and again in 1651 in their joint defence of the unorthodox John Fry, who did not believe in the Trinity, suggest that the rift between them was not so deep as Ludlow implied.

48. *Thomason Tracts* E.1010, no. 5.

49. 'Diary' 28 Dec. 1659.

50. The Commander-in-Chief and his advisers would all have benefited. Instead, Fleetwood lived out his life in oblivion, Berry and Desborough were imprisoned on charges of conspiracy and Vane was executed at Tyburn. Clearly Whitelocke did not know where to find Charles Stuart, who had returned to Brussels from the Pyrenees on 16 December, but information as to his whereabouts and movements could no doubt have been supplied by Thurloe's diligent spies.

CHAPTER XI: 'Bonfires and Joys'

1. Whitelocke may, in any case, have sensed that Hyde would advise Charles against returning to England until he was invited to do so by Parliament.

2. 'Diary' 27 December 1659.

3. Herbert Cokayne Gibbs, *The Parish Registers of Hunsdon Co. Hertford, 1546–1837* (The St. Catherine Press 1915), pp. 13–17 and 19–20.

4. Although two-thirds of the original house has been pulled down and the interior has been much altered, a suite of three small rooms above the present front door has survived, which correspond closely to Whitelocke's description. They would have been in a remote wing of the original house.

5. It is a matter of conjecture whether the papers Mary destroyed related to his work with the Committee of Safety, to correspondence concerning Charles II or to schemes for a republican constitution. Dr. Charles Morton suggested that *Whitelocke's notes upon the King's Writt for choosing Members of Parliament*, which he edited in 1766, may have incorporated part of Whitelocke's and Wildman's

attempt, in 1659, to devise a new style of government for a free state. Whitelocke himself certainly considered the draft constitution incriminating, after the turn of events in 1660, and felt indebted to Wildman for not revealing the contents of their joint paper.

6. *Memoirs of the Verney Family* (Longman, Green and Co. 1907), vol. ii, p. 123. A well-stocked deer park was a highly prized possession.

7. 'Diary' 1 May 1660, also Arthur Bryant, *King Charles II* (Collins 1960), p. 59.

8. 'Diary' 8 May 1660.

9. Add. MS. 32093 fol. 420, also 'Diary' 29 May 1660. Harbottle Grimston, a Presbyterian, had been elected Speaker by the Convention Parliament at the end of April 1660. Colonel James Whitelocke, too, had smartly changed his allegiance and, as Governor of Kings Lynn, promised to secure the town for Charles. *Old Parliamentary History*, vol. xii, pp. 347 and 352.

10. 'Diary' 1 June 1660 and David Ogg, *England in the Reign of Charles II* (O.U.P. 1934), p. 154. On the question of acting against the King, Whitelocke showed some prejudice; during the Civil War Prynne had indeed written in justification of a people deposing their king if he failed in his divine duty, but by December 1648, after Parliament had failed to negotiate a settlement with King Charles on the Isle of Wight, he was anxious that they should effect a reconciliation; after the King's execution, when Whitelocke was praying that God would not show his displeasure against a poor afflicted nation, and was referring to 'the present alterations' brought about by 'unavoidable necessity', Prynne was boldly attacking the Regicides. William M. Lamont, *Marginal Prynne* (Routledge and Kegan Paul 1963), pp. 89, 92-3, 98-9, 101, 182-3.

11. 'He was a learned man of immense reading, but is much blamed for his unfaithful quotations.' Aubrey's *Brief Lives* (ed. Oliver Lawson Dick) (Peregrine Books 1962), p. 314.

12. Whitelocke was chosen Recorder of Oxford in 1646-7. Longleat, vol. ix, fol. 123.

13. 'Diary' I June 1660. Finch (later Earl of Nottingham and of Winchelsea) was an opponent of toleration who 'jeered at "tender conscience" '. He represented Court and Church interests in the House of Commons and was one of the prosecuting counsel at the trial of the Regicides in October 1660.

14. Longleat, vol. xvii, fols. 23, 144; vol. xviii fol. 29; vol. xix, fols. 26, 57. There are also three letters in vol. xix fols. 114, 118 and 120, dated 28 January, February and 10 February 1659[60], in which (1) Whitelocke appealed to Moncke for clemency in connection with his having served, in good faith, on the Committee of Safety and asked the General to write to the Speaker on his behalf. (2) Moncke replied that he resented Whitelocke's speech at Guildhall, traducing his actions, and that it would in any case be improper to write to the Speaker. (3) Whitelocke replied that his Guildhall speech had been mis-reported. (Whitelocke's two letters are draft copies.)

15. 'Diary' 4 June 1660. Moncke was again referring to Whitelocke's Guildhall speech to the Lord Mayor and Common Council in November 1659.
16. 'Diary' 8 June 1660, 30 July 1649 and Add. MS. 37344 fols. 324b and 325. The Septuagint or 'version of the seventy' was the Greek version of the Bible translated by seventy (or seventy-two) learned Jews, the other two copies, dating from the fourth century, being the 'Vaticanus' and 'Sinaiticus'. The 'Alexandrinus' was given to Charles I in 1627 by Cyril Lucar, the Greek patriarch of Constantinople. Whitelocke's integrity in refusing to sell it overseas indirectly enabled George II in 1757 to give this treasure to the British Museum with the rest of the Royal Library. Whitelocke refers to five volumes, although it is generally believed that it was originally in one volume and was divided into four when it came into the possession of Charles I. *The Codex Sinaiticus and the Codex Alexandrinus* (Trustees of the British Museum 1963), pp. 30, 31, 34, 35 and *The Catalogue of Western Manuscripts in the Old Royal and King's Collections in the British Museum* give further details of the 'Alexandrinus'. The references to Patrick Young's representatives (after his death in September 1652) refusing to part with the manuscript until legal proceedings were taken after the Restoration (introduction xxiii) appears to conflict not only with Whitelocke's report but also with a later statement in the introduction xxiv; this is to the effect that Whitelocke, as Keeper of the Library, received a warrant to lend the 'Codex Alexandrinus' to Walton and other editors of the Polyglot Bible, some time after Young's death.
17. The story has variations. John Lord Campbell in his *Lives of the Lord Chancellors* quoted one-and-thirty children; this, he added, must have been an exaggeration. Unfortunately neither he nor Dr. Morton (who quoted the lines in a preface to *Notes uppon the King's Writt*) gave the source, nor does the incident appear in Whitelocke's 'Diary'.
18. 'Diary' 13 June 1660 and R. H. Whitelocke, *Memoirs*, pp. 451–2 and 447. In an exhibition of ecclesiastical art and treasures lent by King George V and the Duke of Gloucester, in Cheltenham, 29 September to 5 October 1928, a fine prayer book was exhibited containing the book plate of John Whitelocke and bearing the royal cipher C.II R. The catalogue described it as 'of the Stuart period 1660'.
19. Longleat, vol. xix, fol. 150.
20. 'Diary' 1 August 1666.
21. That summer books by John Goodwin and John Milton had the distinction of being burned at the Old Bailey at the hands of the common hangman. 'Diary' 5 September 1660 and Goodwin, Milton, *D.N.B.* (The dates do not quite tally.)
22. 'Diary' 12 Nov. 1660. In view of the hatred most Parliamentarians felt for the 'Norman Bastard' this was a decidedly back-handed compliment to Charles II and Whitelocke's comparison between the Norman conquest and the Restoration reflects a degree of hostility towards the King's return. Like Spelman, Cotton

and Selden, Whitelocke was a keen student of Anglo-Saxon history and law. The background to the seventeenth-century view of the Norman invasion is given in Christopher Hill's chapter on 'The Norman Yoke' in *Puritanism and Revolution* (Mercury Books 1962).

23. The six autograph manuscripts (Add. MS. 4749–54) were presented to the British Museum by Thomas Carew of Somerset in 1766, Carew having purchased them from the Duke of Chandos's library (lot 1849) in 1747. It seems from the 'Diary' that they were originally bound in three volumes, and delivered by instalments, the second being submitted in April 1661, the third and last in October. Morton, the first under-librarian of the British Museum, edited the work for publication in 1766. So began his interest in Whitelocke's work which led to his publishing, six years later, *A Journal of the Swedish Embassy*. He referred to the derivative quality of the Notes as if he had caught Whitelocke cribbing; he did not know that the author acknowledged, in his letter to Lord Willoughby and in the 'Diary', how much the manuscript owed to the work of Selden and others. In chapter XCIII Whitelocke referred to the merits of 'mixed monarchy', with king, lords and commons, as it had been delineated by Charles I.

24. The Rev. Samuel Wilkinson was rector of Chelsea Parish Church (now Chelsea Old Church) from 1632–69.

25. The Manor of Fulham (later Fulham Palace) continued to be the residence of the Bishop of London until the year 1972.

CHAPTER XII: Pardon – and Oblivion

1. Since 1611, when Thomas Sutton bought Charterhouse for £13,000, the school's and the hospital's Board of Governors had included Archbishop Laud, Dean John Donne, Bishop William Juxon, His Excellency Oliver Cromwell (appointed like Whitelocke in May 1650), John Bradshaw, Charles Fleetwood and Thomas Lord Fairfax. Again, at the Restoration, the most powerful men of the day joined the board, among them Lord Chancellor Clarendon, George Moncke Duke of Albemarle and Bishop Gilbert Sheldon. James Moore, *Memorials of Charterhouse* (London 1844), p. vi.

2. Venner, *D.N.B.*; John Buchan, *Oliver Cromwell* (Hodder and Stoughton 1935), pp. 431, 440, 466; S.P. Dom. 29, vol. xxviii, fol. 42.

3. 'Diary' February 1661 [2] and February 1662 [3].

4. Frances Whitelocke's mother, Lady Willoughby of Parham, was the daughter of the 4th Earl of Rutland. Kathleen, wife of George Villiers, first Duke of Buckingham, was the daughter of the 6th Earl of Rutland. The great house in Chelsea, later called Beaufort House, had once been the home of Sir Thomas More. In 1627 it was given by Charles I to the first Duke of Buckingham. The second Duke lost

it in 1674 through his extravagance. *G.E.C.* Also L.C.C. *Survey of London* Chelsea Part II, vol. iv, 1913, pp. 18–27.

5. Whitelocke named the Irish stroker as Britridge but it seems more probable that he was the well known faith healer, Valentine Greatraks (Greatrix or Greatrakes), who visited England in 1666 at the request of Lady Conway. He was later summoned to London by Charles II. See *D.N.B.* and *St. Bartholomews Hospital Journal* 1956, **60**, 361–8. Article by R. A. Hunter and I. Macalpine.

6. J. R. Tanner, *English Constitutional Conflicts of the Seventeenth Century* (C.U.P. 1961), pp. 226–7. Although twenty-four independent ministers signed a disclaimer, dissociating themselves from Venner's policy of violence, this group was in general under suspicion.

7. 'Diary' 24 March 1661 [2].

8. During the Civil War Whitelocke had followed the convention of blaming evil counsellors for the King's misdeeds; later he seems to have rejected the concept that 'the King can do no wrong' and that ministers alone were answerable for actions done in a king's name. In Sweden he told Chancellor Oxenstierna 'the king himself, as well as other men, is a subject to the law and an officer under it.' Add. MS. 37346 fol. 187.

9. 'Diary' 27 May 1662.

10. Add. MS. 21099. Tanner, *English Constitutional Conflicts*, pp. 227–9 gives the background to the King's problem.

11. It was said that Harbottle Grimston himself had been appointed Master of the Rolls on payment to the Lord Chancellor of £8,000. *D.N.B.*

12. Colonel Alexander Popham was a grandson of Lord Chief Justice Sir John Popham who had bought Littlecote, on the banks of the Kennet, in 1589. Both Alexander and his brother Edward had fought for Parliament. At the Restoration Alexander swiftly made his peace with the King, but in spite of this change of allegiance he was always a good friend to his neighbour at Chilton Lodge.

13. It is remarkable that so many of Whitelocke's manuscripts have survived in spite of havoc by Prince Rupert's troops, by Mary's conflagration and finally by the Fire of London; some of his inaccuracies may be attributed to these losses.

14. The manor had passed into the hands of Edward Nevill in 1560. Edward had claimed, and his son had successfully asserted, his right to the title of Lord Bergavenny or Abergavenny. The splendid Georgian mansion which replaced the earlier building has for some years been a college of education. D. W. Humphreys (pamphlet) *The History of the Manor of Newton St. Loe*; also Abergavenny (Nevill), *G.E.C.*

15. The second Frances was, in the words of modern psychologists, a 'replacement child' and as such was given her half-sister's name and nickname.

16. The full epigram runs 'They do not easily climb to distinction whose qualities are hindered by cramping poverty at home.'

17. *Debates of the House of Commons From the Year 1667 to the Year 1694* collected by Anchitell Grey (London 1769), vol. i, pp. 182–6, 195–201, 212. On 1 December 1669 Orrery appeared at the bar of the House, crippled with gout, to answer the ten articles of the charge; as he struggled up the stairs he observed to a friend, 'my feet are weak, but if my heels will serve to carry me up, I promise you my head shall bring me safe down again.' The matter was half-heartedly referred to the King's Bench and there was a further, inconclusive debate on the charge before it petered out. David Ogg, *England in the Reign of Charles II* (O.U.P. 1934), vol. i, p. 341 and vol. ii, pp. 397–8.

18. 'Diary' 7 December 1669.

19. Boyle, Roger, Baron Broghill and first Earl of Orrery, *D.N.B.* and *G.E.C.*

20. Katherine (or Catherine), Lady Ranelagh, was the Earl of Cork's fifth daughter. She married Arthur Jones, Viscount Ranelagh, who had served as a Captain under the Commonwealth and of whom it was reported in the Verney *Memoirs*, 'he seldom cometh sober to bed.' A friend of the Verneys wrote of her 'a more brave wench or a braver spirit you have not often met with all' and her close friend, John Milton, expressed equal admiration. At the funeral of her brother, Robert Boyle, in 1692, shortly after her own death, Bishop Burnet recalled in his sermon that she had 'made the greatest figure in all the revolutions of these kingdoms for above fifty years of any woman of our age . . . her great understanding and the vast esteem she was in made all persons, in their several turns of greatness, desire and value her friendship.' *G.E.C.* footnote Ranelagh.

21. 'Diary' 15 April 1670.

22. Whitelocke did Whistler a service in 1655–6 for which the Doctor wrote thanking him ecstatically, but without mentioning the nature of the service. Add. MS. 4992 fol. 145b. Although Whistler married a rich widow it came to light after his death in 1684 that he was deep in debt. The year before he died he was elected President of the Royal College of Physicians. After his death an extraordinary meeting learned that the late President had been defrauding the College. William Munk, *The Roll of the Royal College of Physicians of London* (Longman, Green, Longman and Roberts 1861), vol. i, pp. 230–2. An account in Latin of the committee's proceedings indicates that they impounded such of Whistler's money and plate as they could lay hands on. To avoid an open scandal the new President, Sir John Cutler, seems to have made good the deficit.

23. From the end of January 1644 [45] the 'Diary' and 'Annals' changed from monthly to daily entries; but the vividness and detail of the material in both MSS, from as early as the 1620s, indicate that even in his student days Whitelocke was keeping notes and letter books; he was probably encouraged to do so by the methodical John Selden and by the example of his father, Judge James, who was writing his own autobiography, 'Liber Famelicus'.

24. *Nulli te facias nimis sodalem, gaudebis minus minus dolebis* (Do not make yourself too

friendly with anyone; you will rejoice less but you will grieve less), and *Agnosce multos, cognosce paucos, nulli fides* (have many acquaintances, few friends, trust no one).

25. Longleat, 'History of Persecution', vol. xxvii.

26. 'Diary' 14, 15 June 1671. A copy of Whitelocke's reply is in the library at Windsor Castle, 'Governor's Book' 1668–71 pp. 1–7.

27. Add. MS. 32094 fol. 265. The draft is dated Feb 22 71 [72].

28. Add. MS. 53726 20th year. I am indebted to Dr. Royce MacGillivray for pointing out that some of the material in Whitelocke's printed *Memorials of the English Affairs from the Supposed Expedition of Brute to this Island, to the end of the Reign of King James the First* (London 1709) contains material from Arthur Wilson's *The History of Great Britain being the Life and Reign of King James the First* (1653). It follows that if the history Whitelocke wrote at the age of nineteen was the basis of his posthumously published work it must have been revised after 1653, unless of course Whitelocke lent his manuscript to Arthur Wilson as he lent other papers to Rushworth. It was Whitelocke's intention to insert the History of England in the 'Annals', immediately before his 21st year in which he recorded the accession of Charles I.

29. The Samuel Wilsons still lived comfortably in Bishopsgate and the Cokains in Redcross Street. That part of the City was well stocked with dissenting ministers and conventicles.

30. *Elias Ashmole 1617–1692*, vol. iv, p. 1436. Books of reference give the date of death variously as July 1675 or January 1676 and the place of burial as Chilton Foliat or Fawley. There are tablets in memory of an assortment of unknown Whitelockes in Fawley Church and a florid-faced Bulstrode Whitelocke (the younger) at Chilton. William Penn's introduction to Whitelocke's *History of England or Memorials of the English Affairs* 1713 is probably the most reliable single statement on the subject, coupled with Ashmole's note.

31. R. H. Whitelocke *Memoirs*, pp. 464 and 468.

32. 'Acceptability, or as he called it "acceptance", was to him [Cromwell] the only test of right government . . . in cooler moments he would admit that a government "with something monarchical in it" was probably the most acceptable and therefore the best.' H. R. Trevor-Roper ,'Oliver Cromwell and his Parliaments' in *Essays Presented to Sir Lewis Namier* (Macmillan 1956).

33. Add. MS. 53728 'Upon the new buildings at Chilton Lodge 1667'. This manuscript, not yet foliated, was one of the four manuscripts which the author ran to earth in Dublin. An account of the search is given in the Postscript. *Quench not the Spirit*, a companion volume of Whitelocke's sermons, was published posthumously with an introduction by William Penn (London 1711).

Index

Abergavenny family (see Nevill)

Abingdon, Berks., 46, 61, 63, 64, 70

Abraham, 97

Acts and Bills (see Parliament)

Adson, Dr. John, music teacher to Charles I, 274

Adventurers:
Irish, 81, 85, 206
Merchant, 100, 193

Albemarle, 1st Duke of, (George Moncke), 143, 218, 219, 222, 223, 226, 227, 233, 295, 297

Aldermaston, Berks., 113, 136, 207

Aldworth, Berks., 23, 270

Amaranth, Swedish Order of, 192, 211, 290

Amersham, Bucks., 94

Anabaptists, 172, 287

Anglesey, 1st Earl of, (Arthur Annesley), Lord Privy Seal, 11

Aragon, Queen Katherine of, 27

Armine, Sir William, 89

Arundel, Earl of, (*probably* Thomas Howard), 167

Ascham, Anthony, 117, 137, 155

Ashmole, Elias, 136, 249

Assembly of Divines, 96

Assheton, Sir Ralph, M.P., 225

Astrology, 158 (see also Lilly)

Astrop Spa, nr. Banbury, Oxon., 241

Audley End, Essex, 122

Aylesbury, Bucks., 130
The George, 208

Aymon, Father Jean, 256

Ayscue, Sir George, 283

Babb, Thomas, painter, 47

Bampfield, Thomas, 294

Bankes, Sir John, Attorney General, 68, 72, 90

Barbados, 131, 234, 283

Barnet, Herts., 137

Bartlett, Dr., physician, 51, 52

Bate, Dr. George, 117, 129

Baylie, Dr. Richard, President of St. John's College, Oxford, 64, 96

Beake, Captain, 189, 198

Bearwood, nr. Wokingham, Berks., 23

Beche, de la, family, 23

Bedford, 126, 127

Belvoir Castle, Leics., 65

Bennet, Sir Humphrey, brother-in-law to Whitelocke, 92

Bennet, Rebecca (see Whitelocke)

Bennet, Richard, 211

Berkshire, 1st Earl of, (Thomas Howard), 84, 225, 227, 278

Berry, James, 220, 294

Berwick on Tweed, Northumberland, 218

Best, Paul, 109

Beuningen, Coenraad van, Dutch envoy at Swedish Court, 177, 184

Bishops' Wars:
First, 70
Second, 71

Blake, Admiral Robert, 143

Blunsden, nr. Swindon, Wilts., 131, 233

Blunt's Hall, Essex, 206

Boleyn, Anne, 24, 27

Bonde, Christer, Swedish ambassador to the Commonwealth of England, 204, 205, 207, 208, 292

Booth, Sir George, 216, 294

Bordeaux, France, 24

Borlase (or Burlace), John, 72, 73

Boulogne, France, 55

Bradshaw, John, M.P., president at trial of King Charles I, 116, 123, 124, 213, 297
Braganza, Catherine of, m. Charles II, 243
Braughing, Herts., 205
Breda, Holland, 219, 220
Brentford, Middlesex, 87, 88, 89
Bristol, Glos., 120, 200, 208, 209, 244
British Museum, 257, 260, 282, 296, 297
Broghill, Baron (Roger Boyle) (see Orrery)
Bromham, Beds., 127
Browne, Major General Richard, 100, 219
Buckingham, 1st Duke of, (George Villiers), 33, 34, 35, 38, 48, 55, 298
Buckingham, Duchess of, (Kathleen Manners), dr. of 6th Earl of Rutland, m. George Villiers, 1st Duke of Buckingham, 276, 298
Buckingham, 2nd Duke of, (George Villiers), 113, 121, 167, 233, 234, 298
Bull, Anthony, 45, 273
Bulstrode family, 26, 27
Bulstrode, Elizabeth, m. Judge Sir James Whitelocke (see Whitelocke)
Bulstrode, Colonel Thomas, 190
Burnet, Gilbert, Bishop of Salisbury, 299
Burney, Dr. Charles, 257
Burton, Thomas, M.P., 209, 210
Bute, 2nd Marquess of, 10
Byron, Sir John, (later 1st Baron), 84, 86
Byron, Sir Thomas, 86, 87

Camden, William, author of *Britannia*, 36
Campius, Dr. John, German scholar, 242
Canary Islands, 244
Canterstein, Secretary to Chancellor Oxenstierna, 189
Carisbrooke Castle, Isle of Wight, 111
Carlyle, Thomas, 9, 250, 270
Carr, Robert, 85

Carter, Toucher, 71, 72
Casimir, John, Count Palatine, 188
Catherine, Princess of Sweden, 158, 188
Caversham, Berks., 111
Cely, John, 51, 53
Chamberlain, Dr. Peter, 117
Chancey, tutor, 229, 234
Charles I, King, 33, 48, 50, 61, 64, 67, 69, 70, 71, 76, 78, 80, 81, 82, 89, 90, 93, 100, 101, 102, 103, 108, 109, 111, 114, 115, 278, 280
Charles II, King, 120, 125, 129, 133
    Proclaimed King, 223
    Lands at Dover, 224
    Grants audience to Whitelocke, 228
    Attempts to legalize liberty of conscience, 234
    Consults Whitelocke on indulgence, 237, 279
    also, 230, 243, 292
Charles X (Karl Gustav), Prince, later King of Sweden, 174, 188, 189, 289
Chequers, Bucks., 27, 288
Chilton Foliat, Wilts.:
    Chilton Lodge, 206, 238, 239, 240, 247, 248, 249
    Church, 247
Christina, Queen of Sweden, 141, 152
    Birth and early years, 158–9
    Audiences with, 159, 162–9, 170–1, 174–5, 179, 182, 188
    Exchange of presents with Whitelocke, 182, 184, 189
    Sends portrait to Cromwell, 183
    Welcomes Protectorate, 171
    Attends May-day celebrations, 185
    Invites Whitelocke to wedding at Court, 185
    Abdication of, 174, 185, 187, 191, 289
    Plans to visit England, 200
    Letter to Cromwell, 211

Chute, Chaloner, M.P., 294

Clarendon, 1st Earl of, (Edward Hyde), 31, 47, 48, 50, 52, 54, 56, 64, 65, 67, 70, 79, 81, 87, 88, 92, 94, 102, 105, 106, 183, 215, 229, 230, 233, 234, 235, 236, 238, 240, 297

Clarendon Code (see Parliament: Acts and Bills)

Claypole, Elizabeth, dr. of Oliver Cromwell, 214

Codex:
    Alexandrinus, 228, 296
    Sinaiticus, 296
    Vaticanus, 296
    also: 'Septuagint', 228, 296

Cokain, George, Independent minister, 124, 126, 127, 142, 147, 181, 198, 217, 238, 247, 248

Coke, Lord Chief Justice Sir Edward, 27, 28, 29, 34, 271

Coke, Clement, M.P., youngest son of Sir Edward, 34, 35, 272

Colchester, Essex, 122

Cole, Robert, lawyer, 51, 54, 55, 56

College of Heralds, 290

Colnbrook, Bucks., 33, 87

Commissions of Array, 83, 84

Committee of Privileges, 71, 72, 74

Committee of Safety:
    (i) 82
    (ii) 217, 218, 222

Commonwealth of England, 152, 159, 160, 171, 172

Cooke, William:
    Encourages Whitelocke to remarry, 58–60, 123
    Letter to Frances Whitelocke, 99
    Discusses Whitelocke's appointment to Sweden, 139–40
    Death of, 142–3
    also: 61, 63, 86, 87, 112, 114, 120, 280

Cooper, Anthony Ashley, (later Lord Ashley, then 1st Earl of Shaftesbury), 215, 246, 293

Cooper, Gislingham, m. Ann, granddaughter of Sir William Whitelocke, 255

Coranto, Whitelocke's, 48, 274

Corbet, Miles, M.P., regicide, 98

Cornwall, 89, 102

Cotton, Sir Thomas, 143

Cotton Library, 144

Cotton End, Beds., 126, 136

Council of State, Council, 115, 116, 122, 137, 138, 141, 142, 144, 152, 160, 172, 199, 217, 292

Croke, family of, 27, 41

Croke, Judge George, 27, 35, 45, 73

Cromwell, Henry, 282

Cromwell, Oliver, M.P., Commander-in-Chief, Lord Protector, 103, 104, 105, 110, 112, 114, 115, 116
    Militia Ordinance, 81
    Irish Campaign, 125
    Scottish Campaign, 126–9
    Battle of Worcester, 129–30
    Debate on future government, 130–1
    Consults Whitelocke about royal title, 133
    Dissolves the Rump, 135
    Summons Barebones, 136
    Letter and consultations about Whitelocke's Swedish mission, 137–40, 145
    Assumes title of Lord Protector, 171
    Sends portrait to Queen Christina, 183
    Welcomes Whitelocke home, 199
    Rejects Christina's proposed visit, 201
    1st Parliament of Protectorate, 201
    Instrument of Government, 201, 202, 208
    Dissolves Parliament, 202

Cromwell, Oliver – *contd*
  Ordinance to modify Chancery Court, 203
  2nd Parliament of Protectorate, 208
  Humble Petition and Advice, 210
  Installed as Lord Protector, 210
  2nd Parliament adjourned, 210
  Governs without Parliament, 213
  Ordinance forbidding celebration of Christmas, 213
  Parliament recalled; dissolved, 213
  Death of, 214
  Denzil Holles' opinion of, 280
  Governor of Charterhouse, 297
Cromwell, Richard, Lord Protector, 214, 215, 293
Croydon, Surrey, 234

Dalarö, Sweden, 192
Davenant, Sir William, 216
Denbigh, 2nd Earl of, (Basil Feilding), 103, 107
Denmark, 141, 143, 151, 179, 185
Desborough, Major-General John, 215, 217, 218, 220, 222, 294
Descartes, René, 162
D'Ewes, Simonds, 79
Dieppe, France, 51
Digby, George, son of Lord Bristol, 74, 75, 76
Disraeli, Isaac, 11
Ditton Park, Bucks., 86
Dixon, Cecilia *née* Whitelocke, m. Edward, 28, 45, 46, 281
Dixon, Edward, m. Cecilia Whitelocke, 46
Dixon, Henry, father of Edward, 45, 46, 205
Donne, Dean John, 297
Dorislaus, Dr. Isaac, 116, 137, 155
Dover, Kent, 56

Downing, Sir George, M.P., 198, 208, 209, 290
D'Oyley, Sir Cope, 32, 47
Drake, Admiral Sir Francis, 26
Drake, Thomas, brother of Sir Francis, 26, 270
Drake, Sir William, M.P., 94, 99, 243
Drogheda, Ireland, 122
Dunbar, battle of, 128, 283
Dutch Peace Treaty 1654, 181

Earle, Daniel, Secretary to Whitelocke, 114, 136, 142, 144, 146, 177, 183, 189, 196, 198
Earle, Thomas, Bristol merchant, 244
Earle, Sir Walter, M.P., 74, 75, 76
Eden, Claes, Swedish merchant, 156, 286
Edgehill, battle of, 86, 103
Edinburgh, 218
Edward II, King, Court of, 23
Edward III, King, 23
Edward, the Black Prince, 23
Eliot, Sir John, M.P., 34, 35
Elizabeth I, Queen, 159
Elizabeth, Princess, sister of Prince Rupert, 162
Ellesmere, Lord Chancellor, (Thomas Egerton), 28, 29
Elliot, Dr. Peter [?], 241, 244
Elsinore, Denmark, 151
Elsynge, Henry, Clerk to Parliament, 115, 199
Elsynge, Henry, jnr., 154
Eltonhead, Edward, 190
Enköping, Sweden, 156
Epictetus, 40
Essex, 2nd Earl of, (Robert Devereux), 25, 26
Essex, 3rd Earl of, (Robert Devereux), 85, 88, 95, 100, 101, 102, 104, 106, 109, 111

Eton College, 28, 30, 144, 212, 285
Evelyn, John, diarist, 11, 213, 224, 244

Fairfax, Lord General Thomas, 102, 109, 114, 123, 126, 129, 297
Falkland, 2nd Viscount of, (Lucius Carey), 95
Falkland, 4th Viscount of, (Henry Carey), 227
Fanshawe, Thomas, M.P., 93
Farren, James, tutor to James Whitelocke Jnr., Oxford, 120
Fawkes, Guy, Gunpowder Plot, 25
Fawley, nr. Henley-on-Thames:
  Church, 46, 119, 249
  Fawley Court, 30, 33, 42, 43, 44, 46, 56, 58, 60, 61, 64, 67, 68, 71, 86, 100, 126, 131, 199, 206, 222, 255, 272, 273, 290
Felton, John, 39
Fiennes, James, son of Lord Say & Sele, 71
Finch, Sir Heneage, Solicitor General, 225
Firth, Sir Charles, 11, 250
Firth of Forth, Scotland, 129
Fleetwood, Major-General Charles, Commander-in-Chief, 129, 215, 216, 217, 218, 219, 220, 285, 294, 297
Fleetwood, Colonel George, M.P., regicide, 124, 142
Fleetwood, Sir George, 142, 191, 285, 289
Fleetwood, Sir William, royalist, 142, 219, 285
Fontainebleau, Palace of, France, 211
Forest of Dean, Glos., 32
Forsius, self-styled Astronomer-Royal of Sweden, 158
Forster, Sir Humphrey, 113, 136, 207
Foster, Captain of frigate Phoenix, 146, 147, 150
Fox, George, 208
Fry, John, 294

Gardie, Graf Jacob de la, 176

Gardiner, Dr. S. R., historian, 11
Gascony, Seneschal of, 23
Gloucester, 32, 94, 111
Glyn, John, M.P., barrister, 74, 102
Goodwin, Colonel Arthur, M.P., 84
Goodwin, Dr. John, 229
Goodwin, Dr. Thomas, 235
Gothenburg (Göteborg), Sweden, 141, 151, 152, 153, 156
Gough, Elizabeth, m. Samuel Whitelocke, 241
Grantham, Lincs., 66
Gravesend, Kent, 146, 151, 198, 207
Greatraks, Valentine, Irish 'stroker', 234, 298
Greenlands, nr. Henley-on-Thames, 32, 47, 63, 99, 100, 131, 240, 272
Grimston, Sir Harbottle, 35, 223, 224, 238, 295, 298
Grotius, Hugo, Mare Liberum 285, Latin Eulogy to King James, 286
Guernsey, C.I., 144
Gustavus Adolphus, King of Sweden, 48, 141, 151, 153, 158, 169, 285

Hall, Bartholomew, 45, 65, 123, 126, 127, 128, 142, 190, 239
Hambleden, Bucks., 47, 63, 68
  New House, 60, 61, 69
Hamburg, Germany, 193, 194
Hampden, John, M.P., 34, 67, 68, 69, 73, 75, 80, 84, 88, 94
Hampton Court, 198, 207, 211, 214, 293
Harrison, Colonel Thomas, later Major-General, 126, 129, 135
Harvard College, America, 198, 290
Harvey, Colonel Edmund, father of Samuel, 212, 231
Harvey, Samuel, son of Edmund, m. Cecilia, dr. of Bulstrode and Frances Whitelocke, 212, 231, 237

Harvey, William, M.D., physician, 176
Haselrig, Sir Arthur, M.P., 80, 106, 216, 221, 229, 294
Haynes, Beds., 137
Heads of the Proposals 1647, 111
Hedgerley Bulstrode, Bucks., 26, 27
Henley-on-Thames, Oxon. (see also Fawley, Greenlands, Phyllis Court), 86, 101, 119, 181
  Bell Inn, 45, 46, 99, 280
Henrietta Maria, Queen, 47, 48, 50, 74, 76, 80, 100, 117, 234, 278
Henry VIII, King, 24, 221
Henry, Prince, Duke of Glos., 3rd son of Charles I, 130
Hersham, Surrey, 206
Hertford, 94
Heylin, Dr. Peter, 47
Hill, George, m. Anne, dr. of Bulstrode and Frances Whitelocke, 212
Hinton, Dr. John, 117
Hippesley, Gabriel, 72, 73
Hoby, Peregrine, M.P., 71, 72, 73
Holland, 1st Earl of, (Henry Rich), 63, 108, 112, 113, 119
Holland, Sir John, M.P., 89, 90, 93
Holland, 85, 100, 116, 141, 150, 162, 182
  The Hague, 116
Holles, Denzil, M.P., 80, 89, 100, 102, 103, 104, 106, 107, 108, 110, 280
Holmby House (Holdenby Manor), Northants., 111
Holstein, Governor of, 194
Horton, nr. Colnbrook, Bucks., 33, 43
Hounslow, Middlesex, 199
Howard, Frances m. 3rd Earl of Essex, 85
Howard, the Lady Mary, dr. of 1st Earl of Berks., 227
Howard, Sir Robert, bro. of the Lady Mary, 229

Humble Petition & Advice (see Cromwell)
Hungerford, Sir George, 282
Hungerford, Berks., 238, 239
Hunsdon House, Herts., 221, 294
Hyde, Edward (see Clarendon)
Hydrotherapy, 272

Independents, 61, 96, 97, 109, 114, 234
Ingelo, Dr. Nathaniel, a chaplain to Whitelocke in Sweden and master of his music, 144, 153, 190, 197, 198, 289
Ingoldsby, Colonel Richard, M.P., 134, 221
Ingram, Sir Arthur, 273
Instrument of Government (see Oliver Cromwell)
Inverkeithing, battle of, 129
Ireland, 78, 85, 95, 110, 120, 125, 292
Ireton, Henry, Commissary-General, son-in-law of Oliver Cromwell, 111, 116, 219
Isle of Wight, 60, 111, 114
Isleworth, Middlesex, 121
Ives, Simon, composer, 48, 50

Jamaica, 255
James I, King, 27, 28, 29, 33, 69, 286
Jones, Inigo, 25, 47, 274
Juxon, Bishop William, 30, 212, 297

Keble, Sergeant Richard, a Commissioner of the Great Seal, 115
Kent, Countess of, 90, 108, 167
Kent, Earl of, 112
Kildare, Ireland, 206, 292
King's Lynn, Norfolk, 295
Kitson, Rev. William, Rector of Fawley, 46, 64, 276
Köping, Sweden, 155
Knaith House, Lincs., 66
Kylemore Abbey, Ireland, 258

Lagerfeldt, Swedish agent in London, later served Chancellor Oxenstierna, 150, 160, 174, 175

Lambert, Major-General John, M.P., 126, 129, 142, 216, 217, 218, 219, 220, 222

Land's End, Cornwall, 273

Lane, Sir Richard, Lord Keeper, 99, 279

Lanier, Nicholas, Master of the King's Music, 50, 274

Laud, Archbishop William, 26, 30, 44, 46, 47, 61, 63, 64, 69, 78, 96, 98, 273, 274, 297

Lauderdale, Earl of, (*probably* John Maitland), 111

Lawes, William, composer, 48, 50

Lenthall, William, M.P., Master of the Rolls and Speaker, 94, 109, 112, 203, 204, 217, 221, 222, 229, 294

Lerum, Sweden, 153

Levellers, 132, 172, 201, 291

Lewis, Sir William, M.P., 100, 106, 107, 109

Lichfield, Staffs., 216

Lilly, William, astrologer, 78, 158, 206, 291-2

Lincoln, 4th Earl of, (Theophilus Clinton), 108

Lincoln, diocese of, 273

L'Isle, John, a Lord Commissioner of the Great Seal, regicide, 106, 115, 117, 121, 132, 203, 204, 210, 284

L'Isle, Philip, son of Earl of Leicester, 137, 138, 141, 284

Littlecote, Wilts., 238, 239, 247, 298

Little Rollright, Oxon., 281

Littleton, Sir Edward, Lord Keeper, 81, 90, 278

London and environs:
  Bishops of (see Juxon and Sheldon)
  Common Council of, 87, 218
  Great Fire of, 238
  Lord Mayor of, 50, 95, 123, 130, 210, 218
  Churches:
    Chelsea Old Church (Church of St. Luke), 136, 284
    Pancras, Soper Lane, 42, 124, 143
    St. Dunstan's in the East, 235
    St. Dunstan's in the West, 27, 271
    St. Helen's, Coleman Street, 236
    St. John's, Hackney, 127
    St. Martin-in-the-Fields, 46
    St. Michael's, Crooked Lane, 235
    St. Nicholas', Deptford, 108, 235
    St. Paul's, 232
    The Temple, 108
  Courts of Law:
    Chancery, 121, 201, 203, 291
    Exchequer, 68
    Old Bailey, 233, 296
    Star Chamber, 47, 78, 96, 98
  Districts, Streets, Place names:
    Acton, 88
    Bishopsgate Street, 123, 124, 128, 129, 221
    Bow, 52, 54
    Chancery Lane, 48, 237
    Charing Cross, 48
    Charterhouse Yard, 119
    Cheapside, 43
    Chelsea, 121, 127, 136, 137, 198, 234
    Coleman Street, 80, 229, 232, 233, 235, 237
    Dean's Yard, Westminster, 277
    Finsbury Fields, 84
    Fleet Conduit, 53
    Fleet Street, 23, 27, 237, 239
    Greenwich, 223
    Hackney, 124, 127
    Hammersmith, 88

London—*contd*
Highgate, 94, 98, 137
Hyde Park Corner, 33
Ivy Lane, Westminster, 93
Moorfields, 229
Moor Gate, 80, 84
Old Exchange, 209
Palace Yard, 114, 217
Redcross Street, 300
Salisbury Court, Fleet Street, 47, 48, 53, 56
Scotland Yard, 217
Smithfield, 232
St. James's Park, 133
Temple Bar, 48
Thames Street, 24
Tilt Yard, 50
Tower Hill, 77, 222
Tower Wharf, 146, 204
Turnham Green, 88
Wandsworth, 205
Whitefriars, 178
Halls:
Grocers', 143, 206
Guildhall, 218, 271
Merchant Taylors', 50
Westminster, 33, 74, 210, 217
Inns and Taverns:
The Bear Key, 24
The Dolphin, Ludgate Hill, 247
St. Dunstan's Tavern, 38
Oracle of Apollo, 50
The Ship, Fleet Street, 64
The Sign of the Chariot, Fleet Street, 271
Inns of Court:
Clifford's Inn, 53
Gray's Inn, 49
Lincoln's Inn, 47, 225
Middle Temple, 26, 31, 38, 39, 47, 49, 64, 98, 107, 127, 128, 230, 237

also:
Essex Court, 71; Brick Court, 99
Prisons:
Bridewell, 209
Fleet, 25, 29
Marshalsea, 25
Newgate, 25
The Tower, 23, 25, 35, 47, 77, 78, 80, 81, 98, 204, 212, 216
Residences, Royal and Private:
The Cockpit, Spring Gardens, 145
Dorset House, 205
Ely House, Holborn, 48
Essex House, Strand, 104
Holland House, Kensington, 108
Manor of Fulham, 212, 231, 237, 297
Navy House, Deptford, 100, 106, 107, 108
Somerset House, Strand, 47
St. James's, 122
Whitehall:
Banqueting House, 48, 50
Palace, 48, 198
Schools and Colleges:
Charterhouse, 128, 232, 233, 238, 297
Gresham, 132
Merchant Taylors', 26, 30
Sion, 292
St. Paul's, 30
Westminster, 28, 108
Long, Sir Lislebone, M.P., 294
Loudoun, 1st Earl of, (John Campbell), Lord Chancellor, Scotland, 102, 104, 105
Lovelace, 2nd Baron Lovelace of Hurley, (John Lovelace), 131, 233
Lübeck, Germany, 192
Ludlow, Edmund, M.P., regicide, 218, 294
Lund, Sweden, University of, 288
Luton, Beds., 137

Luton Hoo, Beds., 10
Lützen, Germany, battle of, 158
Lyme Regis, Dorset, 36
Lyndsey, 1st Earl of, (Robert Bertie) (formerly Lord Willoughby of Eresby), 60, 65, 67, 103
Lyndsey, 2nd Earl of, (Montagu Bertie), 103

Madrid, 117
Malaga, nr. Gibraltar, 244
Mallory, Thomas, Independent preacher, 108, 235
Manchester, Lancs., 83
Manchester, 2nd Earl of, (Edward Montague), 102, 104, 232
Marche, Charles de la, a chaplain to Whitelocke in Sweden, 144, 159
Margaret, Queen, 27
Maria Eleanora, Queen of Sweden, m. Gustavus Adolphus, 158, 159
Marlow, Bucks., 71, 72, 73
Marston Moor, battle of, 102, 104
Marten, Henry, M.P., 135
Martin Abbey, 132
Marvell, Andrew, 183, 190
Massey, Colonel Edward, 94
Matthews, Dr., unlicensed German practitioner, 31
Maurice, Prince, nephew of King Charles I, 103
May, Adrian, 233
May, Sir Humphrey, uncle of Whitelocke's first wife, 39
May-day, 184, 185
Mayerne, Sir Theodore de, physician, 117
Maynard, John, M.P., barrister, 72, 74, 104, 105, 107
Mazarin, Cardinal Jules, 293
Mennes, Captain of frigate Elizabeth, 146, 195, 197, 198

Meyrick, Sir John, M.P., 104
Middle Temple (see London)
Militia Bill (see Parliament: Acts and Bills)
Militia Ordinance, 81, 83
Milton, John, 155, 207, 276, 280, 292, 296, 299
'Mixed Government' or 'Mixed Monarchy', theory of, 130, 131, 271, 297
Monaldeschi, Chamberlain to Queen Christina, 211
Moncke, George, (see Albemarle)
Montagu, Colonel Edward, M.P., a commissioner of the Treasury, (later 1st Earl of Sandwich), 204, 205, 207, 274
Mordaunt of Reigate, 1st Baron, (John Mordaunt), 245, 246
More, Sir Thomas, 121, 283, 298
Morton, Dr. Charles, 1st under-librarian of British Museum, 11, 256, 257, 297
Mostyn, Elizabeth, née Whitelocke, m. Thomas, 27, 28, 37, 45, 54, 111, 273
Mostyn, Sir Roger, father of Thomas, 37
Mostyn, Thomas, brother-in-law of Whitelocke, 37
Mulcaster, Richard, 26

Nanson, Joseph, clerk to Whitelocke, 229
Naples, Christina seeks crown of, 290
Napper (or Nappier), Colonel Thomas:
Apprenticed to Whitelocke, 46
Letter to, 53
Leaves Whitelocke's service, 68
Meets Whitelocke at Greenwich, 224
Arranges interview with Charles II; collects reward, 228–9
Naylor, James, 208, 209, 210
Needham, Marchmont, journalist, 172
Netherlands, the, 143

Newbury, Berks.:
    1st battle of, 95
    2nd battle of, 104
Newhall, Essex, 270
Newman, Aurelius, postilion, 144
Newmarket, Suffolk, 111
Newport, I.O.W., Treaty of, 114
Newport Pagnell, Bucks., 216
Newton St. Loe, nr. Bath, 240
Nevill, George, m. Mary, dr. of Bulstrode and Frances Whitelocke, 212, 234
Nevill, George, son of Mary and George Nevill (later Lord Abergavenny), 234
Noble, Mark, *Life of Cromwell*, 249
Norman Conquest, 81, 128, 297
Northumberland, 3rd Earl of, (Henry Percy), 25
Northumberland, 4th Earl of, (Algernon Percy), 89, 90, 105, 108, 121, 232
Norway, 151
Noy, William, Attorney General, 47, 49

Ormonde, 12th Earl, later Duke of, (James Butler), Lord Lieut. of Ireland, 120, 242
Orrery, 1st Earl of, (Roger Boyle, Baron Broghill), 122, 201, 210, 211, 242, 243, 299
Overbury, Sir Thomas, 278
Owen, Dr. John, Independent preacher, 122, 243
Oxenstierna, Axel, Chancellor of Sweden, 168, 169, 170, 171, 173, 180, 182-3, 189, 298
Oxenstierna, Count Erik, son of Axel Oxenstierna, 160, 182
Oxford, 41, 46, 84, 85, 86, 89, 93, 101, 102, 109, 111, 123, 225, 295, also:
    Colleges:
        All Souls, 120
        Christ Church, 89, 90, 93
        Magdalen, 235
        Merton, 90, 92
        Oriel, 120
        St. Edmund Hall, 241
        St. John's, 26, 30, 31, 39, 96
        Whitelocke helps to preserve treasures of, 109
Oxford, 1st Earl of, (Robert Harley), 256

Paget, Lord, 72, 83
Palmer, Geoffrey, M.P., 74, 79, 81, 93, 94, 233
Paris, 51, 52, 53, 54
Parkes, Captain of *President*, 195, 196, 197
Parliament:
    Queen Elizabeth's last, 27
    King James I's, of 1610, 28
    King Charles I's first, 33; second, 33
    Grievances, 34
    Remonstrances of:
        against Buckingham, 35, 39
        Grand Remonstrance, 78, 79
    Dissolved, 35
    Summoned by Charles I after 11 years and dissolved, 70, 71
    Long Parliament, 71
    Prepares for war, 82
    Wages war, 83
    Peace party in, 89
    Sequestration Ordinances 1643, 98
    Hostility against Army, 110
    Great Seal of, 111-12, 115, 222
    The Rump, 132
    Dissolved by Cromwell, 135
    Barebones summoned by Cromwell, 136
    1st of the Protectorate assembles, 201
    'Recognition' of, 201, 202

Parliament – *contd*
  Is dissolved, 202
  Ordinance to modify Chancery Court, 203
  2nd of the Protectorate assembles, 208
  Is adjourned, 210
  Is recalled, 213
  Dissolved by Oliver Cromwell, 213
  Richard Cromwell summons new Parliament, 215
  Humble Representation & Petition, 215
  1659 The Rump recalled by General Council of Army officers, 215
  The Rump dissolved, 217
  The Rump to be reconvened, 219
  Meets before the agreed date, 221
  Dissolves itself, 223
  Convention, 223
  Acts and Bills:
    For the Attainder of the Earl of Strafford, 76
    Against dissolving the Long Parliament without its own consent, 76
    'Root and Branch', 78
    For the Speedy Reducing of the Rebels in Ireland, 80
    For the Union of Scotland and England, 131, 208
    Treason, 1649, 172
    Militia, 208
    For the Registration of births, marriages and burials, 208
    To make the Raising of Money without the consent of Parliament high treason, 216
    Of General Pardon, Indemnity and Oblivion, 224–5
    Clarendon Code:
      Corporation Act, 234
      Act of Uniformity, 235, 237
      Conventicle Act, 248
      Five Mile Act, 248
      For the Better Advancement of the Gospel and Learning in Ireland, 282

Parsons, Philip, tutor to Whitelocke, 30, 90, 272
Pearson, James, tutor to Whitelocke's youngest children, 234, 239, 241, 244, 247, 248, 249
Pembroke, 4th Earl of, (Philip Herbert), Lord Chamberlain, 48, 64, 108, 116
Penn, William, 11, 246, 248, 249, 300
Pepys, John, father of Samuel, 48
Pepys, Samuel, diarist, 48, 225, 244, 274
Peter, Hugh, Independent preacher, 122, 166, 168, 198, 287, 290
Peterborough, 2nd Earl of, (Henry Mordaunt), 113
Phyllis (or Fillets) Court, nr. Henley-on-Thames, 30, 99, 100, 109, 110, 113, 115, 120, 126, 131, 206, 247, 255, 273
Picardy, France, 52, 54
Piccart, French servant to Whitelocke, 53, 56, 61
Pierrepont, William, M.P., 89, 93
Pickering, Sir Gilbert, M.P., 138, 209
Pickes, Jonathan, 178
Pilchard, Mary (see Whitelocke)
Pimentel de Prado, Don Antonio, Spanish envoy at Swedish Court, 157, 161, 162, 165, 176, 192
Piper, John, C.H., 16, 258, 274
Plague, Bubonic, 33, 107, 238
Poland, Christina seeks crown of, 290
Pomerania, 179
Popham, Colonel Alexander, 223, 238, 239, 240, 298
Portland, 2nd Earl of, (Jerome Western), 206
Potley, Colonel Andrew, 153, 189, 192, 289

Presbyterians/Presbyterianism, 61, 95, 96, 97, 102, 104, 106, 107, 108, 109, 110, 111, 114, 126, 201, 208, 212, 218, 239
Price, Thomas, 3rd husband of Joan Whitelocke, 25
Pride, Colonel Thomas, regicide, 114
Priorswood, Co. Dublin, 16, 265, 292
Prisons (see London)
Prujean, Dr. Francis, 117
Prynne, William, M.P., 12, 47, 98, 202, 225, 295
Puritanism, and its critics, 23, 30, 42, 43, 44, 47, 61, 66, 74, 96, 98
Pyle, Francis, son of Sir Seymour, m. Frances, dr. of Bulstrode and Mary Whitelocke, 241, 248
Pyle, Sir Seymour, 238
Pym, John M.P., 34, 72, 73, 74, 76, 78, 79, 80, 81, 82, 83, 89, 95, 100, 105, 117
Pyne, John, M.P., 35
Pyrton, Wilts., 233

Ralegh, Sir Walter, 25
Ranelagh, Viscount, (Arthur Jones), m. Katherine 5th dr. of Earl of Cork, 299
Ranelagh, the Lady Katherine (or Catherine) sister of Lord Orrery, 243, 299
Rathconrath, Ireland, 206, 292
Ré, Isle of, 55
Reading, Berks., 33, 87, 120
'Recognition' of Parliament (see Parliament)
Remenham, nr. Henley-on-Thames, 33
Restoration, 220, 223, 224, 225
Reynolds, Sir John, 219
Richelieu, Cardinal Armand, 52, 275
Riksdag, 185, 187, 191
Robinson, Luke, M.P., 223
Rome, 160

Ross, Lord (or Roos), 243
Rouen, France, 51
Rous, Francis, M.P., Provost of Eton, 212
Royalists, 79, 86, 87, 89, 90, 92, 93, 98, 105, 106, 114, 116, 120, 130, 134, 155, 177, 204, 208
Royal College of Physicians, 299
Royal Library, 122, 143, 228, 282
Royal Masque (see James Shirley)
Rupert, Prince, nephew of King Charles I, 86, 87, 90, 95, 101, 103, 245, 246
Rushworth, John, M.P., 277, 300
Rutland, 4th Earl of, (John Manners), 298
Rutland, 5th Earl of, (Roger Manners), 25, 270
Rutland, 6th Earl of, (Francis Manners), 298
Rutland, 7th Earl of, (George Manners), 60, 62, 65, 66, 67, 270
Rutland, Countess of, wife of 7th Earl, 66
Rye, Sussex, 51

St. Alban's, Herts., 137
St. Ives, Cornwall, 89
St. John, Oliver, M.P., 73
St. Valentine's Day, 175, 178
Sale, river, Uppsala, 181
Salisbury, Bishop of, 249
Salmasius, Claudius, (Claude Saumaise), 155
Savile, 2nd Viscount and Baron of Castlebar created Earl of Sussex 1644, (Thomas Savile), 103, 106, 107
Say and Sele, 1st Viscount of, (William Fiennes), 71, 83, 84, 85, 89, 107, 207, 216, 278
Scott, Thomas, M.P., regicide, 215, 221
Scottish Estates, 120
Scrope, Emanuel, 1st Earl of Sunderland, 68

Selden, John, 28, 29, 31, 32, 47, 73, 90, 93, 96, 108, 122, 144, 167, 177, 178, 199, 202, 285, 300

'Septuagint' (see Codex)

Shakespeare:
  Hamlet, 288
  Romeo and Juliet, 289

Sheafe, Dr. Grindall, Rector of Chilton Foliat, 248

Sheffield Park, Sussex, 212

Shefford, Beds., 126

Sheldon, Gilbert, Bishop of London, 230, 231, 235, 236, 237, 297

Shifda, Sweden, 153

Ship Money, 67, 68, 78

Shirburn Hill, Oxon., 84

Shirley, James, author of Royal Masque *The Triumph of Peace*, 47, 48, 49, 50, 274

Shrewsbury, Salop, 85

Simpson, Edward, trumpeter, 144

Skara, Sweden, 154

Skippon, Major-General Philip, 88, 100, 102

Slough, Bucks., 86, 87, 130

Solemn League and Covenant, 95

Somerset, 1st Earl of, (Robert Carr), 278

Southampton, 2nd Earl of, (Thomas Wriothesley), 90

Spain, 117, 141

Spanish War 1654, 292

Sparre, Ebba, *la belle Comtesse*, m. Graf Jacob de la Gardie, 176, 200, 288

Speed, John, cartographer, 36

Stapleton, Sir Philip, M.P., 88, 100, 104, 107, 109

Stapleton, master of the horse, 146, 189, 198

Star Chamber (see London, Courts)

Stenius, Swedish astronomer, 158

Stirling, Scotland, 129

Stockholm, 142, 152, 190, 192

Stoke Mandeville, Bucks., 67

Stonehouse, Sir George, J.P., M.P., 70

Stora Torget, Uppsala, Sweden, 156

Storks, superstition about, 193, 290

Strafford, 1st Earl of, (Thomas Wentworth) (see also Parliament, Acts and Bills), 73, 74, 76, 77, 277

Strickland, Walter, M.P. and Ambassador, 204

Strickland, Sir William, M.P., elder bro. of Walter, 209

Strode, William, M.P., 80

Stubbes, Philip, Elizabethan pamphleteer, 184

Stubs (or Stubbs), the Rev. Philip, 255

Suffolk, 3rd Earl of and Lord Howard of Walden, (James Howard), 122

Sunderland, dowager Countess of, (*née* Elizabeth Manners), dr. of the 4th Earl of Rutland, m. Emanuel Scrope, Earl of Sunderland, 60, 61, 62, 63, 64, 65, 67, 68, 69, 275, 276

Sutton, Thomas, 238, 297

Sweden, 137, 141, 143, 175, 183, 207

Swift, William, secretary to Whitelocke, 114, 144

Swindon, Wilts., 131, 233

Sydenham, William, M.P., 204

Sydney, Colonel Algernon, bro. of Lord L'Isle, 138

Syon House, Isleworth, Middlesex, 121

Talmud, the, 97

Thame Park, Oxon., 84, 105, 113

Thames, river (or Isis at Oxford), 30, 60, 61, 90, 147, 181, 272

Thirty Years War, 153, 158, 170

Thurloe, John, Secretary of State, 142, 155, 171, 177, 181, 190, 211, 213, 232, 288

Thynne, Mrs., in Countess of Sunderland's household, 62, 63, 64

Thysen, Admiral, Dutch official in Sweden, 152

Tombes, Thomas, preacher, 108

Tott, Count Klaus, 161, 171, 176, 189, 191

Travemunde, nr. Lübeck, Germany, 192

Treason Act 1649 (see Parliament, Acts and Bills)

Trinity College, Dublin, 282

The Triumph of Peace (see James Shirley)

Trumpington, Cambs., 211

Turner, Dr. Samuel, 34, 35, 90, 91, 272, 280

Tully, Dr. Thomas, President of St. Edmund Hall, Oxford, 241

Unton family, 27

Uppsala, Sweden, 152, 153, 156, 158, 180, 181, 182

Archbishop of, 176, 188

Uxbridge, Middlesex, 105, 106

Vanderlin, Monsieur, Master of Ceremonies, Swedish Court, 156, 157, 160, 161, 179, 180, 185, 187, 189

Vane, Sir Henry (Harry), the elder, Comptroller of the Household, 48, 74, 75

Vane, Sir Henry (Harry), M.P., the younger, Treasurer to the Navy, 100, 106, 126, 134, 217, 218, 220, 222, 279, 294

Venice, Italy, 285

Venner, Thomas, 232, 233

Verney, Sir Ralph, M.P., 222

Vernham, Hants., 241

Virginia Water (see Windsor)

Voltaire, 183

Walker, John, steward, 144, 189

Waller, Edmund, M.P., 89, 93

Waller, Sir William, M.P., 108

Wallingford, Berks., 109

Wallingford House Group, 215, 218

Walton, Surrey, 206

Walton, Dr. Brian, Bishop of Chester, editor of English Polyglot Bible, 293, 296

Wanley, Dr. Humfrey, 255

Watlington, Oxon., 84

Welch, Captain, 146

Wenman, 2nd Viscount, Baron Wenman of Tuam, (Thomas Wenman), 84, 105, 107, 113

Wentworth, Sir Peter, 135

Westmeath, Ireland, 206

Wharton, 4th Baron, (Philip Wharton), 85

Whistler, Dr. Daniel, 144, 154, 176, 194, 244, 299

Whitelocke family (*see Tree*), *members grouped broadly by family, in chronological order:*

John, m. Agnes de la Beche, 24

Richard, grandfather of Bulstrode, 24

Joan, (*née* Colte, widow of Brockhurst, later m. Thomas Price), grandmother of Bulstrode, 24, 25, 270

Edmund, Captain, uncle of Bulstrode, 24, 25, 26, 27

Richard, uncle of Bulstrode, 24, 26

William, uncle of Bulstrode, 24, 26

Judge Sir James, father of Bulstrode, 24, 26, 27, 33, 38, 41, also:

m. Elizabeth Bulstrode, 26

Appointments, 28

Bate case, 28, 29

M.P. for Woodstock, 28

Imprisoned, 29

Knighted and appointed Judge, 32

Arranges Bulstrode's marriage, 39

Death of wife, 42

Whitelocke family:
  Judge Sir James – *contd*
    Interest in music, 43, 44
    Illness and death of, 44
    Qualities of, 44, 45
    Will of, 45
    'Liber Famelicus', 45, 300
    Monument to, 46, 47
    William Cooke refers to, 58
    Forced loan, 73
  Elizabeth (*née* Bulstrode), m. Judge Sir
    James, mother of Bulstrode, 26,
    27, 28, 42, 46
  Elizabeth, sister of Bulstrode, m.
    Thomas Mostyn (see Mostyn)
  Cecilia, sister of Bulstrode, m. Edward
    Dixon (see Dixon)
  Sir Bulstrode Whitelocke, M.P.
    (*Selected headings*):
    Family background, 23–7
    Birth and Early Years, 27–33
    Called to the Bar, 38
    Master of the Revels, 38
    Motto, 40
    Royal Masque, 47–50
    Whitelocke's Coranto, 48
    Advice to Hampden on Ship Money,
      67–8
    Illness, 78, 90–2
    Injured near Watlington, 84
    Enlists, 88
    Wills, 112, 142, 249, 254, 285
    Refuses Viscountcy from Oliver
      Cromwell, 213
    Discusses terms for Restoration, 219–
      220
    Appeals for royal pardon, 224, 228
    Last Years, 243–9
    Death of, 249
    His three careers, 250–3
    Handwriting, 13–14

    Belief in freedom of conscience, 61,
      69, 82, 97, 102, 109, 199, 213, 234–
      235, 243, 279
    Knighthood confirmed by Christina,
      293
  Offices held:
    Recorder of Abingdon, 46, 61
    Dep. Lieut., Berks. and Oxon., 83
    Governor, Phyllis Court Garrison,
      100
    High Steward, Westminster School,
      108
    A Lord Commissioner of the Great
      Seal, 111, 115
    Keeper of the Royal Library, 122, 296
    Steward and Recorder of Oxford,
      123, 295
    Governor of Charterhouse, 128
    Commissioner of the Treasury, 204
    Member of Committee for Trade
      and Navigation, 205
    Acting Speaker, 210
    Constable (or Deputy) Windsor
      Castle, 116, 203, 224, 245, 291
    Lord President of the Council, 216
    Member of the Committee of Safety,
      217
  Correspondence:
    Letters to:
    Wife, Rebecca, 41
    Dr. Bartlett, 52
    Mr. Cely, 53
    Thomas Napper, 53
    Sister, Elizabeth Mostyn, 54
    Frances Willoughby, 62
    Mrs. Thynne, 62
    Attorney Gen. Bankes, 68
    Son James, in Ireland, 125
    John Thurloe, 177
    His children, 206
    Sir Harbottle Grimston, 224

Whitelocke, Sir Bulstrode – *contd*
  Lord Francis Willoughby of Parham,
    230
  Lord Ashley, 246
  Letters (or extracts) from:
  Edward Hyde, 52–3, 275
  Oliver Cromwell, 138
  Gilbert Pickering, 138
  Marchmont Needham, 172
  John Selden, 178
  Jonathan Pickes, 178
  George Cokain, 181
  Wife, Mary, 191
  Reflections/Meditations on:
  Hawks, etc., 136
  Ambassadors and Women, 143
  Ambassador Extraordinary to
    Sweden:
  Nomination, etc., 137–40
  Preparations for journey, 141–5
  Voyage to Gothenburg, 146–51
  Journey to Uppsala, 152–6
  Audiences with Queen Christina,
    159–60, 162–7, 168–70, 174–5, 179,
    182, 184, 188
  Interviews with Chancellor Oxen-
    stierna, 170–1, 173, 180
  Signing of Anglo-Swedish Treaty,
    183
  Exchange of presents, 182, 184,
    189
  May-day celebrations, 184–5
  Court wedding celebrations, 185–7
  Abdication of Queen Christina, 174,
    185, 187, 188, 191, 289
  Journey home, 190–8
  Knight of the Order of Amaranth,
    211, 293
  Parliamentary career:
  Enters Parliament as Member for
    Stafford, 33

  Elected Member for Marlow in
    Long Parliament, 73
  Chairman of committee: trial of Earl
    of Strafford, 73
  Chairman of committee: to consider
    the Answer to the 19 Propositions,
    82
  Speaks against civil war, 82–3, 101
  Peace Commissioner to the King,
    89–90, 93, 102–3, 105–6
  Speech to Commons: Laud's trial, 98
  Accused by Savile, 106–7
  Elected Member for Bucks. in Oliver
    Cromwell's 2nd Parliament, 208
  Appointed to prepare new transla-
    tion of Bible, 210
  His marriages:
  1. to Rebecca Bennet, 39
  2. to Frances Willoughby, 64
  3. to Mary Wilson, 127
Rebecca (*née* Bennet), 1st wife of Bul-
    strode, 39, 41, 42, 46, 47, 50, 51,
    52, 53, 54, 56, 59, 77
Colonel Sir James, only child of Bulstrode
    and Rebecca, 42, 43, 52, 54, 56,
    62, 68, 70, 77, 112, 113, 120, 121,
    122, 125, 126, 139, 144, 154, 183,
    189, 206, 211, 212, 215, 217, 224,
    230, 234, 240, 241, 244, 282, 291,
    295
Mary (*née* Pyke, formerly Pilchard),
    m. Colonel Sir James Whitelocke,
    211, 240,
Frances (*née* Willoughby), 2nd wife of
    Bulstrode, dr. of 3rd Baron
    Willoughby of Parham:
  Meets and marries Bulstrode, 61–4
  Visits mother, 65
  1st child, 67
  2nd child, 68
  7th child, 84

Whitelocke, Frances – *contd*
  Moves with family to Middle
    Temple, 99
  Letter from William Cooke, 99
  With family at Navy House, Dept-
    ford, 100
  Husband suspected of high treason,
    106–7
  Birth of 8th child, 107
  Left in charge of Phyllis Court
    Garrison, 109
  Letter to husband re appointment as
    Keeper of Great Seal, 111
  Visit to Thame Park and start of last
    illness, 113
  10th pregnancy, 117
  Death of, 118
  also, 249
Frances, 1st child of Bulstrode and
  Frances, 67, 77, 100, 113, 120, 139,
  202
Sir William, 2nd child of Bulstrode and
  Frances, m. Mary, dr. of Sir
  Thomas Overbury, 68, 77, 112,
  120, 126, 144, 189, 206, 247, 255,
  276, 290, 291
Elizabeth, dr. of Sir William, m.
  William Wiseman, 255
Elizabeth, 3rd child of Bulstrode and
  Frances, 77, 120
Mary, 4th child of Bulstrode and
  Frances, 77, 116, 120, 205, 212,
  234, 240
Anne, 5th child of Bulstrode and
  Frances, 77, 120, 212, 234
Cecilia, 6th child of Bulstrode and
  Frances, 77, 120, 212, 231, 236
Hester, 7th child of Bulstrode and
  Frances, 84, 120, 234
Willoughby, 8th child of Bulstrode and
  Frances, 107, 116, 120, 205, 244, 281

Bulstrode, 9th child of Bulstrode and
  Frances, 120, 206, 239, 244, 281
Mary (*née* Carleton, formerly Wilson),
  third wife of Bulstrode, 123, 124,
  125, 126, 127, 128, 129, 132, 136,
  137, 139, 142, 146, 147, 155, 177,
  178, 182, 190–1, 198, 202, 217, 222,
  225, 232, 240, 245, 247, 248
Samuel, 1st child of Bulstrode and
  Mary, m. Elizabeth Gough, 129,
  131, 206, 234, 241, 291
Carleton, 2nd child of Bulstrode and
  Mary, m. (1) Katherine, dr. of Sir
  Andrew Henley, m. (2) Mary, dr.
  of Herbert Alwyn, 132, 206, 234,
  241, 247, 248, 251, 255, 256, 279,
  281, 292
Major John Carleton, son of Carleton,
  255, 257, 292
George, grandson of Carleton, 250,
  255
Bigley, 3rd child of Bulstrode and
  Mary, 147, 234, 243
Frances, 4th child of Bulstrode and
  Mary, 128, 202, 241, 247, 248
Rebecca, 5th child of Bulstrode and
  Mary, 128, 214, 248, 249
Stephen, 6th child of Bulstrode and
  Mary, 217, 234
Widdrington, Sir Thomas, M.P., 112,
  114, 115, 130, 134, 135, 203, 204,
  210, 290
Wildman, John, M.P., 202, 219, 238, 239,
  295
Wilkinson, Rev. Samuel, 136, 230, 297
William III, King, 290
William I, King (the Conqueror) (see
  Norman Conquest)
Williams, John, Bishop of Lincoln, later
  Archbishop of York, 43, 44, 46, 64,
  273

Willoughby family, 64, 117, 121, 128

Willoughby of Parham, 3rd Baron, (William Willoughby), father of Frances, 60, 65

Willoughby of Parham, the dowager Lady (Frances), dr. of 4th Earl of Rutland, m. 3rd Baron Willoughby of Parham. Whitelocke's mother-in-law, 62, 63, 64, 65, 67, 297

Willoughby of Parham, 5th Baron, (Francis Willoughby), 62, 63, 64, 65, 204, 219, 226, 227, 230, 283

Willoughby, Frances (see Whitelocke)

Willoughby, Colonel William (later 6th Baron Willoughby of Parham), m. Anne, dr. of Sir William Carey, 118, 119, 131, 221, 226, 227, 228, 229, 243, 244

Willoughby, Lady Anne, sister-in-law to Frances Whitelocke, 117, 118, 119, 120, 221

Willoughby, Elizabeth, sister of Frances Whitelocke, 65, 66

Wilson, Arthur, historian, 300

Wilson, Mary (see Whitelocke)

Wilson, Lt. Col. Rowland, M.P., 123, 128, 225, 282, 289

Wilson, Samuel, 124, 127, 142, 147, 190, 199, 233, 239, 243, 244, 247, 289

Winchelsea, 3rd Earl of, (Heneage Finch), 108, 295

Windsor, 86, also:
    Constable of Castle and Keeper of Forest and Great Park, 116, 203, 224, 245, 246, 281, 291
    Keeper of Wardrobe at Castle, 116
    Manor Lodge, 116, 120, 281
    Virginia Water, 116

Winston, Dr. Thomas, 132, 144, 190, 206, 244

Winwood, Richard, M.P., 86, 94, 106, 107, 130, 222, 239, 247

Wiseman, William, m. Elizabeth, granddaughter of Whitelocke, 255

Wolseley, Sir Charles, M.P., 137, 142, 175

Wooburn, Bucks., 27, 43

Worcester, 85, 129
    battles of, 85, 129, 130, 282

Wotton, Sir Henry (Harry), 143, 285

Wrangell, Vice-Admiral, 189, 190, 191, 289

Wren, Sir Christopher, 244, 290

Wright, William, sculptor, 46

Wychwood Forest, Oxon., 69

York, 102, 218, 273

Young, Patrick, 296

Zankey (or Sankey), Sir Jerome, tutor to James Whitelocke jnr. at Oxford, 120, 121, 282